Legal Rules in Practice

Understanding legal rules not as determinants of behavior but as points of reference for conduct, this volume considers the ways in which rules are invoked, referred to, interpreted, put forward or blurred. It also asks how both legal practitioners and lay participants conceive of and participate in the construction of facts and rules, and thus, through decisions, defenses, pleas, files, evidence, interviews and documents, actively participate in law's life. With attention to the formulation of notions such as person, evidence, intention, cause and responsibility in the course of legal practices, *Legal Rules in Practice* provides the outlines of a praxiological anthropology of law – an anthropology that focuses on words, concepts and reasoning as actively used to solve conflicts with the help of legal rules. As such, it will appeal to sociologists, anthropologists and scholars of law with interests in ethnomethodology, rule-based conduct and practical reasoning.

Baudouin Dupret is Directeur de Recherche at the French National Centre for Scientific Research (CNRS) and guest lecturer at the University of Louvain, Belgium. He has published extensively in the field of the sociology and anthropology of law, legislation and media, especially in the Middle East. He is the co-editor of *Law At Work: Studies in Legal Ethnomethods* and the author of *Practices of Truth: An Ethnomethodological Inquiry into Arab Settings, and Adjudication in Action: An Ethnomethodology of Law* and *Positive Law from the Muslim World.*

Julie Colemans is a research engineer at the Faculty of Law, Political Science and Criminology of the University of Liege, Belgium. Her PhD thesis dealt with the decision-making process within the Belgian Council of State. She continued to work on legal reasoning through an ethnography of emotions within law courts, and her current research surrounds the epistemological framework underlying legal doctrine.

Max Travers is Senior Lecturer in the School of Social Sciences at the University of Tasmania, Australia. He is the author of *The Reality of Law, The British Immigration Courts* and *The Sentencing of Children*; and co-author of *Rethinking Bail.* The latter study about bail describes decision-making, and responses to "vulnerable" defendants, in criminal courts.

Legal Rules in Practice

In the Midst of Law's Life

Edited by
Baudouin Dupret,
Julie Colemans and
Max Travers

Routledge
Taylor & Francis Group
LONDON AND NEW YORK

First published 2021
by Routledge
2 Park Square, Milton Park, Abingdon, Oxon OX14 4RN

and by Routledge
52 Vanderbilt Avenue, New York, NY 10017

Routledge is an imprint of the Taylor & Francis Group, an informa business

British Library Cataloguing-in-Publication Data
A catalogue record for this book is available from the British Library

Library of Congress Cataloging-in-Publication Data
Names: Dupret, Baudouin, editor. | Colemans, Julie, editor. | Travers, Max, editor.
Title: Legal rules in practice : in the midst of law's life / edited by Baudouin Dupret, Julie Colemans, and Max Travers.
Description: Milton Park, Abingdon, Oxon ; New York, NY : Routledge, 2021. | Includes bibliographical references and index.
Identifiers: LCCN 2020038337 (print) | LCCN 2020038338 (ebook) | ISBN 9780367495909 (hardback) | ISBN 9781003046776 (ebook)
Subjects: LCSH: Jurisprudence. | Law—Interpretation and construction. | Law—Methodology. | Law—Philosophy.
Classification: LCC K237 .L447 2021 (print) | LCC K237 (ebook) | DDC 340—dc23
LC record available at https://lccn.loc.gov/2020038337
LC ebook record available at https://lccn.loc.gov/2020038338

ISBN: 9780367495909 (hbk)
ISBN: 9781003046776 (ebk)

Typeset in Times New Roman
by codeMantra

Contents

Contributors

Alexis Blouet is a Postdoctoral Research Fellow at Alwaleed Centre in the University of Edinburgh. He obtained a PhD in Law from University Paris I Panthéon-Sorbonne on the topic of constitution-making in Egypt after the January 25th 2011 Revolution. His work received a prestigious award from the Varenne Institute and was published in French by LGDJ editions in 2019. His research interests are focused on how legal theory can contribute to a better understanding of power in the Middle East while trying to refine legal theory's analytical tools through the prism of politics and actors in the area.

Julie Colemans is a research engineer at the Faculty of Law, Political Science and Criminology of the University of Liege, Belgium. Her PhD thesis dealt with the decision-making process within the Belgian Council of State. She kept on working on legal reasoning through an ethnography of emotions within law courts. She is currently working on the epistemological framework underlying legal doctrine.

Marianne Constable is Professor of Rhetoric at the University of California, Berkeley. Her books include *Our Word is Our Bond: How Legal Speech Acts* (2014) and the co-edited *Looking for Law in All the Wrong Places: Justice Beyond and Between* (2019). She has received, among other awards, the Hurst Prize in Legal History from the Law & Society Association; the James Boyd White Award from the Association for the Study of Law, Culture and the Humanities; a Sarlo Award for graduate mentoring; and Fellowships at the Institute of Advanced Study, the Center for Advanced Study in the Behavioral Sciences, and the National Humanities Center. Her current research is on the "new unwritten law" that supposedly exonerated women who killed their husbands in turn-of-the-century Chicago.

Paul Dresch worked extensively in Yemen from 1977 onwards. He taught at Michigan in the late 1980s and then at Oxford. His publications include *Tribes, Government, and History in Yemen* (1989), *A History of Modern Yemen* (2000), and *The Rules of Barat* (2006). He has co-edited several volumes, including *Legalism: anthropology and history* (2012) with Hannah

Skoda and *Legalism: rules and categories* (2015) with Judith Scheele. He is currently an Emeritus Research Fellow at St John's College, Oxford. Among his more recent publications is a reflection on the nature of anthropology, in Judith Scheele and Andrew Shryock (eds.) *The Scandal of Continuity in Middle East Anthropology* (2019).

Baudouin Dupret is educated in Law, Islamic Sciences and Political Sciences. He is Directeur de Recherche at the French National Centre for Scientific Research (CNRS). He is also guest lecturer at the University of Louvain (Belgium). He has published extensively in the field of the sociology and anthropology of law, legislation, and media, especially in the Middle East. He is the co-editor of *Law At Work* (2015) and the author of *Practices of Truth* (2011), *Adjudication in Action* (2011), and *Positive Law from the Muslim World* (2021).

Samer Ghamroun holds his PhD in political science from the École Normale Supérieure of Cachan, in Paris, on the subject of judicial competition between juvenile and sharia judges in Lebanon. He is the co-founder and board secretary, and a scientific editor of the Legal Agenda, a Lebanese Human Rights NGO, and assistant professor at the Faculty of Law and Political Science of the Saint Joseph University of Beirut, where he teaches legal sociology and legal history. His research and publications cover topics such as the religious legal systems for family law and their relationship with civil systems, legal pluralism and the state's normative power, the legal professions, and the relationship between politics, law, and the judiciary.

Michael Lynch is Emeritus Professor of Science & Technology Studies at Cornell University. His major fields are ethnomethodology and social studies of science. He has investigated practical action, visual representation, and discursive interaction in scientific and legal settings, and also has written extensively about conceptual and analytical issues in the social sciences. He was Editor of *Social Studies of Science* from 2002 until 2012, and he was President of the Society for Social Studies of Science in 2007–2009. In recent years, he received two career awards: the 2016 John Desmond Bernal Prize from the Society for Social Studies of Science; and the 2020 Harold Garfinkel and Harvey Sacks Award for Distinguished Scholarship from the Ethnomethodology/Conversation Analysis section of the American Sociological Association.

Youmna Makhlouf is a PhD candidate in law at the Université Paris II Panthéon-Assas. Her dissertation examines the question of the "identity of the individual in the Lebanese private law". She is a teacher and researcher at the Faculty of Law at Saint Joseph-University of Beirut. Youmna is also an attorney at the Beirut Bar Association. Her publications and research focus on gender, identity, nationality, family, personal status, and religious law.

Linda Ross Meyer, Professor of Law, teaches jurisprudence, criminal law, and constitutional law at Quinnipiac University School of Law. She is the author of *The Justice of Mercy* (MIchigan, 2010), *Sentencing in Time* (Amherst, 2017), and numerous articles and book chapters on legal indeterminacy, mercy, sentencing, law and religious revelation, and other spaces at the edge of law-as-rules. She is a past President of the Association for the Study of Law, Culture, and the Humanities and a recipient of that Association's James Boyd White Award. She also co-founded Quinnipiac University's Prison Project and the Quinnipiac/Trinity Higher Education Program at York Correctional Institution.

Marième N'Diaye is a senior researcher at CNRS, based at the institute Les Afriques dans le Monde of IEP Bordeaux. She works at the crossroads of the sociology of law, the sociology of public policies, and gender studies. She is the author of *La réforme du droit de la famille. Une comparaison Sénégal-Maroc*, PU Montréal, 2016. She is currently working, in the context of Senegal, on the working of family justice, cause-lawyering within women rights associations, and debates regarding the decriminalization of abortion and the legalization of homosexuality.

Fernanda Pirie is Professor of the Anthropology of Law at the Centre for Socio-Legal Studies of the University of Oxford. An anthropologist specializing in Tibetan societies, she has used her research into legal practices and legal codes to develop the anthropology of law. *The Anthropology of Law* (OUP, 2013) builds on themes and debates developed in the *Legalism* research group, which she convened with colleagues in anthropology and history (*Legalism*, 4 vols, OUP). As well as studying contemporary Tibetan societies, Fernanda has written on the legal history of medieval Tibet (see www.tibetanlaw.org). She is currently working on a global history of law, to be published in 2021.

Frederick Schauer is David and Mary Harrison Distinguished Professor of Law at the University of Virginia, and has previously been Professor of Law at the University of Michigan, Frank Stanton Professor of the First Amendment at Harvard University, and George Eastman Visiting Professor at the University of Oxford. A Fellow of the British Academy and of the American Academy of Arts and Sciences, and former holder of a Guggenheim Fellowship, he is the author of *Free Speech: A Philosophical Enquiry* (Cambridge 1982), *Playing By the Rules: A Philosophical Examination of Rule-Based Decision-Making in Law and in Life* (Oxford 1991), *Profiles, Probabilities, and Stereotypes* (Harvard 2003), *Thinking Like a Lawyer: A New Introduction to Legal Reasoning* (Harvard 2009), and *The Force of Law* (Harvard 2015).

Thomas Scheffer is professor of sociology with a focus on interpretative social research at the Goethe University Frankfurt (GUF). He did research on various executive, legislative and juridical apparatuses by means of ethnography and discourse analyses. His studies focus on the work invested into discourse contributions, their arrangements, demands and formations. With his object-centered, trans-sequential analysis, Scheffer developed an Ethnomethodology that bridges interaction analysis and work/discourse processes. Currently, Scheffer is member of the Konzil of the German Sociological Association and pro-dean of the Social Science Department at the GUF. He is the author of e.g. *Adversarial Case-Making: An Ethnography of English Crown Court Procedure*, Leident and Boston: Brill, 2010.

Max Travers is Senior Lecturer in the School of Social Sciences at the University of Tasmania, Australia. He is the author of *The Reality of Law* (1997), *The British Immigration Courts* (1999), and *The Sentencing of Children* (2012), and co-author of *Rethinking Bail* (2020). The latter study about bail describes decision-making, and responses to "vulnerable" defendants, in criminal courts.

Michel Troper has been teaching Constitutional Law and Legal Theory since 1969, first at the University of Rouen then at Paris Nanterre. In 1993 he received an appointment to a chair at the Institut Universitaire de France and has been emeritus professor since 2006. He has been a visiting professor or scholar and gave lectures in a number of universities across the world. He held the "chaire Chaim Perelman" at the Université Libre de Bruxelles in 2008–2009 and was a fellow at the Straus Institute for Law and Justice (NYU) in 2011–2012. He has served in several scientific societies and is honorary president of the French Society for Legal and Political Philosophy (SFPJ) and the French Association for Constitutional Law. His main writings deal with constitutional theory, constitutional history, theory of legal interpretation, and legal epistemology.

Barbara Truffin is Professor at the Law Faculty of the Free University of Brussels (ULB). She has specialised in legal anthropology and was trained both in law and in anthropology. She holds a PhD in anthropology (ULB), a Master of Arts in the social sciences (Chicago), a Specialised Diploma in international law (ULB,) and a Master in law (ULB). Currently Director of the Centre of Legal History and Anthropology (ULB), her research interests are related to legal pluralism and ethnography, and specially focused on two fieldworks: the rights of indigenous peoples in Amazonian Ecuador and ethno-national diversity in family conflicts resolution in Belgium.

Ayang Utriza Yakin is Visiting Professor, since 2019, in Arabic and Islamic Studies at the Department of Languages and Cultures, Section Middle-East, Ghent University, and Research Associate at the Research Institute 'Religions, Spiritualities, Cultures, Societies' (RSCS) of the *Université Catholique de Louvain* (UCLouvain), Belgium. He studied Arabic and classical Islamic studies, Islamic law, history, and philology in Indonesia

(1990–2001), Egypt (2001–2002), and France (2003–5 & 2008–13). He was visiting fellow and postdoctoral researcher in Oxford (2012), Harvard (2013), Tokyo (2016), and Louvain-la-Neuve (2016–2019). He has published two books in Indonesian and numerous articles and book-chapters in Indonesian, French, Arabic, and English. He is now co-editing volumes (under review) including *Rethinking Halal: Genealogy, Current Trends, and New Interpretation*" (2021) and *Islamic Divorce in a Global World: Everyday Realities and Practices in the 21st Century*" (2021).

Jean-Marc Weller is a sociologist, researcher at the CNRS (Centre National de la Recherche Scientifique), and member of the LISIS (Interdisciplinary Laboratory Sciences Innovations Societies, Gustave Eiffel University, France). His researches focus on street level bureaucrats' daily work, based on ethnographic inquiries in institutional contexts (justice, agriculture, social policy). These works address different topics: legal practice and decision making in organizational settings, paperwork and governing with rules, public management, and transformation of bureaucracy. They cover various areas of the social sciences: socio-legal studies, theories of public action, sociology of work and activities, infrastructure studies, sociology of organizations, sociology of the State, sociology of law, and STS. He is the author of several books and articles mainly in French, including *L'Etat au guichet* (1999) and *Fabriquer des actes d'Etat* (2018).

Introduction

Legal rules in practice: an exploration into law's life

Baudouin Dupret, Julie Colemans, and Max Travers

General presentation

Legal anthropology has a long, though controversial, tradition. It suffices to mention the name of Henry Maine to be convinced. For reasons related to the nature of the law as issued from the Common Law, however, the division between lawyers and anthropologists was less sharp. The insistence on the judge's work, the development of American legal realism, and the shift toward conflict resolution are all reasons that led legal anthropology to plainly belong not only to anthropology/ethnology but also to the very large domain of law and society studies. The central figure of the judge also largely explains the fact that questions about the nature of law took in this context a less theoretical aspect than in the continental universe. As a consequence, we see the quickly hegemonic rise of the school of legal pluralism, whose extremely variegated forms share in common a minimalist definition of what could be the proper nature and object of law.

French legal anthropology, from which some contributors to this volume originate, is no less ancient. Like legal history, it was mainly the concern of specialists in jurisprudence. Trained in positive law but in contact with the colonies, they felt the need or even the necessity to seek out the law outside the courts and the statutes instituted by metropolitan authorities. Their conception of legal anthropology remained nevertheless marked by the categories specific to their academic and judicial tradition. On the side of anthropologists, it was more sheer ignorance that prevailed, and this was because of a double suspicion: first, vis-à-vis the law, which e.g. the Marxist vulgate confined to the status of a simple superstructure disguising primordial human relationships; and second, vis-à-vis the lawyers, because they seemed to lack the indispensable linguistic and ethnological competences. This division persisted until recently, although the lines started shifting.

Legal anthropology took a new start with the extension of the anthropological perspective to the study of societies that were until then excluded from its investigation scope, that is, mainly Europe and North America. Indeed, it abandoned its questions regarding the forms the law has taken outside its modern understanding and started addressing the practices specific to law in the modern context. In other words, instead of looking for the law in places where legal theory refused to recognize it, legal anthropology undertook to use its own methodological tools and especially ethnography in order to describe and analyze what the law looks like in the concreteness of its practices. In a generic way, one can call this perspective, following the now more than 50-year-old realist expression, "law in action", which must principally be distinguished from "law in the books". The latter would actually correspond to the dogmatic face of the law whose reality would reside elsewhere, for instance, in doorway negotiations, in the euphemizing of power relationships, in authority symbolism, in the patriarchal nature of its functioning, or in its disciplinarization of social relations.

This interest for law's human thickness – and not only for its simple formal enunciation – constitutes certainly an important shift in perspective that enlarges our capacity to seize the legal phenomenon in all of its dimensions. It is, however, striking to observe that a constitutive element of law is still missing, because precisely one wants to escape the dangers of dogmatism. This "missing-what" (Garfinkel, 1986)[1] is the rule itself, but the rule understood not in the mere Kantian or Kelsenian sense as a proposition backed by other statements in a raw logical articulation. It is the rule understood as a compelling point of reference in the concrete work of those who achieve a legal task. One can thus criticize legal anthropology for not taking law seriously, that is, for not taking (enough) into account what constitutes the core or even the purpose of law and of its actors, both profane and professional. In the same way that it seems hard to conceive of an anthropology of health that would take health as a mere pretext or of an anthropology of religion that would not take religious beliefs seriously, it is detrimental to conduct the ethnography of law in all its forms and practices without any consideration for the rules which, in their crafting, interpretation, and implementation, form the ordinary shape of legal life.

Interest for law in context and in action has developed recently. This interest, first of a behaviorist nature, transited through the philosophy of ordinary language before ending up with the social sciences that put interaction at the heart of their analytical approach. One thus shifted from an interest for behavior or the actor's rationality to an interest for action, what can be called a pragmatic or praxeological approach to the social world. This trend of a phenomenological type aims at seizing the law in itself, in its contextual unfolding, in its interactions, in its sense-making activity, in its practices. In a behavioristic way, the realist schools (American realism, Scandinavian realism, new realism) blend the critique of radical positivism with an approach made of the observation of behaviors linked to the law, to the making of legal rules, and to the relationships that are interwoven with them.

In a rather different tradition, the philosophy of language has deeply contributed to the study of law in action, under the impulse of Wittgenstein (1967), on one hand, and of the theory of speech acts, on the other. Interactionist, constructivist, and semiotic trends (symbolic interactionism, ethnomethodology, legal semiotics, narrative theory, Latourian semiotics) have hugely transformed the social sciences of law, putting the accent on legal activities and on the discursive usages that are linked to it. Authors like Mertz (1994, 2007a, 2007b, MacAulay and Mertz, 2013) proposed to study law in the perspective of semiotic anthropology, at the crossroad of social and linguistic anthropology. This approach makes it possible to consider the law through language exchanges, as they integrated in the social context and situated in the legal and judicial arenas.

In a comparable way, works on legal consciousness address the relationships between ordinary individuals and the law. They study how laymen perceive, represent, assess, and mobilize legal rules. They certainly permitted socio-legal studies to get rid of its schoolish and dogmatic vision of law and to enlarge their scope to the manners in which ordinary people bear on law to resolve conflicts of everyday life (Ewick and Silbey, 1992, 1998; Sarat, 1990). Merry (1990) defines legal consciousness as the ways in which people understand and use the law. These works show how the frames of thinking of everyday life operate in the legal sphere, including in the institutions in charge of conflict resolution. This field of research extended to everyday life and to the influence the law exerts in it. Starting from a perspective close to Garfinkel's (1967, pp. 75ff) breaching experiments, these inquiries address the problems as perceived and lived by the people, starting from the principle that the breach in routines and ordinary life disclose legality. Law is thus considered here as a social practice.

It is, however, in the ethnomethodological tradition in the social sciences that praxeological research on law has best developed. This is not the place to discuss this research literature in detail, other than to note that it seeks to explicate the modes of reasoning proper to the members of a given group, what Garfinkel (1967) called "ethnomethods".[2] The praxeological approach to the legal rule, in this perspective, corresponds to the study of the ways the diverse protagonists of law have to refer to such rule, to play with it, to follow it, to apply it or to dodge it, or even to violate it, in sum, to practice it.

The organization of referencing practices finds in texts produced by legal activities a perspicuous setting. For instance, if we take the text of a ruling, we observe that the context of its production evades us. The written document is written for practical purposes that correspond more to its prospective use than to its retrospective historical exactitude. In other words, the ruling is a "polished" version that occults the action that led to its production. From an action to the account of this action, from a verbal exchange to a written narrative, from a record to a report, from a report to a ruling, an enormous transformation operates that created a gap between what happened, what was recorded, and what was given the force of law. However, an ethnographic analysis permits to palliate the deficiencies of an approach limited to formalized texts and to retrieve the uses that presided over the drafting of the ruling, over the formalizing of its retrospective and prospective dimensions, over its dialogical and intertextual constitution assembling in one and the same document multiple pieces and testimonies, over the relating of diverging narratives, and over the emergence of a master narrative. One can thus see how mundane events become legal facts, how terms with fuzzy outlines transform into binding legal provisions, how ordinary personalities evolve into parties to a case, and eventually how commonsense morality can acquire the status of law.

We propose a volume which, taking law in and for itself, develops a sensitivity to legal practices, that is, an anthropology of these practices which refer somehow to a legal rule, be it to apply or interpret it, or even to dodge or violate it. Legal rules do not determine the behaviors of people to which they are supposed to apply, but they serve as their point of reference. It is these referring practices that the many contributions will address: how is the rule invoked, referred to, interpreted, put forward, or blurred? How do legal practitioners and lay participants participate in the construction of facts and rules, conceive the particularity of the former and the generality of the latter, subsume, and articulate the ones to the others so as to produce decisions? How are notions of person, evidence, intention, cause, and responsibility formulated in the constraining context of a trial? By so doing, the contributions to this volume will converge in the production of a praxeological anthropology of law, a socio-anthropology that focuses on words, concepts, and reasoning as used to solve conflicts with the help of legal rules.[3]

This volume

The three parts of the volume are preceded by a chapter in which Frederick Schauer analytically develops and frames the concept of "ruleness". Although non-defeasible (absolute or non-overridable) rules are conceptually possible and occasionally exist, most rule-governed decision-making environments allow some category of decision-makers to defeat a rule when previously unforeseen circumstances appear to demand it. In reality, however, some of these environments are ones in which the weight of the rule as a rule is very strong, and others are ones in which the weight is much weaker. Whether "strong" and "weak" rules can be identified precisely on a continuum through empirical research in legal settings seems less clear: perhaps the studies in this collection about decision-making in relation to facts only describe "weak" rules. Nevertheless, Schauer is helpful in identifying the existence of a variable, which we can call "ruleness", and this chapter explores the conceptual and empirical dimensions of seeing ruleness as a variable rather than a property that does or does not obtain.

Following this conceptual keynote chapter, the volume is organized in three parts. Part 1 addresses the conception of law as a system of rules, its relativity, and its contingency. Part 2 observes the share of materiality, artefactuality, and idiosyncrasy in the practice of rules. Part 3 investigates the issue of interpretation and the role moral and emotional standards play in it.

Part 1 addresses the concept of "ruleness" and its relativity. The critical perspective on law and justice denunciates the formalism implicated by the statement of rule centrality in legal work. Such is the position of American realism whose mark can be observed until now, including in works on legal language (Mertz et al., 2016). Instead of denying the centrality of rules in the practice of the law, there is another approach that wonders how rules manifest their presence in the heart of law's life. Between the pure theory of law's formalism and the realistic theories' sociologism, there is probably room for a theory of rule-based decision making, which considers rules as points of reference endowed with an open texture.

In Chapter 2, Marianne Constable and Linda Ross Meyer offer a critique of ruleness that is interesting to read alongside Schauer's chapter. Drawing on the theories of language, they argue that rules offer, at best, an incomplete account of law. As they explain first, the articulation and use of rules in Western legal texts and decisions involve the use of language and judgment. Law "on the books", that is, results from "action" or speech acts, and such acts cannot be reduced to rules insofar as these acts require judgment. Judgement may or may not be conventional, but it is always situational. Second, they argue that even philosophical accounts that conceive of law as a system of rules ultimately appeal to something outside the rules – whether to the "fact" of official acceptance of rules (e.g. Hart, 1961) or to a "norm" that warrants rules' acceptance (Kelsen, 1967). Third, they illustrate their claim that there is no rule for the application of rules through examples in which judgment occurs – and lawlike institutions are established – precisely when rules appear to run out. This is a relativist critique of the more formalist presentation of rules advanced by Schauer. We would, however, argue that this issue can be re-specified (Garfinkel et al.,1981; Garfinkel, 1986) by conducting empirical research on how rules are employed in actual legal settings (see the final section of the last chapter).

The remaining chapters in Part 1 are authored by legal theorists and anthropologists who have conducted comparative, historico-political studies of law. In Chapter 3, Michel Troper explores the structure of the legal system and its relationship with the emergence of the State. He first asks: What is the influence of legal practice on the law itself? If, by law, we understand merely a set of rules, and by legal practice the behavior that leads to the production or the application of those rules, then the answer is "none", but the law is much more than a set of rules. When we teach law, we also describe all sorts of theories that lawmakers and lawyers use to justify, interpret, and apply the rules, and these theories are not all derived from other theories, from religious, political, or economic doctrines, imported from outside the legal system, and formalized in the law. There is also the possibility that some theories including some that are constitutive of the legal system are being constructed as a result of constraints born out of legal practices. In this chapter, he explores that possibility using the example of the theory of the State and the related concept of Sovereignty emerging from the practice of the hierarchization of norms.

In Chapter 4, Paul Dresch addresses the related issue of equality, hierarchy, and the status of rules in a historico-anthropological perspective. Anthropologists have written on hierarchy and equality, holism and individualism, often not distinguishing the first opposition from the second. The questions that arise involve value and morality. Many involve explicit rules of the kind that law trades in, and thus involve explicit categories. The force of the rule here lies less in its manipulation than in its seeming objectivity and its promise, beyond passing contingencies, of a reasonable life. "Treat like cases alike (and different cases differently)" is an easy principle. But no cases are quite alike. Much debate concerns which differences matter. The problems run deeper. Even displacing equality of outcomes with equality of opportunity leaves us in bind, for we cannot start equal in society as it presently exists. Whether to maintain society or reform it, we turn to government. The "holistic individualism" of state and citizen then threatens an unwanted uniformity. Escaping the bind requires, as Justin Schwartz argued, recognizing different scales of value, such that wealth and honor might be distinguished, or rank and power. This in turn requires further rules. A comparison between nineteenth-century European liberalism and Yemeni tribalism sheds light on rule-bound alternatives to tyranny. In passing it shows that the idea of law without centralised coercion makes sense and that rules need not serve only instrumental ends.

Fernanda Pirie describes, in Chapter 5, a society that turned its back on legal rules. Medieval Tibetan authors wrote approvingly of law, in the context of their political history, and attributed the establishment of a Buddhist polity in Tibet to the introduction of legal rules. Tibetan religious leaders also adopted the Vinaya, an extremely legalistic code of moral conduct formulated in India, which they taught the members of their monasteries. Yet they resisted creating their own legal rules. Even when giving moral guidance to the laity, they turned to a different style of writing, the open-ended and tacit advice offered by stories, examples, metaphors, and proverbs. This chapter contrasts the two styles of guidance offered by legalistic rules and evocative proverbs. Pirie suggests that influential Tibetans had a positive preference for appealing to sensibilities rather than formulating general rules.

The second part of this collection deals with the materiality, artefactuality, and idiosyncrasy of legal practices. Although rule practices are often associated with judicial reasoning, law is not the monopoly of judges. The legal rule is also the basic tool of administration. The centrality of rules in law's life can be observed e.g. through the materiality of its practices, that is, through their relations to documents. Paying attention to the materiality of action allows us to conceive of the legal rule in a manner other than the syllogistic reasoning and demonstrates how the establishment and organization of a file proceed, as in filigree, from a pre-characterization of the cases at stake that furnishes therefore the contextual and cognitive background of their further treatment.

In Chapter 6, Jean-Marc Weller investigates the question of how a legal file is read. He addresses one of the unavoidable activities of any practice of the legal rule when examined in its ordinary accomplishment: reading. More specifically, the chapter deals with the reading of files. How do civil servants who are in charge of the assessment of a situation and of the characterization of the facts constitutive of it read documents contained in corresponding files? On the basis of several inquiries in the activities of agents of the Ministry of Agriculture in charge of defining farmers' payment rights, we shall examine unremarkable situations of bureaucrats' reading of documents contained in files from the time of their first encounter with them. Beyond the issue of potentially diverse practices of reading, one can observe different conceptions of the rule and of public action. Administrative work should be studied "at work" from an ethnographic and anthropological angle. Two perspectives will be discussed. The first one uses the concept of "literacy" as proposed by Goody (2000) and discussed in literacy studies. The second one is in line with the teachings of sciences and technology studies, as inspired by Latour (2002; Latour and Woolgard, 1986). The praxeological and pragmatic specificity of legal practices will be analyzed in this double perspective and on the basis of a contextualized empirical material.

In Chapter 7, Thomas Scheffer explores, through the analysis of the production of accounts in asylum interviews, the contentious passage "from narrative to confrontation". How do officials produce decidability in any asylum case? The production of decidability is intimately linked to the documentation practices during the asylum hearing. Scheffer uses applied conversation analysis and studies of work for this analysis of bureaucratic practice. The analysis mobilizes ethnographic fieldnotes, self-made audio-recordings, and the official record in order to show how officials turn their interviews into valuable accounts. It shows how the officials have to choose between different "disturbing" rhythms of recording: phrase-by-phrase or paragraph-by-paragraph. These interruptions go along with different practical demands: keeping the interview going or keeping the record going. The record as such is formulated in two successive modes: a narrative mode and a confrontational mode. Both record-parts are interactively and textually produced. The first mode is supported by recordings that leave the extra interviewer's parts out. It reduces the interview down to a single question and comprehensive answers. The second (confrontational) mode, in contrast, highlights the interviewer's questions and interventions. It functions as a signaling device, guiding the reader to those parts of the interviewee's self-driven narrative that are doubtful or contradictory. As a result, the asylum hearing brings about a lasting account that makes it possible to reject the asylum application on justifiable grounds. It produces an evidence-based judgement. The accounting anticipates the legal rules and demands for a justifiable and reasoned decision.

Max Travers, in Chapter 8, describes bail decision-making in the lower courts. Tragic events in Australia such as the Lindt Café siege and the Bourke Street rampage have led to calls to strengthen bail laws. A different approach is being pursued in some US courts that seek to augment judicial decision-making with risk analysis. These initiatives have only had a limited effect in changing criminal courts in Australia, partly because traditional craft skills still have legitimacy. They are perceived, at least among practitioners, as generally resulting in fair outcomes. What is missing from these policy debates has been a close, praxeological analysis by social scientists of how bail decisions are currently made. Drawing on ethnographic research being conducted in magistrates courts in four Australian states, this chapter describes some aspects of judicial decision-making: how judicial officers weigh up factors, and interpret and use rules, in applying the law; different approaches among decision-makers; the craft skills involved in ensuring "fair" remands for defendants who re-offend while on bail; and the effect on decision-making of resource and political pressures. It is suggested that algorithms cannot possibly match the craft skills in making these situated decisions. Nevertheless, if introduced appropriately, such tools may perhaps achieve greater consistency among decision-makers, and confidence in criminal courts.

In Chapter 9, Michael Lynch treats the question of evidence as both a topic and a resource in social studies of scientific, legal, medical, and ordinary activities. Such studies examine how participants in the activities they investigate present and make use of discursive, visual, and material evidence (or what counts as evidence). At the same time, such studies use evidence to support their own empirical claims about, and critiques of, the activities they study. In some cases, the same kinds of evidence, such as audio and video recordings, as well as transcripts of such recordings, depositions, and other written records, are used both by participants in the activities studied and by professional analysts of those studies. Of particular interest for the present study are so-called "viral videos" that have touched off public reactions as well as legal investigations in recent decades. The videos, which are often treated in public commentaries as transparent evidence of excessive force (or worse) by police or military personnel, all-too-frequently are "deconstructed" and rendered equivocal by designated "experts" in legal and quasi-legal investigations. In addition to presenting epistemic disjunctures of interest in their own right, the analytical practices used during such investigations reflexively implicate the way videotapes and transcripts are used in social studies of those same practices. This chapter treats particular uses of evidence as a topic that includes professional social studies as well as the activities they study. The aim is not to contribute a meta-study to the philosophy of social science, but to identify and describe practices for selecting, presenting, and analyzing evidence to warrant and illustrate claims made in social studies as well as the activities they study.

The third part of the volume deals with the thorny issue of meaning and emotions in legal interpretation. The question to know whether references to rules, in legal reasoning, obey a purely formal logic is as old as the advent of codified positive law. The ideal of a dispassionate law, applied in a mechanical way, although it weakened from the First World War onward, is observable beyond the process of digitalizing the law. The fourth part of the volume takes the counter of this ideal and tends to show, while underscoring the irreducibly human competences of judges, the limits of a pretense to integral standardization of decision making.

Barbara Truffin, in Chapter 10, investigates the paradoxes and practical achievements of law and justice in family trials in which spouses face conciliator judges. This chapter accounts for legal practices in a context of apparent judicial de-formalization of hearings regarding amicable settlements taking place in Belgian family courts under professional judges' supervision. Based on a detailed ethnography of these hearings' functioning, the chapter re-examines a major stake of modern family justice through the analysis of the practical accomplishments which lead to the production of an agreement between spouses or parents. The empirical description of the context of production of the agreement make it possible to better understand how the equality among parents and spouses – which proceeds from the legislative evolution – does reflect or not in the application and interpretation of legal provisions by judges who have normally no decisional power. The analysis also depicts, from the angle of practices, the movement of de-formalization of family justice, as well as the re-shaping of the respective domains of the private sphere and public regulation.

In Chapter 11, Julie Colemans examines the relationships between law and emotions. The judicial scene is largely described and analyzed through discursive exchanges, and this offers a fine understanding of judicial courses of action. However, few works studied the judicial scene as the locus of multimodal exchanges mixing language, glances, intonations, postures, and gestures. When becoming sensitive to the non-verbal language that completes and indexes discourse, scholars can take the emotional dimension of judicial action into account. While ubiquitous in audiences, emotions are not considered as a relevant object to study practical legal reasoning, since they neither belong to prescribed factual categories nor to the authoritative legal documents. Unless it is constituted as a topic for discussion (remorse, regrets, suffering), emotions are not welcome at the bar. The judicial ritual does not tolerate expression of anger or sorrow. Speech is framed and largely delegated to law professionals who are supposed to adopt a measured posture, while the hearing is deemed to proceed without hitches. Surreptitiously, however, emotional expressions offer precious landmarks to law professionals, especially judges, who extract from them indications as to the veracity of alleged facts, the relevance of pleaded arguments, or the authenticity of the formulated request. Emotions become thus an integral part of the modalities of judicial reasoning. It supposes that judges proceed against the background of shared cultural knowledge, that is, a set of notions, codes, knowledges, standards, and tags within which an ordinary member of society moves in a way that is both competent and unproblematic. After having paved the ground of an anthropological analysis of emotions, the chapter proposes, on the basis of an ethnography conducted in a Belgian court in charge of family disputes, a study of the place of emotions in judicial interaction and in monocultural decision making, which will then be put into perspective with intercultural situations.

In Chapter 12, Baudouin Dupret et al. describe the search for legal grounds in cases of homosexuality in a comparative perspective (Senegal, Egypt, Lebanon, and Indonesia). The authors wonder how judges play by the rules when the law is silent. It appears that, on the one hand, even in cases in which the legal basis is thin or absent, judges are looking for rules on which to ground their decisions. In that sense, judges are positivist legal practitioners who need legal rules to perform their professional duties. However, on the other hand, moral considerations seem to influence deeply the same judges' legal cognition. The chapter examines how this unfolds in the concrete settings of four countries – Indonesia, Lebanon, Egypt, and Senegal – in cases related to male homosexuality. These countries offer in many respects an excellent basis for the comparative inquiry into the morality of legal cognition – Muslim-majority societies, public condemnations of homosexuality, civil-law inspired legal systems, sensitiveness to international discourse on the state of law and human rights. In each of them, it analyzes cases that attracted much public and media attention. It observes in these cases how judges proceeded in situations in which there was no or only elusive rules to ground their rulings. Despite important differences, the cases exhibit striking similarities in the ways in which judges bypass gaps and silences in legislation via the selection of alternate rules that prove efficient in sanctioning morally associated aspects of the accused persons' allegedly deviant behavior.

Do the empirical studies by sociologists and anthropologists support the classical philosophical positions of legal realists and formalists, and contemporary versions by legal philosophers in this volume? We would not see empirical research as necessarily having the capacity to settle debates among philosophers. The chapters do, however, show in detail how legal practitioners use and interpret rules. Although we have not addressed every topic or drawn on every theoretical approach, the chapters demonstrate the value of law and society studies as an inter-disciplinary field. We hope that anthropologists, sociologists, philosophers, and legal researchers will find the combination of approaches interesting. We look forward to further conceptual and empirical studies about legal rules.

Notes

1 See the introduction page vii–viii. There also is a discussion in the 1981 pulsar paper (especially pp. 133–134) about the quiddity of scientific work. He also used haecceity instead of quiddity: see ftn. 16, p. 99 of Garfinkel's Program (2002).
2 For discussion, see Dupret (2011), Colemans and Dupret (2018, introduction), Travers and Manzo (1997), Dupret et al. (2015).
3 It should be noted that all the traditions that contribute to this collection offer distinctive ways of theorizing and researching law. There are, for example, significant differences in sociology between constructivist traditions and ethnomethodology (Button and Sharrock, 1993), or in philosophy between different interpretations of Wittgenstein on rules (see Travers this volume). Our aim in this collection is not to get drawn into these debates, but to explore how a number of theories and traditions can converge in examining rules in practice.

References

Button, G. and Sharrock, W. (1993) 'A disagreement over agreement and consensus in constructionist sociology', *Journal for the Theory of Social Behaviour*, 23, pp. 1–25.

Colemans, J. and Dupret, B. (eds.) (2018) *Ethnographies du raisonnement juridique.* Issy-Les-Moulineaux: Lextenso-L.G.D.J., coll Droit et société, Recherches et Travaux.

Dupret, B. (2011) *Adjudication in Action: An Ethnomethodology of Law, Morality and Justice.* Farnham: Ashgate.

Dupret, B., Lynch, M. and Berard, T. (eds) (2015) *Law at Work. Studies in Legal Ethnomethods.* Oxford: Oxford University Press.

Ewick, P. and Silbey, S.S. (1992) 'Conformity, contestation and resistance: An account of légal consciousness', *New England Law Review*, 26, pp. 731–749.

Ewick, P. and Silbey, S.S. (1998) *The Common Place of Law: Stories from Everyday Life.* Chicago, IL: University of Chicago Press.

Garfinkel, H. (1967) *Studies in Ethnomethodology.* Englewood Cliffs, NJ: Prentice-Hall.

Garfinkel, H. (ed.) (1986) *Ethnomethodological Studies of Work.* London: Routledge & Kegan Paul.

Garfinkel, H. (2002) *Ethnomethodology's Program: Working Out Durkheim's Aphorism*, edited by A. Warfield Rawls, Lanham, MD: Rowman & Littlefield.

Garfinkel, H., Lynch, M., and Livingston, E. (1981) 'The work of a discovering science construed with materials from the optically discovered pulsar', *Philosophy of the Social Sciences*, 11, pp. 131–158.

Goody, J. (2000) *The Power of the Written Tradition.* Washington, DC: Smithsonian Institution Press.

Hart, H.L.A. (1961) *The Concept of Law.* Oxford: Clarendon Press.

Kelsen, H. (1967) *Pure Theory of Law.* Berkeley: University of California Press.

Latour, B. (2002) *La fabrique du droit. Une ethnographie du Conseil d'Etat.* Paris: La découverte.

Latour, B and Woolgar, S. (1986) *Laboratory Life: The Construction of Scientific Facts.* Princeton, NJ: Princeton University Press.

Macaulay, S. and Mertz, E. (2013) 'New legal realism and the empirical turn' in Banakar, R. and Travers, M. (eds.) *Introduction to Law & Social Theory.* Oxford: Hart Publishing, pp. 195–210.

Merry, S. (1990) *Getting Justice and Getting Even, Legal Consciousness among Working-Class Americans*. Chicago, IL: University of Chicago Press.
Mertz, E. (1994) 'Legal language: Pragmatics, poetics, and social power', *Annual Review of Anthropology*, 23, 435–455.
Mertz, E. (2007a) 'Semiotic anthropology', *Annual Review of Anthropology*, 36, pp. 337–353. https://doi.org/10.1146/annurev.anthro.36.081406.094417
Mertz, E. (2007b) *The Language of Law School: Learning to "Think Like a Lawyer."* Oxford: Oxford University Press.
Mertz, E., Ford, W.K. and Matoesian, G. (eds.) (2016) *Translating the Social World for Law: Linguistic Tools for a New Legal Realism*. Oxford: Oxford University Press.
Sarat, A. (1990) '… "The law is all over": Power, resistance and the legal consciousness of the welfaire Poor', *Yale Journal of Law and Humanities*, 2, pp. 343–379.
Travers, M. and Manzo, J.F. (1997) *Law in Action. Ethnomethodological and Conversation Analytic Approaches to Law*. Ashgate: coll. Socio-Légal Studies.
Wittgenstein, L. (1967) *Philosophical Investigations* (transl. Anscombe, G.E.M., Philosophische Untersuchungen [1953]). Oxford and Cambridge, MA: Blackwell.

1 Ruleness

Frederick Schauer

On the idea of a regulative rule

A half-century ago, the philosopher John Searle offered an enduring distinction between two types of rules (Searle, 1969, pp. 33–42).[1] One type he labeled *constitutive*, and it is the type of rule especially familiar in the context of rule-defined and rule-bounded enterprises such as sports and games. In such enterprises, there are rules that define – or *constitute* – certain activities having specified consequences. In football, for example, the rules of the sport tell us what is necessary for some physical action to count as a *goal*, and thus the rules can be said to constitute the very idea of a goal. Without the rules of football, using one's foot to propel a leather or rubber sphere into a net between two posts is just that, and nothing more, but once we are playing football – within the enterprise of football – the exact same physical actions now count as a goal.

The basic idea of a constitutive rule is most easily grasped in those instances in which the label for what the behaviors constitute has no meaning outside of the context and contours of the game. So although there is perhaps some loose relationship between the idea of a goal in football and the ordinary language meaning of having a goal in everyday life, the same does not apply to *castling* in chess, to a *try* in rugby, or to a *trick* in contract bridge. The rules of chess constitute the activity of castling, and without the rules of chess there would be no castling at all. And so too with tries in rugby, tricks in bridge, and countless other rule-constituted activities in everyday life as well as in games.[2] To *prorogue* a legislature is to suspend its session, but without the institution of legislatures there would be no prorogation at all.

Searle offered the idea of such constitutive rules by way of contrast with the perhaps more familiar kind of rule – the *regulative* rule. Consider the typical motorway speed limit, 120 km/hour, for example. Although it is not possible to castle without the enterprise of chess and without the constitutive rules that are part of that game, the same cannot be said of high-speed driving. Even were there no speed limits, it would be possible to drive at 120 km/hour, or for that matter at 200 km/hour, and thus the 120 km/hour rule regulates pre-existing (in the conceptual and not the temporal sense) behavior. Without the rules of chess there could be no castling, but without the rules of driving (the speed limit) there could still be driving in excess of 120 km/hour. Regulative rules thus do not create – or constitute – forms of behavior, but instead only regulate conceptually antecedently existing behavior in ways that constitutive rules do not.

The very existence and idea of regulative rules, however, both entails and presupposes that there can be unregulated behavior. At least as to speed limits, for example, the German autobahns are unregulated domains, leaving a certain form of antecedently possible behavior untouched by external rules. Indeed, and even more commonly, the same absence of regulative rules holds with respect to many of our personal and everyday activities. Some people, for example, put on both socks before they put on either of their shoes, while others put on one sock and then one shoe and then the other sock and the other shoe. But there is no rule in any country that I know of that tells people which of these options to choose.[3] And accordingly, again, putting on one's socks and shoes can be understood as an unregulated or rule-free form of behavior.[4]

Although it might be difficult even to imagine anything understood as a society or culture without at least some constitutive rules, the idea of decision-making without constraint by regulative rules turns out to be well-represented in the theoretical literature as well as in the kinds of everyday activities I have just described. Consider, to take a particularly prominent example, Max Weber's almost certainly erroneous description of so-called *q'adi* (or *khadi*) justice in Islamic law (Weber 1954, p. 351).[5] Putting aside the inaccuracy of locating the idea within Islamic law, Weber posited, as an ideal type, a decision-making regime in which the decision-makers make decisions entirely on the basis of their own rule-free reactions to particular events and particular controversies. Niklas Luhmann (1985, p. 15) describes Weber's picture as depicting "personal arbitrariness," and for Weber this rule-free approach to decision-making marks the earliest stage of legal development, with progressively increasing material rationality and similarly increasing rule-based formality marking the development of what he took to be true legality.[6] And although it is easy to mock Weber's image of *khadi* justice as a caricature not only of Islamic law but also of pretty much any modern decision-making environment, it is worth noting that Weber's picture of rule-free decision-making bears interesting similarities to the modern perspective in moral philosophy known as *particularism*.[7] And perhaps even more relevantly here, it is worthwhile noting the heavily particularized (as well as psychologized) description of judicial decision-making most commonly attributed to Jerome Frank's version of American Legal Realism (Frank, 1930).[8]

Even if extreme particularism, whether from Weber or Dancy or Frank or anyone else, is difficult to fathom, at least today, its theoretical existence serves to remind us that regulative rules are best understood not as necessary or inevitable, but instead as marking a contingent specific approach to decision-making. Indeed, such contingency of rule-based decision-making becomes even clearer once we look at those forms of decision-making that may not be particularistic all the way down, but nevertheless seek to apply one and only one overarching goal or standard or criterion directly to any specific event or decision-making situation. For the act-utilitarian, for example, the correct decision in every single instance is the decision that will maximize utility, however utility (or welfare) is to be measured (Smart, 1956, 1973; Bayles, 1968; Mulgan et al., 2014). All sophisticated act-utilitarians, however, recognize that such case-by-case optimization is beyond the human capacities for thought and decision-making. As a result, most act-utilitarians recognize the importance in some way of having and using *rules of thumb*.[9] Such rules advise the decision-maker on how to decide cases of a certain type but without performing a full utility calculation for each decision. What makes such rules rules of thumb, however, and not rules *simpliciter*, is that for the rule-of-thumb-assisted act-utilitarian decision-maker the result indicated by applying the rule of thumb can be rejected if the decision-maker has good reason to believe that the rule-of-thumb-indicated result will not on this occasion maximize utility (Smart 1956, 1973; Bayles, 1968).

By contrast, so-called *rule-utilitarians* have a more robust conception of rule-based decision-making.[10] For most rule-utilitarians, decisions should be made according to the rule whose following will produce the greatest aggregate utility when followed over time or when followed by an entire population or some relevant subset thereof (Alexander, 1985, pp. 315–332). The rule-utilitarian rejects the "mere" rule of thumb approach because she understands that various cognitive or decisional impairments will produce mistakes for the decision-maker who attempts to maximize utility in the individual case, whether she does so by direct utility calculation or even by applying rules of thumb subject to defeat when the rule of thumb produces something other than the utility-maximizing outcome. It is better to accept some number of mistakes, the rule-utilitarian believes, than to endure an even greater number of mistakes by allowing mistake-prone particularistic decision-makers to attempt to maximize utility in every particular case.

Of rules and reasons

The distinction between act- and rule-utilitarianism allows us, utilitarianism (or even consequentialism more broadly) itself apart, to distinguish act-based from rule-based decision-making.[11] Act-based decision-making seeks to apply whatever reasons, goals, or principles exist in some decision-making environment to particular instances without the mediation of rules. By contrast, rule-based decision-making, even if ultimately based on exactly the same reasons, goals, or principles, does not apply those reasons, goals, or principles directly to the matter at hand, but applies the rules thought to optimize the pursuit of such reasons, goals, or principles across time and across instances, but without any direct recourse to the reasons, goals, or principles themselves in making particular decisions. A rule-based approach to speed limits, for example, even if ultimately based on the goal of maximizing highway safety, would instruct its enforcers and adjudicators (and, *a fortiori*, drivers) not to attempt to determine whether some motorist was or was not driving safely, but only to determine whether that motorist did or did not exceed the posted speed limit rule.

The safe driver who is driving under safe conditions, but who is nevertheless exceeding the speed limit – the rule – can be used to illustrate the basic issue. Although totally rule-free decision-making environments are somewhere between rare and non-existent, the central question in any decision-making environment possessing rules is about just how those rules will be treated by their subjects and, more importantly, how the rules will be treated by those who interpret, apply, and enforce the rules. And at this point in the analysis we can posit two extremes. At one extreme, or pole, a rule would be transparent to its background justification – the *ratio legis*, as it is sometimes put – as with the example of safe driving that still violates the speed limit rule. And if the rule is totally transparent to its background justification, then such safe driving that exceeded the speed limit would not ultimately be considered a rule violation because the justification behind the rule was not violated. At an even greater extreme of transparency, the rules would be transparent even to the best all-things-considered decision. The rules would be treated as a mere rule of thumb, to be discarded when they failed to produce the best result on a particular occasion, or, in the weaker version, when they did not produce the result that would be produced by applying the rule's background justification to the particular act or event. At this pole, all of the rules that exist in a decision-making environment are treated by decision-makers, and even by rule-subjects, as "mere" rules of thumb. And thus the one extreme is the one in which there are rules, but the rules carry no weight in themselves, making them defeasible whenever it appears that they have not or will not produce the best result. At this extreme the rules may exist as useful heuristics based on statistically predominant tendencies, but they have no normative effect themselves.

At the other extreme is an approach to decision-making in which the rules *qua* rules are treated as absolutely dispositive, even if the results they indicate on particular occasions appear decidedly suboptimal, or even wrong. The driver who is driving at 105 km/hour when the speed limit is 100 km/hour is treated as a rule violator, even if the driver is in fact driving safely given the conditions, or even if the driver has a very good reason for exceeding the speed limit. In the vernacular of some of modern legal theory, treating the rules in this way would be a form of *formalism*.[12] To be formalistic in this sense is to follow the linguistic indications of a rule, and to ignore the possibility that those indications might be generating a bad all-things-considered result, or might be generating a bad result when compared to the result that would be generated by direct application of the reason or rationale or justification lying behind the rule.

Ruleness

We have now identified an important feature of governance by rules. Because rules imperfectly reflect their background justifications, and thus and necessarily align also imperfectly with the best all-things-considered rule-independent decision, there will inevitably be instances in which the rule-indicated outcome diverges from either the background-justification-indicated outcome or the best all-things-other-than-the-rule-considered outcome. At one extreme it is possible, as just explained, to treat the rule-indicated outcome as dispositive, even when there is divergence with the background-justification-indicated outcome or, even more commonly, the best all-things-considered outcome. Joseph Raz (1975), relevantly, refers to the best all-things-considered outcome as the best outcome on the "balance of reasons." Raz, representing at best only a slight variation on what I have marked as one pole or one extreme, takes rule-based decision-making as excluding certain otherwise eligible reasons,[13] and thus understands rule-based decision-making as necessarily diverging from balance-of-reasons decision-making.

There is no reason to suppose, however, that governance by rules need be this kind of all-or-nothing affair, whether, as I describe it, as an "extreme," or in Raz's version. Instead, we can posit that a rule can have a degree of *weight* against the pressures of what seems to be a better decision. A police officer, for example, might believe that the speed limit rule has sufficient weight to prevail against the claims of a safe driver on a clear day attempting to get to her office on time, but not against the claims of someone rushing an injured person to the hospital. A judge might think that a filing deadline has sufficient weight to prevail in a case in which a missed deadline caused no injustice but was nevertheless caused by forgetfulness, but not so much weight as to prevail when again the missed deadline caused no injustice but was the product of an unexpected natural disaster.

The upshot of the foregoing is the conclusion that a rule can have some degree of weight as against the best all-things-considered decision, and some degree of weight against the decision indicated by the rule's background justification, but that this weight need not be either negligible or, on the other hand, infinite. Indeed, this "some degree" can be represented in terms of different verbal formulas for presumptions of different strengths in favor of a rule or, from the opposite direction, for different burdens of proof or burdens of justification for setting aside the rule-indicated outcome. One possibility, therefore, is that there would be a strong presumption in favor of the rule-indicated outcome, an outcome that would be set aside only if it were clear, or, even stronger, clear beyond a reasonable doubt, that the rule-indicated result was inferior either to the justification-indicated result or to the all-things-except-for-the-rule-indicated result. Somewhat weaker would a presumption in favor of the rule, but one that could be overcome when it appeared reasonable to conclude that the rule-indicated result was suboptimal. And somewhat stronger would be a presumption in favor of the rule that could be overcome only when it was absolutely clear that the rule-indicated result was inferior. Rules derive their strength from the extent of their *entrenchment*, but rules can be more or less entrenched, requiring more or less effort, to extend the metaphor, to unearth them.

All of this is to suggest that a range of possibilities exist between the one extreme of absolute rule dominance – formalism, in one sense of that word (Schauer, 1988,1999, pp. 527 ff.) – and the opposite extreme of the pure rule of thumb with little or no weight. And once we recognize this range of possibilities, we can give a label to the weight or degree of resistance that a rule possesses against the reasons for reaching a seemingly preferable result that diverges from the rule-indicated result. And this label, I want to offer, is *ruleness*. Ruleness, however, is not a feature of rules themselves, but rather of how we treat the rules that do exist. Just as Wittgenstein reminded us that no rule can determine its own application (Bogen, 1972, pp. 183–184; McDowell, 1984) – an arrow on a highway sign does not tell us whether we should head in the direction of the point or of the tail – so too do the rules in any decision-making environment not tell us just what weight those rules should have.[14] The weight of the rules must come from something outside of the rules themselves about how we will treat the rules, and the "something," a variable, is what I have labeled "ruleness."

It is tempting to think of that which provides the degree of weight that rules will have as still another rule, or a second-order rule. But that would be an oversimplification. The weight that first-order rules would have *could* be determined by another rule – a second-order rule[15] – but it could also be determined by that amorphous collection of behaviors and normative reactions to those behaviors that we call a *practice*, again in the Wittgensteinian sense of a practice. These practices in terms of how we treat our rules may not be crystallized in a concrete formulation, and they may not even be crystallize-able (Schauer, 2012, pp. 1–7). Moreover, the practices may change over time, at times dramatically and at times – more commonly – slowly and almost indetectably.

This dimension of ruleness – whether we think of it as another rule or, preferably as just described, as a practice – may be understood either individually or societally. That is, individuals may treat the rules directed to them, the rules of which they are subjects, as being of greater or lesser strength. Some people, for example, treat speed limits, "Don't Walk" signs, and a host of rules of etiquette as little more than suggestions. They exceed the speed limit whenever they think it safe to do so; they cross against a "Don't Walk" sign whenever they detect no vehicles approaching; they jump the queue if they suspect that they can get away with it; and they end sentences with prepositions with impunity. Other people, however, are just the opposite, and they stand obediently at street corners when signs say not to walk; they drive at or below the speed limit even on clear, dry days with no traffic; and they pay little attention to the rules of etiquette or grammar.[16] And much the same variability as exists for individual rule-subjects may also exist for individual enforcers and individual adjudicators. Different police officers and different judges may have widely variant views about the rigidity with which they enforce or adjudicate the rules applicable to the issues that come before them.

More importantly, especially in the context of this volume, just as individual rule-subjects or rule-enforcers or rule-adjudicators may treat the rules that apply to them (or that they are tasked with applying) with varying degrees of weight, so too may groups, cities, countries, legal systems, and less formally delineated aggregations of individuals have varying degrees of ruleness collectively. Just as it is well known that different businesses have different so-called corporate cultures, so too might different communities (or, for that matter, businesses) have different rule cultures – different collective views or collective practices with respect to how much strength that community will attribute to the community's rules. In other words, different communities, societies, cultures, subcultures, and legal systems may have different degrees of ruleness – they may be more or less "ruly."

I do not mean to suggest by offering this particular measure of ruleness that there are not other dimensions along which we might evaluate rules.[17] In particular, some number of scholars, especially in the United States, are fond of distinguishing between "rules" and "standards."[18] This distinction, which is also scalar rather than polar, distinguishes crisp and precise directives – rules – from broad, vague, and open-ended ones – standards. "Drive at 100 km/hour or slower" is a rule; "Drive prudently and safely" is a standard.[19] "All legal actions must be filed within three years of the date on which the cause of action arose" is a rule, and all "all actions must be filed in timely fashion so as not to disadvantage the opposing party" is a standard. But although the distinction between rules and standards is valuable in its place, and although we might choose to label the degree of precision in a rule-formulation as the degree of "ruleness" of that directive, the sense of ruleness I offer here is different, and is a property of an individual's or society's attitude about rules, and of an individual's or society's method of treating rules, rather than a linguistic or semantic property of individual directives.

Nor is the conception of ruleness I offer here about the extent of regulation in a society or of a domain of activity. Certain social domains are heavily regulated and thus might be considered rule-heavy, while others are largely free of regulation. This again is a useful distinction, and in many contexts it would be important to distinguish those areas of human activity in which there is a pervasive density of rules (and thus in which there are few unregulated behaviors) from those areas in which rules do not have much of a presence and in which behavior remains largely unregulated. Again, I do not want to detract from the potential value of viewing different domains of human activity in just this way. But the distinction I offer about how rules will be treated when they appear to produce a poor result is different, and it is one that offers a potentially valuable way of evaluating the degree of formal legality across cultures.

Towards systematic empirical inquiry

When the late Judith Shklar (1986) wrote about "legalism," she was writing, critically to be sure, in an empirical mode. She based her criticism on the view that societies, or at least certain societies at certain times in certain respects, should be condemned for preferring legality to morality, for treating the obeisance to form as a value superior to the value of doing the right thing, and for treating law and morality as largely separate domains. And in much the same vein, Henry David Thoreau (1980(1849), p. 228) in the nineteenth century sought to emphasize that "it is not desirable to cultivate a respect for the law, so much as for the right."

Both Shklar and Thoreau, along with scores of others,[20] have taken to the systemic level one end of the distinction I discuss here. Insofar as legal systems are comprised of written laws, and insofar as written laws are rules, then there will invariably be instances of divergence between what the law – rules writ large – requires and what is simply the right thing to do. What concerned Shklar, Thoreau, and many others was the existence of a culture at a particular time and pace in which the legal rules were taken to have considerable resistance against what is, the law apart, right.

There is, of course, another side to this debate, if we can call it that. Theorists of the Rule of Law, perhaps Albert Venn Dicey (1982(1915)) most prominently,[21] have glorified the rule of law (in perhaps a different sense of "rule") over the "rule of men," as Dicey and others put it a century and a half ago, precisely because of a worry not only about self-dealing by political leaders but also because of the degree of variation in what people in power might think was, the law apart, the right thing to do. For Dicey and others, the law and its rules might function as a second-best alternative to a system in which those in power were authorized to embody their own sense of what is right, a sense that turns out often not to be right from a larger perspective. As against an extreme version of Thoreau's preference for the right over the law, the tradition of celebrating the rule of law would ask, skeptically, just whose understanding of the right should prevail.

This is no place to resolve these issues. It is, however, perhaps the place to recognize that different cultures have resolved these issues and debates in different ways at different times. And one window into examining these different resolutions is to ask the question of how a society sees the strength of the claim of its rules, of its laws, and of its legal system generally against the claims of, to oversimplify, the right. And although normative inquiry into what different cultures ought to do in this regard can be valuable, so too can empirical examination of just how different cultures have addressed the question I put forth here – and thus the degree of ruleness that exists within different cultures at different times. The "Don't Walk" sign has a different strength against the pedestrian's own estimation of safety in Helsinki than it does in Naples, and this is as much about attitudes towards rules in general as it is about attitudes towards law.

My casual comparison between the residents of Helsinki and those of Naples is but a hint at what could be a serious inquiry. One such inquiry was undertaken by Patrick Atiyah and Robert Summers (1987) more than 30 years ago, when in a largely impressionistic way they compared the United States and the United Kingdom, or at least the judges in those countries, on just the dimension I describe here. Not surprisingly, they concluded, to use my terminology and not theirs, that there was a substantially greater degree of ruleness in the domain of the British judiciary than there was in that of their American counterparts.

In the time since Atiyah and Summers addressed these issues, the methods of comparative law and comparative sociology have become substantially more sophisticated. As a result, we can now imagine an inquiry similar to theirs in aim but which employs rigorous survey methodology, another that uses experimental methods, still another that looks for cross-cultural or cross-national natural experiments, and yet another that uses qualitative or case study approaches disciplined by the way in which even qualitative research can rest on basic principles of social science (King et al., 1994). This essay is of course not the place to describe, let alone perform, the kinds of research I have just suggested. It is to be hoped, however, that understanding the dimension of ruleness might provide the basis for formulating hypotheses about the degree of ruleness that prevails in a given legal culture, which in turn might provide an important way of evaluating just what rules do, when they do it, and how they do it.

Notes

1 For a recent recapitulation, see John R. Searle (2018, pp. 51–54). A particularly valuable commentary is Frank Hindriks (2009, pp. 253–275). As Hindriks explains, the rudiments of the idea of constitutive rules had been suggested earlier by Elizabeth Anscombe and John Rawls (and, I might add, H.L.A. Hart (1954, pp. 37–60) and Max Black (1962, 1958, pp. 95–139), but Searle properly gets the credit for full development of the idea. Joseph Raz (1975, pp. 108–113) objects to calling these things "rules," arguing that they are not rules at all but only "act-descriptions," but nothing in this essay turns on resolving the terminological dispute between Searle and Raz.

2 And, of course, in law. See Hart, *op. cit.* note 1. Without the system of rules that we call law, there would be no "corporations." Corporations exist because of the law, and only within the law. Accordingly, the word "corporation" is defined by the rules of the legal system in which corporations exist.

3 The example comes from a now-famous scene in the 1970s American television comedy series *All in the Family*. What makes the scene so funny is precisely the fact that Archie Bunker believes that anyone who does not do it the way he does it is doing it "wrong."

4 In another sense of the word "rule," a rule is simply a regularity or habit with no normative dimension. See Hart (1961, pp. 9–12). I could say that "as a rule" I put on both of my socks before putting on either of my shoes, but this is not a rule that can be either broken or violated. Nor, for that matter, can it be followed in

any strong sense of following, or obeying. If I switch from the two-socks-then-two-shoes practice to the one-sock-one-shoe-other-sock-other-shoe approach I have not violated any rule, because the "as a rule" behavior I have engaged in in the past had no normative weight behind it. From here on I will ignore this sense of a "rule" as a habit or regularity, and focus instead only on rules with normative dimensions.

5 For application and discussion, see, for example, Ansbach and Monsen (1989), Morris (1958), Silbey (1981).

6 See Kalberg (1980), Trubek (1972).

7 See Dancy (2004), Hooker and Little (2000), McKeever and Ridge (2008).

8 See also Hutcheson (1929). For discussion, see Schauer (2009, pp. 124–141). For Frank, particularism in judicial decision-making was both a psychological inevitability as well as being normatively desirable, but others have advocated particularistic judicial decision-making – focusing on the equities of particular disputes – without taking on Frank's dubious psychological and psychiatric baggage. See, for example, Bartlett (1990) and Sunstein (1999).

9 See, for example, Regan (1980). For a general discussion of rules of thumb, see Schauer (1991, pp. 105–109).

10 See Brandt (1959), Hare (1981), Hooker (2000), Urmson (1968, pp. 3–39).

11 See generally Schauer (2009).

12 See Schauer (1988, pp. 509–548). But because "formalism" is so commonly considered pejorative, and because there are multiple meanings of both "form" and formalism," it is probably best to avoid this distracting terminology. "As everyone knows, there is no expression more ambiguous than the word 'formal' . . ." Weber (1977), as quoted in Summers (2006, p. 40 n.3).

13 And thus, in the Razian scheme, rules operate as second-order exclusionary reasons excluding some first-order reasons. For discussion, explication, and criticism, see Alexander (1990), Clarke (1977, pp. 252–255), Edmundson (1993, pp. 329–343).

14 See, analogously, in the context of the law of evidence, Barzun (2008, pp. 1957–2018).

15 Note Hart's designation of rules of recognition, rules of change, and rules of adjudication as "secondary rules." Hart, *op. cit.* note 1, pp. 76–79, 91–99. See Guest (1972, pp. 417–425).

16 I am not ignoring the role of sanctions, social pressure, criticism, and other forms of external pressure and incentives. I just at this point want to emphasize that different people may have different internal attitudes towards the force or strength of rules, and so too might different people have different reactions to how they react to the possibility of sanctions or other external forms of pressure. But this is not to deny that the degree of compliance with rules will also vary with the extent of enforcement – by formal legal sanctions or otherwise – will also determine the strength that rules have within a particular culture. See Schauer (2015).

17 For a list of some dimensions, see Baldwin (1995, pp. 7–11). And still another way of situating the role and operation of rules is to be found in Conley and O'Barr (1990).

18 See, for example, Gillette (1996), Kaplow (1992), Korobkin (2000), Sullivan (1992).

19 For an illuminating analysis of a shift from numerical speed limit rules to vague standards and then back again, see King and Sunstein (1999).

20 See, for example, Cover (1984), Luban (1988).

21 Useful overviews include Ronald A. Cass (2001), Craig (1997), Fallon, Jr. (1997), Rubenstein (2018), Waldron (2008).

References

Alexander, L. (1985) 'Pursuing the good – indirectly', *Ethics*, 95, pp. 315–332.
Alexander, L. (1990) 'Law and exclusionary reasons', *Philosophical Topics*, 18, pp. 5–22.
Ansbach, D.F. and Monsen, S.H. (1989) 'Determinate sentencing, formal rationality, and khadi justice in Maine: An application of Weber's typology,' *Journal of Criminal Justice*, 17, pp. 471–485.
Atiyah, P. and Summers, R. (1987) *Form and Substance in Anglo-American Law*. Oxford: Clarendon Press.
Baldwin, R. (1995) *Rules and Government*. Oxford: Clarendon Press.
Bartlett, K.T. (1990) 'Feminist legal methods', *Harvard Law Review*, 103, pp. 829–888.
Barzun, C.L. (2008) 'Rules of weight', *Notre Dame Law Review*, 83, 1957–2018.
Bayles, M. (ed.) (1968) *Contemporary Utilitarianism*. New York: Doubleday.
Black, M. (1962) *Models and Metaphors*. Ithaca, NY: Cornell University Press, pp. 95–139.
Bogen, J. (1972) *Wittgenstein's philosophy of language: Some aspects of its development*. London: Routledge.
Brandt, R. (1959) *Ethical Theory*. New York: Prentice-Hall.
Cass, R.A. (2001) *The Rule of Law in America*. Baltimore, MD: Johns Hopkins University Press.
Clarke, D.S. Jr. (1977) 'Exclusionary reasons', *Mind*, 86, pp. 252–255.
Conley, J.M. and O'Barr, W.M. (1990) *Rules versus Relationships: The Ethnography of Legal Discourse*. Chicago, IL: University of Chicago Press.
Cover, R.M. (1984) *Justice Accused: Antislavery and the Judicial Process*. New Haven, CT: Yale University Press.
Craig, P. (1997) 'Formal and substantive conceptions of the rule of law: An analytical framework', *Public Law*, pp. 467–87.
Dancy, J. (2004) *Ethics without Principles*. Oxford: Clarendon Press.
Dicey, A.V. (1982[1915]) *Introduction to the Study of the Law of the Constitution*. E.C.S, 8th ed. London: Macmillan.
Edmundson, W.A. (1993) 'Rethinking exclusionary reasons: A second edition of Joseph Raz's', *Law Philosophy*, 12, pp. 329–343.
Fallon, R.H. Jr. (1997) '"The rule of law" as a concept in constitutional discourse', *Columbia Law Review*, 97, pp. 1–56.
Frank, J. (1930) *Law and the Modern Mind*. New York: Brentano's.
Gillette, C.P. (1996) 'Rules, standards, and precautions in payment systems', *Virginia Law Review*, 82, pp. 181–251.
Guest, F.D. (1972) 'Hart's primary and secondary rules', *Otago Law Review*, 2, pp. 417–425.
Hare, R.M. (1981) *Moral Thinking: Its Levels, Method and Point*. Oxford: Clarendon Press.
Hart, H.L.A. (1954) 'Definition and theory in jurisprudence', *Law Quarterly Review*, 70, pp. 37–60.
Hart, H.L.A. (2012[1961]) *The Concept of Law*, 3rd ed. Edited by Bulloch, P. A., Raz, J. and Green, L. Oxford: Oxford University Press.
Hindriks, F. (2009) 'Constitutive rules, language, and ontology', *Erkenntnis*, 71, pp. 253–275.
Hooker, B. (2000) *Ideal Code, Real World: A Rule-Consequentialist Theory of Morality*. Oxford: Oxford University Press.

Hooker, B. and Little, M. (eds.) (2000) *Moral Particularism*. Oxford: Oxford University Press.
Hutcheson, J.C. (1929) 'The judgment intuitive: The function of the "Hunch" in judicial decision', *Cornell Law Quarterly*, 14(3), pp. 274–288.
Kalberg, S. (1980) 'Max Weber's types of rationality: Cornerstone for the analysis of rationalization processes in history', *American Journal of Sociology*, 85, pp. 1145–1179.
Kaplow, L. (1992) 'Rules versus standards: An economic analysis', *Duke Law Journal*, 42, pp. 557–629.
King, G., Keohane, R.O. and Verba, S. (1994) *Designing Social Inquiry: Scientific Inference in Qualitative Research*. Princeton, NJ: Princeton University Press.
King, R.E. and Sunstein, C.R. (1999) 'Doing without speed limits', *Boston University Law Review*, 79, pp. 155–91.
King-Utz, E. (Martin Albrow, trans) (1985) *Introduction to N. Luhmann, a Sociological. Theory of Law*. London: Routledge & Kegan Paul.
Korobkin, R.B. (2000) 'Behavioral analysis and legal form: Rules vs. standards revisited', *Oregon Law Review*, 79, pp. 23–60.
Luban, D. (1988) *Lawyers and Justice: An Ethical Study*. Princeton, NJ: Princeton University Press.
McDowell, J. (1984) "Wittgenstein on Following a Rule," *Synthese*, 58 (1984), 325–63.
McKeever, S. and Ridge, M. (2008) 'Preempting principles: Recent debates in moral particularism', *Philosophy Compass*, 3, pp. 1177–1192.
Morris, C. (1958) 'Law, reason and sociology', *University of Pennsylvania Law Review*, 107, pp. 147–65.
Mulgan, T., Eggleston, B. and Miller, D. (eds.) (2014) *Cambridge Companion to Utilitarianism*. Cambridge: Cambridge University Press.
Raz, J. (1975) *Practical Reason and Norms*. London: Hutchinson.
Regan, D.H. (1980) *Utilitarianism and Co-operation*. Oxford: Clarendon Press.
Rheinstein, M. (ed.) (1954) *Max Weber on Law in Economy and Society*. New York: Simon & Schuster.
Rubenstein, D.S. (2018) 'Taking care of the rule of law', Georg*e Washington University Law Review*, 86, pp. 168–230.
Schauer, F. (1988) 'Formalism', *Yale Law Journal*, 97, pp. 509–548.
Schauer, F. (1991) *Playing by the Rules: A Philosophical Examination of Rule-Based Decision-Making in Law and in Life*. Oxford: Clarendon Press.
Schauer, F. (1999) 'Formalism revisited,' *University of Chicago Law Review*, 66, pp. 527ff.
Schauer, F. (2009) *Thinking Like a Lawyer: A New Introduction to Legal Reasoning*. Cambridge, MA: Harvard University Press.
Schauer, F. (2012) 'Is the rule of recognition a rule?' *Transnational Legal Theory*, 3, pp. 1–7.
Schauer, F. (2015) *The Force of Law*. Cambridge, MA: Harvard University Press.
Searle, J.R. (1969) *Speech Acts: An Essay in the Philosophy of Language*. Cambridge: Cambridge University Press.
Searle, J.R. (2018) 'Constitutive rules', *Argumenta*, 4, pp. 51–54.
Shklar, J.N. (1986) *Legalism: Law, Morals, and Political Trials*. Cambridge, MA: Harvard University Press,

Silbey, S.S. (1981) 'Making sense of the lower courts', *Justice System Journal*, 6(1), pp. 13–21.

Smart, J.J.C. (1956) 'Extreme and restricted utilitarianism', *Philosophical Quarterly*, 6, pp. 344–54.

Smart, J.J.C. (1973) 'An outline of a system of utilitarian ethics' in Smart, J.J.C. and Williams, B. (eds.) *Utilitarianism for and Against*. Cambridge: Cambridge University Press, pp. 1–74.

Sullivan, K.M. (1992) 'The justices of rules and standards', *Harvard Law Review*, 106, pp. 22–123.

Summers, R.S. (2006) *Form and Function in a Legal System: A General Study*. Cambridge: Cambridge University Press.

Sunstein, C.R. (1999) *One Case at a Time: Judicial Minimalism on the Supreme Court*. Cambridge, MA: Harvard University Press.

Thoreau, H.D. (1980[1849]) 'On the duty of civil disobedience' in *Walden and "Civil Disobedience."* New York: Signet Books, p. 228.

Trubek, D.M. (1972) 'Max Weber on law and the rise of capitalism', *Wisconsin Law Review*, 1972, pp. 720–753.

Urmson, J.O. (1968) 'The interpretation of the moral philosophy of J.S. Mill' in Bayles, M. (ed.) *Contemporary Utilitarianism*. New York: Doubleday, pp. 3–39.

Waldron, J. (2008) 'The concept and the rule of law', *Georgia Law Review*, 43(1) pp. 1–61.

Part 1

Ruleness and its relativity

Scholars address the concept 'ruleness' in contrastive manners, according to disciplinary perspectives (e.g. legal theory, historical anthropology, language studies, law in action) and personal sensitivities. Whereas the critical perspective on law and justice denunciates the formalism implicated by the statement of rule centrality in legal work, other approaches wonder how rules manifest their presence in the heart of law's life. Between the formalism of the pure theory of law and the sociologism of realistic theories, there is a whole spectrum of intermediate stances as well as some room for a theory of rule-based decision making that considers rules as points of reference endowed with an open texture. While it is not the stance taken by the coeditors of this volume, it might also be the case that disciplines do not really speak to each other and that the merits of each research tradition should be appreciated in its own terms.

Exploring the issue of rule-following and rule interpretation, Marianne Constable and Linda Ross Meyer underscore and refine the double claim made in this volume's introduction that legal rules do not determine the behaviors of people to which they are supposed to apply, but serve as their point of reference. They stress the classical point that law is not and cannot be exhausted by statements of rules, or codes. They argue further that presuming that rules or codes are sufficient to explain law or to explain conduct is to expect too much of them. Much remains unsaid and much else remains unsayable in the following of rules and in the learning, knowing, telling, hearing, and doing of law in action.

Michel Troper questions the influence of legal practice on the law itself. If, by law, one understands merely a set of rules, and by legal practice the behavior that leads to the production or the application of those rules, then the answer is 'none'. However, the law is much more than a set of rules. Teaching law means describing all sorts of theories that lawmakers and lawyers use to justify, interpret, and apply the rules, some of them being constructed as a result of constraints born out of legal practices. Such is the case of the theory of the State and the related concept of Sovereignty emerging from the practice of the hierarchization of norms.

Fleshing out the concept of equality, Paul Dresch also addresses the contingency of law and legal systems, but in the opposite perspective, that of cultural relativism. In Western societies, anthropologists often do not distinguish the opposition between hierarchy and equality from that between holism and individualism. Certainly this generalized fascination with equality and inequality is unusual. Explicit rules of the kind that law trades in involve explicit categories, and these categories determine what kinds of similarity and difference count for what purposes. In Western societies, where law stresses the equivalence of generic, isolated persons, there is an affinity between explicit rules and the formal equality of individuals. Informally, rules exclude discussion of substantive difference.

As a kind of counter-example, Fernanda Pirie describes a society that turned its back on legal rules. Medieval Tibetan authors wrote approvingly of law, in the context of their political history, and attributed the establishment of a Buddhist polity in Tibet to the introduction of legal rules. Tibetan religious leaders also adopted an extremely legalistic code of moral conduct, which they taught the members of their monasteries. Yet they resisted creating their own legal rules. Even when giving moral guidance to the laity, they turned to a different style of writing, the open-ended and tacit advice offered by stories, examples, metaphors, and proverbs. This contrasts ruleness and another style of normative guidance, that of evocative proverbs.

2 No rule for the application of rules

Marianne Constable and Linda Ross Meyer

Within Anglo-American legal scholarship, philosophers often define law as a system of articulated rules and take seriously debates as to the paradoxes and extent of rule-following. Sociolegal studies, by contrast, criticize philosophers' emphasis on law as rules. Early twentieth-century legal realism challenged what they perceived as the dominant view in U.S. law schools that law was determined by, or consisted of, formal statements of rules and their application. Legal realists and the social scientists of law who followed them generally turned to what they considered the reality or actuality of law to emphasize how judges, no less than other legal officials and actors, rely on social interests, public policies, personal predilections, and other more nefarious factors, in decision-making. Their studies famously distinguish the rules of law "on the books" from the *realpolitik* law "in action."

In this paper, we bring a different challenge to claims as to the foundational role of statements of rules in law. Grounded, like legal realism, in the actuality of how persons conduct themselves and decide or know what to do, we focus, unlike much legal realism, on the language and learning of law.[1] We argue, in keeping with many others in cross-disciplinary fields of law and humanities, that in law as elsewhere, both statements of rules – as acts of speech – and the application of rules – as acts of judgment – involve practices that cannot be fully described or properly understood as codes of rules, however detailed. If law in the broadest sense involves acting or knowing what to do, one can ask how law happens: how it is learned, told, and heard, and what knowing law must be.

Our concern is as much with law as with rules, about which we make three basic points below. First, learning law is not a learning "that" certain rules are law, but learning "how" to do things with legal situations, legal words, and legal materials. Correspondingly, judgment is never logically determined by a preexisting rule but involves an expert assessment of a situation, or case, from a standpoint of care for justice. Second, law includes customs and practices that cannot be completely stated in codes, both because the "said" always depends upon much context and background that is "not said," and because words are always open-ended, moving from past context to future application by analogy, rather than by logical entailment. Third, insofar as law aspires to fairness or justice, self-restraint and humility guide and moderate the exercise of its power. Fully articulating these aspirational features of law in written rules, or even in propositional language, would eliminate the possibility of law becoming better, and its practitioners wiser, in an as-yet-unknowable human future.

Part I (Learning what to do) presents some background underlying our claims that law appears largely as a practice or set of activities involving language which must be learned and which may be done in more or less skilled ways that transcend knowledge of code-like rules. Part II (Judging cases) offers examples of how knowing law involves much more than statements and applications of rules. Rules may be an aspect of an activity or practice, but they are never enough. Part III (Expectations of rules) then explains why one cannot expect to formulate rules, or a set of rules, to fully guide behavior or to cover all instances. Confusing, as some do, the rule of law with a system of rules, Part IV (Rule of law as law of rules?) concludes, fails to do justice to the responsibilities of officials and of others in their encounters with law and in their judgments as to how to act according to law.

Learning what to do

The claim that there is "no rule for the application of rules" is by now familiar to many, even if there is disagreement as to whether the argument comes from Kant, Wittgenstein, Arendt, or others. The point is that to follow rules, like following recipes or applying formulas, requires prior knowledge, and that to ask for a rule for the following of rules is like asking for a recipe for following recipes. The analogy of law to cooking suggests that engagements with rules happen not only in formal or official domains, but also in everyday activities. Answers to questions about how to follow rules, like those about recipes, at best offer rules of thumb and, if insisted on, foreclose action or generate an infinite regress.

If there is no rule for the application of rules though, how do persons, judges, officials, know what to do? They learn in the same ways that they learn other things. A beginner may indeed actually begin with some acontextual features and rules for engaging in an activity or skill, as Dreyfus and Dreyfus (1986, p. 111) argue but, as persons become more skilled, they come to recognize situational aspects of the activity that are not covered by the rules. Their growing competence comes to depend not only on their following basic rules then, but also on their involvement in the activity: on making choices as to perspectives and plans when they encounter situations not (clearly) covered by the rules and taking responsibility for successes and failures entailed by their choices. (With experience, one's discernment develops: is this wheat flour a little drier than usual and shall I compensate with a tad more liquid?)

Dreyfus offers learning to drive or to play chess as examples of "skill acquisition" and points to the various emotions that accompany choice and responsibility: anticipation, fear, and anxiety; joy or elation at doing well;

shame or sadness at making mistakes as one learns (Dreyfus, 2004). He argues that as one moves beyond the first three skill levels – novice, advanced beginner, and competent performer – to proficiency, one comes to rely increasingly on one's own judgments as to the situations in which one finds oneself. Ultimately, he argues, the expert has encountered such an array of possible situations that his or her decision as to how to act has become a matter of "intuition" in which rules are forgotten in favor of situational judgment. Even if Dreyfus and Dreyfus are not quite right that the expert "forgets" the rules and even if it is rather the case, as others have argued, that expert performance itself involves a kind of "chunking" and categorizing or classifying of aspects of situations into something more akin to provisional rules of thumb, the point is that expertise requires more than propositional knowledge of rules or their logically-entailed application (Gobbet and Chassy, 2009).[2] Becoming an expert juggler, for instance, is not so much a matter of learning to throw mechanically or of developing more complex routines, although this may be part of it, but rather involves learning to deal increasingly well with throws that are slightly off as one engages in increasingly skillful performances (Wilson, 1999).

In short, learning to do something well is a matter of practice and skill that involves at least in part the development of intuition and flexibility of performance. But such learning also involves – even prior to the beginners' rules – some understanding of context. To explain to a novice driver the rules for shifting gears makes no sense if the novice does not know what a car is or does; to explain the rules for moving chess pieces on a board makes no sense if the beginner does not somehow grasp that he or she is a player in a game (Wittgenstein §31). Learners of second languages who begin with rules (generally) already speak a mother tongue. And that mother tongue was likely not learned, at least initially, through rules of grammar or parts of speech, but through experience. Indeed one might argue that in learning *to* speak a first language, children learn what language is and *does* (ibid. §32). Even thinking and perceiving, philosopher Alva Noe (2012) argues, in rejecting a representational account of knowledge, are skills for accessing the world that one must learn to do.

So too, interpretation or, rather, the interpreting that goes on in legal contexts is an activity that one learns *to* do. Indeed, the bulk of legal activities – speaking and hearing, reading and writing, researching, arguing, and representing – must be learned. Law schools teach students to read, write, speak, question, and answer in particular ways (Mertz, 2007). As future practitioners, students must learn how to make particular kinds of "speech acts" and what makes those of others matter. What makes an act of complaint, defense, objection, rebuttal, offer, acceptance, agreement, appointment, holding, or appeal, the act that it is? What makes a particular act successful or, in J.L.Austin's terms, "felicitous" (Austin, 1962)? Students learn that particular kinds of utterances must meet particular conditions that others need not. Contracts unlike verdicts, for instance, require offer and acceptance. Offer and acceptance must be within the power of the parties; parties must articulate – and then each carry out – the terms of their agreement in particular ways. Verdicts too must conform to particular conventions and be declared by an authorized hearer. Students learn also to characterize utterances made in particular situations as instances of more general rules – A's response constituted acceptance – even as they learn that the features of any given situation make its conformity to a given rule a matter of gradation – was there really acceptance if the time zones were different? (Essay exams confirm a student's sense of the variability of situations; exams in which all questions are designed to have one correct answer suggest, on the contrary, the transparency of situations and reinforce perceptions of the clearcut character of rules.) As advanced students learn to offer interpretations of increasingly complicated hypothetical situations and to make increasingly sophisticated arguments, they come to realize, again paraphrasing Austin, that for something to count as a particular legal speech act, it must fulfill particular conventions, be carried out correctly and completely, by an appropriate authority, and involve the appropriate intentions and uptake. No matter how brilliant a student's rewriting of a court opinion, that is, it does not have the legitimacy or validity of the opinion of the issuing court. No matter how well-justified a motion, it fails if not filed on time.

And yet, even when all of the conditions and general rules for a successful speech act are met, the act may "fail": a valid objection may be overruled, a procedurally correct verdict overturned or a legitimate appeal denied. And conversely, even an act that does not strictly follow the rules – an insincere promise, for instance – may be binding. How can this be? How is it that following the rules of felicitous performance is not enough to warrant success? Again there appears to be no ultimate rule for the following of rules.

Judging cases

Judgment occurs when rules run out. This thought is a corollary of the idea that there are no rules for the application of rules. At the very least, one must judge that "this case" is one to which the rule applies. And the rule cannot tell you that.

One traditional way to think about this is to argue that rules have both "clear" applications in some cases and "fuzzy" or "penumbral" applications in others. Legal positivism rests on the presumption that these categories of cases are distinct. It maintains a distinction between cases in which judges do not exercise any judgment because the case is "easy" or "clear" and other cases in which judges are "free," or at least "freer," to exercise judgment. Sometimes one speaks as though judges in "clear" cases are merely "applying" or "bound by" rules, and judges in "penumbral" cases, by contrast, are "making up" or "legislating" new rules (even if only in the "interstices" or "cracks" of the clear rules). But it is not that a *rule* is clear in some cases and not in others, but that the *context and application* are deeply familiar in some cases but not others. Judgment about the appropriateness of applying the rule in *this* context is required whether a case seems easy or hard.[3]

These distinctions, between easy and hard cases and between "applying" law and "making" law, have morphed into a political debate about what kind of interpretive strategy judges should pursue, and some commentators and judges claim that judges should decide only "clear" cases and avoid "judicial legislation" in penumbral cases, instead waiting for further legislative clarification or deferring to the interpretation of an executive branch that is more democratically controlled. The Federalist Society, for example, includes as part of its mission statement that "it is emphatically the province and duty of the judiciary to say what the law is, not what it should be."[4]

One feature of this debate is that the "clear cases" are understood to be "clear" because they fall within a "standard instance" or "dictionary definition" of a rule. This presupposition imagines the meaning of words to be abstracted from their use, as though words were boxes containing things. Yet a central feature of Wittgenstein's discussion of words is that words do not work like containers. Instead, words are often extended metaphors or analogies that point to similarities and differences, but do not create closed categories. His famous example of the impossibility of defining "game" in a way that perfectly describes all and only those practices we call games makes this point (Wittgenstein, 1967).

If words are not perfect categories that preexist use in context, then rules made up of words are also not perfect categories that identify "clear" cases by way of a set of dictionary definitions. Yet we do have the *experience* of more and less obvious applications of rules. How can that be explained if not by whether or not a case falls within the "standard instance" of a word or a rule?

As Lon Fuller (1958) argues in "Fidelity to Law," the "more or less obvious" application of a rule has as much to do with the customs and context within which the rule is operating as with the standard meaning of its words.[5] He called the former the "purpose" of the rule. He understands "purpose" not in the sense of a rule-maker's private intentions, but rather as the evident reason or justification for the rule in its context, based on deep cultural understanding of past practice and existing norms. A rule forbidding sleeping in a train station, for instance, would naturally be applied to the wide-awake person in a sleeping bag, but not to the nodding-off commuter, even though the "plain language" or "standard meaning" of "sleeping" would countenance an opposite conclusion. Francis Lieber and William Hammond (1839) made the same point about the importance of context a hundred years earlier, referring to "nursery stories" in which people who "are prompted by a pedantic anxiety to speak with absolute clearness … only entangle themselves in endless explanations, one upon the other, until the whole story ends with an utter inability of the pedant to ask for the commonest thing, and he dies of hunger." In the English-speaking world of children's books, the Amelia Bedelia books have made a franchise of this point, as has

Lemony Snicket (Parish, 1993; Snicket, 1999).[6] The rules-literalist Amelia is forever sprinkling dust on the furniture, drawing [portraits of] the drapes, and dressing the chicken [in adorable suits].

To give a less frivolous example, the U.S. Supreme Court in *Bond v. United States* (2014) confronted a case in which a woman had been charged with a violation of the Chemical Weapons Convention Implementation Act, which forbids, among other things, using "a chemical weapon."[7] "Chemical weapon" is defined by U.S. law the same way as it is defined by international law: "any chemical which through its chemical action on life processes can cause death, temporary incapacitation or permanent harm to humans or animals." 18 U.S.C. 229F(8)(A). Carol Anne Bond, the defendant, discovered that her best friend, Myrlinda Haynes, was carrying her husband's baby. She stole an arsenic-based compound from her employer and ordered a vial of bright orange potassium dichromate from Amazon. She then spread the chemicals on her rival's car door, mailbox, and door knob, hoping Haynes would develop a rash. The chemicals were easy to see, and Haynes received only a minor chemical burn on her thumb, which she rinsed with water. When local police took no action in response to Haynes' complaints, she complained to the U.S. Postal Inspectors, who filmed Bond's activities, and federal prosecutors charged her with two counts of possessing and using a chemical weapon, a charge which could be sentenced "for any term of years." 18 U.S.C. 229A(a).

The Supreme Court held that even though Bond's activity met the "plain language" of the statute – she was, after all, using chemicals that *could* cause permanent harm – the statute was not meant to cover crimes like hers. The Court noted that "[p]art of a fair reading of statutory text is recognizing that 'Congress legislates against the backdrop' of certain unexpressed presumptions. … For example, we presume that a criminal statute derived from the common law carries with it the requirement of a culpable mental state – even if no such limitation appears in the text … we presume, absent a clear statement from Congress, that federal statutes do not apply outside the United States … The notion that some things 'go without saying' applies to legislation just as it does to everyday life."[8] Hence, the background "principle of federalism," "the deeply serious consequences of adopting such a boundless reading," "the lack of any apparent need to do so in light of the context from which the statute arose – a treaty about chemical warfare and terrorism," the fact that "the chemicals in this case are not of the sort that an ordinary person would associate with instruments of chemical warfare," and the fact that "no speaker in natural parlance would describe Bond's feud-driven act of spreading irritating chemicals on Hayne's door knob as 'combat'" counseled dismissing the charges.[9]

In other words, like Lon Fuller's sleeping commuter, *Bond* was a "clear case" warranting dismissal, despite the fact that the "clarity" of the application did not turn on the dictionary definition of the words, but on the obviousness of background norms and customs in the context of the case.

Moreover, this "clear" case, just as much as a "difficult" case, required judgment, that is, the thoughtful and situational attention to background norms and practices as well as attention to the future consequences of deciding the case in a certain way. At the same time, however, it would be a stretch to say that this case was decided "politically" or based on a judge's "personal" or "idiosyncratic" normative views. Indeed, the case was unremarkable, and its very obscurity demonstrates that the result "went without saying" precisely because the background normative practices were so clear in the context.

Bond did provoke disagreement from the "plain language" interpreters of statutes, Justices Scalia, Thomas, and Alito. The resolution they proposed, that Congress needed to rewrite the statute in a narrower fashion, could be argued for, however, in any case. For every case requires a situational determination of whether or not that case is sufficiently "like" the terms of the statute to be brought under its guidance. And that determination of "likeness" inevitably requires judgment, for it depends upon picking out the salient from the non-salient factors of the case: if the statute's plain language does not expressly say that it applies to crimes committed on Tuesday, then is this case, which occurred on Tuesday, covered? Even a "plain language" version of interpretation has its own unexpressed background presumptions, e.g., that statutes which do not specify which day of the week they are to cover are interpreted to apply to all days of the week. Relative clarity and ambiguity are here determined by background legal practices and customs, not by features of the statement of the rule. The rule is clearly applicable on Tuesday not because of how the rule is stated, but because the background practice is uncontroversial.

Expectations of rules

If rules are only helpful against a background and in context, some may ask, then what is their use? If a rule is vague or incomplete, then how can it guide at all?

The problem one comes up against here is not with rules, but with one's expectations of them. Early statutes were enacted to solve problems that arose – not to solve all possible problems. Even in an age of extensive codification, statutes do not exhaust "the law." A law school may have a Student Handbook, for instance, but nowhere in the handbook does it forbid students from dancing on their desks during class.

Such silence, like legislative or statutory silence, is always ambiguous (Constable, 2005, pp. 1–7). Perhaps silence means that there is no law. Perhaps silence means that whatever is not prohibited is permitted. Perhaps silence means that whatever is not permitted is prohibited. As in the example of dancing on the desks, which we would all recognize as a violation of classroom "law," the rule has never needed stating because the background norms are so strongly followed. In other words, it "goes without saying" that dancing on the desks (singing opera, playing baseball, burning trash, etc.)

during (a law school) class is forbidden and need not be written into the student handbook (although dancing on a desk may be part of a class spoof or even a class in performance studies). Likewise, there is no rule or statute or caselaw that we are aware of that explicitly sets forth a rule that lawyers must make legal arguments and not draw cat pictures, that courts must write reasoned opinions and not just tweet out winners, that courts must follow caselaw precedent and not folktales, that courts must not roll dice to decide who wins, or that Presidents must move out of the White House at the end of their Term of Office. If one expects rules to cover *every* situation, one is asking for the impossible. The absence of rules keeps open the possibilities of action, as Arendt might argue.[10]

But such absence cuts both ways. The absence of explicit statements of rules as to the norms of Presidential conduct is precisely what has allowed the forty-fifth U.S. President to modify expectations of that office.[11] When we consider rules to be helpful guides *in contexts in which they were articulated to clear up problems or misunderstandings in that context*, then we acknowledge their usefulness without asking too much of them. Wittgenstein (§87) again helpfully explains: "One might say: an explanation serves to remove or to avert a misunderstanding – one, that is, that would occur but for the explanation; not every one that I can imagine." J.L.Austin (1979), in "A Plea for Excuses," suggests analogously that adverbs work by specifying the particular manners in which the acts or verbs they modify do not occur in the usual or expected ways.

Rules are issued or enacted in response to a context-specific misunderstanding or a problem that arises. They are useful in the context of that problem but, as the *Bond* case illustrates, not in every context. If I am playing chess and can't remember what the rule is for moving the Queen, the chess rules will be helpful. But the rule about the chess Queen will not be helpful in playing Monopoly.

Sometimes, lawyers try to invoke the "plain language" of rules in order to use the definition of a word in one context to solve a problem in another context. In one of the now-infamous "torture memos," for example, the Legal Counsel's Office tried to use statutory discussions of "severe pain" that had been developed in the context of recompensing emergency rooms for emergency care, to confine the definition of "torture" to situations involving "death, organ failure, or the permanent impairment of a significant bodily function."[12] The memo acknowledges that the purpose of the health care statute was to "treat severe pain as an indicator of ailments that are likely to result in permanent and serious physical damage in the absence of immediate medical treatment."[13] Under the terms of the health care statute, hospitals are told: if you see severe pain, then you may infer a probable emergency involving a need for immediate medical attention. But a conditional doesn't imply the biconditional – that there is no severe pain unless there is a medical emergency. Moreover, while "death, organ failure, or the permanent impairment of a significant bodily function" would be quite relevant to a need for emergency medical treatment, these factors, taken out of context, are not at all obviously relevant to how much pain may be inflicted by an interrogator on a prisoner. A decision about which cases are "like" or "unlike" depends not merely on the dictionary meaning of words of a rule, but on whether the case or situation is analogous along vectors of practice, purpose, and custom.

The further corollary is that – despite codification movements in both civil and common law – one can never have a completely codified system of law. The "Rule of Law" (Scalia, 1989) cannot be a "law of rules."[14] There are three reasons why this is so: 1) If rules are only useful in the context in which they arose, they cannot themselves identify that context. Someone must identify "this case" as a case of the right sort, that is, or as being within the context in which the rule applies. 2) Language itself is not a closed system, but a system of open-ended regularities, so the words we use to articulate rules mean something themselves only through context. Therefore, there is no way to reduce a word to a "standard instance" so that its meaning will never change no matter the context in which it is used. If words have no context-free "standard instance," then they cannot be used to formulate rules with airtight boundaries or context-independent "core" meanings. 3) When humans develop rules, they act in time, drawing on a past experience and normative context to imagine a future of what "should be." Living in time, humans therefore cannot imagine every future case all at once in order to decide what the rule should be for an as-yet unimaginable case. Hence, law is always in progress and imperfect, pointing toward something that has not yet been determined. As Professor Daube (1947) noted in his study of ancient codes, the first attempt at writing them usually begins with a broadly written general "code," which is then followed by later "codas." "Codas" refine the first efforts of a rule's articulation, as the legislator begins to see the unexpected consequences or unforeseen cases that arise in the code's wake.

This temporal point is twofold: the unexpected or unforeseen case may be novel or it may be due to interpretations that have varied from the earlier expected understanding of the rule. Sometimes a later "coda" is due to a genuinely new discovery about what rules are needed (a situation we couldn't imagine – like rules about cellphone use and privacy). Sometimes the later "coda" is added due to misinterpretation. Daube points out that these "codas" in ancient law are often not understood or incorporated as "amendments" to an earlier provision that was considered "wrong" in some respect, but are appended later, almost like caselaw, as though they are explications of how that code should be understood in specific contexts that later arose.

So too, as in Wittgenstein's example, when we tell someone to play a game with children, we do not "mean" to allow gambling, even if that example never occurred to us until someone did it. We expect the later interpreter of our rule to interpret it in light of background norms, and when that expectation is defeated, we add a more specific explication. So "play a game with the children" is not wrong or even incomplete simply because it omitted "but not gambling." Instead, we may decide we need to add "but not gambling" only if that unexpected situation arises because the rule-applier makes a "mistake" in interpreting the rule. The interpreter does a better job of avoiding the need for "codas" when she applies background norms than when she uses "plain meaning" approaches. If I direct my son to buy "fruit for pie" and he comes home with oranges, I have a right to be annoyed with his decision, even while making sure to be more specific next time. But a more specific direction, like "berries or apples" may not necessarily be a better "rule," since I would now leave out lots of other options, like pears, peaches, and rhubarb.

This example likewise explains why qualified immunity should not turn on whether an officer's conduct is forbidden by "clearly established law." Just as a student does not need the Student Handbook to understand that it is wrong to dance on the desks during class, an officer does not need a judicial decision to know that it is wrong to shoot a small child in a park or to steal from a crime scene. When one expects a rule to specify every instance to which it applies, an officer who commits an act that is so outrageous that its wrongfulness "goes without saying" will be immune, because no one before had ever thought to act so wrongly as to force a judge to explicitly forbid such conduct in a "clearly established" ruling (Meyer, 1996).[15]

Behind the obvious catch-22, however, is a deeper point: law runs ahead of rules, and rules are often admonitions rather than prescriptions, written after law-breakers have destroyed the trust of what "goes without saying." Written law often surfaces, describes, reminds, or admonishes us about "best practices" and "just action"; it does not invent them. And an interpretation of written law that purports to ignore that same background of "just action" fails to interpret justly. The "ground" of positive law lies outside positive law itself: law as "just practice" undergirds law as rules or statements of rules.

That more specific rules are not necessarily better has been more apparent to some codifiers than others. According to a mid-twentieth-century writer on the history of codification,

> The approach of the French codifiers was directly opposed to the absurd ideas of the Prussian legislators. The spirit which guided the drafters of the French codes is well explained in the *Reasons for the Civil Code*, written by Portalis. [note omitted] "The purpose of the statute," we read in the *Reasons*, "is to regulate causes which arise most frequently. Accidents, unexpected and extraordinary cases cannot be the subject matter of a statute." This is a far-reaching proposition which delimits the proper scope of legislative enactments. But even in matters which should be dealt with by the legislator, according to Portalis, "it is impossible to regulate everything by strict rules. It is a wise prediction to realize that it is not possible to foresee everything."(Wagner, 1953)[16]

To whom are codes or bodies of rules useful? Just as rules are useful to beginners learning what to do, so too instruction manuals are helpful to those who do not have familiarity or practical knowledge of what otherwise appears as a mass of undifferentiated detail. Codes of law may restate diverse customs (Roman) or they may serve as appropriately balanced general statements, aiming to compensate for uncertainty while also allowing flexibility (nineteenth century). If we expect codes to be complete however, the subsumption of a proliferation of local knowledges of what to do into non-indigenous categories in restatements no longer does justice to the particularity of circumstances; the expectation of a systematicity of rules in modern codes forecloses otherwise desirable possibilities of action.

Rule of law as law of rules?

So far we have argued that the rule of what is conventionally considered law is not and cannot be a seamless or exhaustive system of rules. And yet some of the most respected twentieth-century legal philosophers, such as H.L.A. Hart (1961) and Hans Kelsen (1967), consider law to be a system of rules. If the rule of law is not a law of rules, then what is it?

Even Hart and Kelsen, it turns out, ground their systems of rules elsewhere – Hart in the "fact" of official acceptance of rules; Kelsen in a higher *Grundnorm*. Even to those for whom law is a system of rules then, law is not a closed system – or, if one were to consider it so, its closure comes about via appeal to an outside "ground" or "fact." Of what does an appeal beyond rules consist? For Hart, the "force" of rules comes in recourse to the "fact" of official acceptance of a rule of recognition for identifying rules. Maintaining (correctly) that the rules of a positivist legal system are not necessarily moral or just, Hart grounds the legitimacy and obedience of the modern legal system in the social and normative "pressure" that individuals internalize (here as elsewhere conflating his original distinction between "obligation" and "being obliged"). Hart (1961, pp. 92–93) also argues much too reductively that "as a matter of history," the unification of rules occurs in two steps: the "mere reduction to writing of hitherto unwritten rules" and "the acknowledgment of reference to the writing or inscription as authoritative, i.e. as the proper way of disposing of doubts as to the existence of the rule." To Hart, "hitherto unwritten rules" share the defects that Hart accords to primary rules: they do not change; in cases of conflict, they require adjudication; and they are uncertain. But these are characteristics of written statements of rules, not of "customs" as such – unless one expects those customs to be written. As in Sally Falk Moore's account of the colonial situation in Tanganyika, the emergence of a Hartian positivist legal system is eternally deferred: either hitherto-unwritten propositional statements of rules already exist and are written and transformed into or replaced by another lawlike system of rules or there is nothing – since one must begin with rules – from which the positivist system can step. (Moore, 1992, p. 11).[17]

While Hart grounds what he considers the system of rules that is modern law in an appeal to a fact of official acceptance which is on a continuum with the imposition of force, Justice Scalia maintains that judicial appeal to "facts" as a "totality of circumstances" in a case shows that the rule of law as a law of rules extends only so far. When judgments of law become matters of assessing a totality of circumstances, he argues, legal judgment reaches the edge of law as a system of rules. At this limit, judgment – whether by judges and formal legal officials or by others – is no longer rule-following.

At the limits of rule-following, then, judgment appears to be, as it is for Dreyfus and Dreyfus's expert, a right-brained matter of knowing what to do that judges may nevertheless articulate as rational factors and balancing tests. Judgment appears, as Desmond Manderson writes of decision in *Kangaroo Courts* (his reading of D.H. Lawrence's *Kangaroo*), to be neither a matter of choosing one side or the other, nor a compromise.[18] It appears unexpectedly through a process that is irreducible to one of two sides. Judgment lies, as Kundera might put it, "somewhere behind" the rules.[19]

To what must law be faithful, if not rules? Lon Fuller describes the rule of law as a form of "fidelity." Fuller points to a kind of legal Kantianism of treating like cases alike, a transparency of public opinion-writing that tries to formulate neutral principles from case to case, and a style of interpretation that interprets rules in light of just purposes. Sociolegal scholar Tom Tyler (1990) points to "procedural justice" – that is, that people perceive law to be lawful when they have the opportunity to be heard, when they are treated politely and respectfully, when the decisionmaker appears neutral, when they understand how the decision has been made, and when they perceive the decisionmaker as interested and understanding.[20] Keally McBride (2016), in her historical investigation of the rule of law in imperial England, argues that hard, detailed investigation of a situation, self-restraint of power, and humility in judging are more likely to curb colonial abuse than a system of rules, however comprehensive. She contrasts the self-restraint, self-questioning, and situational knowledge of a "Sisyphean" ruler with the scientific efforts of a "clockmaker" ruler, who aims to use power counterbalances and codification to put the "rule of law" on autopilot. The story McBride tells in the context of British imperial control of India suggests that codification merely allowed power imbalances to flourish beneath the apparent equality of rules unequally applied. The rule of law did not constrain; the self-restraint of rulers did (Meyer, 2018).

Rule of law, then, becomes more about the self-restraint of the powerful in exercising power and about the humility of the judge in exercising judgment than about the completeness of a code or the application of statements of rules. Self-restraint is a way of acting that is itself learned and with time may become expected and manifest in customs. Fidelity to law thus becomes, as with expert juggling, not mechanical adherence to rules, but rather a practical knowledge or reason, an Aristotelian *phronesis* or learned know-how, that requires involvement and commitment to the activity. In the case of officials entrusted with enacting or deciding law, it involves respect for office, as Dorsett and McVeigh (2012) might put it; humility, self-control, and good character. As legal practitioners and everyday persons learn to act according to law, they become persons of virtue, faithful to justice and its rule, neither deafened by nor deaf to it.

Notes

1 Some sociolegal scholars, such as Elizabeth Mertz (2007) and Ewick and Silbey (1998), admittedly address issues of learning and language. They do so largely under the rubric of "legal consciousness," with which they fill an ostensible "gap" between law as statements of rules and law as action. We consider statements and applications of rules themselves to be acts of language and judgment.

2 Our point here may resemble that of Baudouin Dupret (2011), who in effect argues that learned practice involves more than enunciable rules.

3 "Following rules blindly" was used in Wittgenstein's text to refer to cases in which we don't stop to think about all the alternative interpretations available because the context is so familiar: 1+1, 2+2, 3+. We know the answer is 3, but not because the rule logically "requires" it, but because it is such a familiar context. As Wittgenstein points out, the "logic" of the rule does not require the answer to be 3, because we could imagine a different pattern: 1+1, 2+2, 3+1, 4+2. Nonetheless, we know what to do, because we've done it a hundred times before, not because the "rule" is clear.

4 "The Society is founded on the principles that the state exists to preserve freedom, that the separation of governmental powers is central to our Constitution, and that it is emphatically the province and duty of the judiciary to say what the law is, not what it should be." https://fedsoc.org/about-us

5 See also Perelman (1984).

6 Klaus correctly and felicitously accuses Count Olaf of planning to marry Violet not figuratively, but literally – and legally – in the play that Olaf and Violet will perform, because the nuptial laws require no more than "the presence of a judge, a statement of 'I do' by both the bride and groom, and the signing of an explanatory document in the bride's own hand." (Snicket (1999), pp. 96–97)

7 Bond v United States, 572 U.S. 844 (2014).

8 Id. at 857.

9 Bond, pp. 858–866.

10 See Chiara Ricciardone on why Arendt refused to answer the question "what are we to do?" online at "medium" as "What Do We Do Now?" https://medium.com/quote-of-the-week/what-do-we-do-now-83a9921428bd, downloaded 3/8/19

11 Likewise, as Chris Kutz (2014) has argued in the context of the laws of war, norms underlie the positive law's prohibitions on torture.

12 Memorandum from Jay Bybee to Alberto Gonzales, Counsel to the President, August 1, 2002, archived at: https://nsarchive2.gwu.edu/NSAEBB/NSAEBB127/02.08.01.pdf

13 Id. at 5–6.

14 Compare Lieber, supra note at 42: "No code can possibly provide for all specific cases … nearly every case in reality is a complex one; because the various relations of men are forever changing."

15 Jessop v. City of Fresno, 936 F.3d 937 (2019), *cert. denied*, __ U.S. __ (May 18, 2020). (Holding officers had qualified immunity because no clearly established law that it violated the 4th Amendment to steal over $200,000 from a crime

scene. "Although the City Officers ought to have recognized that the alleged theft of Appellant's money and rare coins was morally wrong, they did not have clear notice that it violated the Fourth Amendment." Id. at 942.)

16 http://www.repository.law.indiana.edu/facpub/2324 350

17 For more detailed argument, see Constable (2005, pp. 29–32; 1994, pp. 67–95). For further examples, see much work on colonial legal systems.

18 Desmond Manderson, *Kangaroo Courts and the Rule of Law* (2012).

19 As Milan Kundera (1988) writes of Kafka, citing Jan Skacel's poem: "Poets don't invent poems/The poem is somewhere behind/It's been there for a long long time/The poet merely discovers it."

20 But see Jenness and Calavita (2018).

References

Austin, J.L. (1962) *How to Do Things with Words*. Oxford: Oxford University Press.

Austin, J.L. (1979) 'A plea for excuses' in Austin, J.L., edited by Urmson, J.O. and Warnock, G.J. (eds.) *Philosophical Papers* (3rd ed). Oxford: Oxford University Press, pp. 175–204.

Constable, M. (1994) *The Law of the Other: The Mixed Jury and Changing Conceptions of Citizenship, Law and Knowledge*. Chicago, IL: University of Chicago Press.

Constable, M. (2005) *Just Silences: The Limits and Possibilities of Modern Law*. Princeton, NJ: Princeton University Press.

Daube, D. (1947) 'Codes and codas in the Pentateuch', *Studies in Biblical Law*, pp. 74–99.

Dorsett, S. and McVeigh, S. (2012) 'Conduct of laws: Native title, responsibility, and some limits of jurisdictional thinking', *Melbourne University Law Review*, 12, p. 470.

Dreyfus, H.L. and Dreyfus, S.E. (1986) 'From Socrates to expert systems: The limits of calculative rationality', *Philosophy and Technology*, 2, p. 111.

Dreyfus, S.E. (2004) 'The five stage model of adult skill acquisition', *Bulletin of Science, Technology and Society*, 24, p. 177.

Dupret, B. (2011) *Adjudication in action: An ethnomethodology of law, justice, and morality*. Dartmouth, Aldershot: Ashgate.

Ewick, P. and Silbey, S.S. (1998) *The Common Place of Law: Stories from Everyday Life*. Chicago, IL: University of Chicago Press.

Fuller, L.L. (1958) 'Positivism and fidelity to law: A reply to Professor Hart', *Harvard Law Review*, 71, pp. 630–672. https://doi.org/10.2307/1338226

Gobbet, F. and Chassy, P. (2009) 'Expertise and intuition: A tale of three theories'. *Minds and Machines*, 100–111. https://doi.org/10.1007/s11023-008-9131-5.

Hart, H.L.A. (1961) *The Concept of Law*. Oxford: Clarendon Press.

Jenness, V. and Calavita, K. (2018) '"It depends on the outcome": Prisoners, grievances, and perceptions of justice', *Law and Society Review*, 52(1), pp. 41–72.

Kelsen, H. (1967) *Pure Theory of Law*. Berkeley, CA: University of California Press.

Kundera, M. (1988) *The Art of the Novel*, New York: Perennial Library.

Kutz, C. (2014) 'How Norms Die: Torture and Assassination in American Security Policy,' *Ethics & International Affairs*, 18(4), pp. 425–449.

Lieber, F. (1839) 'Legal and political hermeneutics, or principles of interpretation and construction in law and politics: With remarks on precedents and authorities'. Republished William G. Hammond, ed. (3rd ed., 1880) St. Louis: F.H. Thomas.

Manderson, D. (2012) *Kangaroo Courts and the Rule of Law: The Legacy of Modernism*. Abingdon, Oxon: Routledge.

McBride, K. (2016) *Mr. Mothercountry: The Man Who Made the Rule of Law*. Oxford: Oxford University Press.

Memorandum from Jay Bybee to Alberto Gonzales, Counsel to the President (August 1, 2002). Archived at: https://nsarchive2.gwu.edu/NSAEBB/NSAEBB127/02.08.01.pdf

Mertz, E. (2007) *The Language of Law School: Learning to "Think Like a Lawyer."* Oxford: Oxford University Press.

Meyer, L.R. (1996) 'When reasonable minds differ', *New York University Law Review*, 71, pp. 1467–1518.

Meyer, L.R. (2018) 'Sisyphus and the Clockmaker: Two Views of the Rule of Law in Keally McBride's *Mr. Mothercountry: The Man Who Made the Rule of Law* (March 28, 2018). Available at SSRN: https://ssrn.com/abstract=3151957

Moore, S.F. (1992) 'Treating law as knowledge: Telling colonial officers what to say to Africans about running "their own" native courts', *Law and Society Review*, 16, p. 11.

Noe, A. (2012) *Varieties of Presence*. Cambridge, MA: Harvard University Press.

Parish, P. (1993) Amelia Bedelia. New York: Scholastic.

Perelman, C. (1984) *Le raisonnable et le déraisonnable en droit. Au-delà du positivisme juridique*. Paris: LGDJ.

Ricciardone, C. (2019) "What Do We Do Now?" (March 8, 2019). Available at https://medium.com/quote-of-the-week/what-do-we-do-now-83a9921428bd

Scalia, A. (1989) 'The rule of law as a law of rules', *University of Chicago Law Review*, 56(4), pp. 1175–1188.

Snicket, L. (1999) *A Series of Unfortunate Events*. New York: Scholastic.

Tyler, T. (1990) *Why People Obey the Law*. New Haven, CT: Yale University Press.

Wagner, W.J. (1953) 'Codification of law in Europe and the codification movement in the middle of the nineteenth century in the United States', pp. 335–359. Articles by Maurer Faculty. Paper 2324. http://www.repository.law.indiana.edu/facpub/2324 350.

Wilson, Frank R. (1999) *The Hand*. New York: Vintage Books.

Wittgenstein, L. (1967) *Philosophical Investigations* (trans. Anscombe, G.E.M., *Philosophische Untersuchungen* [1953]). Oxford and Cambridge: Blackwell.

3 The structure of the legal system and the emergence of the state

Michel Troper

Seen from the perspective of legal positivism, especially in its Kelsenian version, the law and the practice of the law are ontologically different. The law belongs to the realm of *ought* and the practice of the law to that of *is*. This is also true from an epistemological point of view since law is an object for the normative sciences, while the practice of the law can be studied by the social sciences and only the latter can study their object in the light of the principle of causality, while the normative sciences do it in the light of a principle of imputation. It has even been argued that, because each science constitutes its specific object, the normative and the social sciences have different objects, to the effect that we should distinguish sharply between on the one hand legal science, whose object is the law, the system of rules, and on the other hand, legal sociology, whose object is the practice or practices leading to the production or the application of rules.

Even the less radical positivists make a distinction between rules and practice. They define practice as the application (or infringement) of the rules or as the set of intellectual and physical actions necessary to produce a rule. Rules and practices are thus closely connected while remaining conceptually separate. The practices are not produced nor implied by rules, since rules cannot apply or be implemented by themselves, but only through humans who conform to the rules. Nor do rules arise from practices only, because the production of rules must have been authorized by a higher rule. *Ex facto jus non oritur.* Thus, it does not suffice that the law orders some action for that action to take place and it does not suffice for someone to issue a command for that command to be a rule. Only the Law can produce law. Yet, in spite of that vision, shared by most jurists, it is not impossible to conceive of situations where the law emerges from practices alone.

Obviously, we must put aside the case of custom, as it is usually defined: a practice repeated over a certain period, a plain fact, and believed to be mandatory, also a fact. It may thus seem that a rule has emerged from the combination of these two facts. However, something cannot be a legal rule unless it is *valid,* i.e. unless it is an element of a legal system and this is only possible if the rule has been issued according to a higher rule. A proposition has the meaning of a legal norm only if a higher norm has made a certain fact the condition for the production of a norm, e.g. a statute is valid if the constitution has made the fact that a majority of the members of a parliament has voted in favor of a certain text a necessary and sufficient condition for the production of a valid law. Similarly, there is a valid customary rule only if a higher norm has ordered that one behaves according to a certain practice, generally believed to correspond to a binding rule.

Thus, there can be no connection between practices understood as social practices and law understood as a set of rules, but there is no reason to stick to such narrow definitions. First, when we think about the law, we do not focus only on rules. When we describe a legal system, we merely describe not only rules, but most importantly all sorts of discourses that justify the rules, without which we could neither make sense of them, nor interpret or apply them. Take a sentence like article 3 of the present French constitution "national sovereignty belongs to the people". None of these words can be understood by reference to ordinary language, but only by relying on at least one theory of sovereignty. Such theories are about the law itself, its function, its relation to politics, morality or society; they make use of concepts such as property, the state, human rights and many others. They are also in connection to practices, first by social, political, economic, or religious practices, by various ideologies, but also by legal practices. The term "legal practices" refers here to the different ways in which rules are being made and applied, and more generally to the type of relations between rules, namely the form or structure of the legal system. In modern legal systems, this structure is best described as a hierarchy, which is a practice, because it happens when rules are produced on the base of higher norms and they empower lower authorities to apply them.

I will attempt to show that this practice has a strong connection to the production of legal discourse and legal concepts, taking the example of the theory and concept of the State, that emerged in the seventeenth century. It is in the seventeenth century that we see the structuring of the legal system in a hierarchy and the development of the modern State.

Naturally, we must start from a definition of the State, but such definition poses many problems. I will use a point of departure: Kelsen's well known and much criticized theory of the identity of Law and State. Kelsen's thesis (1928) is directed against the traditional dualist theory that holds that they are different entities, and either views the State as an objective and independent being that produces law or alternatively considers that it is the law that constitutes the State by empowering its authorities to act and produce law. He blames the dualist theory for resting on two assumptions both wrong: that the law that empowers the State is some form of natural law and that the State can be defined in any other way than as a legal order.

He objects that natural law does not exist and, on the other hand, that it is impossible to give an independent definition of the State. First it is impossible to give a sociological definition of the State, because, any attempt at such a definition will inevitably rely on legal elements. For example, Max Weber defines the State « as an entity which successfully claims a monopoly on the *legitimate* use of violence », but this monopoly is obviously not a *de facto* monopoly, because there are many acts of violence that are not committed by the State; it is a monopoly of the legitimate use of violence. The word "legitimate" does not imply that the use of violence by the State is just or in accordance with certain fundamental values. It means that acts of violence are performed according to legal rules. On the other hand, the State is an abstraction and thus incapable of exercising violence. Only human beings can exercise violence, but the acts accomplished by some individuals are imputed to the State and this is only made possible by way of legal rules that ascribes which acts by which individuals will be imputed to the State.

Secondly, it is impossible – according to Kelsen – to give a purely legal definition of the State. If we look at the traditional definition by elements (a people, a territory, a public government) we can see that it is impossible to define these elements taken one by one without a tautology: a people is not an objective entity that could be defined independently of the State; the people of France do not possess any common psychological, religious or ethnic characteristic. They can only be defined as the class of human beings who are subject to the French State or, in other words, to the same legal order; similarly, the territory of the State can only be defined as that portion of space that is subject to a particular State or, in other words, to the legal order of that State; moreover, it is the State that decides on the content of the class of subjects that constitute the people or on the limits of the portion of space that constitutes its territory; finally, the public government is the government of the State or the highest power in the legal order and what constitutes the government of a State is also decided by the State. Thus, these three elements cannot define the State because they are themselves defined by the State and since we can in each case substitute in the definitions the words "Legal order" or "Law" for "the State", they are just two names for one and the same reality. To say that the State is just another word for the law is not denying the hard reality that it uses force, that there are bureaucrats, police and prisons. It only means that such institutions are empowered by legal norms, act by means of legal norms, and that all those norms can only be identified because they are elements of a legal system. For Kelsen, the monist theory has an enormous advantage, that of dissolving the problem of the relation between the Law and the State, i.e. the question whether the State can be subject to Law.

We are left, however, with another problem: we can certainly replace the words "the French State" with "the French legal order", but we cannot replace "the international legal order" by the "international State". Kelsen is therefore constrained to introduce in his definition a new element: centralization. Some legal orders are centralized, i.e. they include specialized organs, such as a parliament, an executive, a system of courts; they have a monopoly of the production of the most general norms, that are valid for the entire population, on the entire territory, and whose addressees are the subjects, whereas others, like the international legal order, are decentralized because the norms are produced, interpreted and applied by the addressees themselves. Thus, the French or the German legal orders are states, but the international legal order is not.

Unfortunately, this distinction does not really help because, taken together, the central organs of the legal orders constitute precisely what the classic dualist theory called a "State". Kelsen is forced to admit that there are two different concepts of the State: the State *lato sensu*, which is identical with the legal order, and the State *stricto sensu,* which is the system of organs that have the power to produce norms. But then we are left with the same puzzles. If Law and State are one and the same thing, then the question of their mutual relation is obviously nonsensical, but the State *stricto sensu* is not the same thing as the Law and we are thus confronted with the same initial questions: is this State the source of law or is the law the basis of the State? can the State be limited by the law that it has created?

Thus, Kelsen (1928) seems to have failed. However, this failure is a *felix culpa.* It provides what seems to be a fruitful opportunity to analyze the relation between the State *lato sensu* and the State *stricto sensu.* In a brief introduction to the second edition of his "*Der soziologische und der juristische Staatsbegriff*", Kelsen remarks that the former concept is presupposed by the latter.

He probably understood this as a purely logical or conceptual connection because one cannot think of the State *stricto sensu* without conceiving it as the set of those organs that produce the norms that are at the top of the entire legal order, i.e. at the top of the State *lato sensu.*

Nevertheless, we can also view it as a real historical and possibly also causal connection. Such a connection, however, is only possible if both are historical phenomena. According to a common view, this is true for the State *stricto sensu,* the modern State, which has emerged some time at the end of the sixteenth or in the seventeenth century, but not for the Law, which is usually supposed to have existed in every human society. This view is not only that of natural law, but of positivists also. For example, Kelsen defines Law simply as an immanent order of constraint, a definition that works equally well for national legal systems, international law, feudal law or the law of primitive societies. However, when we consider not the general definition but the main characteristic of the legal system, as we know it, namely its hierarchical structure, described in Kelsenian terms as a hierarchy that is both static and dynamic, the general and universal definition loses its validity: all legal systems are not structured in this manner. It is only towards the end of the sixteenth or in the seventeenth century that we find a hierarchy resembling that model.

Naturally, this is not enough to allow us to speak of a causal connection, but I want to test the hypothesis that it is the emergence of the legal system that led to the emergence of the State, so that it is not the State that creates the law but the law that creates the State.

The State is not understood here merely as a complex of organs but as a type of justificatory discourse held by agents in a specific political system. As was the case with Kelsen's definition of the State as the legal system, defining it as a discourse does not mean a denial of its political and material reality. It allows to distinguish it from other forms of political systems. In every political system, power is exercised by force, but in the State the use of force is regulated by law and justified by specific principles, different from those invoked in other systems. The State is thus a system of constitutive principles, in the sense that we recognize a State when agents play the game of State, i.e. justify their decisions by invoking such principles as sovereignty, representation, distinction between the office and the office holder, distinction between public and private law, between State and civil society, personality or continuity of the State, etc. In this essay, however, I focus mainly on "sovereignty".

The hypothesis has two branches. Firstly, the law, understood as a hierarchy of norms, has emerged as the result of an autonomous and spontaneous process that had started in the late Middle Ages and was almost accomplished at least as an instrument of legal argumentation by the end of the sixteenth century. Secondly, the emergence of the hierarchy of norms has given rise to the emergence of the constitutive principles of the State.

One last remark: I will not consider the emergence of these principles from the point of view of a history of political thought, studying e.g. Bodin, Hobbes, in order to construct a genealogy of concepts. Great thinkers have played a decisive role in the development of the theories of the State, and an analysis of their works is indispensable, but it has already been done by the most excellent scholars. Moreover, we still need to explain why these ideas have been discovered at this particular moment. It is not sufficient to look at political thought as an autonomous sphere where ideas are transmitted from one author to the other or appear as replies to others as well as responses to political problems of their time. There is also a need to understand why they were so quickly received and put to use by political and legal agents.

Nor will I consider these developments from the point of view of a history of institutions – this also has already been done – but from that of legal argumentation on the assumption that the hierarchy of norms is a specific style of legal argumentation.

I will proceed in three steps; first, I will examine the methodological difficulties that historians face when they examine the date for the emergence of the State, in particular, the difficulty in finding a definition; I will propose a definition based on the hierarchy of norms. Secondly, I will then look for a hierarchy of norms in the Middle Ages and in the modern period; Thirdly, I will attempt to relate the two elements and explain the emergence of sovereignty.

The problem of the definition of the state

Any theory on the origin of the State must rely on a definition. Reflecting on the trends of French historical research on the State, the legal historian Albert Rigaudière (2003) remarks that during the major part of the twentieth century, "legal historians have limited themselves to a history of institutions, mostly without any deep analysis on the concept of State...they have described the nuts, bolts and wheels rather than the global mechanism and the entity that this mechanism constitutes". Only after 1980, have they started to analyze the medieval conception of the State.

This distinction between institutional and conceptual analysis is not as clear as one might wish. When traditional historians describe institutions of the late middle ages such as the King, the courts or the *curia regis*, they cannot avoid relying on political ideas and using expressions drawn from the language of the time. It would indeed be impossible, for instance, to relate the dispute between the French King Philippe le Bel and Pope Boniface VIII in 1296 without referring to arguments used by both parties, i.e. to their respective doctrines (Chénon, 1926–1929, pp. 933ff)[1]. On the other hand, those authors who, like Rigaudière, profess to analyze the medieval conception of the State use not only medieval terms derived from Roman law like *imperium, majestas, jurisdictio, regimen*... but inevitably they too must rely on modern ones. Rigaudière himself uses terms such as "State", "sovereign' or "legislative power", which, needless to say, appeared much later.

Historians are thus confronted with a dilemma: either they use ancient concepts and they have no way of knowing whether these concepts are related or not to a construction that we may rightly call a State or they can try to use later concepts and find that they correspond neither to the language nor to the reality of the Middle Ages.

The only way out of the dilemma is to devise a meta-concept that would allegedly be timeless and call "State" any political form that roughly fits the definition and deny that qualifications to those that do not. But, as historians are well aware, the choice of a definition predetermines the answer to the question of the emergence of the State. If the definition is too broad, almost every political entity with a territory is a State, except primitive societies. Naturally, most historians will seek to narrow the definition as have all those quoted above, and find characteristics not of the State but of the "modern" State.

Unfortunately, the same difficulty arises with the definition of the modern State. Even for the modern State, as we know it in the twenty-first century, there is no generally accepted definition. Some historians who have studied the Middle Ages generally rely on simplified versions, based on the existence of a public taxation system, differentiated institutions, centralization, a circumscribed territory, monopoly of violence, a centralized courts system, professional lawyers... (Genet, 1997; Hall, 1994; Holmes, 2000). Others will recognize the emergence of the State when they see "sovereignty" or the signs of sovereignty, such as a legislative power (Rigaudière), or the fact that power cannot be appropriated and is depersonalized.

Some of these definitions may lead to strange results. Take for instance Genet. He mentions as a key element a public system of taxation, accepted by political society. However, how do we define "acceptance"? Is it the simple fact that there is no effective resistance against taxation and that taxes are actually being collected? But in that case whenever there is an effective tax system, there is acceptance and we must call "State" the Assyrian or the Aztec empires. Or does it mean, as Genet himself asserts, representative government or at least some form of dialogue with civil society and in that case the absolutist State ceases to be a State?

In any case, the defining terms must always be defined, and the intermediate definitions also predetermine the answer to the question of the origins. For example, if one considers that the State emerges with the enactment of general rules, one may find a State in Western Europe as early as the twelfth century (Giordanengo, 1989). If, on the other hand, one sees the essence of the State in a centralized bureaucracy, then we will have to wait until the sixteenth century.

Centralization itself is not a very clear concept.

In the same way, we may use sovereignty as a criterion of the State, but there are many different ways to establish that the State is sovereign. We may, for instance, assume that the State is sovereign when we discover the presence of the words "sovereign" and "sovereignty" in the writings of a certain period. However, many questions remain: what if these words appear at different moments and in different contexts, as it is indeed the case? What kind of writings are we looking at? Those of the great thinkers, but how do we know whether when they say that the State is sovereign, they describe the actual State of their time, they seek to magnify the power of the King, recommend the creation of a strong authoritarian State or provide arguments for some current legal dispute? Moreover, the presence of the word proves nothing if these authors do not refer to the same reality or the same concept (Courtine, 1985).

Alternatively, it may very well be that the words were different, while the reality or the concepts were the same (David, 1996)[2]. For example, historians sometimes claim that "*auctoritas*" or "*potestas*" or "*imperium*" or "*majestas*" were parts of a more general concept of sovereignty, for which there was no word or that they had the same functions.

Thus, most of these definitions have been chosen with the purpose of proving some thesis: either that the State was created in the Middle Ages (some even give a precise date) or that it has emerged later, in the sixteenth century (Saint Bonnet, 2000; Renoux-Zagamé, 2010; Di Donato, 2011).

But historians or political theorists may have other powerful ideological interests at stake. Depending on whether they favor an authoritarian or a moderate State, the role of legislation or that of the judiciary, they will try to show that the State has been created by statutory law or by courts or by centralization or by wars, that the "true" characteristic of the State is that it is absolute or alternatively that it is subject to higher law, that it is related to Christianity or to secularism, that it is a force that requires external countervailing mechanisms such as courts or alternatively that courts are part of the State and thus constitute internal checks. It is naturally impossible to falsify part – or all – of these definitions, unless we believe that there is an essence of the State. They are not descriptions of an objective reality but stipulations. It does not follow that they should be dismissed altogether. Stipulations are not susceptible of being true or false, but they can be evaluated for their capacity to help in the discussion of some specific problem.

Naturally the stipulated definition should not predetermine the outcome and we must be aware of committing the Gorenflot fallacy: In his novel, *La Dame de Montsoreau,* Alexandre Dumas portrays a monk, brother Gorenflot, who, being very hungry on a Friday during Lent, and wishing to eat a capon without sinning, finds a wonderful solution in baptizing the capon "carp"[3].

In order to avoid the Gorenflot fallacy and test the hypothesis that the State is a form of political power exercised through law and that it emerges as a consequence of the structuration of a legal system, we must define it by some other criterion than the structure of the law itself.

Sovereignty is an interesting candidate. It has often been mentioned as a constitutive element of the State. "Constitutive" generally means "essential" and most lawyers would agree that all states are sovereign and no entity that is not a State is fully sovereign. However, the term can also be understood in Searle's sense of a constitutive rule, one that defines the game that is being played (Searle, 1969). In the present case, we can see that in the modern State authorities use arguments resting on the theory of sovereignty in order to justify their decisions. This is one of the principles that define the game of the State, sovereignty, the distinction between public and private law and a reference to the rule of law. In the present chapter, I must limit the analysis to sovereignty in order to ascertain the extent to which sovereignty as a constitutive principle emerges as a result of the hierarchical structuration of the law.

The emergence of a hierarchy of norms

What is a hierarchy of norms?

As we have seen, the State can be characterized as a type of political system where power is exercised through or by means of the law. This is the reason why Kelsen could rightly say that "*Jeder Staat ist ein Rechtsstaat*" (every State is a State of law). Law is thus a means of political power because of its specific structure, the hierarchy of norms.

The term "hierarchy of norms" is obviously a metaphor that is commonly used to describe a great variety of relation between norms that are not of equal value. Sometimes, we speak very loosely of a hierarchy between two norms merely when, in case of a conflict, one is made to prevail over the other, whatever the basis for that prevalence, but in a strict sense, we speak of a hierarchy between two norms whenever one of them is only valid when it is based on the other and in case of a conflict the prevalence of one norm over the other depends not on their respective content but solely on the fact that it has been produced by a higher authority or in a higher form. For example, in French law there is a hierarchy between the constitution and statutes because the constituent power is a higher authority that has empowered Parliament to enact statutes and because statutes must conform to the constitution.

However, in order to understand the way in which political power operates by means of the law, we need to consider not two single norms but the more complex structure of the whole system. Kelsen has described this structure as a hierarchy that is at the same time static and dynamic.

A static hierarchy is one in which a lower norm is valid, meaning that it belongs to the system, if and only if its content conforms to the content of a higher and more general norm. There are several possible conceptions of conformity, but it is usually thought that it need not be a logical relation, where the lower norm is deduced from the higher norm and that it suffices that the content of the lower norm can be subsumed under the higher norm or simply that it does not contradict it.

A dynamic hierarchy is one in which the lower norm is valid, is an element of the system, if and only if it has been produced according to the procedure laid out and by the authority empowered by a higher norm.

Kelsen's theory of the hierarchy of norms has brought an entirely new perspective: instead of defining the law as a collection of legal norms – which requires an impossible definition of the single legal norm as a command backed by threat or as a hypothetical judgment – the legal norm is defined or identified by the system of which it is an element (Bobbio, 1960). A norm is a legal norm when it belongs to a legal system, and it belongs to a legal system when it is an element of static and a dynamic hierarchy.

It follows that a given act, whether a court decision, a command by an officer, a contract, a marriage, is valid when it has been accomplished by someone who has been granted by a higher norm the power or the right to produce it and when it is not contrary to the same or another higher (substantive) norm. How do we know that this is the case? When the authority that accomplishes the act claims that it is valid and another authority does not successfully challenge that claim. If it is challenged, then it is on the basis that the former authority has not been empowered to produce the act or that it has exceeded its powers or that the act is contrary to some higher substantive norm.

The emergence of a hierarchy of norms in the sixteenth century

We witness the slow structuration of a hierarchy, at the beginning of the fifteenth and sixteenth century. The hierarchy is constructed both from the top and from below. From the top, it is obviously legislation that plays a major part. Other factors of the construction of the State, like administrative centralization, a court system, taxes, armies, are themselves products of legislation.

Legislation does not produce a hierarchical legal system merely because it consists in general rules, but only because these rules authorize directly or indirectly the production of all other rules, regulate their content and constitute the sole basis for their validity. This happens when by legislation other sources are integrated into one legal system. Naturally, what we will be describing here is not an empirical reality. The hierarchy of norms is not an empirical phenomenon. When we say that norms are objectively valid because they ultimately have their basis in a law, we only refer to an argument that they are valid in that sense. Indeed, this is precisely the claim made by the king. The argument may or may not succeed rapidly and success obviously results not only and even not primarily from the quality of the argument but from relations of power, but it is sufficient to recognize that it is in the king's best interest to use it and sometimes in best interest of other actors to accept it.

The most important source to be integrated is custom. At the end of the hundred years war, in 1453, Charles VII enacts the ordinance of Montil-les-Tours, to mandate that all customs of the kingdom be written down. This move means that from now on customs will be binding not because they are ancient but because the king has ordered that they be applied. The ordinance explicitly forbids "all attorneys of the kingdom to invoke or propose other customs than those which will have been written and granted"[4].

From now on, at least in principle, there is no longer a distinct and autonomous order of customary law, but customary law is a subsystem of the unified legal order. Thus, in case of a conflict between a statute (a law emanating from the king) and a custom, the former prevails. Customary law is thus integrated in one legal system and the same happens with ecclesiastic law. Thus, the whole domain of private law is indirectly under statutory law.

In Kelsenian terms, we now tend to have a hierarchy with three levels: statutory law, custom, courts decisions. The hierarchy is both dynamic and static. It is dynamic because the higher level, the ordinance or statute, has prescribed the writing and the reformation of customs. What counts as custom is what has been written down according to the king's ordinances. It is static because the custom will be binding only if its content does not conflict with the content of an ordinance – indeed some ordinances have abolished customs considered to be unreasonable – and because the content of court decisions must derive from customary rules.

The second source to be integrated by legislation is judge-made law. The king gradually develops a system of royal courts that gradually acquires a quasi-monopoly of adjudication. Thus, in 1539, by the Ordinance of Villers-Cotterêts, Francis I limits the jurisdiction of ecclesiastic courts over lay persons exclusively to matters pertaining to spiritual matters such as sacraments. In the same ordinance, he offers feudal lords to buy their power to render justice. When they keep it, this will be only by delegation from the king, so that they will exercise that right not in full sovereignty but only in the name of the lord sovereign" ()[5].

In 1566, the ordinance of Moulins strictly limits the jurisdiction of city courts to matters of police. The royal ordinances that set up civil and criminal procedure make clear that the power of the courts derives from the king. Civil and criminal courts also are considered as delegates of the king. Even when judges own their offices (because they have bought or inherited them) and when they hold them in perpetuity, they are still delegates, because the rule of perpetuity has been established by the king and it is the king who mandates the application of ordinances and customs (Sève, 1985).

The king exercises his control over the courts' decision by several means. One is that he can always evoke a case pending before a court and decide it in his council. The other is the procedure of cassation, which to this day is an essential characteristic of the French legal system. Cassation is different from an appeal. It is not a dispute between the same parties than in the lower courts but between the decision of a lower court and the law. It does not include a new examination of the facts of the case, but only of legal reasoning on the grounds that the law had been violated (Godin, 2010). If the lower court has misapplied the law or a custom, the king may reverse the decision.

A similar movement to integrate the courts in one legal system can be observed in other countries than France, e.g. in England (Brand, 2000, p. 133; Holmes, 2000, p. 315) or in Germany (Nehlsen Von Stryk, 2000, p. 165).

Thus, a court decision becomes a third level in the hierarchy of norms: it is valid both from a dynamic point of view (because it has been made by a court acting as delegate of the king, within the limits of its powers, according to the rules of procedure established by law) and from a static point of view because its content must not be contrary to any superior law.

For example, the charter of the *Compagnie des Indes occidentales*, created by Colbert in 1664, included a provision mandating the appointment of judges. These judges were "bound to decide cases following the laws and ordinances of the realm". On the basis of the same, provision officers of the crown were also bound to follow and conform to the custom of Paris that would also rule contracts made by individuals. Neither officers nor individuals were permitted to introduce any new custom, so as to avoid diversity[6].

When making decisions, courts thus appear to be applying a superior rule, statute or custom as prescribed by a statute. Naturally, when a statute is not available, lawyers will cite catholic sources or Roman law, but when there is such a statute, lawyers will use the same kind of syllogistic reasoning that was later theorized by Beccaria and Kant and is still prevalent today; whereas the techniques of interpretation also resemble those that are being used today for statutes (Mac Cormick & Summers, 1991).

What has been said of custom can be said of ecclesiastic law. It had been an autonomous source of law, but was integrated into the legal system and became binding not because of the authority of the pope or the council but because of the authority of the king and to the extent that it did not conflict with royal ordinances.

Thus, the Ordinance of Villers-Cotteret 1539 mandates priests to keep registers of baptisms and marriages and limits the jurisdiction of ecclesiastic tribunal and the Ordinance of Blois of 1579 regulates in detail the organization of the church, in particular the appointment of bishops, archbishops and abbots and determines the various age when priests can be ordained. More generally, Canon law was applicable only on the basis of the king's explicit or implicit authorization (Duccini & Hermann, 2000; Martin, 2009b, p. 313).

It is easy to see how the king can take advantage of these developments. Not only does he now have a monopoly of the production of general rules, but also, he is not forced to produce laws that would go deep into details, something that could be technically difficult or politically challenging because it could encounter resistance. He can now choose between giving reception to previously autonomous sources, such as custom, empowering lower authorities authorizing discretion in the process of application. As Bernard Guenée (1968) rightly notes, legal centralization is not the enemy of decentralization and decentralization was not an obstacle to the construction of the State. Quite the opposite: by accepting the creation of provincial parliaments, the king achieved two results: he established his authority over these parliaments, which exercised a delegated power and applied his laws; he gained political acceptance of his authority by the provinces.

But the hierarchy of norms is also constructed from below, because it enables those who produce local or particular rules to justify them by invoking not only morals, religion, or tradition, but also a superior legal norm that can ultimately be traced to the king. This is the case with administrators, courts and local authorities. The courts in particular contribute to the creation of a hierarchy as a means to increase their power, because of the necessary latitude that they will necessarily enjoy in the process of adjudication, especially because they have to interpret the law. A law is but words on paper. It is not a legal norm until these words are interpreted as having the meaning of a legal norm. Of course, the lawmaker himself gives it precisely that meaning, but, as Kelsen puts it, this is only a "subjective meaning". Its "objective" meaning can only be provided by the legal system as a whole, i.e. by an authority empowered to give an authentic interpretation, such as a court. Thus, judges may decide that a given text has the meaning of a legal norm, determine its nature, its level in the system and what its content is (Troper, 2001, p. 69). Interpretation implies a wide margin of discretion. Very often, but not always, that authority is a court. Once the court has thus created the norm and applied it, this norm is the basis for the validity of the lower norm i.e. the court's decision.

When they exercise their power of interpretation, the courts create, manipulate and maintain a hierarchy in two ways.

First, by interpreting a text as having the meaning of a superior norm to be applied in a case, they create that superior norm. One might think – and this was indeed many lawmakers' concern – that the law's supremacy would be lost because of the power of the court to interpret and that the hierarchy would be reversed, because the superior norm would be not the text enacted by the king, but the norm that is the meaning of the text, as determined by the court, to the effect that instead of constructing a hierarchy, the power of interpretation seems to have the opposite effect, since the law is being recreated by the court.

However, the supremacy of the law remains, but we must understand it differently: a hierarchy of norms is not necessarily a relation between norms laid down by different authorities. Such a hierarchy can also obtain between norms created by the same authority whenever the first is used as an argument to justify and assert the validity of the second. This is the real hierarchy behind the apparent official one. It gives the courts a power that is all the greater for being hidden (Di Donato, 2010).

The second mode of constructing a hierarchy is by deciding that a text or a practice has the meaning of a legal norm and determining the level at which it is placed in the hierarchy.

One classical example in contemporary French Law is that of the Declaration of the Rights of Man of 1789. After it was enacted, it was not considered as a set of binding legal norms, but rather as a philosophical basis for the constitution or a political agenda. It was not until 1971 that the Constitutional council decided that it was a legal norm, that it was part of the constitution and that it was binding on Parliament (although not on the people voting in a national referendum).

However, Parliaments did something similar in France, starting in the sixteenth century, making a distinction between rules that the king could amend and those that he could not (rules of succession to the throne and the inalienability of the royal domain), and thus attempting to create a new superior level in the hierarchy. The distinction meant that some of these rules were upgraded to a super legislative level with the purpose of allowing Parliaments to exercise a form of judicial review over ordinary legislation by means of a confrontation of royal ordinances to these fundamental laws (Di Donato, 2003). Although the king fought such attempts by Parliament to invalidate his laws, he did acknowledge the principle. Thus, that there were some laws that he could not amend. After Louis XIV's death, his testament legitimizing his bastards was abrogated in the form of an edict of the new king, the little Louis XV, by which he proclaimed that "the fundamental laws of the realm leave us in the fortunate powerlessness to alienate our crown's domain… we take pride in acknowledging that we are not at liberty to dispose of our crown" (Mousnier, 1980, p. 503)[7].

Some historians (Mestre, 1992; Renoux-Zagamé, 2003; Di Donato, 2003; Krynen, 2009; Saint Bonnet, 2000) have recently claimed that these immutable rules of the realm were the equivalent of a modern constitution, so that the review by parliaments of the king's ordinances could be interpreted as prefiguring judicial review. This view misses the important point that a modern constitution expresses the will of a constituent power and is always amendable, while the fundamental laws were for the most part customary and unamendable even by the sovereign. However, the important point is that the courts have indeed created a superior level of norms.

The structuration of the legal system and the hierarchy of norms may explain the emergence of the modern concept of sovereignty.

Sovereignty

The idea that Sovereignty is an essential character of the modern State is commonly accepted. This classical definition is precisely the reason why those who have recently argued that states have lost their sovereignty or that their sovereignty has been limited, qualify this development as the decline of the State[8]. This is also the reason why most historians who defend the view that the State has emerged in the Middle Ages are constrained to claim that the king already exercised sovereignty long before Bodin coined the theory.

They use a variety of arguments. Some rest on words. Most historians agree that the word "sovereignty" only appeared in the sixteenth century, but some stress that the adjective "sovereign" referring to an authority is more ancient or that, although the substantive "sovereignty" was not in use until the sixteenth century, other terms such as *maiestas, potestas absoluta, summa potestas, imperium* conveyed the same meaning or at least part of that meaning. Others maintain that, even if in the language of the Middle Ages there was no term that was the exact equivalent of sovereignty, the type of power that was exercised at the time could nevertheless be rightly described as sovereign. In order to prove that point, they have to rely on a definition of sovereignty that is necessarily anachronistic. In the same way that some of them use Weber's definition of the State when they look for a medieval State, others use a later concept of sovereignty when they analyze the medieval legal system and most often it is Bodin's. However, when looking at the emergence of the modern State we cannot take for granted that Bodin invented once and for all the modern theory of sovereignty. We need a truly modern theory that can provide us with a meta-concept. Once we have defined that meta-concept, we can then ask whether it fits the concepts that we can find in the Middle Ages, and later in the sixteenth and seventeenth centuries.

Before going further, we stress an important point that could easily be overlooked: sovereignty is a legal theory. It is part of reality only to the extent that theories and language are part of reality, but no more. It follows that for a polity or a man to be sovereign means that they have certain legal capacities, not that they have real political, economic or military power, so that we cannot falsify the theory that the king was sovereign in the Middle Ages just by showing that he did not exercise effective power over such and such group or such and such part of his kingdom, nor that he was constrained to seek the consent of some other group.

However, as a legal theory, it does not exist only in a world of ideas and the fact that some thinker has developed some elements of a theory of sovereignty at one moment in time is not sufficient for us to say that sovereignty "existed" at that moment. It exists only in so far as arguments from the theory are those that count as valid arguments to justify decisions made by actors in the system.

We can thus identify sovereignty when we find actors using concepts derived from a theory of sovereignty. The modern theory that can provide the necessary meta-concepts is that of Carré de Malberg, who breaks the notion of sovereignty into three concepts:

"In the original sense, the word 'sovereignty' refers to the supreme character of the State's power. In a second sense, it refers to the whole range of the powers included in the State's authority and it is therefore synonymous with that authority. Thirdly, it is used to characterize the position occupied within the State by the highest organ of the State's authority and in that sense, sovereignty is the same thing as the power of that organ" (Carré de Malberg, 1920, p. 79).

Carré de Malberg (1929, p. 86) stresses that the French language is poor and contains only one word for these three concepts of sovereignty. The same could be said of English. However, the German language has three words, one for each of these senses. *Souveranität* corresponds to sovereignty in the first sense, i.e. the supreme character of the State on the international as well as on the domestic level. *Staatsgewalt* is the power of the State in the second sense. *Herrschaft* is the power of domination by an organ. Carré de Malberg believed that these distinctions could help us discover the "true nature" of sovereignty. Such a belief may be naive, but the distinction is nevertheless useful to clarify a few traditional puzzling questions.

One of these is whether it is possible to divide sovereignty. On the basis of Carré de Malberg's distinction it is easy to see that sovereignty in the third sense, the quality of the highest organ of the State, is indeed indivisible, because, as soon as one divides it between several organs, none is the highest[9]. On the other hand, if sovereignty in the second sense is the range of powers that can be exercised by the State, it is perfectly divisible. It is even possible to divide them by their subject matters (the power to wage war, to control a currency, to render justice, etc.) as Pufendorf (1706) did with the *partes potentiales* or by the type of legal acts that are necessary to exercise them (like legislation, execution and adjudication). Separation of powers is precisely a division of sovereignty in this sense.

In the same way these distinctions help to understand why some sentences using the concept of sovereignty, which seem incompatible or contradictory can nevertheless be simultaneously true. Thus, at the time of Carré de Malberg, during the French Third Republic, it was possible to answer the question "who is the sovereign", by any one of three sentences: "the French State is the sovereign", "the French Parliament is the sovereign", and "legislation is a sovereign power". In the first sentence, sovereignty refers to the supreme character of the State's power, which enables it to act on the international level and interfere with other sovereigns, or to dominate the church or any other institution.

In the second sentence, sovereignty is a quality of an organ of the State, and in the third sentence it is one of the powers that the State may exercise.

However, Carré de Malberg's distinction does not give sufficient account of some sentences that we find in constitutional and political discourse. Take for example, "the sovereign is the French people" or, "sovereignty belongs to the people" (Constitution of the 5th Republic, 1958, art 3). Such a sentence obviously does not mean that the French people *is* the State and effectively acts on an international level, nor that it exercises a power of domination and certainly not that the people alone can really exercise a range of powers. These propositions do not refer to any reality and they are only used to justify other sentences: e.g. in French legal discourse "sovereignty belongs to the people" was used during the Third Republic to justify "Parliament is sovereign" or "the law is sovereign". It meant that Parliament exercised a sovereignty that was not its own, but belonged to the people and was exercised *in the name of* the people, or that statutes were presumed to express the general will, i.e. the will of the sovereign and were therefore supreme. In this context, when imputed to the people, the word "sovereignty" is thus used in a fourth sense: it refers to the quality of a being in whose name some power, in any one of the first three senses, is exercised. Indeed, the theory of sovereignty generally implies a distinction between the essence and the exercise of sovereignty. Because of the hierarchy of norms, what is imputed to a sovereign is not only legislation or decisions in international affairs, but also every single act, presumed to have been performed in virtue of a delegation. This is why e.g. justice is rendered in European countries "in the name of" the French, Italian or German people as it was before "in the name of the king". To Carré de Malberg's three concepts, we must therefore add a fourth: the doctrine of sovereignty is a principle of imputation. A sovereign in that fourth sense is the entity presumed to possess the essence of a sovereignty that is exercised by others in its name and thus to be the author, direct or indirect, of every single norm in the system.

Using this distinction between four different concepts of sovereignty, we can see that whereas sovereignty in the Middle Ages is discernible only in two senses of the word, it is only in the sixteenth century that it exists in the full four senses.

Sovereignty in the modern age

From the sixteenth century onwards, sovereignty is much closer to Carré de Malberg's analysis and corresponds to the four concepts. First, as was already the case in the Middle Ages, the king claims to possess a power supreme in the sense that there is no other power above his own, so that neither the pope nor the emperor could produce legislation on temporal matters that would be binding in the realm.

Secondly, also as in the Middle Ages, he was the highest authority within the realm, but what was different were the type and the range of powers that the king could exercise and which now extended to all human affairs, including private law, notably family law, and religious matter. As Loyseau writes "it is difficult to assuredly list the rights of sovereignty, as ancient philosophers have almost not mentioned it, because in their time sovereignties had not been well established". The novelty of this concept of sovereignty lies precisely in the fact that the sovereign holds – and is indeed defined by – the power of intervening in every possible domain (Sève, 1985), including religion or the subjects' properties.

Finally, the fourth concept of sovereignty, imputation, also appears in the sixteenth century. Previously, such an idea had been inconceivable because of the plurality of legal orders, but now institutions do not rest on separate basis and all possible legal norms are finally either laid down by the king, by an authority explicitly or implicitly delegated by him or tacitly authorized. Imputation is thus simply an expression of the hierarchy of norms.

It is remarkable that the concept of imputation can refer both to the ascription of an attribute or an action to a person and to the relation between two norms. Kelsen (1973) clearly shows that it is one and the same relation. The statement that a crime is imputed to a person means that she is legally considered as having committed the crime and that a sanction can be inflicted upon her. Imputation is therefore the relation between crime and sanction. This relation is not a causal one, because it is not necessarily the case that when someone has committed a crime she will be punished. It is a relation created by a norm that states that if a crime has been committed then the person who committed it ought to be punished. But more broadly imputation is the relation between the two elements of the norm "if x, then y ought to be". It is the internal structure of the norm (Kelsen, 2005(1960), p. 67). It follows that the concept also helps to characterize the structure of the whole legal system, because a higher norm empowering an authority to produce a lower norm can be read "if the authority x makes a decision then that decision is legally valid", e.g. "if a court finds that one of the parties to a contract did not consent, then the court ought to declare the contract void". The relation between the higher and the lower norm is a relation similar to that between crime and sanction and we can say that the lower norm is imputed to the higher and the latter to an even higher norm. In the end, they are all being indirectly imputed to the highest norms and to their author who, not having been empowered by any other superior legal norm, must be presumed to be sovereign.

The hierarchy of norms and sovereignty

Sovereignty thus appears to be a concept that one is bound to encounter whenever there is a hierarchy of norms that are thought of as produced by the will.

It can best be understood by analogy with Kelsen's theory of the *Grundnorm*. It is well known that for Kelsen the validity of every norm is based on a higher norm, which in turn is based on an even higher one and so on until one reaches the highest norm in the system. Since it is the highest there is no higher norm on which it could be based and yet if it is not valid, it cannot serve as the basis for the validity of the lower norms. This is the reason why we have to assume that the highest norm is valid on the basis of a *Grundnorm*, which states: "the highest norm is valid". Everybody is of course perfectly aware of the fact that there is no such norm and Kelsen does not pretend that there is. On the contrary, he calls it a fiction. But this fiction is necessary because without it we could not treat any norm as valid.

However, Kelsen's theory rests on an ontology of norms, conceived as ideal entities that are not and cannot be produced by the will, because they belong to the sphere of "ought" whereas the will is a fact and belongs to the sphere of "is". The validity of a norm can only be based on another norm, not on a fact. When an authority wills a rule, that rule is not valid because of the will, but only because the higher norm that empowered that authority has prescribed that if the authority expresses the will to create a rule, then the rule is valid and binding. Thus, if no rule is derived from a will, neither is the Grundnorm. It is not willed but presupposed.

But, the legal system in sixteenth century France rests on a very different ontology, that law is an expression of the will (Alchourrón and Bulygin, 1981). In that case, every decision or norm in the system is valid because it has been willed by an authority delegated or authorized by a legislative rule, but this rule must also express the will of some entity, a will that has not been authorized by any earthly authority (Martin, 2009a). Just as with the Grundnorm, we must therefore assume that this entity (whether the people, the king or an aristocracy) possesses an inherent quality that enables it to produce law without having been authorized. This quality is sovereignty.

It is therefore not surprising that lawyers easily made that assumption. Sovereignty has not been invented by Bodin or by anybody else, just as Kelsen did not invent the Grundnorm, no more than he could have discovered it in positive law. He only claimed that it was an assumption or presupposition of any lawyer who purports to treat something as valid law and that he, Kelsen, just brought this hidden assumption to consciousness.

However, if Bodin did not invent sovereignty, he did not describe positive law either and there is no clear correspondence between his conception of legislation and the practices of the sixteenth century (Martin, 2009a). And he did not describe actual processes of argumentation of his time. Rather, his was an interpretive theory in Dworkin's sense: what he did was discover the best possible argument to justify the power of the entity to whom all the norms in the system are imputed, the argument that was assumed by the whole legal process and bring it to consciousness. The argument was that this entity was sovereign and that he possessed a godlike quality.

The argument that sovereignty implied the monopoly of power had been discovered by the king before Bodin's Republic. For instance, in the édit de Moulins 1566, he justified a prohibition to any other authority to raise taxes by asserting that "to do otherwise would undertake on our authority and majesty" (art. 25).

It was overwhelmingly used after the publication of his book, both by the king or his counselors or his subjects urging him to adopt new legislation. Kings expressly claimed the godlike quality. James I, who had read Bodin, in a famous speech addressed to Parliament in 1609 insisted that "Kings are not only God's lieutenants upon earth, and sit upon God's throne, but even by God himself they are called gods", an idea also expressed later by Bossuet preaching before the court "you are gods".

One of the strong points of Bodin's theory is that it works just as well whether the sovereignty bearing entity is a king or the people or a mere abstraction, whether sovereignty derives from god's delegation, as it does in the case of the king, or is based on the nature of the sovereign, as in the case of the people. This is because the king's godlike quality is not related to his personal virtue but only to the nature of his power. It is not his godlike quality that makes him a sovereign but sovereignty that makes him a god.

This is the reason why the theory of sovereignty, in spite of the references to the divine right of kings, is essentially secular. The sovereign king is not the person who happens to be on the throne, it is the institution. One of the most certain signs of the secularizing role of the theory of sovereignty is the change in the function of the coronation. At the end of the period, he did not need to claim anymore the charismatic quality that allowed him to cure the sick people by touching them and the formula that he used. Instead of saying, "the king touches you, God heals you", Louis XV said, "the king touches you, may God heal you" (Mousnier, 1979, p. 655).

That there is a necessity because of the hierarchy of norms to use the argument of sovereignty as a principle of imputation is shown clearly in the eighteenth century struggles between the king and the *Parlements*. The *Parlements* claimed the right to refuse the registration of the King's ordinances when they conflicted with their interpretation of the fundamental laws of the realm. As we have seen, this was an attempt to extend the hierarchy by creating a new level above the king. Such an attitude was difficult to reconcile with the doctrine that the king was sovereign. The most efficient way to attempt such reconciliation was to claim that since the *Parlements* were delegated by the sovereign, when they exercised a check on the king, they still acted in the name of the sovereign[10]. When they refused the registration of a law, they did not oppose the king's will, because such a law only expressed the king's apparent will, the will of the individual who happens to be on the throne, not the real will of the king as an institution. The real will was thus expressed by the *Parlement*. The unity of the system was thus preserved. This solution carries two further benefits. It provided a possible answer to the question "Why can't the king, if he is sovereign, change the fundamental laws of the realm?" The answer could be "the king as an individual cannot, but the king as an institution definitely could, but, thanks to the *Parlements,* he is wise enough not do it". On the other hand, it provides a solution to the problem of checks to the power of the sovereign. The difficulty lies in the idea that if a sovereign is checked he is not a sovereign. The solution is in replacing the idea of external checks, such as those which were found in various institutions like the church, the "*corps intermédiaires*" or the courts, by internal checks that form an integral part of the sovereign. Sovereignty thus remains unlimited, but each of its components is limited. This type of arrangement is the core principle of constitutional government.

Conclusion

The thesis that the State and, in particular, its main constitutive element, sovereignty, emerges as a consequence of the hierarchy of norms faces several possible objections. Two are closely linked: firstly, we have not explained in that way the formidable development of the King's power, which results from many social, political, religious or economic factors; and secondly we could not explain why the hierarchy of norms grew in France and not – or not the same degree – in other parts of Europe, or why it has produced an absolute monarchy in France, but not in England. The answer is that the thesis does not pretend to describe the actual or effective organization of power, but only the type of argumentation that characterizes the State. This answer should come as no surprise. When we speak of States in international law and when we describe them as sovereign, we call "State" any entity that fits the definition, regardless of its size, strength or actual capacity to act independently, China or the United States as well as Monaco or Andorra.

The same is true of the hierarchy of norms in the sixteenth and seventeenth century. The King may face resistance from other institutions. He might even fail to impose his will. The fact remains that he claims that courts have been empowered by him, that they are his courts, that they should apply his laws, that he can overrule their decisions or that marriages are to be celebrated according to his rules. The hierarchy of norms is a type of argument that one makes about the reason why a rule is valid or binding and these arguments are being used by various authorities. They can be more or less successful but the simple fact that they are being used is evidence for the existence of a legal system. Similarly, the existence of a hierarchy of norms leads to the argument that there is a sovereign, whether the claim is made by the sovereign himself or by another authority. The argument may be thought persuasive or not. The fact remains that it is being made, unlike what happened in previous political systems, where different kind of arguments drawn from canon law, custom or feudal relations were used by those who wished to impose their authority. The power that is being exercised by means of arguments that there is a hierarchy of norms and a sovereign can thus be identified a State.

However, one could agree that there may be some causal relation between the development of a hierarchy of norms and the emergence of a concept of sovereignty and still deny that the former has produced the latter. One could argue that the opposite is true and that it is the sovereign who produces the hierarchy of norms, e.g. when the king orders the writing of customs, makes rules regarding marriages or mandates the application of ordinances by the courts. However such an the objection is based on a confusion between the king's political might and sovereignty, and takes too seriously the idea that the king "is" sovereign. Sovereignty is not a quality like physical strength or intelligence or prestige that the king possesses and that he can use to do certain things. It is only an argument that he is constrained to invent in order to justify what he does, e.g. producing a hierarchy of norms. The State as political form emerges precisely when the type of rules and of relations between rules are justified by the concept of sovereign.

Notes

1 Chénon and Olivier-Martin are precisely the target of Rigaudière's critique.
2 The same view had been held by other historians, notably by Wilks (1963), for a contrary opinion, see e.g. Quaritsch (1986).
3 In English "Chicot the jester (la dame de Monsoreau) 1956, London, Collins, Chap. 8: "In the name of Bacchus, Momus, and Comus, trinity of the great saint Pantagruel, I baptize thee, carp," said Gorenflot.
4 Cited in Sève (1985). The full text is to be found in Isambert, T. ix, pp. 252–253.
5 Loyseau (Discours de l'abus des justices de village) quoted by Sève (1985).
6 Art. 34. "Seront les juges établis en tous lesdits lieux, tenus de juger suivant les loix et ordonnances du royaume; et les officiers de suivre et se conformer à la coutume de prévôté et vicomté de Paris, suivant laquelle les habitans pourront contracter, sans que l'on y puisse introduire aucune autre coutume, pour éviter la diversité». The charter has been reproduced in Pauliat (1887, p. 221); see Fioravanti, 2012.
7 Halevy R., (2009) La déconstitution de l'Ancien Régime. Le pouvoir constituant comme acte révolutionnaire, in, *Jus Politicum* n°3,. http://www.juspoliticum.com/La-deconstitution-de-l-Ancien.htmls.
8 Among many others Cassese (2002), Van Creveld (1999), Fioravanti (2001) contra: Troper (2010).
9 However, several organs could exercise sovereignty jointly, *see below*.
10 See the works of Francesco Di Donato mentioned above.

References

Alchourrón, C.E. and Bulygin, E. (1981) 'The expressive conception of norms' in Hilpinen, R. (ed.) *New Studies in Deontic Logic: Norms, Actions, and the Foundations of Ethics*, Netherlands, Dordrecht: Synthese Library. Springer, pp. 95–124. https://doi.org/10.1007/978-94-009-8484-4_4

Bobbio, N. (1960) *Teoria dell'ordinamento giuridico*. Torino: G. Giappichelli,.

Brand, P. (2000) *La formation du système juridique anglais, 1150–1400*. Paris: PUF, Justice et législation.

Carré de malberg Raymond, 1920, Contribution à la théorie générale de l'Etat; spécialement d'après les données fournies par le droit constitutionnel français, Paris, Sirey, réimpr. CNRS, 1962, nlle édit. Dalloz, 2003, Vol. I., p. 79.

Cassese, S. (2002) *La crisi dello stato*. Roma-Bari: Laterza.

Chénon, E. (1926) *Histoire générale du droit français public et privé des origines à 1815. Tome, Période gallo-romaine – Période franque – Période féodale et coutumière.* Paris: Hachette.

Courtine, J.-F. (1985) 'L'héritage scolastique dans la problématique théologico-politique de l'âge classique' in Méchoulan, H. (ed.) *L'État baroque: regards sur la pensée politique de la France du premier XVIIe siècle.* Paris: Vrin, p. 91.

David, M. (1996) *La souveraineté du peuple.* Paris: PUF.

Di Donato, F. (2003) *L'ideologia dei robins nella Francia dei Lumi. Costituzionalismo e assolutismo nell'esperienza politico-istotuzionale della magistratura di antico regime (1715–1788).* Napoli: Publicazioni della Facoltà di Economia.

Di Donato, F. (2010) *La rinascita dello Stato – Dal conflitto magistratura-politica alla civilizzazione istituzionale europea.* Bologna: Il Mulino.

Di Donato, F. (2011) 'La costituzione fuori del suo tempo' in *Dottrine, testi e pratiche costituzionali nella Lunga durata*, in Quaderni constituzionale, (4), pp. 895–928.

Duccini, H., Hermann, C. and Barbiche, B. (eds.) (2000) *Textes et documents: les monarchies française et espagnole du milieu du XVIe siècle à 1714.* Paris: Temps.

Fioravanti, M. (2001) Sovereignty, constitution. The European model in the late nineteenth and the early twentieth century' in Cazzaniga, G. M. and Zarka, Y.C. (eds.), *Penser la souveraineté à l'époque moderne et contemporaine.* Pise – Paris: Edizioni ETS – Vrin, tome II, p. 509 ff.

Fioravanti, Marco. (2012) « Le préjugé de la couleur. François-André Isambert et l'administration de la justice aux Antilles françaises pendant la Restauration », *Les Cahiers poitevins d'Histoire du droit*, IV, pp. 113–152.

Genet, Jean-Philippe. (June 1997) La genèse de l'État moderne, in *Actes de la recherche en sciences sociales*, (118), pp. 3–18.

Giordanengo, G. (1989) 'Le pouvoir législatif du roi de France (XIe–XIIIe siècles): travaux récents et hypothèses de recherche', *Bibliothèque de l'École des Chartes, t.*, 147, pp. 283–310.

Godin Xavier. (2010) « La procédure de cassation au XVIIIe siècle ». *Histoire économie & société*, 29(3), pp. 19–36.

Guenée, B. (1968) 'Espace et État dans la France du bas Moyen Âge', *Annales. Économies, Sociétés, Civilisations*, 23(4), pp. 744–758.

Halevy, R. (2009) La déconstitution de l'Ancien Régime. Le pouvoir constituant comme acte révolutionnaire, *Jus Politicum*, 3. Available at: http://juspoliticum.com/article/La-deconstitution-de-l-Ancien-Regime-Le-pouvoir-constituant-comme-acte-revolutionnaire-141.html

Hall John, A. (ed.) (1994) *The State: Critical Concepts* (Vol. 3). London and New York: Routledge, p. 331ff.

Holmes Clive. (2000) Les instruments juridiques du pouvoir et l'Etat dans l'Angleterre du début de l'époque moderne, in Padoa-Schioppa, A. (ed.) *Justice et législation*,Traduit de l'anglais par Marie-Anne de Kisch. Paris: PUF, p. 315ff.

Kelsen, H. (1928) *Der soziologische und der juristische Staatsbegriff; Kritische Untersuchungen des Verhältnisses von Staat und Recht*, 2nd ed., Tübingen: Scientia Verlag.

Kelsen, H. (1960) *Pure Theory of Law.* Clark, NJ.Lawbook.

Kelsen, H. (1973) *Essays in Legal and Moral Philosophy* (selected and introduced by Ota Weinberger). Dordrecht-Holland and Boston, Reidel, Chapter VII "Causality and Accounting."

Krynen, J. (2009) *L'état de justice: France, XIIIe-XXe siècle.* Tome 1 L'idéologie de la magistrature ancienne. Paris: Gallimard.

Mac Cormick, N. and Summers, R.S. (eds.) (1991) *Interpreting Statutes. A Comparative Study*. Dartmouth: Aldershot.

Malberg, R. C. (1920) *Contribution à la théorie générale de l'Etat; spécialement d'après les données fournies par le droit constitutionnel français*. Paris: Sirey, réimpr. CNRS I, 79.

Martin, F. (2009a) 'Jean Bodin et les formes' in. Leveleux-Teixeira, C., Roussel et-Pimont, A., Bonin, P. and Garnier, F. (eds.) *Normes et normativité. Études d'histoire du droit rassemblées en l'honneur d'Albert Rigaudière*. Paris: Economica, pp. 233–253.

Martin, F. (2009b) *Justice et législation sous le Règne de Louis XI. La norme juridique royale à la veille des Temps modernes*. Paris: LGDJ.

Mestre, J.-L. (1992) L'évocation d'un contrôle de constitutionnalité; 'Les maximes du droit public français', Actes du Colloque de l'AFHIP, Toulouse. 11–13 of april 1991, L'Etat et le pouvoir. Idées européennes, vol. VIII, Aix, Presses universitaires d'Aix-Marseille III, pp. 21–36.

Mousnier, R (1979) *The Institutions of France under the Absolute Monarchy, 1598–1789*. Chicago, IL: University of Chicago Press.

Mousnier, R. (1980) *Les institutions de la France sous la monarchie absolue*. Paris: PUF.

Nehlsen Von Stryk, K. (2000) 'Centralisation de la justice et formation d'une hiérarchie judiciaire dans l'Etat du début de l'époque moderne' in Padoa-Schiopa, A. (ed.) *Justice et législation*. Paris: PUF.

Pauliat, L. (1887) *La politique coloniale sous l'Ancien Régime*. Paris: Calmann Levy.

Pufendorf (1706) Le *droit de la nature et des gens* (traduit du latin par Jean Barbeyrac). Livre VIII: "Où l'on traite des principales parties de la souveraineté" Amsterdam.

Quaritsch, H. (1986) *Souveränität: Entstehung und Entwickung des Begriffs in Frankreich und Deutschland von 13 Jh. bis 1806*. Berlin: Dunker & Humblot.

Renoux-Zagamé, M.-F. (2003), Du droit de Dieu au droit de l'homme. Paris: PUF.

Renoux-Zagamé, M.-F. (2010) 'Juger la loi au nom du droit naturel: fondements et portée du contrôle des Parlements de la monarchie' in Cahiers du Conseil constitutionnel n° 28, July 2010. Available at: https://www.conseil-constitutionnel.fr/nouveaux-cahiers-du-conseil-constitutionnel/juger-la-loi-au-nom-du-droit-naturel-fondements-et-portee-du-controle-des-parlements-de-la-monarchie.

Rigaudière, A. (2003) Penser et construire l'État dans la France du Moyen Age. XIIIe-XVe siècle, Comité pour l'Histoire économique et financière de la France. Paris: IGPDE.

Saint Bonnet, F. (2000) 'Un droit constitutionnel avant le droit constitutionnel ?', *Droits*, 32, pp. 7–20.

Searle, J.R. (1969) *Speech Acts: An Essay in the Philosophy of Language*. Cambridge: Cambridge University Press.

Sève, R. (1985) 'Le discours juridique dans la première moitié du XVIIème siècle' in Mechoulan, H. (ed.) *L'Etat baroque: regards sur la pensée politique de la France du premier XVIIe siècle*. Paris: Vrin, pp. 119–146.

Troper, M. (2001) *Le droit, la théorie du droit, l'Etat*. Paris: PUF.

Troper, M. (2010) 'The survival of sovereignty' in Kalmo, H. and Skinner, Q. (eds.) *Sovereignty in Fragments. The Past, Present, and Future of a Contested Concept*. Cambridge: Cambridge University Press, pp. 132–150.

Van Creveld, Martin. (1999) *The Rise and Decline of the State*. Cambridge; New York: Cambridge University Press.

Wilks, M.J. (1963) *The Problem of Sovereignty in the Later Middle Ages*. Cambridge: Cambridge University Press.

4 Equality, hierarchy, and the place of rules

Paul Dresch

Equality recurs often in discussions of law despite the fact that, as Jeremy Waldron notes (2002, pp. 1–2), "there is … little … on the background idea that we humans are … one another's equals".[1] Waldron himself is thus drawn to Dworkin's "equality of concern and respect" (Waldron, 2017, pp. 13, 51). The world of course contains good people whom I may indeed respect, but the world (let's be honest) contains also rogues and fools whom I do not, in the word's normal sense, respect at all; agreed, beyond this, there are things I would not do or have done even to persons who are evil, and the reasons range from fear that abusing them corrupts public values to insistence I not imperil my soul, but "equal concern and respect" is a thoroughly misleading phrase. It is used, of course, in societies where care for equality of wealth or longevity is not conspicuous,[2] and, in Anatole France's words, "*la majestueuse égalité des lois … interdit au riche comme au pauvre de coucher sous les ponts, de mendier dans les rues et de voler du pain.*"

Anthropologists have had almost as unhappy a time with the topic. Some have taken equality as somehow the natural state of things, while others take the fact that equality is mainly a fib in our own societies to mean it must be so everywhere (Robbins, 1994, pp. 21–24). The question is really which differences count in what connection. Anthropologists' concern with comparison allows us at least to examine what assumptions colour our debates, and in the present paper we must prise apart equality and individualism on the one hand, holism and hierarchy on the other. The place of rules, I hope, then comes into focus. Both historians and anthropologists in recent years have been reluctant to admit that rules inhere in social existence (Dresch and Scheele, 2015), and legal theorists (e.g. Schauer, 1991) are far more rewarding on the subject. Yet the latter tend not to ask why explicit rules, such as those that we speak of as law, are conspicuous in some times and places, not in others. Their answers, when pressed, turn on an equation of moral order with political order, which fails to allow for the prevalence of law in settings where no centralised authority is recognised (Dresch, 2012a, pp. 32, 33, 35). With or without an idea of centralised authority, I shall argue, such rules recur in many settings where equality is valued. Often they define what measure of equality is apt in which circumstance and when it is that commensurability does not apply.[3]

India, ourselves, and other places

In 1966 Louis Dumont published a book on India entitled *Homo hierarchicus: essai sur le système des castes*, which foregrounds equality's opposite. Caste, says Dumont, is ordered by an opposition between pure and impure, with Brahmans at the top of the status-scale and Untouchables at the bottom, while specific castes (*jâti*s) are spoken of widely in terms of the classical *varna*s, of which there were four: Brahmans (very roughly, priests), Kshatriyas (roughly, kings and warriors), Vaishyas (merchants, or, earlier, cattle-herders), and Shudras (servitors, cultivators). Both *jâti*s and *varna*s, says Dumont, take their value from hierarchy, by which he means, unexpectedly, a relation of "encompassment" whereby "the elements of a whole are ranked in relation to the whole" (1970, p. 66). He finds here a sequence of limiting inclusions. Thus Brahmans dominate care for transcendent matters, and they legitimate the kings or warriors; Brahmans and Kshatriyas together have dominion over all; and Brahmans and Kshatriyas and Vaishyas are all "twice born," which Shudras are not. Together, says Dumont, these four, or present-day groupings spoken of in such terms, form a rational whole as caste society. Untouchables, the least pure (even impure), although they too comprise *jâti*s, are treated as marginal to the caste world.[4]

Not surprisingly, explicit rules are evident. In parts of southern India, for example, an Untouchable should not approach within 96 paces of certain Brahmans, although how, asks Dumont (1970, p. 82), would one ever notice? There have been detailed and explicit caste-rules, rules made by kings, and rules that set the larger moral world in order; there seems not to have been the political integration of rules we associate with state-centred law, however. The law of *dharma* (that is, of right-ordering beyond the transitory faults of this group or the other) is instead that of Brahmanical theory, in which *varna*s figure and with which Dumont's view of hierarchy aligns.[5]

Much follows from the idea that the "priestly function" comes first. Not only is power devalued in Sanskritic learning, but those playing the Kshatriya role as power-holders often show little interest in markers of purity, while groups lower down a local ranking may obsess about such markers. "As the mantle of Our Lady of Mercy shelters sinners of every kind ..., so the hierarchy of purity cloaks, among other differences, its own contrary" (1970, p. 78), and Dumont's approach, therefore, cannot be refuted by empirical counting of exceptions. It is not, though, the only way in which caste has been understood. A.M. Hocart (1938) – again, in his way, a holist – thus placed kings, not Brahmans, at the centre of analysis. An alternative to both approaches is through what Anastasia Piliavsky (2020) calls "patronage." The source of patronage can be priestly, political or neither (many patrons in Piliavsky's sense are deities; see also Piliavsky, 2015), but one's worth derives from attachment to a superior, who provides one's *khandân* – a term that sometimes translates as identity or substance. In a local scheme, a dominant caste might be recognised by others on grounds of one paramount value (purity, power, auspicious wealth), but the idea of asymmetrical moral dependence recurs whatever the value is. Indeed, *contra* Dumont, no societal whole need be invoked.[6]

Elsewhere than India one finds a principle that Austronesianists have dubbed "precedence," whereby the order of the world is structured through asymmetric pairs – elder/younger, for example – applied recursively such that points of origin become important, and the principle, which itself is not holistic, can produce hierarchy in Dumont's sense or undermine it (Fox, 1994). The more general idea that inequality is a basis of moral value recurs, however, far more widely. One may need to be not only connected with other people to be a person oneself (true even in the present North Atlantic world, where autonomy of persons is so much emphasised),[7] but linked with a superior to have worth, and in parts of Africa it was therefore thought better to be a slave than unattached (Miers and Kopytoff, 1977). In Europe, professedly holistic visions of society may recede with the divine right of kings, but there is nonetheless routinised acceptance until close to our own time of deference (from below) and condescension (from above).[8] Whatever the detail of these cases, they are scarcely egalitarian. We are not, note well, arguing about whether people in whatever degree are bigger, stronger, or richer than those around them; we are reporting that, unlike Waldron and the authors he cites, all these traditions treat inequality as right and proper.

Equality is a much rarer value, which Joel Robbins (1994) pursues in New Guinea. Here formalised exchange is important and should be symmetrical, so a "big man" does not come to prominence through uneven trade, at least not ideally, but his personal skills – oratory, pig-raising, yam-growing and the like – allow him to maintain more relationships of exchange than other men. Big men then find themselves dominating transactions between groups; the cohesion of groups (itself something valued locally) may depend on them doing so. Success, though, is a poisoned chalice, and the moral contradictions that arise lead not infrequently to the implosion of local communities and the self-immolation of big men (ibid. 49–53). Robbins's attempt to put equality in first place is intriguing. He confronts, however, a set of cases where pursuing equality requires endless work. Hierarchy in India or precedence in Austronesia, or rank until recently in Europe, do not; a particular set of relations may well require effort to maintain, but inequality as a moral fact is given.

Equality or autonomy

A more exact opposite to Dumont's India might be tribalism in northern Yemen. Practical inequality among households is obvious at most periods (some ate well and others starved), but the sources of wealth and power lie mainly beyond tribal territory, and considerable autonomy, along with formal legal equality, exists at home; rarely do prominent families among tribes north and east of Sanaa extract significant wealth from people immediately around them. Equality of status between one tribe and the next is meanwhile suggested by an image of shared genealogy, different tribes being "sons" of some common ancestor and sons being nominal equals. Nor is authority of some men over others well established in practice or in local theory.[9]

Even separating out "tribalism" from all else that is going on, no-one could pretend that this is a simple world. Tribes (*qabâ'il*) are indefinitely divisible, down to the level of the household, and parts of tribes can opt out of disputes that appear to implicate them, while blood-debts that imply vengeance may be engrossed in structures of guaranty that mean vengeance is indefinitely postponed. (On both counts sociality is law-bound in that binding rules are invoked; also, law is decentred in that no sovereign power is recognised as standing over all). How much is really paid to whom in settling debts is usually unclear. But what strikes one forcibly is the purported exactitude of compensation when stated. Here is a case from a fight between tribes in the late 1950s:

> Muhammad 'Alî al-Rubû'î is due his wound-money, for an internal wound and a flesh-wound, of 271 riyals plus a quarter and one half of one eighth ... Hamîd Yahyâ al-Rubû'î is due 71 riyals and a quarter and half of one eighth ... 'Alî Husayn Sa'îd of Dhayfân is due wound-money of 119 riyals less one eighth (of a riyal)...
>
> (Dresch, 1989b, p. 85)

There were 40 brass *buqshah*s to a silver riyal, and two or three riyals might have bought a goat. A presumed (but unremarked) equality between victim and offender is disturbed by an offence, and the imbalance must be restored, in accordance with explicit rules, to the value of a few brass coins.[10] At the moment of settlement, though not always in other contexts, rank is excluded or denied.

The word "egalitarian" is often used, of course, of cases where rank does not arise to start with. Among hunter-gatherers, for instance, wealth is not accumulated and domination of most sorts is unlikely; egalitarian means simply not unequal. In other cases, however, we must think what sort of claim is being made.

> To say that two objects are equal implies that that they possess the same value, are equivalent, with respect to a specific criterion, usually implicit. But clearly it does not imply that they are equivalent in all ways, or they would be identical. In the interaction between the ways in which persons are equals and the ways in which they are not lies the source of the problem.
>
> (Pitt-Rivers, 1963, p. 229)

This is easily lost sight of. Although a rhetoric of legal equality in our own societies casts a burden of explanation on those invoking difference of any kind, it is in itself empty (Westen, 1982),[11] and, well beyond law, we are everywhere faced with at least two questions.

The first is the criterion (more usually, criteria) invoked to judge value. We have already mentioned purity in India. One cannot read far in nineteenth-century English literature without noticing that birth and wealth provide different rankings. Again, certain chiefs in Polynesia could banish commoners from their island ("a condemnation to suicide") but could not make commoners dig the chief's garden (Pitt-Rivers, 1963, p. 230). Even when criteria of status are systematically muddied – as "life chances," let us say, in contemporary jargon – different types of equality or inequality may be invoked: of opportunity, condition, or outcome (Robbins, 1994, p. 33). Waldron's concern is with what some call "ontological" equality. More straightforwardly, he himself (2017) refers to "basic equality," non-negotiable equality of a kind which, as many have noted, allows inequality of other sorts. The one thing that cannot be measured in a bureaucratic state may discount the importance of all that can be measured.

The second question is how measures are applied, and whether they can be applied. The Polopa in New Guinea, for example, whom Robbins mentions, comprise a collection of shifting "communities" who feast each other and feud with each other as a matter of prestige. But their reckoning of both these is ordinal (or relative), not cardinal, each gift of "good things" or each act of vengeance being thought of as greater or less than the last, such that "one debt is settled only by creating another" and "equivalence in exchange is inconceivable ..." (Brown, 1979, p. 717). So too, then, is established rank or its denial, despite what looks to be obvious commensurability.

Equality, as such cases suggest, is seldom the key concept. Often autonomy is more the issue, whether in parts of Borneo (Helliwell, 1995) or of the Middle East (Dresch, 1998), and is rarely what theorists of law envisage. If, for example, Helliwell's Dayak friends have a notion of "standing" (*diri*) which sounds like self-sufficiency, it depends on cosmological ideals of hearths and origins, and some groups lack such standing in that they depend on the hearths of others for ritual protection.[12] In less holistic schemes, the same "mutuality of persons" (Helliwell, 1995, p. 365) is common. De Tocqueville's report on the modern world is therefore unusual. Egotism is nothing new, he says, but individualism perhaps is – "a mature and calm feeling, which disposes each member of the community to sever himself from the mass of his fellows and to draw apart with his family and friends..." (Tocqueville [1840] 1945, pp. ii, 104). The individual, meanwhile, figures as what Dumont calls the "locus of morality."[13]

In Dumont's view, "the individual of the modern type" and society of the hierarchical type are not related as part to whole but are homologues, each representing "the essence of man": moral arguments in the one case begin from the individual, in the other from society as a whole (1970, p. 10). This does not cover all that concerns us. Collective identities are invoked that foreclose certain arguments, as "identity politics," for example, obscures issues of wealth (Dresch, 1995); individual tastes, proclivities, and fate are then rolled into such identities under the rubric of equality (Hobsbawm, 1996, p. 428).[14] Nonetheless, it is commonly the case in our own world at present that appeals to individual experience trump appeals to a collective good (ibid. p. 334).

The importance of the individual is grounded by philosophers, meanwhile, in the potential young children represent (Waldron, 2017, pp. 60, 160, 176, citing Arendt), in the human capacity for reason (ibid. p. 94, 96, 121–122, citing Locke), or in our capacity for happiness. But that is not the anthropologist's focus. Rather, each of two opposed ideologies, one holistic and the other individualistic, leaves a "residue" in life as lived (Dumont, 1970, pp. 232–234), and in the modern West the existence of a residue is plain. For one thing, our economic arrangements are complex and "the ideal of the autonomy of each person became established among men who were dependent on one another for material things to a much greater extent than all their predecessors" (ibid. p. 11). Nor is it only "the modern West." Tribal populations in the Arab world depend on a broader field of exchange but commonly speak as if each tiny group were free-standing even with regard to marriage (Dresch, 1998). Claims to autonomy, like those to equality, assume always an unstated background which is readily obscured.

As Christine Helliwell argues (1994, 1995), Western discussions of equality rest often on a distinction between natural and social that does precisely this. Differences in "natural" capacity might justify differences of wealth, prestige, and influence in a way that differences of birth (perhaps oddly, these count as "social" differences) might not, and recognition of natural capacity would produce what Locke called "a just precedency" (cited Helliwell, 1994).[15] Caste, of course, makes precedence by birth natural (Bailey, 1996, pp. 24–25, 28). Social science, however, is usually content with its parochial visions, and even groups in Borneo some of whose households rank formally above others thus count as egalitarian because rank is somehow achieved, not given (Helliwell, 1995, p. 361). This is very much de Toccqueville's "equality of conditions," a phrase that runs through his account of early America ([1835] 1945, pp. i, 48, 53, 301, and *passim*), meaning first an absence of formal status by inheritance, then a turbulence of rank among families, and, occasionally, the fact that, with a modicum of effort, land was available to all because its original inhabitants could be swept aside.

Individualism (in effect, a claim to autonomy; indeed, Waldron's "basic" equality) might in cases of this kind justify practical inequality, as it does in a recent language of "fair competition":

> if the best man wins, it follows that he who loses is not the best man. Success, no longer the sign of Divine Favour as in Max Weber's analysis of the Protestant Ethic, is now the testimony of individual excellence.
> (Pitt-Rivers, 1963, p. 232)

In early America or in Britain, an alternative was to seek a "competency," safe means to live a (moderately) independent life (Vickers, 1990),[16] where comparison of rank was blunted. The last few decades, with their dramatic increase of income-inequality most notably in the English-speaking world, have forced many people away from such modesty towards the logic Pitt-Rivers describes, and the counter-argument on behalf of those not favoured remains only that of the Putney debates [1647]: "the poorest he that is in England has a life to live as the greatest he" (quoted Waldron, 2002, p. 127). Where dependence of persons on their fellows is so little stressed, key terms may be placed at odds, as liberty and equality often have been.

Liberty, even in its reduced current form of "choice," represents a capacity to act as one wishes. In the Anglophone world, more particularly in the United States, autonomy appears to trump equality as a public value (Robbins, 1994, pp. 29, 30–31, 33),[17] and curiously it encourages a justificatory claim that "differentiation" is of basic interest (ibid.p. 32) and "similarity" is thus anathema (ibid.p. 36, cf. Lucas, 1965, pp. 297, 303). This is largely nonsense. Beeman, with an eye on de Tocqueville, thus describes a common paradox with respect to advertising: "Near the top of the list [of things which Americans agree are important], along with mother and apple pie, lies 'freedom of choice' ...," yet they "recognize and actualize their integration with others ... through making the same choices" (Beeman, 1986, p. 59), and not to do so, one should add, provokes distrust. America has seldom been famous for its tolerance. Its thinkers from the start have feared forced conformity, not from alien authority but from their neighbours, and "Beeman's paradox," if we may call it that, recurs elsewhere.

The appeal of equality, meanwhile, derives from autonomy's denial. An example comes near the end of Barbusse's depiction of World War One. Losing people to anonymous slaughter in a swamp of filth, the remnants of "the squad" mutter about a just world. There are great ideals available. Liberty, equality, fraternity. But only equality can be relied on:

> L'égalité (sociale, car les individus ont chacun plus ou moins de valeur, mais chacun doit participer à la société dans la même mesure, et c'est justice, parce que la vie d'un être humain est aussi grande que la vie d'un autre), l'égalité, c'est la grande formule des hommes.
>
> (Barbusse, 1916, p. 369)

The idea that one life is as important as another (despite the fact that each of us has "more or less value" in other ways) may allow space for liberty and fraternity, or may not. But equality comes first. When one of the soldiers wonders why we make war, he says we don't know; but for whom we make war, that's easy. For privileged people (a "gilded caste," in fact) who pursue fame and profit at our expense. Demands for "equality of respect" result from domination of a kind that ignores one's moral worth.[18]

Frames of reference

Barbusse employs a language of group identity (of class, not rank) and of a unified field of comparison, but how pressing comparison may be within such fields will depend on circumstance. American small-holders were thus in somewhat the position of Middle Eastern tribesfolk, obtaining from a broader world even the tools they worked with yet carving out for themselves a livelihood. A distant view of autonomy and interdependence (an overview of cash-flows in New England *circa* 1800, let us say; an overview of cash-flows in Yemen at the time) may not be the view of people with immediate lives to lead, and class inequality may therefore form little part of local rhetoric.[19] Again,

> La fraternité islamique repose sur une base culturelle et religieuse, elle n'a aucun caractère économique ou social... Le mendiant est mon frère en effet; en ce sens, surtout, que nous partageons fraternellement la même approbation de l'inégalité qui nous sépare.
>
> (Lévi-Strauss quoted Pitt-Rivers, 1963, p. 231)

Yet when people are subject to homogenising forms of exploitation (steel-mills in Egypt, oil-fields in Arabia), Muslims are no slower than others to adopt class politics. Let us try to reach a little deeper, and consider how equality and inequality are judged.

The ranking of castes in India was always cause for argument. Endless law-suits in recent times have concerned traditional precedence at festivals (Dumont, 1970, p. 230), petty kings would once have been arbiters of rank locally, and the British, by arbitrating rank on a wider scale, are said by many to have "let the jinn out of the bottle."[20] But a basic problem, under any regime, "springs from the multiplicity of concrete criteria and from the necessity of ranking them in relation to each other" (ibid. p. 57). Local assertions by a dominant caste of a "social whole," where this occurs, provide an arbitrary answer by promoting one criterion above others, which not everyone locally will find compelling. But even agreement on criteria need not mean settled rank. With the Polopa in New Guinea, groups are commensurable, as well as comparable, in that all recognise the same terms of rivalry, without which the groups themselves lack meaning (Brown, 1979, pp. 712, 726). They do not, though, and possibly cannot, sum exchanges between groups. Nor, then, are equality and inequality very useful terms.

In our Yemeni case one can sum at least the state of blood-debt. Or one could do if alternative accounts of "who started it" did not go back indefinitely far. And if all could agree which groups were implicated, which is rarely so because each element of a set (a tribe such as Banî Suraym, for instance) can deny responsibility for the actions of another element within that set or, as easily, respond to an implication affecting some larger set (Hâshid, for instance, which includes Banî Suraym, is distinct from a set of tribes named Bakîl). The assumption of equality that underpins Yemeni arguments is meanwhile precisely that, an assumption. It is not an ideology in Dumont's sense, not a claim to the world's right ordering but rather grounds for a claim when denied; as so often, "equality" is of interest in its breach, recuperating which is the matter of explicit rules.

We have already mentioned distinctions between an internal wound (*jâ'ifah*) and flesh-wound (*mutalâhimah*). We could go on to distinguish wounds that touch bone, those that only draw blood, those that cause bruising in this degree or that. Law proclaims an ideal equality of compensation. In other cases, such as Anglo-Saxon England (Lambert, 2017), it may distinguish one rank of people from those of another rank yet proclaim the same equivalence within each. What it also proclaims is the circumstance in which rank and equivalence matter, that of an offence of person against person, and certain types of offence are commonly picked out, such that the idea of *mundbryce* (breach of protection), for example, recurs in many forms of law, as does *hambryce* (breach of house-peace). The moral standing of tribesmen in Yemen, like that of freemen in Anglo-Saxon law, rests on the idea of spaces within and between which commensurability on most grounds does not apply but violation of which requires amends, and tribal Yemen in the time that I worked there (on and off, roughly 1977–2007) was oddly "tolerant": what you did in your space as householder, member of a tribal section, member of a tribe, was very much your business. It was only impinging on other spaces that gave rise to claims.[21] What in one sense is an egalitarian form of law is in another sense a form that denies commensurability, which is true of our contemporary arrangements in America and Europe.

A rhetoric of compensation in the Yemeni case fails to translate into a general comparison of households or persons. The fascination with exchange that characterises much of New Guinea fails also. The further one reads in Indian material, the more convinced one becomes, *pace* Dumont, that a widespread acceptance of inequality, at the other extreme, produces no one criterion by which equality or its denial could be measured. Our rhetorical conventions in the modern North Atlantic world place equality first, of course, but theorists' arguments then collapse into further argument over what sort of equality, or inequality, should count in which circumstance for what purpose. One ends up, perhaps, with a simple claim that like cases, whatever the criterion for likeness, should be treated alike (Westen, 1982, pp. 570, 575).

Ethnographic comparison suggests, in brief, that a generalised concern with equality and inequality is a special case and that much of what theorists take as given (as "human nature," perhaps, or the nature of society) is peculiar to our own obsessions. What is it in our world, then, that allows liberty and equality to be set at odds under the rubric of individualism, or oppression and inequality to be equated, or conformity and difference culturally to displace more intransigent questions of exploitation? Part of the answer, surely, is that some more or less explicit whole imposes a common frame of reference in which commensurability of persons or of groups is not avoidable. One such frame is conventionally dubbed political, another dubbed economic.

Equality and law

The French Revolution provides Dumont's type-case of inability to deal with difference, each instance of which is likely to be seen as a form of inequality and thus betrayal of the social whole. The whole at issue is the nation or state, which Dumont rather loses sight of.[22] Rhetorics of equality (along with quite other rhetorics) covered a state-centred terror which at critical junctures in the late eighteenth century found popular support in Paris, and presumably it is this that de Tocqueville has in mind (1945, pp. ii, 101–102) when he fears that all may be equal in subjection to a chosen master and that people may prefer equality to freedom. Two factors, he says, saved America from the fate of Revolutionary France. The first is religion, which one might think in the American case has contributed to the problem as often as relieving it, and the second is a reverence for law. Yet law in a democracy is itself unstable (ibid. i. 213, 267, 437). Indeed where the sovereign people "has the right both of making and of executing the laws" (ibid. i. 273) law offers scant assurance of liberty.

In India, for example, post-1947 "temple entry acts" (Dumont, 1970, p. 231) granted Untouchables, as equal citizens of a modern state, entry to Brahman temples. In the old scheme, impure activities (tanning and the like) could go on in close proximity to more prestigious form of life on condition of explicit inequality and difference, but in the new dispensation of universal rules the obvious response was to drive such activities out of town and to impose a nominal purity on all in the form of regional laws that everyone be vegetarian.[23] Already by J. S. Mill's day (Mill [1859] 2015, pp. 86–87), American demands that all be teetotal by law had caused alarm. Yet law is also the promise of salvation. If the constitutions of American states had mainly changed more than once by Tocqueville's time, the federal constitution, perhaps unexpectedly, remained in place, and the concern with individual rights in its amendments and its later interpretation requires no stressing.[24] Presumably the cult of law in de Tocqueville's time rested on more localised concerns. There seems little doubt, however, that Americans were willing to "go to law," and that law involved centralised authority, the centre both before and after independence being commonly the township.

Yemeni tribal law, both in concept and in practice, is thoroughly decentred (there is no bounded set of arbitrators; no separable group exerts coercion), and enforcement turns on ideas less of obedience than of reputation and loss of standing. The final "sanction," if one thinks in such terms, was outlawry. Even that was a localised, decentred question. Loss of standing in law results most obviously, however, from refusal of amends for breach of protection, and wronging one's guest, to take the basic case, requires a multiple of the usual recompense for harm. Such asymmetric relations could be handed off to others, as in the case of escort (Dresch, 2012b, p. 149), just as common responsibility could be formally denied (Dresch, 1989a, pp. 86–87). The categories at issue are host, escort or fellow tribesman, not simply person, and "secondary" rules that govern their application (when do the rules of escort apply to me, when do they not?) are at least as prominent as "primary" rules prescribing how many riyals for an ear or finger (Dresch, 2012b, pp. 150, 165). Given the absence of centralised authority, what are explicit rules doing here? Simply put, they define what matters: "moral likeness is established only when people define categories" (Westen, 1982, p. 545), and categories of this kind are coincident with explicit rules.[25]

Definitions elsewhere may formalise inequality, of course, although sometimes in unexpected ways. For example, one version of Sanskritic law suggests a scale of fines that rise with the status of the wrongdoer, such that Shudras should pay eightfold for theft, Vaishyas 16-fold, and Kshatriyas 32-fold (Lingat, 1973, p. 67). Elsewhere again, sumptuary laws might enforce rank or deny it. Many forms of law will define penalties or compensation according not only to rank but to degrees of relatedness between the parties (classical China is the obvious case; MacCormack 1996). Modern law, if we may call it that, is thus unusual on several grounds, and as Robbins argues (1994, pp. 37, 55), people in our own world are equal (or, of course, unequal) not with regard to each other but "with regard to the state or to society …," which is only to say equal before the law (cf. Lucas, 1965, pp. 299–300). The 14th amendment of the US constitution, from which American legal arguments so often start, thus speaks of "equal protection of the laws," not of those laws' substance. Indeed the imagined autonomy of subjects or citizens is in large part law's own creation.

Persons in current legal rhetoric are meant all to be of the same kind and somehow of the same value, such that distinguishing "sorts" of people is thought wrong, although differences of "conditional" status imposed by law, such as bankruptcy, are considered fair (Waldron, 2017, pp. 6–8). This obscures a good many issues. There may indeed be sorts of people who deserve distinguishing,[26] while conditional status may in effect be permanent and destroy people's lives, as observers of American probation or felony-law cannot fail to notice. Beyond this, "basic" equality (equality which is present by definition) leaves morality as a separate issue that must somehow be tacked on to discussion.[27]

Such "tacking on" is difficult if one foregrounds prescriptive equality. For example, the New Testament injunction to take in the stranger, minister to the sick, and visit those in prison (Waldron, 2017, p. 75, citing Matthew 25) assumes that the righteous, at the time of asking, are in a better position than those needing help. Even if we concede that "equality" is a way to speak of common humanity (Lucas, 1965; Westen 1982), such common humanity need demand no more than politeness with strangers. It is inequality, the opposite condition, that motivates compassion, charity or care. Kant's famous essay on "Perpetual peace" [1795], with its secular equation of autonomy and equality, thus produces a notoriously thin set of rights, for if all of us owe duties in general to people in general, there is no obvious reason why I in particular should help someone wronged or in need and not leave doing so to you or humanity at large (Dresch, 2012a). The Yemeni tribal scheme is conspicuously different. The idea of honour (*sharaf*), here doing very much the work that Waldron (or for that matter Lucas) wants done by "respect," inserts people in a moral field, but the honourable man is obliged to take in the stranger, at least for three days, and to protect the oppressed. To wrong the guest or protégé, once taken in, requires multiple amends. The difference between such amends being due and ordinary compensation being due is given by what we could call "situational inequality."

In an explicitly holistic world situational inequality fits a language of "levels and reversals"[28] in the manner of Kipling's nineteenth-century Canada within Britain's empire: "Daughter am I in my mother's house / But mistress in my own." The Yemeni case is not hierarchical in this sense. Instead, it echoes Pitt-Rivers's account of hospitality, whereby reciprocity, unlike the reciprocity of violence, resides "not in an identity but in alternation of roles" (Pitt-Rivers, 1977: 102). I can be your host, or protector, in my space today, you can be my host in your space tomorrow; and our moral equivalence consists in our mutual recognition of each other's capacity to do so. The separation of spaces is the key to this, and with it the place of law as providing definitions among shifting groups each able, potentially, to coerce the other. The only obvious form of "hierarchy," beyond the domestic sphere, is meanwhile a vague sense of branched genealogy or nested identity, making all of us related but some sets of people more closely implicated than others in the actions of a given group. This is scarcely holism. Yet nor is "individualism" the right word for a world in which the actions of others so obviously implicate one's reputation and safety.

Without some concept of the State or of bounded community as the source of authority and comparison, it is difficult to oppose not only individualism to holism but equality to hierarchy, let alone to elide the first opposition with the second in the manner of Dumont. Indeed much of anthropologists' discussion falls into place as a series of appeals to some imagined condition that would form an alternative to our own.

The liberal world

Our analytical and moral problems in North America and Western Europe remain those of nineteenth-century governance. They are posed, though they were never resolved, by classical liberalism,[29] and the key-stone of liberalism was surely a distinction between public and private space: do what you like at home, but don't do it in the street and frighten the horses. If the distinction is less clear than it once was (Dresch, 2012b, p. 154), this is due in part to endemic abuse of power within domestic space. But a rightful concern with such abuse has scarcely touched the broader problems of liberty and equality under state-centred law, not least because our language to discuss the issue is restricted.

The equation of holism and hierarchy that Dumont seeks in India is largely absent from our current North Atlantic states. His distinction, and that of de Tocqueville, between religion and politics – the very basis of "value" in Dumont's scheme and thus of "encompassment" as coterminous with rank – has meanwhile collapsed in favour of political order, making religion only part of "civil society." But nineteenth-century authors found more immediate cause for worry. Whether in the essays of Bagehot or the novels of Trollope, one finds a concern with securing Locke's "just precedency" against the anonymous power of wealth. In our own time, one realises, wage-scales are one of those "frames of reference" we referred to earlier as forcing on us questions of equality and inequality. The idea of a "competency" (or an "independence" or a "permanency" in novels of the nineteenth century) has all but disappeared, and an older *pudeur* about income dissolves in the face of competitive success and rank that is measured in monetary terms.

A common style of cross-cultural comparison, of course, grounds the notions of equality and inequality themselves in material scarcity. This is rarely the local view, however. Helliwell's Dayak companions, for example, treat rice as quasi-human, and producing sufficient rice to gain "standing," or *diri*, is likened to having many children. The symbolic goods required for *diri* include flowering plants whose practical use is obscure, none of these groups was so poor as to go hungry, and land for new cultivation of rice was reckoned plentiful (Helliwell, 1995, pp. 363, 366, 369). Again, raising pigs in New Guinea no doubt required effort, but anyone could do it: in the Polopa case, "material dependence between communities in consuming pork is created out of material independence in producing pigs" (Brown, 1979, p. 718). Neither rice nor pigs are a simple "commodity." Nor was land in that part of early American experience that so fascinated De Tocqueville.[30] When money is the salient mean of reckoning, however, which in itself is nothing new, all things may be thought commensurable and all persons, too, in conditions where, by definition, everything is in some degree scarce.

The root of the problem that results is apparent in the opening sections of Mill's *Political Economy* [1848, 1871], where he starts to set out his arguments against mercantilism. Even land has no special status in the jostling for rank and precedence. Nor do specific status-goods, nor yet a person's command of goods at a given time:

> We really, and justly, look upon a person as possessing the advantages of wealth, not in proportion to the useful and agreeable things of which he is in the actual enjoyment, but to his command over the general fund of things useful and agreeable...
>
> (Mill, 2006, p. 6)

Those things include the services of others. We may purchase the labour-power, and indeed the subservience, of less well-off people although we are not any longer allowed to buy the people themselves, and several types of good are thought improperly fungible. We also distinguish "sectors" of life, such as politics and economics. For all the dishonesty of usage (a certain constituency complains of politics "interfering" in economics; another denounces that distinction as itself a political claim), these terms recur in attempts to manage a supposed democracy. To take an obvious case, there are laws against buying the verdict of jurors or buying electoral votes.[31] Yet the individual who is subject to, if not wholly created by, modern law is allotted only "equal protection of the laws," omitting most practicalities.

In a piece that deserves a far wider readership, Justin Schwartz (2001) addresses the elision of equity and equality in our own world by examining Rawls's *Theory of Justice*. Rawls, of course, pursues an ideal of "fair equality of opportunity"; the fact that we raise children in families means that opportunities are by no means equal, however, and strict consistency would require that we do away either with the family or with Rawls's particular ambition of fairness.[32] Indeed, towards the end of the piece Schwartz mentions Marx's claim that in conditions of structural disadvantage talk of "right" (or law) can only mean "a right of inequality." In an attempt to take the edge off this dilemma, which is that of Locke, Schwartz then points out that opportunity, deserts and outcomes are compounded on a unitary scale that elides forms of good we might better keep separate:

> Surely opportunities to be physicians or attorneys should be confined to those who have the requisite talents. Why though, should medical or legal talent translate into wealth, security and political power in a way denied to those whose talents run to auto mechanics?
>
> (Schwartz, 2001, p. 112)

Power, comfort, status (leisure, job-satisfaction; the list goes on) need not all go to the same people.[33] But to keep them distinct would now require explicit rules.

Few of us wish a world where mechanics wear one colour of dress and lawyers and doctors wear another, while lawyers are distinguished from doctors by a hat with a tassel, although other societies than our own have tended towards something like this (classical China again comes immediately to mind). We have contented ourselves, instead, with a world of rules about generic persons and their interactions. Within that logic, not elsewhere, lies what Max Weber might have called an "elective affinity" between rules (treat like cases alike) and a notion of basic equality among persons (treat no-one differently from another); what Lucas (1965) calls "formal equality" is readily confused with recognition of common humanity. The first of these is entailed in rational administration and in laws. The second tells us little of law's content. We could impose what laws we see fit, of course, – and we do so, for instance through tax-codes – but the absence of moral holism makes discussion difficult.

Decisions on imposing rules or on applying rules appear always arbitrary. Weber confronts this when he speaks of a contradiction, under individualistic rhetoric, between an ethic of ultimate ends and an ethic of responsibility, such that all one can say when one acts for the common good is, "Here I stand; I can do no other" (1958, p. 127). Almost in despair he turns to an imagined India, much as Dumont does later. If am Kshatriya then coercion is my rightful business, and if I am Brahman then my concern is with a larger order of which kings' affairs are a part but are not my immediate concern. Absent this hierarchical order, contradiction is centred on the individual politician as scapegoat or saviour.[34] The alternative ("a government of laws, not men") is explicit rules, and rules about rules *ad infinitum*, which is strikingly our own condition.

The state of Massachusetts, says de Tocqueville with surprise (1945, pp. i, 267), had already, by the 1830s, passed sufficient laws in 50 years to fill "three stout volumes." By present standards, of course, one can only stand amazed at their moderation, for the sheer amount of law – the number and complexity of rules – in current society is the stuff both of practice and of myth, and we are often told, for instance, that the US tax code now runs to more than 70,000 pages. Actually the code is about 2,600 pages (quite enough, one might think) and the larger figure applies to a standard compilation containing previous codes and a mass of case-law.[35] Nonetheless, only a specialist would claim to understand it. If the number of "general public Acts" in the UK is large compared with, say, the eighteenth century, we should remember that parliament used to pass a great many Acts to deal with particular marriages, rights of way, or plots of land. On the other hand, a general Act will typically produce vast amounts of delegated legislation, such as rules set by ministers without reference to parliament.[36] Calculate as you will, however, we live in a world of endlessly multiplying rules, the totality of which seems always inadequate.

The prevalence and place of rules

Individualism and equality, as we have seen, are not the same thing. Nor need holism be the opposite of either, although few societies go as far as ours in obscuring what Helliwell calls the "mutuality of persons." Holism itself, in fact, comes in different degrees. For example, the "circle of justice," whereby the ruler's soldiery need money, which needs a productive peasantry, which needs justice enforced by the ruler through his soldiery if the state is to thrive (London, 2011), requires little elaboration of rank or function. Nor is the supposed whole very closely bounded. Indeed boundedness is more a feature of modern states. The modern state, however, like many older states in the Middle East, lacks an exhaustive cosmology to rationalise its usage, which perhaps is not unusual. There is really no need for all of life to obey one overarching logic, yet academics of many kinds pursue it.

In the second English edition of *Homo Hierarchicus*, Dumont supplemented his earlier formulation of hierarchy – "a relation between that which encompasses and that which is encompassed" (Dumont, 1970, p. xii) – with a claim that hierarchy is "the encompassment of the contrary" on the model of the English terms "man" and "woman": at one level, set and subset, at another level simply opposites (Dumont, 1980, pp. 239–240). This is surely a special case, yet it caught the attention of anthropologists elsewhere in a way the more modest formulation had not. As Robbins notes (1994, p. 31), the idea of levels, and thus "reversals of value" (a man who is vassal of his lord in public life could himself be lord of his household), might apply both to an indigenous cosmology and to an analyst's ambitions. Many anthropologists would like to gather the ends of their ethnography and tie a bow so that seeming anomalies all form part of a coherent whole. Whether they should do so is a different question.[37] While certain social formations themselves employ an exhaustive scheme of levels and reversals, most do not, and over-interpretation is all too likely.

In our own world – that of North Atlantic "democratic" states – law has at least an ambition of coherence. It sometimes has little option but to produce an appearance of completeness comparable to that of overly-ambitious anthropologists. Yet one distinctive feature of our states is the starkness of opposition between the totality of supposedly separate individuals and the centralising power that claims to allow their peaceable coexistence. The link between them is equality before the law. Its substance is that of generalised explicit rules, as if procedural equality would give substantive justice. Yet formal equality of this kind disadvantages the many. I cannot myself see a formula to escape our problem, and rules about rules will no doubt continue spreading in a futile pursuit of order, but the issue is akin to Pitt-Rivers's point (1963, p. 229) that the poll-tax was entirely equal and therefore unjust.

Notes

1 This opening quotation is lifted from a forthcoming book on India (Anastasia Piliavsky's *Nobody's People: hierarchy as hope in a society of thieves*) that explains, in the teeth of fairly severe opposition, why inequality may be a moral value, not a sin or failing.

2 To mention longevity is to invite suspicion of exaggerated rhetoric. I can only recommend Marmot (2015). The fact that the risk to a cohort of teenage girls, through the course of their reproductive lives, of dying in childbirth is about ten times greater in the United States than in Italy surely deserves notice. I am unfair to Dworkin in that "concern and respect" in his analysis are properties of government, not private persons, but that only gives further point to Marmot's arguments.

3 Ignoring ethnographic variety produces what Lévi-Strauss once called "*une sorte de métaphysique pour midinettes*." Few readers of this volume will be anthropologists. I have therefore looked for references (Helliwell, Piliavsky, Robbins) which make sense if read alone but have good bibliographies. My approach to "law," meanwhile, is not that of all anthropologists, and some may favour quite other views. See Dupret (2016).

4 In southern India, even 30 years ago 68% of places in educational institutions and jobs in the public sector were already reserved, on constitutional grounds of equal opportunity, to "the backward classes" (Srinivas, 1986, p. 131).

Add these classes together and it is often a majority of the population, from which many writers deduce that equality now is (or should be) the dominant issue both between castes and within them. This sounds well and good until one opens an Indian newspaper.

5 For law in classical India see Lingat (1973), Davis (2010). Again, of course, some may prefer not to use the word "law." My sympathies lie with Davis. For a useful note on *dharma* and Dumont's view of totality, meanwhile, see Rio and Smedal (2009, pp. 32–33).

6 What is invoked in some cases is clarity of attachment to a patron. Combined with something like the Elizabethan fear of "masterless men," the fact that the people with whom Piliavsky lived had no clear attachments encouraged their neighbours to treat them with amoral violence.

7 The idea of a pre-social individual is always illusory (for one thing, we are language-users), but claims to a measure of autonomy are not. Nor are they straightforward. As Hart points out (1983), appeals to the "separateness" of individuals are common to such different writers as Nozick and Dworkin, and the latter's "equality of concern and respect" provides no solid means to argue either for what we think right or against what we think wrong. See also Finegan (2015).

8 Those at the lower end of such rhetoric were often discontented. But everywhere that rank was not displaced by class (Briggs, 1960), which for decades was most of life, it was rank that formed the basis of moral demands. Rank allows more easily a multiplicity of criteria, but also it applies to specific persons and relationships, where class is far more anonymous. As Briggs makes clear, the change in vocabulary was provoked by genuine changes in the world, not least the growth of industrial cities.

9 For an account see Dresch, 1989a. The population here depended largely on rain-fed farming, in areas with little rain. One cannot stress too much the salience in the region's history of wars, famine and migration, and tribal values are not at all the only values at issue. But tribalism in the sense I have sketched shows remarkable longevity. The word tribe (*qabîlah*) is usually applied in areas north of Sanaa to quite large sets of people, these days of easily 50-100,000 each, and "tribal Yemen" counts millions. We are not discussing "small-scale" or "face-to-face" society.

10 Lists of values for wound-money are copied and kept quite widely. Throughout what records we have, blood-money is the same for all Muslim men and that for Muslim women is half this. Many points in the present paper are addressed also in the conclusion to Dresch, 2006, which unfortunately is now hard to find. I have therefore placed it on academia.edu.

11 Compensation, one notes, is in common-law practice a matter for juries more than for stated rules. Although there are tariffs for industrial injuries and the like, assessment of injury more broadly, and thus of the victim's worth, presents itself as a matter of intuition, while the rhetoric of equality can always be reduced to other terms.

12 Groups that lack *diri* seem not to depend on other groups economically, nor to contribute wealth to those groups. The "standing" of groups that grow sufficient rice to maintain a permanent dwelling and a hearth, is more like the English and American "competence" or "independence" that we shall touch on later. All groups meanwhile think themselves dependent on a wider cosmology of gods and people.

13 This phrase can sound too abstract for comfort. For an unreflective, and therefore useful, account of individualism one could look at Robert Bellah's best-seller (1985). His American interviewees have problems maintaining marriages (to take an obvious case) because no language is available for discussing the long-term grind of duty; if all one can say in the face of life's troubles is that

one's personal development is compromised, then one's partner can only say the same and disaster follows. An unrequited longing for "community" meanwhile colours the whole book.

14 "LGBTQ rights" are thus presented as an "equality issue." They may be an issue of tolerance, of separating public and private spheres, or any number of important issues, but scarcely of equality. The acronym, which many hold strongly should contain yet further symbols (the criteria denoted in the first string already overlap), does not denote a set comparable to, say, black or female, but turns upon a claim to individual difference that denies the very ground of comparison.

15 If Waldron's attempt (2017) on "basic equality" as such seems thin, his analysis (2002) of Locke is compelling. One would be hard pressed to deny that Locke's notion of equality depends on a holistic scheme whereby the value of persons derives from God by way of the capacity for reason. What counts as "natural capacity" beyond this, apart from "age" or "virtue," and thus justifies "precedency," is obscure. Perhaps, arbitrarily, the clerkly skills of people who write books, whether Locke or our present readers.

16 The units in Vickers's work, as in theorists from Locke to Rawls, are not single persons but households and families. This makes little difference to the present argument but reminds us how ignorant we are of our surroundings. For example, in the United States at present how much wealth is transmitted by descent of which kind, how much by affinity, how much by way of distant kin-links? Financial statistics work by households but give no clue what a family is.

17 In American jurisprudence they still form a complementary pair (see e.g. Ginsburg, 1985; Post, 1997). Nor should the value of equality in popular culture be discounted; the spectacle of politicians pretending to be "regular guys" has long had its fascination, and plutocratic populism (or populist plutocracy, whichever it is) thrives on denouncing supposed élites.

18 This is not the only context in which a rhetoric of equality is used, of course. It can be deployed against neighbours who by no stretch of the imagination are one's oppressors; indeed mere difference of taste and interest may result in accusations of "getting above oneself," and there is often a nasty taste of unfocused resentment. Nonetheless, if people complain of inequality then a problem usually needs addressing.

19 Elsewhere in Vickers's work (1994 as well as 1990, pp. 20–21) one finds how illusory independence often was, in that attempts to better one's lot encouraged a search for credit; small wonder that banks and currency form such a feature of nineteenth-century American populism. The equivalent in Yemen was that tribal wealth came always from non-tribal areas of the country, sometimes by way of a state, such as the Zaydi imamate, sometimes otherwise.

20 Older work (e.g. Singer and Cohn, 1968) makes clear both the complexity of caste over wide areas and the frequent indeterminacy of local ranking. The British, although they used no single criterion of rank, tried to produce a pan-Indian "table of precedence." As so often, a centralising state raised questions of comparison that earlier would have been difficult to conceive, and recent legal arguments over ritual precedence put one strongly in mind of minor notables in de Tocqueville's *L'Ancien regime.*

21 Households rest on inequalities of sex and age; larger identities in the Yemeni case use much of the language applied to households (Dresch, 1989a, pp. 57, 80, 81), and an older convention of feminist analysis might rest the very language of wider equality on domestic hierarchy. Yet that hierarchy can be removed and leave untouched the conceptual problems of equality and autonomy.

22 The contrast between ideology and residue that we mentioned earlier is depicted in a famous diagram (Dumont, 1970, p. 233) with *Homo major*'s hierarchical

or holistic ideology and individualist residue played off against the inverse for *Homo minor*. On very thin grounds, the "nation" ends up on the line between residue and ideology. When the diagram is reproduced (e.g. Robbins, 1994, p. 27) the nation or state is often lost entirely. For Dumont's later attempts to give the state its due see Dumont (1986), Chapters 2 and 6. For a more useful view of French republican language see Descombes (1984).

23 For an engaging account of temple-entry legislation at village level in Orissa see Bailey (1996). The title of his book denotes a major problem of our time, finding somehow, within a nation state, "The civility of indifference."

24 The development of "constitution worship" must be left to historians. It is not conspicuous in de Tocqueville's day. As to individual rights, a generous count might conclude that more than half the first ten constitutional amendments deal with these, but the later use of the fourteenth amendment, of all things, to protect employers from labour-unions leaves mute the resources of ordinary language. The use of its juristic complement, the first amendment, has sometimes been just as odd.

25 Some will argue, in broadly the terms of Austin, that morality and law are distinct. So they are. But if explicit rules are a feature of law, as I would argue they are more often than is unified sovereignty, then Westen's point applies *a fortiori* to almost anything I would call "law".

26 As Sedley (2019) points out, disability and age allow discrimination in both US and UK law. Elsewhere the results of equality-rhetoric are striking. An obvious case, the very mention of which will produce discomfort, is the distinction between men and women. For the moment, at least, it remains the case that women get pregnant, not men, and women, less ineluctably but pretty constantly, get stuck with responsibility for child-rearing. The language of prescriptive equality means that most arrangements to relieve the "sortal" burden rest "conditionally" on less well-off women, and mainstream feminism has become the preserve of well-off persons (cf. Hobsbawm, 1996, pp. 316–318).

27 Beginning from "basic" equality, as Waldron does, makes arguing for reform cumbersome. If we begin from our practical treatment of others (Sangiovanni, 2017), certain arguments become clearer: often we are acting cruelly, for which there is no excuse. *Pace* Sangiovanni, however, I cannot see that a formal concept of equality is needed to recognise bad behaviour or that the concept is implied by such recognition.

28 Robbins (1994, pp. 53, 56. This is from a later phase of Dumont's thought that we can touch on at the end of our discussion. For a useful account of later Dumontian hierarchy across cultures see, again, Rio and Smedal eds. (2009).

29 "Liberal" is now often used where I would say "neo-liberal" (it has long been used distinctively in French, of course). Nonetheless, throughout the nineteenth century it is fairly clear what people are discussing in the British case. There is certainly a concern for property. There is a concern for individual freedom. More problematically, there is an assumption of unilinear progress (Mill's comments on barbarism need no repeating). But neither among theorists nor politicians, one has to say, is there much sign of *laissez faire* government as a doctrine. Indeed, the whole point of liberalism derives from a perceived need to regulate society.

30 De Tocqueville, 1945, pp. i, 303. "Every culture needs its lies," says Vickers (1990, p. 28), and supposedly empty land was one of these in the American case (without the displacement or eradication of Indians, the history of the United States makes no sense). As to the next stage, through the Homestead Act of 1862, one need only consult the classics of American historiography, such as Hofstadter, to see how land became the commodity *par excellence* and a powerful new source of practical inequality.

31 Or at least, there were such laws. I am genuinely unsure what to make of *Citizens United v. Federal Election Commission* 558 US 310 (2010), whereby corporations are equated with natural persons and their money with speech, thus allowing unlimited political spending under the first amendment. But even the US Supreme Court seems not to condone exchanging individual votes for cash. A tribute paid by vice to virtue? The equation of corporate with natural persons, going back to the 1880s, suggests the problem may run deep.

32 Much as one admires the consistency and patience of Rawls's approach, his role is that of a latter-day Isaiah Berlin: if one happens to be a comfortably middle-class person in North America or Western Europe, he explains why one can justly feel pleased with oneself. Nonetheless, his famous claim that "the arbitrariness of the world must be corrected for" is appealing. Forty years later, when arbitrariness seems all the rage, it sounds almost radical.

33 The issue should be familiar to academics. Until quite recently, the tacit assumption was that one elected a career whose monetary rewards were not great in return for being left alone to do something more interesting. The soul-destroying triviality of commercial life brought material reward.

34 "Politics as a vocation" is dull to read, and only a few pages (Weber, 1958, pp. 118–127) are gold-dust. But the lecture was delivered in extraordinary circumstances where the rhetorical contradiction of ends and means was acute: as mayor of Munich do you order the police to fire, thus killing perhaps 30 people, or not to fire, perhaps allowing a riot in which 300 could die? As with later "trolleyology," whatever you do is somehow wrong. The language available to rationalise or justify your choice is thin.

35 This is published by the Commerce Clearing House, based in Illinois. Presumably it is these days used as a resource on-line.

36 The acts providing these endless governmental powers to make rules are often referred to, with no detectable sense of irony or worry, as "enabling acts." Compare the German *Ermächtigungsgesetz*. For a list of "general public acts" see https://www.legislation.gov.uk/ukpga.

37 Caton, in no sense a Dumontian, thus claims that piety comes before honour in tribal Yemen, as if invoking a scale of values (Caton, 1990, pp. 26–27). In my own experience, however, if I suspect a tribesman is pulling my leg and I ask him is something true "by God," he will happily continue with a falsehood; if I ask him is it true "on your honour," he never will. Yet no-one, if asked, will deny religion's primacy. Which value trumps which, if we wish to use such terms, depends on who is speaking to whom in what setting. I cannot see that a unified set of levels and reversals gets us anywhere. In parts of Austronesia perhaps it would.

References

Bailey, F.G. (1996) *The Civility of Indifference: On Domesticating Ethnicity*, Ithaca and London: Cornell University Press.

Barbusse, H. (1916) *Le feu: journal d'une escouade*. Paris: Flammarion.

Beeman, W.O. (1986) 'Freedom to choose: Symbols and values in American advertising' in H. Varenne (ed.) *Symbolizing America*. Lincoln: University of Nebraska Press, pp. 52–65.

Bellah, R.N. et al (1985) *Habits of the Heart: individualism and commitment in American life*. London and Berkeley: University of California Press.

Briggs, A. (1960) 'The language of "class" in early nineteenth century England' in Briggs, A. and Saville, J. (eds.) *Essays in Labour History*. London: Macmillan, pp. 43–73.

Brown, D.J. (1979) 'The structuring of Polopa feasting and warfare', *Man* (n.s.), 14/4, pp. 712–733.

Caton, S. (1990) *"Peaks of Yemen I summon": Poetry as Cultural Practice in a North Yemeni Tribe*. Berkeley and Los Angeles: University of California Press.

Davis, D.R. Jr. (2010) *The Spirit of Hindu Law*. Cambridge: Cambridge University Press.

Descombes, V. (1984) 'Pour elle un français doit mourir', *Revue européenne des sciences sociales*, 22(68), pp. 67–93.

Dresch, P. (1989a) *Tribes, Government, and History in Yemen*. Oxford: Clarendon Press.

Dresch, P. (1989b) 'Keeping the Imam's peace: a response to tribal disorder in the late 1950s', *Peuples Méditerranéens*, special issue on "Yemen-Sanaa", 46, pp. 77–95.

Dresch, P. (1995) 'Race, culture and – what? Some pluralist certainties in the United States' in James, W. (ed.) *The Pursuit of Certainty* (ASA Decennial volume). London and New York: Routledge, pp. 61–91.

Dresch, P. (1998) 'Mutual deception: Totality, exchange, and Islam in the Middle East' in James, W. and Allen, N (eds.) *Marcel Mauss: A Centenary Tribute*. Oxford and New York: Berghahn, pp. 111–133.

Dresch, P. (2006) *The Rules of Barat: Tribal Documents from Yemen*. Sanaa: Centre Français d'Archéologie et de Sciences Sociales, Deutsche Archäologisches Institut.

Dresch, P. (2012a) 'Legalism, anthropology, and history: A view from part of anthropology' in Dresch, P. and Skoda, H. (eds.) *Legalism: Anthropology and History*. Oxford: Oxford University Press, pp. 1–37.

Dresch, P. (2012b) 'Aspects of non-state law: Early Yemen and perpetual peace' in Dresch, P. and Skoda, H. (eds.) *Legalism*. Oxford: Oxford University Press, pp. 145–172.

Dresch, P. and Scheele, J. (2015) 'Rules and categories: An overview' in Dresch, P. and Scheele, J. (eds.) *Legalism: Rules and categories*. Oxford: Oxford University Press, pp. 1–27.

Dumont, L. (1970) *Homo Hierarchicus; The Caste System and Its Implications* (Mark Sainsbury trans., French original 1966). Chicago, IL: University of Chicago Press.

Dumont, L. (1980) *Homo Hierarchicus: The Caste System and Its Implications* (second, expanded, edition). Chicago, IL: University of Chicago Press.

Dumont, L. (1986) *Essays on Individualism: Modern Ideology in Anthropological Perspective*. Chicago, IL and London: University of Chicago Press.

Dupret, B. (2016) 'Réflexions sur le concept de droit à partir de quelques cas limites', *Droit et société*, 94(3), pp. 645–662.

Finegan, T. (2015) 'Dworkin on equality, autonomy and authenticity', *American Journal of Jurisprudence*, 60(2), pp. 143–180.

Fox, J.J. (1994) 'Reflections on "hierarchy" and "precedence"', *History and Anthropology*, 7, pp. 87–108.

Ginsburg, R.B. (1985) 'Some thoughts on autonomy and equality in relation to *Roe v. Wade*', *North Carolina Law Review*, 63(2), pp. 375–386.

Hart, H.L.A. (1983) 'Between utility and rights' in *Essays in Jurisprudence*. Oxford: Clarendon Press, pp. 198–222.

Helliwell, C. (1994) '"A just precedency": The Notion of Equality in Anthropological Discourse', *History and Anthropology*, 7, pp. 362–375.

Helliwell, C. (1995) 'Autonomy as natural equality: Inequality in "egalitarian" societies', *Journal of the Royal Anthropological Institute*, 1(2), pp. 359–375.

Hobsbawm, E. (1996) *The Age of Extremes; A History of the World 1914–1991*, paperback edition. New York: Vintage Books.
Hocart, A.M. (1938) *Les Castes* (trans. E. Levy and J. Auboyer). Paris: P. Guethner.
Lambert, T. (2017) *Law and Order in Anglo-Saxon England.* Oxford: Oxford University Press.
Lingat, R. (1973) *The Classical Law of India* (trans. J. Duncan Derrrett). Berkeley: University of California Press.
London, J.A. (2011) 'The circle of justice', *History of Political Thought*, 32(3), pp. 425–447.
Lucas, J.R. (1965) 'Against equality', *Philosophy*, 40(154), pp. 296–307.
MacCormack, G. (1996) *The Spirit of Traditional Chinese Law*, Athens, and London: University of Georgia Press.
Marmot, M. (2015) *The Health Gap: The Challenge of an Unequal World.* London: Bloomsbury.
Miers, S. and Kopytoff, I. (1977) 'African "slavery" as an institution of marginality' in Miers and Kopytoff (ed.), *Slavery in Africa: Historical and Anthropological Perspectives.* Madison: University of Wisconsin Press, pp. 3–81.
Mill, J.S. (2006) 'Principles of political economy' in Robson, J.M. (ed.) *Collected Works of John Stuart Mill*, vols. 2 and 3. Indianapolis, IN: Liberty Fund.
Mill, J.S. (2015) *On Liberty, Utilitarianism, and Other Essays* (M. Philp and F. Rosen eds.). Oxford: Oxford University Press.
Piliavsky, A. (2015) 'Patronage and community in a society of thieves', *Contributions to Indian Sociology*, 49(2), pp. 135–161.
Piliavsky, A. (2020) *Nobody's People: Hierarchy as Hope in a Society of Thieves*, Stanford, CA: Stanford University Press.
Pitt-Rivers, J. (1963) 'The egalitarian society', *VIe Congrès international des sciences anthropologiques et ethnologiques.* Paris: Musée de l'homme, vol. 2 part 1, pp. 229–233.
Pitt-Rivers, J. (1977) 'The law of hospitality' in *The Fate of Schechem, or the Politics of Sex.* Cambridge: Cambridge University Press, pp. 94–112.
Post, R. (1997) 'Equality and autonomy in first amendment jurisprudence', *Yale Law School Faculty Scholarship Series*, paper 197.
Rio, K. and Smedal, O. (eds.) (2009) *Hierarchy: Persistence and Transformation in Social Formations.* New York and Oxford: Berghahn.
Robbins, J. (1994) 'Equality as a value: Ideology' in Dumont, Melanesia and the West, *Social Analysis*, 36, pp. 21–70.
Sangiovanni, A. (2017) *Humanity without Dignity: Moral Equality, Respect, and Human Rights.* Cambridge, MA: Harvard University Press.
Schauer, F. (1991) *Playing by the Rules: A Philosophical Examination of Rule-based Decision-making in Law and Life.* Oxford: Clarendon Press.
Schwartz, J. (2001) 'Rights of inequality: Rawlsian justice, equal opportunity, and the status of the family', *Legal Theory*, 7, pp. 83–117.
Sedley, S. (2019) 'Short cuts', *London Review of Books*, 41(3), pp. 14–15.
Singer, M. and Cohn, B.S. (eds.) (1968) *Structure and Change in Indian Society.* Chicago, IL: Aldine.
Srinivas, M.N. (1986) 'Comment on André Béteille. Individualism and equality', *Current Anthropology*, 27(2), pp. 129–130.
Tocqueville, A. de. (1945) *Democracy in America* (ed. H. Reeve, further revised by P. Bradley), 2 vols., New York: Alfred A. Knopf.

Vickers, D. (1990) 'Competency and competition: Economic culture in early America', *The William and Mary Quarterly*, 47(1), pp. 3–29.

Vickers, D. (1994) *Farmers and Fishermen: Two Centuries of Work in Essex County, Massachusetts 1630–1850*. Chapel Hill, NC: University of North Carolina Press.

Waldron, J. (2002) *God, Locke, and Equality: Christian Foundations in Locke's Political Thought*. Cambridge: Cambridge University Press.

Waldron, J. (2017) *One Another's Equals: The Basis of Human Equality*. Cambridge, MA: Belknap Press.

Weber, M. (1958) 'Politics as a vocation' in Gerth, H.H. and Wright Mills, C. (eds. and trans.) *From Max Weber: Essays in Sociology*. New York: Oxford University Press.

Westen, P. (1982) 'The empty idea of equality', *Harvard Law Review*, 95(3), pp. 537–596.

5 Laws and proverbs

The making and unmaking of moral rules in historic Tibet

Fernanda Pirie

Societies are more or less legalistic. Some have a tendency to subject aspects of human behaviour to legal rules, mapping out the ways in which people ought to behave, morally, socially, or politically. Others seem content to allow social interactions to follow custom and tradition, individual negotiation, or the directions of a small number of influential individuals or institutions. The variations are endless and the examples often surprising: complex and bureaucratic societies, such as those of ancient Egypt and the Aztecs, appear to have made no explicit laws, while scribes in tiny medieval Irish and Icelandic farming communities wrote down intricate legal rules. What accounts for these differences?

In this chapter, I use material from medieval Tibet to explore a society that seems to have turned its back on legal rules. Between the tenth and seventeenth centuries no indigenous ruler centralized power for any length of time, although a literate class flourished. Mainly concerned with religious doctrine and philosophical debate, these scholars were aware that Tibetan kings had earlier established a relatively bureaucratized polity on the plateau, and that they had created laws. The kings had also adopted the Vinaya, an elaborate code of moral conduct brought from India, which regulated life in the Buddhist monasteries. Later scholars wrote historical accounts, albeit with a firmly religious slant, which described how these kings had made laws on the basis of Buddhist moral principles. After this, their realm had increased, the economy had flourished, and their people had lived peaceful and moral lives. Law-making had, on this account, formed the basis for a successful kingdom. Yet neither the medieval scholars nor the clan leaders who controlled different parts of the plateau tried to emulate the early kings by creating their own laws. It is almost as if they shied away from making legal rules. It was not until the thirteenth century that Mongol invaders brought more bureaucratic practices to the plateau. And even then, Tibetan leaders were more inclined to support local practices of mediation than create a legalistic judicial system or promulgate sets of general laws, as the early kings had done.

Historical, administrative, and religious texts from this period give us the opportunity to consider a society that seems deliberately to have turned its back on law-making, then. In this paper I explore the terms in which medieval writers described the historic Tibetan laws. And I ask why, when they formulated their own moral guidance for the laity, they turned instead to narrative and aphoristic styles. Contrasting these different resources and styles of moral guidance, I suggest here, sheds light on Tibetan attitudes towards legalism and, hence, on the place of law within their society.

Following recent developments in the anthropology of law, I use the term 'legalism' to refer to general rules and abstract categories and the practice of using them to describe and direct human conduct (Dresch, 2012; Pirie, 2013, ch. 5). As an analytic concept, legalism is more precise, albeit broader, than the notoriously vague English-language category of 'law' and, hence, a better starting point for comparative scholarship. The tendency to appeal to abstract and general rules and categories is a recurrent feature among examples of law, so it often points to important and distinctive aspects of legal phenomena. It marks out a useful distinction between law and custom, for example, enabling us to distinguish explicit and precise rules and laws from imprecise and changeable customary norms and practices. At the same time, the concept of 'legalism' extends beyond law. The constitutional rules of clubs and societies may be legalistic, for example, as are many moral rules. But rather than worrying about the distinction between laws and rules and the concern of legal theorists to differentiate 'mere rules' from 'proper law', or between law and morality, this paper takes the concept of a legalism as a means to reflect on the importance of rules in legal practices. The medieval Tibetan material allows us to consider the legalism of moral rules and contrast it with the alternative moral resources to which Tibetan scholars seem to have been drawn. And this, in turn, sheds light on the appeal simultaneous and refusal of law among Tibetans.

The early polity in Tibet

During the seventh to ninth centuries, the sparsely-occupied, high-altitude desert of the Tibetan plateau was largely inhabited by farmers and nomadic pastoralists. But a number of tribal leaders were gradually able to dominate others and bring a large proportion of the population under their control, eventually establishing themselves as 'kings'. They developed centralized and bureaucratic administrative structures, instituted judicial processes with some complexity, and made laws (Dotson, 2015). Surviving texts contain detailed lists of blood money and wound prices, while others are concerned with penalties for theft. They make firm distinctions between levels of social status and types of wrong-doing, specifying requisite forms of evidence and possible defences to certain charges. They were clearly sets of laws.[1] They also seem to have been part of a wider political project on the part of the kings to undermine tribal autonomy and revenge-based conflict, incorporating potentially autonomous tribal leaders into a unified system of status and rank (Pirie, 2015). Chinese models might well have inspired the Tibetan laws-makers: penal codes had been used by Chinese rulers for centuries, becoming more elaborate under the Qin and Han at around the turn of the millennium and culminating in the great Tang code of the seventh century. The Chinese laws, which were probably known to Tibetans, had a firmly penal and disciplinary character (Johnson, 1979, 1997). The Tibetan laws focused on compensation more than punishment, but they were evidently part of a larger political project on the part of the kings to establish centralized authority.

Buddhism was by now flourishing in parts of China, as well as India, and in the late eighth century the Tibetan king, Tri Song Detsen (Khri Srong lde btsan),[2] announced that he was adopting the religion. He founded monasteries, adopted new funerary rituals, patronized Buddhist scholars, and ordered the translation of Buddhist texts, including the Vinaya. This extensive set of rules for monastic conduct had been formulated on the plains of India almost a millennium earlier (Gombrich et al., 1984). It is largely made up of quasi-historical examples, from which a rule, a moral category, or the definition of an offence is extracted. This is a form of casuistry, an important – if short-lived – style of reasoning in Christian moral theology, also found in the Islamic world (Johnson and Toulmin, 1988; Johansen, 1995). As well as basic proscriptions on causing harm and directions for ritual conduct, the Vinaya offers rules relating to the ways in which monks and nuns can engage in commerce and property relations, many of which are complex and specific. Nuns, for example, should not 'prosecute for seizure on a promissory note', or 'call in loaned property', and the various property offences they could commit – joint ventures, loans on interest, commodity loans, and so on – are carefully defined (Schopen, 2014). The Vinaya offers complex and legalistic rules, that is, which are evidently the product of Indian scholastic thinking. The moral guidance offered to the laity was far less elaborate. *The Chapter on Ethics* in Asanga's *Bodhisattva Stage*, translated into Tibetan at around the same time, set out a code of ten virtues for the laity which simply consisted of ten basic prohibitions (Tatz, 1986). There were three bodily prohibitions – killing, stealing, and sexual misconduct; four relating to speech – lying, divisive speech, aggressive speech, and slander; and three of the mind – avarice, malice, and wrong (religious) views. Texts setting out these 'virtues' were widely disseminated in Tibet (van Schaik, 2016, pp. 61–62). Both homegrown and imported legalism were, that is, features of early Tibet.

The imperial regime went into a period of decline in the ninth and tenth centuries. After an anti-royalist revolt in the 840s, the ruling family fled from central Tibet, Buddhists were persecuted, and the region was not unified again under a Tibetan ruler for almost 900 years.[3] A text known as the *Scripture from the Sky*, which probably dates from the ninth or tenth centuries, laments the passing of this great polity. The historic empire had flourished, it claims, after the early kings had received a document on Buddhist doctrine, which fell from the sky.[4] By adopting its ideas, the text claims, the kings increased the bounds of their dominion and ensured that harvests were good and their people became respectful, kind, honest, steadfast, truthful, and courageous. But this happy state was followed by a period of decline, during which Tibetans lost their sources of guidance: the path of truth and the practice of virtue; the discipline of the Vinaya; the laws (*khrims*) of the kings; and the oral wisdom of wise elders. This text sets the scene for the historical narrative of later Tibetan writers by attributing the greatness of the now-crumbling Tibetan polity to the receipt of Buddhist ideas. These had, in turn, produced different sources of guidance for the people. On this account, religious doctrine (the path of truth) and the moral code for renunciates (the Vinaya) were supplemented by the laws of the kings. The memory of law had not, that is, disappeared with the imperial regime.

The religion was not entirely wiped out, however. Throughout the subsequent period of political disunity, new monasteries provided a home for Buddhist scholars, who continued to work with Indian materials, and Tibetans writers continued to insist on the glories of the imperial past and the importance of its laws.

The historical narratives

Law as discipline

From the 'fragments' of the empire (as Tibetan writers put it) new political regimes gradually emerged, generally headed by leaders of the most powerful clans. Although administratively disunited, Tibet saw a great flourishing of religious institutions and intellectual thought during this period, as a second wave of Buddhist texts and teachings swept into the region. Monastic establishments built up power and influence, religious masters were invited from Kashmir and India, and Tibetan scholars made the arduous journey over the Himalayas to Buddhist centres in northern India. The bulk of the new texts was religious, but Tibetan writers also turned to their own past to contemplate their history as a Buddhist land. As in the *Scripture from the Sky*, the authors attributed the greatness of the earlier kingdom to the introduction of religious doctrine and texts from India. The eleventh-century *Washé* (*dBa' bzhed*), for example, recounts how the early kings had received sacred texts, which fell from the sky.[5] In order to read them, the king, Songtsen Gampo (Srong btsan sgam po), sent a minister to India to develop a Tibetan script.[6] After this, he was able to create laws (*khrims*) on the basis of the ten virtues. The virtues are not set out in any detail – indicating that they were still familiar to a Tibetan audience – but the text adds that killing and stealing were to be addressed through compensation payments, lying through the taking of oaths, and sexual misconduct through mutilation penalties. In this way, the first four of the virtues were mapped onto what must have been contemporary customs for dealing with practical disputes. Maybe not surprisingly, the author makes no attempt to elaborate on any laws that might have been designed to enforce the much vaguer injunctions to avoid avarice, gossip, wrong views, and so on. On this account, then, the kings made laws to ensure that people would comply with the basic virtues of Buddhism. It seems likely that the authors were inspired more by the example of the Vinaya, with its legalistic rules for monastic conduct, than the detail of the imperial laws, themselves, which was in no way influenced by Buddhist ideas (Pirie, 2017).

The same basic story runs through a series of subsequent historical narratives. They place increasing emphasis on the work of religious teachers in the introduction and dissemination of Buddhist doctrine, but the core account of the foundation of the Tibetan empire by the early kings is retained and elaborated. The *Pillar Testament*, [7] probably composed by a religious scholar in the twelfth century, asserts that Songtsen Gampo made laws (*khrims*) based on the ten virtues. In creating these laws, it continues, he adopted the example of the 16 great principles for human conduct (*mi chos chen po*) (pp. 108–109). Lists of these moral and social principles were circulating in various forms at the time (Roesler, 2015), and they are set out in a longer, and near-contemporary, compilation of religious and historical writings, known as the *Mani Kabum*. In its account of law-making by Songtsen Gampo, the king explains the 16 principles in the following terms (p. 205):

> The subjects under my dominion ought to generate faith in the Three Divine Jewels. They ought to practise and accomplish the true doctrine. They ought to repay the kindness of their parents. They ought to respect those who have (good) qualities. They ought to respect the upper classes and elders. They ought to be honest with relatives and friends. They ought to give help to their fellow countrymen and neighbours. They ought to talk straightforwardly and with humility. They ought to follow the nobility assiduously. They ought to be careful about food and wealth. They ought not to cut themselves off from those who have previously been kind. Debts ought to be repaid on time and there should be no deception with *bre* and *srang* measures. They ought to act fairly towards everyone and without jealousy. They should not listen to the bad things that close friends say, but maintain their own judgement. They should speak gently and discreetly. They ought to act with forbearance and magnanimity. In this way, the 16 pure human principles will establish the basis of the law.

Two things are particularly notable about these principles. The first is the uncategorical nature of the main concepts. Two of the principles urge people to be respectful, for example, but give little guidance as to how this might be demonstrated, save to list those to whom respect is due. It is left to the individual to judge whether or not his or her behaviour is properly respectful. Concepts of honesty, humility, forbearance, and so on, have a similar character. Secondly, the rules are almost entirely positive, unlike the prohibitions of the ten virtues. The king's laws are here associated with rather open-ended moral exhortation.

A rather different tone is struck in other parts of the same texts.[8] In more than one passage, the *Pillar Testament* suggests that ordinary people had had to be tamed before they would behave as moral beings. 'Their intellect does not lean towards religious knowledge', the king is supposed to have declared. Nevertheless, 'they will be tamed by my religious and royal laws', which will bring the ignorant inhabitants of Tibet to study and develop faith (p. 258). On this account, not only did people need moral guidance, they also needed firm discipline. Similar ideas are found in Nyang ral's *Nectar of Flowers*, also from the twelfth century. This author describes how Songtsen Gampo made his laws to prevent people engaging in sinful activity, which would lead to their rebirth in the lower realms, and he emphasized that punishment would be applied for any breach of his laws (pp. 174–175). This is a rather different account of ethical behaviour from the positive and open-ended ideals of the 16 principles. It assumes that people needed to be directed to obey moral rules on pain of punishment. In the *Mani Kabum*, too, where the standard account of Songtsen Gampo and his law-making is presented twice, each time stating that the laws would bring about good behaviour on the part of Tibetan people (pp. 204, 375–376), the text also emphasizes the need for discipline. It recounts that, after Songtsen Gampo had established his kingdom, his queens arranged for 1,000 emanations to enact horrific physical punishments on the sinful, in order to intimidate people into obeying the king's laws (p. 277). Another passage recounts how the young king realized that many Tibetans were uncivilized, being the descendants of a monkey and a rock ogress, so they needed to be tamed by being punished severely (p. 374). Later, he is said to have created the royal laws and meted out punishments on emanated people – cutting off heads and limbs and gouging out eyes – in order to intimidate and control them (p. 407). Law is here the activity of a controlling king, designed to discipline ordinary people into good behaviour.

In these texts, moral guidance is given by the king, in some sections described in terms of moral exhortation, while in others it is implemented through punitive rules. In this latter aspect, the writers may have been inspired by the example of the Chinese legal codes, which were thoroughly disciplinary in character. It is also possible that some of the writers were attempting to justify contemporary practices of punishment, which were probably organised locally by monastic authorities, village leaders, and ruling families. On these accounts, then, moral behaviour consisted in obedience to rules and ill-disciplined subjects needed to be forced or terrified into becoming good human beings. The kings are praised for the 'strictness' of their laws (Nyang ral, p. 251).

It is notable that, at the same time, Tibetan writers made no real attempt to elaborate on what these royal laws might have consisted of, beyond rather vague references to compensation payments, oaths, and punishments. Nor did they to set out rules for practical guidance in any detail. One might expect the writers to have tried to elaborate on the prohibition of killing by, for example, describing exceptions for cases of self-defence or duress, or to have described more explicitly what constituted sexual misconduct, or given practical guidance about what amounted to slander or divisive speech. The laws composed in the early polity went to some length to draw distinctions, for example between instances of intentional and accidental killing (Dotson, 2015), and the medieval writers were implicitly describing the sort of Buddhist polity that could, and ideally should, be recreated on the plateau. But their texts shied away from the sort of second-order reflection on the content and ambit of the rules that characterize complex laws, and which is found plentifully in the Vinaya. This suggests that contemporary writers were not interested in, maybe because they were not familiar with, legalistic rules and practices. Nor, as far as we are aware, did any Tibetan political leader attempt to establish systematic laws during this period. The twelfth-century Lama Zhang referred to 'the yoke, the law, and the seals' when describing his activities as ruler, but his biographies give no indication that he ever promulgated detailed rules (Yamamoto, 2012, pp. 194–203). We might plausibly suppose that the problem of punishment deterred monastically-trained writers from elaborating more precise laws.[9] Nevertheless, the idea that disciplinary laws were imposed by a strong ruler seems to have lingered into this period, presumably reinforced by Chinese examples.

Law as moral guidance

Subsequent texts indicate a more pronounced turn away from legalistic rules, despite the introduction of new bureaucratic practices onto the plateau. By the middle of the thirteenth century, Mongol forces had established themselves as the dominant military power in central Asia and the charismatic Tibetan religious leader, Sakya Pandita, secured his appointment as spiritual adviser to the Qubilai Khan. As the Mongols consolidated their regime in China, establishing the Yuan dynasty, Qubilai and his successors extended their administrative control over Tibet, establishing offices and officers, a census, a system of taxation, and postal stations. They also introduced documentary practices, with standard forms for legal agreements, and convened courts (*khrims sa*).[10] But, although the Yuan administration made a code of law for their Chinese dominions (Ratchnevsky, 1937, p. 151), there is no evidence that they tried to implement it in Tibet. We must assume that their 'courts' largely engaged in mediation, producing written agreements about land, tax revenues, and so on, many of which have survived (Everding 2006) although powerful administrators could doubtless also mete out punishments.

During this period, Tibetan authors continued to write historical texts, largely following older precedents. Sakya Lama Dampa's (Sa skya bla ma dam pa) *Mirror of the Royal Genealogies*, written in the mid-fourteenth century, follows the pattern of earlier histories by describing how Songtsen

Gampo directed his ministers to create laws based on the ten Buddhist virtues. These provided that:

> rewards are to be given to the good; punishment to be inflicted on the bad; … the highland water to be collected in reservoirs; the lowland water to be conducted into channels; weights and measurements to be established; fields to be divided into plots; men to be taught to write; horses to be marked; exemplary customs to be established; those who instigate quarrels to be punished; proportionate compensation to be paid by those who kill; … those guilty of sexual misconduct to be banished, having had limbs cut off; liars to have their tongues cut.
>
> (p. 74)

This list, implicitly aimed at government officials, is followed by another set of directions, implicitly guidance for ordinary people, which reflect the 16 principles. People were:

> to seek refuge in the Three Jewels, to have faith and show them devotion; to repay the kindness of their parents by treating them with respect; … not to quarrel with nobles and members of the upper classes, but to yield and follow their noble works and deeds; to concentrate on religion and its texts, so as to understand their meaning; to have faith in the law of karma; to avoid completely the non-virtues; to help friends and neighbours and not harbour malicious thoughts towards them; … to consume food and *chang* appropriately and act modestly; ….
>
> (p. 75)

Lama Dampa presents these two sets of rules as the 'laws' (*khrims*) of early Tibet, which the king based on the example of the ten virtues. Although more elaborate than in earlier texts, the detail of these 'laws' is still barely legalistic. Many express matters of general principle, advocating vague ideas, such as 'exemplary customs'. The second set presents a vision of ideal human conduct, based on abstract ideas of respect, gratitude, honesty, and so on. The reference to blood money seems to reflect the historical laws, but the text provides no detail.

At around the same time, another religious figure, Urgyen Lingpa (O rgyan gLing pa), presented a historical account with a rather different emphasis. In *The Five Chronicles*, his major text, he describes how Songtsen Gampo based his laws on the ten virtues, which made all living beings happy (p. 116). Tibet flourished at this time, he says, because the king made his decrees on the basis of careful consideration, using succinct words, concise meanings, implications, contrasts, and metaphors. It was important, Urgyen Lingpa asserts – apparently directing his words towards a contemporary audience – that people should not blindly apply the law and impose improper punishment, but should investigate each matter (pp. 149–150). He expresses concern about the potential harshness of the law and the need for a king to act wisely. He is, here, voicing the sort of criticism often levelled at over-legalistic practices in other contexts. The kings' ministers, too, should provide, or rely upon, examples, on the directions of people's lineages, and on knowledge of good and bad, he says. They should act according to examples and take advice from those who have experience and insight (pp. 442–443). While ostensibly describing a historical period, Urgyen Lingpa seems to be articulating concerns about the way in which Tibet was then being governed and he emphasizes the need for officials to act wisely to examine their own actions (p. 469). He continues by describing daily activities, which should involve respectful speech, good manners, and the avoidance of lies, fighting, threats, cheating, and so on (pp. 443–444).

Urgyen Lingpa adopts a similar tone in his other major text, the *Pema Katang*, a biography of the Indian sage Padmasambhava. Here, he describes how Tri Song Detsen made different types of laws in order to ensure that 'deeds should come to fruition', implying that the object of the laws was to bring about the sort of moral behaviour that would ensure favourable rebirth (p. 397). He then launches into a long description of good behaviour: everyone should learn how to read and write; they should recite, train in, and explain the Buddhist doctrine; they should not neglect the needs of old people; and so on. There is considerable emphasis on mental activities: virtuous laymen should be directed to the (Buddhist) teachings; people should be even-minded about things that are said and things that happen; and it demands respect for scholars, religious masters, lords, parents, elder brothers, and husbands. Towards the end of the section, the author launches into a list of fierce punishments and directs that the consequences (of the laws and of breaking them) should weigh upon the mind (pp. 400–401).

Urgyen Lingpa is, thus, emphasizing the need for both kings and those who apply the laws to use judgement and he appears cynical about the capacity of laws to produce justice. In the *Five Chronicles*, he implicitly distinguishes laws, rules, and obedience, from justice, social knowledge, and judgement, placing the emphasis on mental training and wisdom. Like Lama Dampa, he is evidently trying to work out the relationship between the kings' laws and the moral behaviour of ordinary people, which they are supposed to bring about. And both authors describe the laws in terms of moral principles and idealistic images of good behaviour, rather than providing detailed rules for conduct, of the sort found in the Vinaya. For Urgyen Lingpa, even the laws are supposed to consist of implications and metaphors, that is, turns of speech that are not legalistic, and he recognizes the importance of custom and tradition, referring to lineage traditions as a source of moral guidance. Above all, he emphasizes the mental aspect of moral behaviour, the need to listen to advice, to read religious texts, to respect scholars, and to let the consequences of bad behaviour weigh upon the mind.

This aspect of ethical behaviour is even more prominent in a text written some 200 years later, known as the *Feast for Scholars*. In its account of law-making, there is a distinct emphasis on the need for judgement and it ends with an image of the peace and happiness brought about by the enactment of 'the strict laws of the ten virtues' (p. 194):

> men were brave, horses were fast, and material wealth was equal to that of the gods; regarding everyone as their parents, people avoided disputes; reading and writing flourished and everyone adopted the religion; there were no taxes; through the nectar of timely rainfall, the seeds multiplied, the branches of all trees became fully grown, the birds sang carefree and melodious songs, and the contentment and happiness of the people of Tibet was like that of the gods.

In this text, the idea of laws that provide categorical rules for moral behaviour, which can be imposed on pain of punishment, has been eclipsed by the emphasis on the mental aspects of ethical behaviour, directed towards the image of an ideal society and, implicitly, the favourable re-birth that this will bring about. Many of these 'laws' (*khrims*) are now described in terms that make them seem barely law-like. It is as if Tibetan writers felt that they ought to be describing a disciplinary world, in which individuals could refer their conduct to strict and detailed rules, but that in practice, they found it more appealing to dwell on images of ideal conduct and the contented lives it would produce.

Law as mediation

The idea of political legalism was not, however, abandoned by Tibetan writers. Shortly after the fall of the Yuan empire in 1368, Tibetan political leaders created a legal treatise, which affirmed the idea of historic Tibetan laws. *The Mirror of the Two Laws* was probably created by or for the Pakmodru (Phag mo gru), then the most powerful family in Tibet, as its members were trying to enhance their shaky political position (Pirie, 2020). This text repeats the familiar story about the creation of the early Tibetan polity and goes on to describe how the 'kings' laws' should be implemented, implicitly by the Pakmodru officials. In practice, it does little more than describe the sorts of issues faced by mediators, offering guidance about how they should approach cases of killing and injuries, divorce and sexual misconduct, disputed allegations of theft, insults, revenge relations, and so on. It clearly reflects contemporary practices, often explicitly recording what 'wise men' and 'elders' have told the authors and recognizing a variety among local customs. It reads like a first attempt to standardize practices of mediation. In fact, there is no evidence that the Pakmodru ever established a more systematic judicial system, or of the way this text was used in practice, if at all. It is a long way from the disciplinary laws described in the earlier narratives and bears only the loosest connection to the ten virtues.

The Pakmodru did not hold on to power for long and for the next 200 years different factions vied for political control in central Tibet. In 1631, the leader of the Tsang family, which then controlled a large area, used the Pakmodru text as the basis for another legal treatise, the *Legal Code (Khrims yig) in Sixteen Sections.*[11] The Tsang were soon defeated by the Gelukpa, who went on to establish the regime that governed central Tibet into the twentieth century. Their leader, the Fifth Dalai Lama, adopted and reproduced the Tsang treatise, but this text is also barely legalistic, giving few specific directions and not being particularly explicit in its categories and distinctions. Versions continued to be circulated to Tibetan administrators throughout the next three centuries, and although it has come to be referred to as a 'law code' (French, 1995), it is really a discussion of legal practice and advice for mediators. That this is the closest that Tibetan rulers came to promulgating a general set of laws simply highlights their turn away from legalism.

The legshé

While we might understand this move away from rule-making in terms of the political dynamics of the rather chaotic and uncentralized medieval period, what is, perhaps, more of a puzzle is that Buddhist writers also seem not to have been interested in elaborating moral rules for the lives of the laity. This is, after all, what the historical narratives claim led to the flourishing of the early polity and what was supposed to secure a favourable rebirth. The Vinaya continued to be taught in the Tibetan monasteries so why did religious leaders not follow its style in making more detailed moral rules for the laity? The answer to this question may shed some light on the Tibetans' attitude to law and legalism, more generally. My suggestion is that the contrasting positive and open-ended style of moral guidance found in the historical narratives resonated more closely with Tibetan ideas about ethical activity and how it should be practised, particularly among the laity.

From the time Buddhism was first adopted, the Tibetan kings constructed and patronized monasteries and nunneries as places in which renunciates could live and practise, removed from the concerns of daily life. The separation must not be overemphasized (Mills, 2003), but at least part of the time renunciates could, and were expected to, remove themselves both physically and morally from lay life. The Vinaya, with its legalistic rules, marked a separation between these two realms. The laity, meanwhile, had other moral resources. The ninth century *Scripture from the Sky* listed the 'oral wisdom of wise elders' alongside the Vinaya as sources of guidance available to Tibetans. Urgyen Lingpa also referred to metaphors, customs, and traditions in his description of Tri Song Detsen's laws. In practice, proverbs and sayings were an important source of popular wisdom in Tibet from pre-Buddhist times. Documents dating from the imperial period include proverbs about 'good' and 'bad' parents and children, using images from pastoralist settings. Aphorisms and adages are found throughout Tibetan literature, both religious and popular, including biographies, histories, songs, and epics (Thomas, 1957; Cüppers and Sørensen, 1998, pp. xi–xiv). By the eleventh century, religious masters, too, were writing maxims and tales to enhance popular understanding of Buddhist truths and teachings, often drawing from Indian sources, in a genre known as the *pechö* (*dpe chos*, religious examples) (Roesler, 2012). Several anthologies were brought together over the following centuries, many written in the vernacular, or even in dialect, indicating that they were meant to be transmitted orally amongst ordinary people (Cüppers and Sørensen, 1998).

In the thirteenth century, a genre of texts known as *legshé* (*legs bshad*), literally 'beautiful' or 'elegant' sayings, became popular in Tibet. These consisted of short, pithy quatrains, a style of writing based on the Indian *nitiśāstra* literature. They concerned what might be regarded as matters of common sense and social dynamics, such as relations between family members, teacher and pupil, master and subordinate. They also included matters of polity and statecraft, alongside the characteristics of the good and learned, and aspects of ethics and religion, including reflection on the principles of karma and the theory of liberation (Pathak, 1974). Tibetans seem to have been particularly attracted to the Indian texts and translated many of them (Pathak, 1974, ch. 5; Davenport, 2000, pp. 4–8). They also caught the attention of religious leaders. In the thirteenth-century, Sakya Pandita composed his own text in this style, which he called the *Jewel Treasury of Beautiful Sayings* (*legs par bshad pa rin po che'i gter*) (the Sakya *legshé*). Clearly influenced by the *subhāsitas*, the Indian sub-genre that aspired to elegant language and images, his text was widely read, extensively copied, and commented upon, effectively engendering an indigenous Tibetan tradition of similar writing (Bosson, 1969, pp. 1, 7; Davenport, 2000, pp. 8–13).

The Sakya *legshé* consists of 457 quatrains, each made up of seven-syllable lines. They are divided into nine chapters, the majority of which concern good and bad behaviour. The first four specifically relate to wisdom (*mkhas pa*). One chapter contains more practical advice – about being careful and cautious and not being over demonstrative, with examples of how to deal with friends and enemies. The last chapter reflects upon death and the operation of karma. In practice, there is considerable overlap between the sections. A typical example uses a concrete image to illustrate an abstract idea:[12]

> 2 People may or may not be knowledgeable
> But the wise have the capacity to discriminate.
> A magnet is able to extract
> Iron filings that are mixed with dust.[13]

They often emphasize the importance of judgement over rule-following:

> 21 When they are commanded,
> Even animals can understand.
> Those who know what to do
> Without being directed are wise.[14]

> 125 It is possible that what helps one
> May cause harm to another.
> At moonrise, the water lily blossoms,
> But the lotus flower closes.[15]

Several verses concern the qualities proscribed by the rules of the ten virtues, while others concern the sorts of moral ideas found in the 16 principles.

> 144 Like a mountain that absolutely nothing can move,
> Great people are steadfast.
> Like wisps of cotton wafted around by the slightest thing,
> Inferior people behave erratically.[16]

They praise those who are skilful and discerning:

> 119 Some think they have achieved things through talking [about them];
> Others silently pursue their objectives.
> An inferior dog [simply] barks at his enemy;
> While the cat silently ambushes the waterfowl.[17]

Many verses highlight the complexity of human nature, presenting paradoxes and difficulties. They emphasize the need for care, discretion, and judgement, evoking the complexity and subtlety of moral behaviour and the dilemmas that can arise for those who try to act well. For example:

> 193 When appointed to a high position,
> Few people know what to do.
> Though one has eyes to see others,
> A mirror is required to see oneself.[18]

> 195 It is possible for honest (literally, 'straight') speech to be wrong
> And for dishonest speech to have good qualities.
> A straight path can lead to material ruin,
> While the white conch shell, curling to the right, brings good fortune.[19]

The author points out that it is important to do the right thing, even if it achieves the wrong result:

> 126 Although a goal may be achieved through wrongdoing,
> Why would the wise desire that?
> Although something done well may go wrong,
> The wise do not feel ashamed.[20]

The verses repeatedly explain the importance of being discerning about friends and those from whom one takes counsel.

Sakya Pandita was the most influential and respected religious figure of his day, but his *legshé* do far more than explain the principles of karma and other matters of Buddhist doctrine. They are directed towards what we could call 'everyday ethics', providing guidance for daily life in a very different form from the legalism of explicit moral rules and the formalistic directions and categories of the Vinaya. Aphorisms can be memorised and the Sakya legshé were probably repeated, embellished, and circulated orally, alongside other proverbs and the examples of the *pechö*. If Sakya Pandita chose this form to set out his moral guidance for the laity, was it because he considered this to be more suitable than the detached, abstract, and categorical rules of the Vinaya?

Rule-following and judgement: law and proverbs

The more esoteric provisions of the Vinaya are only studied, and only supposed to be observed, by monks and nuns who have already undertaken many years of practice and reached the higher levels of training (Dreyfus, 2001, pp. 113–118). The most detailed moral rules are, that is, a privilege reserved for those engaged in Buddhist practice – the more advanced the practice, the more numerous and more stringent the rules. Legalism goes with self-discipline.[21] In the European Middle Ages, too, knights were subject to very many more rules than ordinary freemen (Southern, 1953, pp. 104–107). These were rules that restricted them, but in a way people considered to be rational, and which also provided them some protection against the arbitrary actions of others. It was a privilege to have recourse to laws in the way it was a privilege for Buddhist practitioners to observe the more extreme legal provisions of the Vinaya. The Tibetan laity was also supposed to be guided by a set of basic moral rules, but a quite different type of ethical activity was demanded by the stories, examples, metaphors, and proverbs that circulate among them. What, then, do these different types of ethical resource demand of their audiences, and can this shed light on Tibetan attitudes to law and legalism, more generally?

Societies have made moral rules since ancient times: Moses gave the ten commandments to the Israelites; the laws of Leviticus contain famously precise dietary prescriptions (Douglas, 1966, ch. 3); Islamic scholars created the complex rules of the Islamic *fiqh* (Hallaq, 2009); Indian brahmins specified duties and privileges according to caste and life-stage in the *dharmaśāstra*s of the Hindu tradition (Davis, 2010); and Christian penitentials contained detailed rules on sin and penance (Mahoney, 1987). Moral, like other, rules tend to objectify, putting ethics and other types of behaviour into categories, promoting reflexivity and deliberation and allowing for excuses and justifications (Keane, 2010; Dresch, 2012). As Mahmood (2005, pp. 25–31) and Clarke (2015, pp. 246–247) have described, rule-following is often a sign of commitment, the result of an ethical decision, an aspect of what some call 'moral cultivation' (Mahmood,

2005, pp. 151–152).[22] In the morally hierarchical world of Buddhist Tibet, moral rule-following indicated commitment to an ethical way of life.

While the Tibetan renunciates were supposed to have the discipline to follow strict rules, then, the laity was offered examples and images to encourage them to act ethically, and even the most intellectual religious scholars also gave moral advice in the form of metaphors, examples, and stories. These offered tacit, rather than explicit, forms of ethical guidance, appealing to sensibilities rather than formulating transcendent rules. Durkheim (1974, p. 45) long ago expressed the view that moral norms cannot be merely a matter of duty or obligation. They must also be 'desirable and desired', as he put it. Similarly, Turner (1967, p. 30) described ritual as, among other things, 'a mechanism that periodically converts the obligatory into the desirable'.[23] In a similar way, the *legshé* offer poetic images and conjure up an aesthetics, portraying the desirable world that moral behaviour will bring about. As Ricoeur (1972) has emphasized, metaphors work by interpreting reality. They are not just ornamental, but generate layers of perception, impression, and meaning. The images of the *legshé* render their ideas concrete and alive, embodied in examples from the natural world.

Making similar points in his account of human thought, psychologist and philosopher Iain McGilchrist (2009) draws a distinction between schematic, logical, and propositional reasoning, on the one hand, and metaphorical, inclusive, and particularistic thought, on the other. Logical and schematic thought brings things into focus, he says, rendering the implicit explicit. It is detached and simplified, setting out what can or ought to occur, in terms that transcend the ambiguous and multi-layered nature of reality. It renders what it knows 'denatured and decontextualised' (2009, pp. 181, 195). Metaphorical and particularistic styles of thought and writing, by contrast, present the world as individualized, changing, and interconnected. In the same way, the *legshé* conjure up images of individuals who accept apologies and practise serenity, self-criticism, and generosity; they present people and things as part of the real world, not detached from it, using images of barking dogs, blossoming lilies, waterfowl, bees, mirrors, and conch shells. As McGilchrist puts it, this style of thought presents ideas that are both implicit and incarnate, encouraging reflection and appreciation. They also bring dilemmas and tensions to life, presenting uncertainties and paradoxes in a series of partly overlapping ideas, rather than logical schemes of thought.

As scholars have noted in other contexts, narratives and proverbs demand judgement. An image invites reflection, metaphors demand interpretation, and careful juxtapositions express tensions and paradoxes. In *The Use of Pleasure* (1985) Foucault contrasts the penitential systems of early Christianity and their rules of sin and penance with what he calls the 'practical texts' of the ancient Greeks – records of speeches, dialogues, treatises, and collections of proverbs. The Greek texts, he says, demanded that individuals make decisions and judgements about which course to take, rather than simply following a rule. They advocated restraint and moderation and offered models for self-reflection, self-knowledge, and self-examination. They did not tell people in categorical terms what to do (1985, p. 29). Aristotle's Nichomachean Ethics, for example, concentrates on ethical decision-making, which should be guided by the idea that life has a proper end or character, a telos, a vision of human nature as it could be (1985, pp. 29–30).[24] Many Tibetan texts, similarly, emphasize intellectual virtues and Sakya Pandita places a substantial discussion of wisdom in the opening chapters of his text. This is also what Urgyen Lingpa demanded of rulers and officials. The Tibetan legshé, like other stories, narratives, and images, may use concrete and everyday images, but they require thought, reflection, and judgement.

When Tibetans adopted the legalistic rules of the Vinaya, they did not displace these other types of moral resources, which demanded very different things of their audiences. In fact, by restricting the Vinaya to those at the higher levels of monastic practice, they indirectly confirmed the importance of the moral advice given in the form of stories, proverbs, and aphorisms. When the historians constructed the image of a polity in which the kings made disciplinary laws on the basis of moral principles, they were masking a much more complex moral world. Tibet is not the only society to have offered very different moral resources to its people. Alongside legalistic penitentials, medieval Christianity produced an extensive literature on saints' lives, exemplary tales of fortitude, chastity, and virtue (Campbell, 2008). The 'practical texts 'of classical Greece included detailed dietary rules (1985, p. 109). Examples of the Prophet's and other lives are important subjects in Islamic texts (Clarke, 2015, p. 247) while the rules of the *shari'a* encompass a whole range of norms, legal, moral, and ritual (Hallaq 2009, p. 19). In classical Rome, too, *exempla* illustrated the enactment of virtue, providing people with the opportunity to observe and assess the moral decision-making of an exemplary figure (Langlands, 2011, p. 122). What is distinctive about Tibet is the ubiquity of the stories and proverbs and the fact that the more legalistic resources, the moral rules, came to be confined to such a small sphere of activity.

Conclusion: rules and legalism in historic Tibet

What are the implications of these contrasts for Tibetan law and law-making? As I have described here, in the earliest polity to flourish on the plateau, Tibetans made laws and developed legalistic practices, quite possibly inspired by Chinese models, as well as embracing the moral legalism of the Indian Vinaya. Over the next centuries, however, the idea of law, or political legalism, became progressively vaguer, gradually replaced by the image of kings who indulged in moral exhortation and descriptions of the ideal state they were able to bring about. I have suggested that there may have been pragmatic reasons for this. In the politically chaotic and decentralized period that followed the collapse of the early polity, the rulers would have had little use for a system of bureaucratic administrative rules. Even the Dalai Lamas, when they established a more centralized polity in the seventeenth century, recognized that disputes were resolved by mediation and political legalism never regained the central role it had in the early polity (Pirie, 2016). Tibetan rulers never again promulgated general rules supposed to apply to the population at large.

But the evidence presented in this paper suggests that there may have been deeper cultural reasons for these developments. During the same period, religious leaders built on a long tradition of both oral and written proverbs and examples to create moral resources for the laity. Turning away from the legalism of the Vinaya, they presented people of all classes and backgrounds with an array of stories, proverbs, images, and metaphors, for both religious instruction and general moral guidance. These seem to have been designed to make moral behaviour attractive, more than compulsory, contrasting with the obedience and discipline demanded by the moral rules of the Vinaya, which were taught only within the most elite spheres of religious activity. This suggests that influential Tibetans had a distinct preference for metaphorical and particular moral guidance over logical, schematic, and legalistic rules. The examples of the Chinese legal codes and the Indian Vinaya may have encouraged some Tibetans to think about law and legalism as aspects of a successful polity and disciplinary religious practices, respectively, and writers were clearly aware of the possibilities offered by the bureaucratic practices of the Yuan, which they emulated over the following centuries. Moreover, the Pakmodru seem to have thought that creating a legal text would enhance their status and authority. Yet most writers resisted any temptation to create new legalistic resources, whether moral codes or legal rules.

Tibetans never entirely turned their backs on the idea of legal rules. The documentary evidence indicates that both political and moral legalism continued to be, at least theoretically, attractive into the modern period and the concept of *khrims* resonates clearly with the English-language concept of law. Yet the turn away from rules in a series of historical narratives, written from the tenth century onwards, and the evident attraction of the legshé indicate that even the most scholastic writers remained more comfortable with metaphor and narrative. Medieval Tibetans never became wholly comfortable with the schematic, logical, and legalistic aspects of written law.

Notes

1 The immense cache of documents found in Dunhuang, an entrepot on the silk routes to the north of Tibet, which was governed by Tibet for a part of the eighth and ninth centuries, contains texts that must have originated in central Tibet, along with a great many in Chinese and other central Asian languages. It is evident that during this period important documents were read and transmitted widely throughout a large area.

2 I mainly transcribe Tibetan names and words phonetically, adding the Wylie transliteration in brackets.

3 The historical details in this section are largely drawn from Kapstein (2000, 2006) and van Schaik (2010). Beyond religious texts, many of which were reworked over centuries, historical evidence from the following centuries is extremely sparse, and the context of the texts discussed in the following sections remains sketchy.
4 This important text has been discussed by Richardson (1977), Stein (1986, pp. 173–180), and Kapstein (2000, p. 57–58).
5 This is one of a series of chronicles of the dBa' clan, which had been powerful under the early kings and seems to have retained influence in later centuries (Pasang Wangdu and Diemberger, 2000).
6 Songtsen Gampo ruled until approximately 649. There are, in fact, no records of law-making from this period, although other texts indicate that literacy was flourishing during his reign (Dotson, 2009).
7 Primary sources are listed separately in the bibliography. Page numbers refer to the editions listed there.
8 Like most of the narratives written during this period, they draw heavily on earlier precedents – some could even be regarded as compilations – so their ideas are not always consistent.
9 This had been of considerable concern to Indian Buddhist writers (Zimmerman, 2006).
10 The historical details in this section are largely drawn from Petech (1983) and Czaja (2013). There is little detail on the practices of the courts.
11 This text is widely reproduced, for example in the *Bod kyi snga rabs khrims srol yig cha bdams bsgrigs*, 1989.
12 The Tibetan transliterations are those published by Bosson (1969).
13 *skye* bo yon tan yod med pa'i/ blang dor blo gros ldan pa mkhan/ rdul dang 'dres pa'i lcags phye rnams/ khab len rdo yis len pa shes.
14 smras shing bskul bar gyur pa na/ dud 'gro la yang go ba skyes/ ma skul gzhan gyis ma smras par/ bsam pa shes na mkhas pa yin
15 gcig la phan par 'gyur ba yi/ bya ba gzhan la gnod pa srid/ zla ba shar na ku mu da/ kha 'byed 'gyur gyi padma zum.
16 lhun po cis kyang mi sgul ba/ de bzhin bdag nyid chen po brtan/ shing bal chung ngus g.yo ba ltar/ dman pa'i spyod pa 'gyur ldog che.
17 kha cig smras pas grub par rtsi/ la la mi smra don la 'bad/ khyi ngan dgra la khus 'debs te/ chu skyar byi la sgra med 'jab.
18 bdag nyid dpon du bskos gyur na/ de yi bya ba shes pa dkon/ gzhan la lta ba'i mig yod kyang/ rang nyid lta na me long dgos.
19 drang srong smra ba'i skyon bcas dang/ 'khyog sgra yon tan ldan pa srid/ lam drang 'ga' zhig nor 'jig la/ dung dkar g.yas 'khyil bkra shis byed.
20 nyes pa la las don grub pa/ byung yang mkhas rnams ga la smon/ legs par bsgrubs kyang skyon srid mod/ de la mkhan rnams khrel ba med.
21 Monasteries also made sets of rules to manage their institutions but these were, of course, places set aside from ordinary life (Jansen, 2018).
22 Robbins (2004) has described complex dietary and other taboos formerly important to the Urapmin of Papua New Guinea, while rules appear to hold considerable attraction for modern Pentecostals (Robbins, 2010). In Islamic societies, too, moral rules and directions are important for many people, who seek *fatwa*s from the *mufti*s (Mahmood, 2005; Clarke, 2010, 2015).
23 I am indebted to Robbins (2016, pp. 779–780), who makes these points in his pertinent critique of 'ordinary ethics'.
24 This writing has generated an important literature on 'the anthropology of ethics' (Laidlaw 2010, 2017; Lambek 2010, 2015). But anthropologists have only recently turned to historical sources to expand their debates (Clarke and Corran, forthcoming).

Primary sources

The Pillar Testament (bKa' chems ka khol ma)

A Collection of Rediscovered Teachings Focussing upon the Tutelary Deity Avalokiteśvara (Mahākaruṇika), reproduced from a print from the no longer extant Spuṇs-thaṇ blocks. 1975. Trayang and Jamyang Samten (eds), New Delhi.

A ti sha, sMon lam rGya mtsho (ed.) 1989. *bKa 'chems ka khol ma*. Lanzhou: Kan su'u Mi rigs dpe skrun khang.

Bod kyi snga rabs khrims srol yig cha bdams bsgrigs. 1989. Lhasa: Bod ljongs mi dmangs dpe skrun khang.

Lama Dampa's *Mirror of the Royal Genealogies (rGyal rabs gsal ba'i me long):*

Nyang ral nyi ma'i 'od zer. 1988. *Chos 'byung me tog snying po sbrang rtsi'i bcud*, (1st[st] ed.) Lhasa: Bod ljongs mi dmangs dpe skrun khang.

Nyang ral's *Nectar of Flowers (Me tog snying po sbrang rtsi'i bud)*:

O rgyan gLing pa. 1997a. *bKa' thang sde lnga*. Lhasa: Mi rigs dpe skrun khang.

O rgyan gLing pa. 1997b. *Pema Katang (Padma bka' thang):*

Orgyen Lingpa's *Five Chronicles (bKa' thang sde lnga):*

rGyal rabs gsal ba'i me long. 1981 [2002]. Beijing: Mi rigs dpe skrun khang.

The Mani Kabum (Ma ṇi bka' 'bum):

U rgyan gLing pa. 1987. *Padma bka' thang*. Chengdu: Si khron mi rigs dpe skrun khang.

References

Bosson, J. (1969) *A treasury of Aphoristic Jewels: The Subhāṣitaratnanidhi of Sa skya Paṇḍita in Tibetan and Mongolian*. Bloomington: Indiana University Press.

Campbell, E. (2008) *Medieval Saints' Lives*. Cambridge: D.S. Brewer.

Clarke, M. (2012) 'The judge as tragic hero: Judicial ethics in Lebanon's shari'a courts', *American Ethnologist*, 39, pp. 106–121.

Clarke, M. and Corran, E. (forthcoming). *Legalism: Ethics and Conscience*. Oxford: Oxford University Press.

Cüppers, C. and Sørensen, P. (1998) *A Collection of Tibetan Proverbs and Sayings*. Wiesbaden: Franz Steiner Verlag.

Czaja, O. (2013) *Medieval Rule in Tibet*. Vienna: Verlag der Österreichischen Akademie der Wissenschaften.

Davenport, J. (2000) *Sakya Pandita's Treasury of Good Advice*. Somerville: Wisdom Publications.

Davis, D. (2010) *The Spirit of Hindu Law*. Cambridge: Cambridge University Press.

Dotson, B. (2009) *The Old Tibetan Annals: An Annotated Translation of Tibet's First History*. Wien: Verlag der osterreichischen Akademie der Wissenschaften.

Dotson, B. (2015) 'Introducing early Tibetan law: Codes and cases' in Schuh, D. (ed.) *Secular Law and Order in the Tibetan Highland*. Andiast: IITBS, pp. 267–314.

Douglas, M. (1966) *Purity and Danger: An Analysis of the Concepts of Pollution and Taboo*. London: Ark.

Dresch, P. (2012) 'Legalism, anthropology, and history' in Dresch, P. and Skoda, H. (eds) *Legalism: Anthropology and History*. Oxford: Oxford University Press, pp. 1–37.

Dreyfus, G. (2003) *The Sound of Two Hands Clapping: The Education of a Tibetan Buddhist Monk*. Berkeley: University of California Press.

Durkheim, E. (1974) *Sociology and Philosophy* (trans. D.F. Pocock). New York: Free Press.

Everding, K-H. (2006) *Herrscherurkunden aus der Zeit des mongolischen Grossreiches für tibetische Adelshäuser, Geistliche und Klöster*. Halle: International Institute for Tibetan and Buddhist Studies.

Foucault, M. (1985) *The Use of Pleasure: The History of Sexuality*, 2 (trans. R. Hurley). London: Penguin.

Gombrich, R., Lamotte, E. and Joshi, L.M. (1984) 'Buddhism in ancient India' in Bechert, H. and Gombrich, R. (eds) *The World of Buddhism*. London: Thames and Hudson, pp. 77–98.

Hahn, M. (1982) *Nagarjuna's Ratnāvali*, Vol 1. *Basic Texts*. Bonn: Indica et Tibetica.

Hallaq, W. (2009) *An Introduction to Islamic Law*. Cambridge: Cambridge University Press.

Jansen, B. (2018) *The Monastery Rules: Buddhist Monastic Organization in Pre-Modern Tibet*. Berkeley: University of California Press.

Johnson, W. (1997 [1979]) *The T'ang Code*. Princeton, NJ: Princeton University Press.

Kapstein, M. (2000) *The Tibetan Assimilation of Buddhism*. Oxford: Oxford University Press.

Kapstein, M. (2006) *The Tibetans*. Oxford: Blackwell.

Keane, W. (2010) 'Minds, surfaces, and reasons in the anthropology of ethics' in Lambek, M. (ed.) *Ordinary Ethics: Anthropology, Language and Actions*. New York: Fordham University Press, pp. 64–83.

Laidlaw, J. (1995) *Riches and Renunciation: Religion, Economy, and Society among the Jains*. Oxford: Oxford University Press.

Laidlaw, J. (2010) 'Social anthropology' in Skorupski, J. (ed.) *The Routledge Companion to Ethics*. London: Routledge, pp. 369–383.

Laidlaw, J. (2017) 'Fault lines in the anthropology of ethics' in Mattingly, C. (ed.) *Moral Engines: Exploring the Ethical Drivers in Everyday Life*. New York: Berghahn Books, pp. 174–193.

Lambek, M. (2010) 'Introduction' in his *Ordinary Ethics: Anthropology, Language and Actions*. New York: Fordham University Press, pp. 1–36.

Lambek, M. (2015) *The Ethical Condition: Essays on Action, Person, and Value*. Chicago, IL: Chicago University Press.

Langlands, R. (2011) 'Roman exempla and situation ethics: Valerius Maximus and Cicero de Officiis', *Journal of Roman Studies*, 101, pp. 100–122.

MacIntyre, A. (2007 [1981]) *After Virtue*. London: Bloomsbury.

Mahmood, S. (2005) *Politics of Piety: The Islamic Revival and the Feminist Subject*. Princeton, NJ: Princeton University Press.

Mahoney, J. (1987) *The Making of Moral Theology*. Oxford: Clarendon Press.

McGilchrist, I. (2009) *The Master and His Emissary: The Divided Brain and the Making of the Western World*. New Haven, CT: Yale University Press.

Pasang Wangdu. and Diemberger, H. (2000) *dBa' bzhed*. Wien: Verlag der Österreichischen Akademie der Wissenschaften.

Pathak, S.K. (1974) *The Indian nītiśāstras in Tibet*. Delhi: Motilal Banarsidass.

Petech, L. (1990) *Central Tibet and the Mongols*. Rome: IsMEO.

Pirie, F. (2013) *The Anthropology of Law*. Oxford: University Press.

Pirie, F. (2016) 'State, law, and morality in traditional Tibet' in Bischoff, J. and Mullard, S. (eds), *Social Regulation: Case Studies from Tibetan History*. Leiden: Brill, pp. 231–249.

Pirie, F. (2017) 'Buddhist law in early Tibet: The wmergence of an ideology', *Journal of Law and Religion*, 32, pp. 406–422.

Pirie, F. (2020) 'The making of Tibetan law: The Khrims gnyis lta ba'i me long', in Bischoff, J., Maurer, P., and Ramble, C. (eds) *On a Day of a Month of a Fire Bird Year*. Lumbini: International Research Institute.

Pirie, F. (2015) 'Rules, proverbs, and persuasion: Legalism and rhetoric in Tibet' in Dresch, P. and Skoda, H. (eds), *Legalism: Anthropology and History*. Oxford:-Oxford University Press, pp. 105–128.

Ratchnevsky, P. (1937) *Un code des Yuan*, vol. 1. Paris: Ernest Leroux.

Richardson, H. (1998) "The dharma that came down from heaven": A Tun-huang fragment' in Richardson, H. and Aris, M. (eds) *High Peaks, Pure Earth: Collected Writings on Tibetan History and Culture*. London: Serindia, pp. 74–81.

Ricoeur, P. (1972) *The Rule of Metaphor*. London: Routledge.

Robbins, J. (2004) *Becoming Sinners: Christianity and Moral Torment in a Papua New Guinea Society*. Berkeley: University of California Press.

Robbins, J. (2010) 'On the Pleasures and Dangers of Culpability', *Critique of Anthropology*, 30, pp. 122–128.

Robbins, J. (2016) 'What is the matter with transcendence? On the place of religion in the new anthropology of ethics', *Journal of the Royakl Anthropological Institute*, 22, pp. 767–785.

Roesler, U. (2012) *Fruhe Quellen Zum Buddhistischen Stufenweg in Tibet*. Wiesbaden: Dr. Ludwig Reichert Verlag.

Roesler, U. (2015) '16 Human Norms (mi chos bcu drug) - Indian, Chinese, and Tibetan' in Czaja, O. and Hazod, G. (eds), *The Illuminating Mirror: Tibetan Studies in Honour of Per K. Sorensen on the Occasion of His 65th Birthday*. Wiesbaden: Dr. Ludwig Reichert Verlag, pp. 389–409.

Schaik, S. van (2011) *Tibet: A History*. London: Yale University Press.

Schaik, S. van (2016) *The Spirit of Tibetan Buddhism*. London: Yale University Press.

Schopen, G. (2014) 'On the legal and economic activities of Buddhist nuns: Two examples from early India' in French, R.R. and Nathan, M. (eds.) *Buddhism and Law*. Cambridge: Cambridge University Press, pp. 91–114.

Stein, R.A. (1986) 'Tibetica Antiqua IV: la tradition relative au début du Bouddhisme au Tibet', *Bulletin de l'Ecole française de l'Extrême-Orient*, 75, pp. 169–196.

Tatz, M. (1986) *Asanga's Chapter on Ethics*. Lewiston: The Edwin Mellen Press.

Thomas, F.W. (1957) *Ancient Folk-literature from North-Eastern Tibet: Introductions, Texts, Translations and Notes*. Berlin: Akademie-Verlag.

Yamamoto, C.S. (2012) *Vision and Violence: Lama Zhang and the Politics of Charisma in Twelfth-century Tibet*. Leiden: Brill.

Zimmerman, M. (2006) 'Only a fool becomes a king: Buddhist stances on punishment' in Zimmerman, M. (ed.) *Buddhism and Violence*. Lumbini: International Research Institute, pp. 213–242.

Part 2

Materiality, artifactuality and idiosyncrasy of legal practices

The centrality of rules in law's life, although qualified in different ways as we observed in Part 1, can be observed through the materiality and artifactuality of their practice, that is, through their relations to various media through which they are achieved. Paying attention to the materiality of action allows us to conceive of the legal rule in a manner other than the syllogistic reasoning through which general and abstract rules are applied to contingent facts. It also demonstrates how the establishment and organization of a file proceeds, in the background, from a pre-characterization of the cases at stake, which furnishes, therefore, the contextual and cognitive background of their further treatment.

Jean-Marc Weller shows that, whereas rules lean on texts, they cannot be dissociated from some practical work whose material dimension is paramount. If, to tell the law, judges must continuously manipulate pieces, read and write, they do it with paper, screens and files, that is, with documentary resources whose forms and nature must be accounted for. The issue of rules must be discussed in the perspective of e.g. the judges' capacity to find their way among the many intermediary accounts of these cases, given their differentiated uses of computer devices and of the ordinary or simplified versions of the criminal procedure to which they refer.

Thomas Scheffer's chapter deals with the legal rule's specific performativity. Efforts are invested in order to produce accountable facts for the case to be decided. Interviews are documented, following certain translation rules or maxims, from which officials produce decidability and rejectability. The procedural apparatus mobilizes a number of authoritarian knowledges, practical skills, and formal vocabularies in order to produce the relevant features needed in every case. Rules are applied through a 'testing ceremony' which disregards personal specificities, meaning to treat the case-at-hand as any other case 'impersonally', and this, in turn, serves the production of a rule-bound result.

Looking at routine decision making in the lower courts, Max Travers reminds us that, although much jurisprudential literature focuses on how judges apply and interpret cases and legislation, judicial officers in the lower courts often have a high level of discretion. For the most part magistrates making bail decisions employ common-sense knowledge and methods of reasoning to assess risks within a legal framework. They also interpret and can work around what might seem the strongest rules guiding their decisions in legislation. Travers offers a view of legal practice from within, without drawing on resources or assumptions from constructionist or critical traditions in social science.

Michael Lynch contrasts the admission, presentation, and adjudication of evidence in a judicial course of action with the way in which the production of evidence in ordinary circumstances might be taken as transparent and unremarkably obvious. Rules of evidence, such as those that limit 'hearsay' evidence, and criteria of proof such as 'beyond a reasonable doubt' in criminal trials, are justifiable as means for avoiding prejudice and maximizing fairness. However, in some cases, in which for instance evidence seems to demonstrate something that 'anybody can see', rules of evidence and, more broadly, legal formalism and proceduralism can provide a refuge for the accused to avoid prosecution and conviction. In such situations, rules entrenchment in the hands of legal experts makes it difficult to achieve justice.

6 Reading case files

The material organization of cases and the work of judges

Jean-Marc Weller

Building on the body of research describing legal work, to which the various anthropological traditions have contributed, this chapter studies the material organization of case files and the way they are used. The focus is thus on the reading and writing activities performed by judges. An important argument for ethnographic analyses is their ability to capture the process of elaboration of a judgment, the writing concluding a case. This process, which turns an initial event into a final text, follows a formal procedure, regulating the stages over the course of which each case is processed, step by step. But it also involves a whole range of intermediary documents without which judges' ability to take up a case, to conduct it in court and to deliberate in order to deliver justice would be far more difficult: folders, slips, summaries, notes, files, etc. We here endeavour to better understand the nature and organization of this bureaucratic equipment, characteristic of any case file: in what way does it contribute to the characterization of situations and their processing?

To answer this question, we examine cases where work situations are faced with a change in this material environment. Such is the case of penal orders, considered in this chapter. These orders concern minor offences with no victims for which there is sufficient evidence, such that the public prosecutor is authorized to refer them to the court for a decision without a hearing. This so-called "simplified" procedure, which is quicker than the ordinary trial procedure, is used extensively in a growing number of cases, particularly including traffic fines and offences that generate huge volumes of litigation.[1] Without going into the literature analysing the genesis and implementation of alternative procedures designed to remedy the slowness of the judicial system,[2] our contribution stems from an observation: the introduction of penal orders has gone hand in hand with significant change in the working tools used by judges, with increased use of computer tools (filing and inputting of cases, assistance in drafting judgments, computer-assisted decision making, etc.). To what extent can these developments also be seen as contributing to the acceleration of the decision-making process? What are these transformations doing to the work necessary to enforce the law? This link between judges' ability to rule on events and the material organization of case files is at the core of our discussion, focused on the concrete activities that judges carry out when studying the multiple documents involved (handling, leafing through, typing, striking out, listing, copying, signing, etc.).

To this end, this chapter draws on the findings of a study carried out in France several years ago, with small claims court judges in charge of the least serious offences and directly affected by the rise in the number of penal orders.[3] In the first section of the chapter, we emphasize the importance of the material frameworks inextricably linked to reading and writing activities, and essentially to case files. We discuss two key points, drawn from science and technology studies and new literacy studies respectively (**Part 1**). We then venture into the office of a judge, whose work we follow through two emblematic situations, the one relating to the processing of penal orders, and the other to ordinary proceedings. This second section particularly focuses on the material configurations of the case file, the activities involved to process it and their consequences on legal reasoning (**Part 2**). Finally, we highlight some of the main properties of the case file and how they have evolved, taking into account its status under both procedures (**Part 3**).

Technologies and texts

The study of legal work through the meticulous observation of the scenes in which it is actually performed is no longer new territory. A wide range of research exists on the activities performed by legal professionals, studied on the ground. Alongside the analysis of the interactions opposing different protagonists in contexts organized by criminal procedure (cross-examination, defence speech, deliberation, etc.), precise studies have investigated the reading of documentary material, the preparation of certain administrative documents (police reports), and the mobilization of textual resources.[4] But what is the place of the case file itself in this context? Since the first studies in ethnomethodology,[5] two particularly relevant areas of research have emerged: science and technology studies (STS) and literacy studies. These research pathways, which both place emphasis on situated action, help to further our understanding of case files.

The case file as a technology

Science and technology studies are probably the better known of the two research areas. To describe the production of scientific knowledge, a host of studies have focused on the writing and reading practices actually performed by researchers. This ethnographic research, anchored in laboratories (Latour and Woolgar, 1988; Knorr-Cetina, 1981; Lynch, 1985), attributes a central role to administrative writings, visualization processes and, more broadly, all graphic artefacts: memos, scribbled notes, statements, tables, reports, boards, maps, drawings, and so on. And with good reason, for they are at the heart of the production of scientific statements, the steps of which consist in gradually translating a reality into text. In light of this, the importance of the case file has been emphasized. This seemingly insignificant object actually plays a decisive role, insofar as it allows documents to be assembled and circulated (Latour, 1987, pp. 255–256).

This has offered an inspiring perspective for studying the work of bureaucrats in charge of pronouncing the law. As in the laboratories or medical departments where they have served as a common thread to investigate professional practices (Heath, 1982; Berg, 1996; Bruni, 2005), case files have been scrutinized over the course of their processing. They have been described as material equipment inextricably linked to the activities that staff must perform to qualify situations, handle cases and reach a decision. In this respect, Bruno Latour's ethnographic study of a French supreme court seems emblematic. Meticulously followed the case files, the sociologist described the long process through which judges reached their decisions, the particularities of their reasoning, and the work that they had to carry out (Latour, 2010). Beyond the multiple material devices available to trace, project and visualize a phenomenon, he stressed the importance of "inscriptions", for it is through this intense production of traces that judges are able to pronounce the law: "in the same way that we do not understand anything of Science if we think that words are distant from and opposite to things, in the same way we do not understand anything of Law if we seek to pass directly from the norm to the facts of the particular case without this modest accumulation of papers of diverse origin" (ibid.: 90). In light of this, the role of case files is central. Owing to its ability to bring together heterogeneous elements of a case and thereby bring into relief an overall picture, it stands out as the necessary vehicle for judges to legally qualify cases by articulating duly constituted material facts and legal texts, as required by the Penal Code. The case file, a sort of small vehicle to move from one end of a case to the other without losing sight of the final text to be constructed, appears to be a technology that is both "mobile" and "immutable".[6]

The file as text

The second significant area of research partly builds on this observation. As it was developed in dialogue with the work of the anthropologist Jack Goody, it is significant that for Goody, syllogistic reasoning – the discriminating criterion supposed to reveal a society's capacity for abstraction, and of which law is an emblematic activity – refers not to a specific form of thinking, but to technologies of the intellect and the reading and writing operations they make possible: tables, formulas, lists, and so on (Goody, 1977). The same is argued to apply to case files. Through the formal, cognitive and linguistic operations they allow, case files have become essential material supports inextricably linked to legal reasoning. More broadly, they contribute to the very organization of the law, through the standardization of the observations they organize, the critical perspective they afford on statements stabilized through writing – as evidenced by the activity of signing, for example – and the accumulation and memory of precedents that they make possible (Goody, 1986, pp. 127–170).

This analysis of literacy, understood as the ability to read and write, has not gone unchallenged. In the 1990s, building on the early studies of the effects of writing on cognition and uses of reading in diverse societal contexts,[7] Goody's analysis was criticized for being too general, for attributing too much autonomy to literacy, and for its ambiguous relationship with technological determinism (Cole & Cole, 2006). In fact, the *New Literacy Studies* current was born out of the call to document situated practices and the complex relationships they have with the spoken word, based on the observation of "literacy events".[8] Studies that adopt this perspective on reading and writing practices specifically in relation to administrative documents, and more crucially to case files, remain rare.[9] Still, they are consistent with other ethnographic explorations, equally attentive to writing and reading practices and endeavouring to describe these bureaucratic objects, within specific contexts, as texts, documents made of language, the creation and use of which correspond to literary genres (forms, letters, etc.) and organized situations (input, instruction, etc.). In order for an administrative document to take on the performative force of law and to act, it must conform with specific practical conditions that need to be described.[10]

These different orientations, all attentive to the material and textual dimension of writing in different ways, offer a useful extension of the praxeological perspective. With regard to case files in particular, they call for a study the multiple statuses that these files potentially take on in the action as it unfolds since the latter consists in producing a decision. In medical activity, ethnomethodology has stressed the role that case files play in: equipping attention; regulating interaction in consultations; maintaining the continuity of the patient as a case as their body transforms with the care provided; coordinating with the multiple care providers; and allowing for the distribution of tasks in a hierarchical context (Garfinkel, 1967, pp. 186–207; Berg, 1996). In judicial activity, the questions that apply are similar: what role do case files play in the documentary production of the final judgment? What role do they play in the necessary coordination work with the multiple protagonists involved in a case (prosecutor, victim, accused) or actors in charge of managing it (judges, registrars, bailiffs)?

The bundle and the stack: two reading and writing situations

The two situations through which we examined reading and writing activity were part of a study on small claims court judges. This study, carried out about ten years ago, closely monitored the work that these judges had to carry out in penal cases to produce their judgment. While the study was concerned with understanding a new jurisdiction,[11] this was also one of the first jurisdictions to be affected by the rapid increase in penal orders, massively used by the Public Prosecution at the time to process traffic fines and offences. To gain insight into the impact of this introduction of penal orders on the work of judges, we focus on judges' reading and writing activities.[12] What role do documents play, in view of the evolution of formats (typed documents, computer screens)? How do these transformations affect the interpretative activity that these judges must carry out? How are the elements that make up cases approached? To answer these questions, we examine the work performed by a same judge for two cases which, though subject to the same legal texts, were processed differently: while the first case fell under the simplified procedure, which is largely automated and leads to a computer-assisted decision, the second one, in accordance with ordinary procedure, was examined manually.

A young person getting carried away during a police check

The first case falls within the "penal orders" that judges must process. It is important to remember that this is criminal litigation involving minor offences with sufficiently conclusive elements and no victims, such that the proceedings initiated lead to a judgment without adversary proceedings. The case of Kevin De Suza[13] falls under this simplified procedure. Consider the desk of the judge in charge of examining the case.

The first noteworthy formal element is that the case file was in a specific stack of such files on the judge's desk, that he had been to collect from the Registry of the Court office that day. The stack, bound to others with a rubber band, was invariably part of a batch of 25 stacks. Within this framework, the summary slip, written by the Prosecution, forwarded to the Registry of the Court and placed at the top of the bundle, stated the elements motivating the proceedings for each case: the last name and first name of the accused; the date, place and description of the facts; the laws applicable and the amount of the demand. These are the three essential elements for any offence, without which the offence would not exist. For a prosecution to take place, there must be: (i) legal texts defining the prohibited conduct (criminal law), in accordance with the principle that *nullum crimen nulla pœna sine lege*[14]; (ii) the material facts charged, given that in order to exist, just like in the case studied here, the offence must be materialized by an act such as: "NOISES DISTURBING THE PEACE OF THE NEIGHBOURHOOD"; and (iii) the identity of the defendant.[15] These elements – which penal literature refers to as legal, material and moral, respectively – thus define the legal framework of an offence laid out in the summary slip, the purpose of which is to summarize the batch of cases held together. However, this summary has no legal value, and the slip itself is not linked to the bundle in any way: it only serves as a summary.

To study the case itself, one needs to be familiar with the elements of which it is comprised. In this case, these consist of a set of several pages firmly stapled together, as though to give them substance and act as a reminder that they are the voice of one single entity: the Public Prosecution. This set of pages is comprised of three elements. The "demands", through which the public authorities intend to enforce the law in the name of the general interest, base their conclusions on the other elements attached to the document. The "police statement", in the form of a literal account in which a sergeant – a police officer or a *gendarme* – records the facts observed, contains all the information deemed useful for describing the facts, explicitly referencing the legal text authorizing them to draw up a report. Finally, the actual police report, in the form of a pink card, mentions a certain amount of information detailed in the statement, along with the identities of the sergeant reporting the offence and the offender, and their respective signatures. Of course, all this information is not always as complete and accurate as expected. It can happen that the sergeant, while trying to describe the offence as accurately as possible, reports the offending behaviour under an unsuitable category. It can also happen that the offender refuses to sign. In fact, this is what Kevin De Suza decided to do, when he was stopped by the police that day for driving "his vehicle (...) on the pavement and up a one-way street". The man protested vigorously, and in his outburst, seems to have expressed his anger in colourful language. The sergeant reporting the offence, who transcribed some of these words.[16] determined that this constituted offensive disturbance of the peace, and reported the offender.

These were the only elements documenting the penal order. The case did not include any other elements, nor did any of the other cases in the bundle. The judge we observed, who told us that a growing number of cases were dealt with in this way, stressed the automated nature of this procedure. Thus, after taking several bundles out of a metal cabinet where she stored them, and putting them all on her desk, she turned to her computer and opened a program called MINOS. The outline of an ancient temple against a blue background appeared on the screen. After entering her login details and recording the summary slip number, the judge could then proceed to examine the case – or rather cases, for she processed all of the cases in one go, checking that the elements appearing on the screen did indeed match the information stated on the slip. Her examination of those elements revolved around the key question that she asked herself in that moment: is the action admissible? In other words: are the formal elements of any offence, which are stated on the summary slip, properly described?[17] Once she had completed this formal check, the judge validated the information. Before pressing the key on her keyboard, it was her duty to establish that adversary proceedings were indeed unnecessary and that she could rule by order. But as the judge admitted, "that never happens". She attributed this to procedure: first, the processing of a bundle never called for in-depth inquiry into the cases and, second, the defendant could challenge the decision issued by the ruling, therefore forcing adversary proceedings to take place to judge the case. The judge therefore launched the program. After just a few seconds, the empty columns were filled with new information about the nature of the decision (the sentence) and the penalty amount that was calculated automatically.[18]

The judge then printed out the decisions, also drafted automatically, read them out to formally check the wording (identity of the defendant, address, texts, etc.), and signed them. The case discussed here was no exception: De Suza was to receive a fine of €190 (Excerpt no. 1). However, based on our observations, at no point were the elements that made up the case examined more closely than when the references were checked to ensure that the data on the screen matched the content of the bundle.

Excerpt no. 1 Police Court Observation M2a 27.04.08[19]

Time		*Comment by the judge*	*Material device*
03:20:19	01	you want to see how it looks right now?* yes yes * these are... then we'll see on the computer... it's case files that come up... these are case files... you'll see... [gets up to pick up two bundles stored in a compartment of a metal cabinet]	filing cabinet compartment
03:22:54	02	here you go, this is what I'm going to collect from where we went yesterday [a room of the Court Registry reserved for the reception of the cases] well... it's always like that, I often have several of them I put them there [points to the cabinet] but I'll show you...	bundle
03:23:35	03	the slip... it lists the 25 offences that are here. it's always like that... they're pending. I have to start the computer... [the Minos program launches] I put in my login and my password... there you go. I have to enter the slip number here... *batch 00265*... here you go	computer
03:25:43	04	so there you see the 25 cases... there... I need to check that I have everything on the slip in the table... there, I check I have the... *5722 5723 5724 5727 28 5732 33 37 5741* hmmm *5747*... well even normally the judge can refuse to put a case in PO [Penal Order] eh but... * you're basing yourself on...?* no but no... that never happens... now I see it's fine... I validate...	summary slip table
03:26:12	05	[the empty boxes corresponding to the decisions and the amount of the sentences are filled in] * it's incredible though... how does it calculate?* the computer compares the cases to the average sentence for the same type of offense... but maybe there are discrepancies with the demands it's on that basis... *and they're all the same?* (same amounts)?* yes yes here they're grouped together... (by type of offense)	table completed
03:27:02	06	so now I can start printing for the Registry of the Court... let's be straight, it's real mindless work!... I hate doing it. I've got loads of them waiting [points to the compartments of the filing cabinet] ... you don't become a small claims court judge to do that.	printing

The friend of a motorist in a fight with police officers on rollerblades...

The second case was rather similar in substance: it concerned an individual who got carried away, following the illegal parking for which his friend, the driver, was fined, such that he himself ended up being ticketed for offensive disturbance. But the case followed ordinary procedures this time: the judge familiarized herself with the elements ahead of the hearing, which was to take place the next day. This difference materialized formally from the distribution of the case files covering her desk, forming another stack consisting of a set of cardboard folders, each of which contained the documents necessary for each case. It is worth emphasizing the nuance: while for penal orders, the judge must manage a batch, processing a flow, the elements of which are connected by a rubber band, and working through the slips, for adversary proceedings, each case must be considered individually, without any particular connection with any of the case files of the day, even if they will be tried in the same hearing. Although the general movement differed, the elements relating to the making of the judgment remained the same: on each case file, the sheet attached listed the characteristics of the case, from the general grammar of any penal offence, successively stating the identity of the accused, the nature of the offence, and the relevant legal norm. Obviously, however, only the content of the folder mattered from a legal standpoint, which the judge was about to study.

Like all the others, the case file concerning Edmond Jaquier was comprised of three distinct sets of documents. The first one, which the judge checked perfunctorily, was made up of all the elements attesting to the admissibility of the proceedings initiated (demands, summons to appear, serving). The judge ensured that the proceedings were valid, that the court had jurisdiction and that the accused had been reached. The second set of documents, which required that the substance of the case be studied, concerned the offence itself (police statement, police report). The judge assessed the acts of which the offender was accused and the validity of the legal texts used by the Public Prosecution to qualify them. Finally, the third set of documents was made up of all the other information produced by the defendants, and sometimes the victims (medical certificate, employer's letter, employment contract, public service certificate, etc.). In this respect, the Jacquier case file appeared to have been reduced to a minimum: no elements other than those in the first two sets of documents featured, except for the check on the defendant's criminal background, which is always included, and the document concerning it, attached to the back of the cardboard folder. The information, which the judge noted down as she formally inspected the documents, was important because in this case, the accused had a criminal record. She noted its presence on the file that would serve as a memo for her to conduct the hearing, stating the reason ("he has a record… insulting a police officer"). Once she had entered the formal elements of the offence on her computer, she examined the case more thoroughly.

The case related to the ticketing of a driver for "disorderly parking", in the middle of a public road and blocking access to an underground car park. More specifically, it concerned Edmond Jaquier, a friend of the driver in question who, after interfering with the police check and getting so carried away that he uttered colourful language, was himself ticketed for offensive disturbance. The judge took into account these elements by reading the police statement, which was written by the rollerblade patrol that had carried out this police check. Her reading was precise: while she endeavoured to reconstruct the facts based on the report of a sergeant detailing the circumstances of the situation that had led to the sanction, she did so based on the rule called for by the statement itself, asking herself whether it really "held up". At this stage, the judge doubted the solidity of the proceedings: in what way did the unkind words uttered by the offender ("I'll go where I want… we're on a public road"… "don't touch me… go on… go rollerblading") constitute an insult? And even if the defendant had had a few run-ins with the police and was quick to quarrel ("the guy doesn't like them… that's clear"), could what he said that day really be considered offensive? The judge could however only hypothesize at this stage, given the uncertainties of the hearing (Excerpt no. 2).

Excerpt no. 2: Police Court Observation M2a 26.04.08

Time		*Judge's comment*	*Material device*
02:21:30	01	so 19… we're up to 19.	folder
02:21:45	02	then this one's *Jacquier…* [turns to her computer and types on the keyboard] J-A-C-Q-U-I-E-R [spells out each letter]	word file
02:21:53	03	so what's his deal [examines the case file folder] … *offensive disturbance…* that's daytime disturbance again… [opens the folder and checks the time mentioned on the requisitions, then turns the cardboard folder over] ah ah … he's got a record: *insulting an officer* … [grabs the sheet with the requisitions] *250 euros* … well he's got a record though	folder requisitions criminal record
02:22:19	04	[turns to computer and types in the information regarding the qualification of the offence and the criminal record] … *it's not nightly disturbance* [types DISTURBANCE in capital letters] … *offensive offensive disturbance. [*types OFFENSIVE]	word file
02:22:34	05	Offensive disturbance on a public road… *at 1:55 pm…* what's going on? [reads the police statement aloud] … Ah! *Rollerblade patrol… Saint Honoré market… a vehicle illegally parked…* [reads aloud at a fast pace] *after having checked the administrative documents of the vehicle and those of its driver… the driver's friend started shouting at me … he found it inadmissible that his friend was being fined for disorderly parking… I should specify that the driver had parked…* What's going on here?	police statement

(*Continued*)

Time		*Judge's comment*	*Material device*
02:23:10	06	[reads address from the police report mumbling very quickly, then goes back to the statement]... okay.	police report
02:23:14	07	*at the aforementioned address in the middle of the traffic lane thus preventing vehicles from entering the underground car park.* Oh yes, I know this parking garage... *while my colleague was writing the ticket, the friend in question kept arguing... interfering in the police check. I asked him several times to step away and stay out of the police check to let us get on with our work and... not to let the police check turn sour. This individual did not want to stay out of the police check, so I tried to get him to move away by taking him with my arm, explaining to him for the umpteenth time that he had to move away for our safety and his own. This individual replied: I'll go where I want... we're on a public road...* that's not insults hey... *I continued to push him away gently but the man got even more angry and he shouted as he spoke to me informally: "DON'T TOUCH ME ... GO ON... GO ROLLERBLADING"* [written in capital letters in the statement] It's not offensive eh... I say it's not offensive... *I asked him for his ID card* [continues reading briefly]	police statement
02:24:25	08	Well on the other hand [reading the criminal record] it's sure that the guy has already been sentenced for insulting an officer so obviously it's a bit of an issue... *insulting a person in charge of public authority* well for sure... the guy doesn't like them... that's visible... but there's no insult though...	criminal record
02:24:43	09	[turns to the computer and inputs her comment, in capitals] NO?	word file
02:24:46	10	[then returns to the police report] because I'm sorry, let's unpack this again: Captain Michel, he's going to find me in the same space as the other day [refers to the Public Prosecution officer probably speaking at the next hearing, referring to a previous hearing] *"I'll go where I want... we're on the public highway" ... "Don't touch me... go on... go rollerblading"* that's not an insult, that's a poor charge! If there was a rebellion, that's one thing, but... that doesn't hold up!	police statement
02:25:20	11	well, for this case, on the face of it I'm strongly in favor of the defendant but... imagine that at the hearing he pipes up saying they're all idiots... I'm going to change eh... it is just a cold reading ... the tables can turn! That's the point of a debate... so that everyone can explain [saves file]	word file

The case hearing was held the next day. Though it was established that the defendant was aware of the summons to appear addressed to him, he did not attend. The adversary proceedings did nevertheless take place, in accordance with the procedure. Like all other cases of the same type, the discussion with the Public Prosecution was delayed to the end of the public hearing. When Case No. 19 was reopened, the deputy public prosecutor restated the charges. The judge questioned the validity of the qualification: was this really offensive disturbance as defined by Article 623-2? Did the words transcribed in the police report really constitute an insult? The Public Prosecution officer went on to consult the penal code, such that a discussion ensued: even if an invective was devoid of insults, could it not be considered as offensive, just like a noise? Could the intention to disturb the police check not be interpreted as a moral element that should make it possible to punish the perpetrator? The judge ultimately sentenced Emile Jacquier to a €200 fine, which was less than the penalty set by the code. She wrote down this decision in the record (court registry) handed to her by the court clerk, stating the formal aspects of the offence. She signed the record, which would be used by the Registry of the Court to enter the information to draft the final judgment, the document of which is generated by a dedicated computer program.

The two cases recounted above certainly describe contrasting situations. The scene seems similar, involving a judge in her office, with a computer and cases. In both situations, she must legally qualify criminal acts committed by a perpetrator whom the Public Prosecution intends to prosecute, within the same criminal system. However, although the offences concerned involved the same laws and shared a number of common features, their processing involved different reading and writing activities. In terms of material media, first of all, cases linked to penal orders are part of a flow, arrive in a bundle and are examined by a judge whose computer plays a central role (automatic inputting, calculation of the penalty). Those linked to ordinary proceeding, on the other hand, constitute a stock; they form a pile and require case-by-case processing where the computer's role appears to be peripheral (note taking). As for reading activities, for the former, they are limited to the formal aspects that appear on the screen, with the graphic arrangement of the writings presented facilitating this work (table, software design). For the latter, they involve a longer process, requiring the articulation of all the pieces organized precisely inside a folder. With regard to writing activities, even though the actual drafting of the final judgment is automated in all cases, the work to reach this stage involves equally different forms and media (printing, proofreading and signing for orders; stylized notes, preparation of the Registrar's notes in court, then inputting by the Registry of the Court, printing, proofreading and signing for adversary proceedings). As for the legal reasoning itself, it did not take into consideration the criminal qualification of the offence in the first case when, on the contrary, the judge weighed up the validity of the second one. Yet the judge could have consulted the police statement, assessed the content of the words spoken and formulated as many questions about them as she had about the motorist's passenger: were they really offensive? Did the situation not call for considering the particular circumstances of the police check, given the uncertainty surrounding the "vehicle", the use of which on a pavement was not formally called into question.[20] Does the law not stipulate that the judge's assessment remains sovereign? Finally, in both cases, moral concerns were present, but not in the same place. While the judge did not question the legitimacy of a sanction without adversary proceedings, let alone the amount of the penalty, she was not insensitive to the meaning of what she was accomplishing. While signing the notifications and admitting to the researcher that it was "really mindless work", she delegated to procedure the task of repairing any decision taken too quickly: the order amounts to a penalty proposal, which the defendant can challenge. Conversely, in the case of adversary proceedings, she herself was responsible for the promise of reparation, believing that the hearing should be educational; it was not enough to state the sentence for it to be heard, it had to be explained.

Having noted these observations, it is important to stress the role of case files in each of the two situations. Evidently, their examination did not receive the same attention. But beyond the acceleration of processing made possible by the elimination of adversary proceedings, what do these differences tell us about the way legal decisions are produced?

The properties of case files in action

From the bundle to the stack, in light of the research areas calling for case files to be considered as technologies and texts respectively, praxeological specification brings three particular results into relief.

Assembling

A first result stems from the finding that a case file is first and foremost an extraordinary entanglement of material and language. Made of paper, cardboard, rubber bands and staples that can be handled, it also contains documentary entities that can be read. This assembling appears significant, for through this reading activity, it participates in the very production of the case. The case file is not just the medium for recording information that is already there, but rather a powerful instrument for formatting situations, turning them into a reality that is compatible with the thinking from which legal activity stems.[21]

In this respect, the comparison of the two cases is a reminder that one of the important properties of the case file is its ability to bring together heterogeneous documents within a single container; it acts through what it offers up for reading. Opening the cardboard folder of a case, such as that of the passenger of the motorist who was fined for offensive disturbance, one finds heterogeneous documents assembled for the first time, which force one to describe the offence from a perspective that has never been so broad. Through the writings it reveals, or even through what these writings preclude from understanding, due to the very fact of being compiled in this way in the same container, the case file produces the capacity to ask questions, by offering up a new collection of points of view that it brings together and which are potentially complicated to grasp as a result of their juxtaposition: "so what's his deal?", "what's going on?". This activity, deployed at the place of the documents to anticipate the fate of the case and to test the solidity of the qualification provided by the sergeants, is inextricably linked to the material qualities of the case files: through handling, skimming through, opening and closing them, they allow for reading documents in possibly multiple ways. Here, the case in question did not lend itself to further examination other than by the Public Prosecution alone, for lack of additional documents. But the judge could not know this without opening the case file, and the examination of the documents did not prevent her from questioning things, rereading the police report, examining the criminal record, and positing potentially hostile though not offensive behaviour. However, given that the case file seemed to be limited to a single sheet of paper, summarized by a line written on a computer, and that the procedure provided for the possibility of a challenge by the defendant, a detailed examination of the case file seemed less useful. Moreover, the optical resources offered by the screen, allowing one to see the bundle all in one piece, encouraged this limitation. And in that context, the reading was reduced solely to the space in a table that could not be interfered with in any way other than to validate it.[22]

The significance of the increase in interpretations facilitated by the perspective afforded by case files through the multiple writings they contain has been pointed out in the literature (Latour, 1990; Weller, 2018a). But it also echoes another argument, put forward by literacy studies, of the polyphonic nature of the case file: the writings contributed by the various parties allow the reader to understand the situation of which they discover the elements from a multiplicity of voices, without there necessarily being any convergence. Referencing the work of Mikhail Bakhtin, this contrapuntal dimension of the case file as a text has also been highlighted (Fraenkel, 2008; Hull, 2012, p. 150). What is more, this marks a difference with the case of orders, the material elements of which are by definition confined to the sole voice of the police.

Circulating

A second finding relates to the ability of any case file to circulate. From hand to hand, from folders to hard disks, it is read by several professionals and, as it journeys on, is handled and transcribed in various ways. It does not designate a stable entity, fixed once and for all. On the contrary, it is an entity intended to circulate, given the division of labour that governs the legal treatment of situations. This applies from the time it is created at the Public Prosecutor's Office, through to the Registry of the Court and the judges of the competent court, and finally its archiving. Its processing – classifications, annotations, post-it note additions, etc. – must thus be mindful of the fact that others will read it. This observation, which has been widely described in relation to police records (Meehan, 1986; Komter, 2006), highlights two findings. The processual and distributed nature of the production of a judicial decision entails a specific documentary production, designed to equip any case file with a memory of what has been done up until that point and to force those in charge of processing it to coordinate with one another. The notion of boundary object, as envisaged by Susan Star and James Griesemer (1989) with regard to scientific work is a reminder here of the importance of intermediary representation mechanisms. Though they have no legal value in the strict sense of the term, these mechanisms are involved in the management of information: reference numbers written on the folders and a number of documents allowing all the actors of the penal procedure chain to find the case; summaries attached to the folders; slips; updatable computer tables showing the elements of the cases for penal orders; and court records which, during the adversary proceedings, circulate between the Registrar and the judge, so as to keep a record of elements relevant from a legal standpoint, used to draft judgments. But this ability for these professionals to coordinate with one another is also owed to the literary and graphic form of each case file. Bakhtin stresses the importance of speech genre, which, by using an impersonal tone and stylistic figures that neutralize any involvement of the writer, ensures the homogeneity of writings and enables the professionals to understand and coordinate with each other (Bakhtin, 1986, pp. 62–63).

In the two disturbance cases discussed here, the case file thus circulated differently. The writing work carried out by the judge appears to be minimal: reduced to the act of the signature in the first case, it takes the form of more personal typed notes in the second one, with the judge noting down some details regarding the case and her reasoning in order to recall the case in court the next day. In both cases, however, the writing appears to be highly standardized: it is the institution writing, not a person.[23] It is also highly automated. Nevertheless, the making of the final decision – a notification or a judgment – differs from one procedure to the other. For penal orders, the table generated by the software plays a major role in the way the reading is formatted and thus at the same time allows for the coordination of the actors of the penal procedure chain. With adversary proceedings, the process is sequential and driven by the writing of the court record which, although standardized, is nevertheless handwritten and literal.

Immobilizing

A third property, finally, is the ability that the case file affords the reader to prepare a single final text. Whether it is the notification under the simplified procedure, which becomes a final judgment only after a period of time during which the defendant is able to file an opposition, or the judgment resulting from adversary proceedings under ordinary proceeding, these documents require a precise form: the "statement of reasons", which sets out the charges against the defendant and states the laws applicable (the grounds for the judgement); followed by the "pronouncement", which states the decision reached by the court. The latter documents thus materialize a deductive reasoning, whereas what has been duly established ("Whereas Mr. X. is being prosecuted for having...", "whereas it has been sufficiently established that Mr. X. did indeed commit the acts of which he is accused...", "charged with having committed the following offence on XX/XX/XX...") precipitates a perfectly logical judicial decision ("finds Mr. X. guilty..."), "we sentence him to a fine of Y euros..."). This demonstration, which attests to a positivist conception and is founded on legal syllogism, nevertheless appears to be a reconstruction established after the fact. That is not to say that it is itself artificial, but it says nothing about the situated interpretive work that had to be done for it to be seen as natural, as though the facts had simply been observed and qualified, based on a perfectly established criminal standard.[24]

Both cases are a reminder that this process is not so mechanical and may take different paths. Did the case of the driver's passenger, who was fined for the colourful words he uttered to the police officers ticketing his friend, not cause the judge to doubt the validity of the qualification ("It's not offensive, eh... I say it's not offensive...")? Did she not acknowledge, on the strength of the elements that she discovered by reading the criminal record, that the movement that inspired the offender was probably not the result of a best intention ("the guy doesn't like them... that's clear") but that the remarks he made to the police officers did not constitute an insult ("*'I'll go where I want... we're on a public road... 'Don't touch me... go on... go rollerblading'* that's not an insult!")? And, when the hearing was held, was the consideration of possibly dropping the charges ("That's bad prosecution!") itself not reversed, based solely on the elements of the case file and the relevant laws, even though the defendant did not appear in court? While the way of moving from the scarce documents contained in a case file to a final text certainly cannot be reduced to the reasoning described in the final document, it takes different paths depending on the cases studied. In the case of simplified procedure, the material facts are associated with legal texts by means of a calculation; in the case of adversary proceedings, this is done by outlining a narrative. Admittedly, in the first case discussed here, the final decision was not entirely automatic: there was still a human in the loop. But the judge only felt the need to check the legal conformity of the elements entered into the computer so that the program could precipitate a decision. In the second case, she had to be able to assess the coherence of the documents gathered, by producing a plausible scenario of what happened, and assessing its consistency with the legal qualification that had been proposed.

*

These different findings regarding the properties of case files call for three concluding remarks. By focusing attention on the material substance of judicial work, this chapter, first of all, reminds us that the ability of judges to grasp events and to qualify them from a legal standpoint relies on tools, first and foremost case files, which allow for the collection, storage and transportation of documents. One of the aims of the ethnographic study was to capture its multiple nature, comprised of paper and electronic material. A second finding shows that, in order to move from the scattered documents that make up any case to the production of a legal decision, an approach limited to formalized texts does not make it possible to understand the way in which legal facts are developed. Thus, between the two so-called "simplified" and common versions of criminal procedure, orders are characterized not only by the elimination of adversary proceedings, as provided for in the law, but also the way in which the multiple documents of a case are successively examined to arrive at a judgment, by way of calculation and no longer based on a narrative. This finding, which owes nothing to procedure, is a reminder of the importance of the materiality of case files, in terms of the ability to reasoning and to act with which they endow their users. Finally, a third finding begs us to consider the impact of such "infrastructure" on the forms of production of the law (Weller, 2018b). Depending on the information production processes that characterize them, case files reveal possible inconsistencies in a case through the documents they contain or of which they homogenize the content using ready-to-use tables, forcing the judge to relate what they are reading to case law built up through experience, or automate the comparison with other cases deemed similar by calculation. In short, case files do not literally "form" the same cases, even if they involve the same texts. The standardization of decisions and the massive volumes of processing that seem to be handled by computer tools call for investigation of the situated conditions of enunciation of the law that they enable or prevent. The case of penal orders examined here speaks volumes: while the procedure provides that the judge may refuse to rule by order and may refer the case back for adversary proceedings, or that the defendant may object to the notification they receive, our research has shown that in practice such contention is very rare.[25]

Notes

1 Introduced in 2003, criminal penal orders are now the most widely used tool for relieving the courts. They are the second most used prosecution procedure (in numbers) and, at the time of the study, accounted for over a quarter of all prosecutions (Roussel, 2014).

2 These procedures to expedite justice, such as instituting proceedings without a hearing, need to be situated within the context of countries with a continental tradition. They are inspired by the mechanisms characteristic of *common law* countries, such as *plea bargaining,* which reduce the procedural stage and the role of the court. For a comparative perspective on these measures in continental Europe, see Cécile Vigour (2018).

3 The court in question had civil jurisdiction over disputes for less than €4,000 (minor everyday disputes) and criminal jurisdiction over offences liable to fines

of less than €750 (minor offences against the rules of life in society). Created in 2002 and made up of lay judges, it was definitively removed in 2017.

4 This includes namely the preparation of police reports and the juvenile police (Meehan, 1986), the filing of documents and the organization of reading practices at a law firm (Suchman, 2000), the pre-hearing interview for immediate trial (Gonzalez-Martinez, 2006), and the preparation of testimony (Lynch, 2015).

5 Namely the pioneering work of Harold Garkinkel on patient orientation based on the review of clinical records (1967, pp. 186–207) or of Don Zimmerman (1969) who wrote his thesis on the paperwork of social services staff in a US federal agency.

6 On this notion of "mobile immutable", an expression which became very popular, see Latour (1990).

7 These studies on literacy in traditional societies were undertaken by psychologists, linguists and anthropologists. They focused namely on the Vai people of Liberia, in relation to whom Sylvia Scribner and Michael Cole (1981) questioned the intellectual effects of writing taught in school (English), different from everyday life (Vai) and Koranic schools (Arabic); and the uses of writing in Iran since the 1980s, studied by Brian Street (1984). Béatrice Fraenkel is credited with introducing these studies to French-speaking academia (Fraenkel and Mbodj-Pouye, 2010).

8 A paradigmatic example of these literacy events is the bedtime story, studied by Shirley Heath (1982). Beyond the work of Street (1984), considered to be foundational, see David Barton, Mary Hamilton and Roz Ivanič (2000).

9 One example is the scriptural activities surrounding the management of cattle at auctions, studied by Kathryn Jones (2000).

10 Regarding the production of legal documents, Béatrice Fraenkel's French work on signatures or chains of writing (2007 & 2008) offer a key source of inspiration. Another example is the study by anthropologist Matthew Hull (2012) of the planning services of the city of Islamabad.

11 The investigation followed the processing of just over 200 cases, based on the observation of work scenes before and during the trial (picking up case files from the Registry of the Court, preparing before the hearing, conducting the hearing itself, final drafting and signing). The cases observed as part of this study related to criminal offences that fell within the jurisdiction of the Police Court. These were violations with a degree of seriousness that could neither incur penalties exceeding €750 nor result in imprisonment, except in specific cases provided for in the procedural code. They involved a range of litigation (road code, disturbance, violence, etc.), with a clear prevalence of traffic offences. At the time of the study, the judgment of these offences fell under an autonomous jurisdiction, which has since been removed.

12 In addition to interviews with judges and other professionals involved in the management of their cases (bailiff, Registry of the Court, president of the district court, conciliator, prosecutor, professional judges) (n=54), the research methodology consisted essentially in observing the work activities of several judges (n=9) in two key settings: the courtroom and the judges' office. We drew on a corpus of criminal cases (n=212) representative of the court's significant litigation, from which we drew the two cases discussed here. During this observational research, office scenes were studied through an original lens: recording were made of the judges' comments, spoken out loud at the invitation of the sociologist who was there to observe them, on the files they had to process. Where possible, this recording was also supplemented with photographs of the documents.

13 The last names have been anonymized, but retain their original connotations.

14 No crime, no punishment without law. This customary and fundamental rule is reiterated in the Penal Code: "No one may be punished for a felony or for a misdemeanour whose ingredients are not defined by statute, nor for a petty offence whose ingredients are not defined by a regulation" (Art. 111–113)

15 Criminal liability applies when a causal link is established between the acts committed and the damage caused by the contravention of a criminal legal norm. In the case of misdemeanours, offences are presumed to be unintentional, characterized by recklessness or negligence. For this reason, there is no need to prove culpable intent, only force majeure being able to nullify the offence.

16 Excerpt from the police report: "IS THAT ALL YOU give a shit about, fining a poor WORKING KID? go to the HOUSING ESTATES instead of BOTHERING us on the road" (in capitals in the text).

17 This information, provided in the form of a table, concerns respectively the program's processing reference number (Column no. 1), the enrolment number stated by the Public Prosecution (Column no. 2), the identity of the defendant (Column no. 3), the type of offence recorded (for example, Code 13313 refers to noise made on a public road, disturbing the peace of the neighbourhood or human health) (Column no. 4), and a coefficient indicating the number of offences recorded (Column no. 5).

18 According to the judge we met, this amount is the result of a calculation based on sentences already pronounced over the last year for the same type of offence. But other elements are also stated, such as the fact that discrepancies between demands and sentences pronounced are taken into account, without any further investigation having been carried out. The fact is, in this case, the sentence matched the conclusions of the Public Prosecution.

19 The table shows respectively the sequences, comments and the material devices involved in the judge's activity. In square brackets, we provide information about certain details of the scene, such as body movements or manual operations performed. In parentheses, we mention contextual elements. Between two *, we indicate the observer's comments, interacting with the person concerned. In italics, we indicate the excerpts read aloud, taken from the material media (documents, screen). Underlined text corresponds to phrases pronounced with heavy emphasis.

20 This brings to mind the canonical example given by Hart (1961, p. 126) about the "No Vehicles in the Park" rule, which was not certain to apply to bicycles or tanks, especially since the police statement did not specify the nature of the vehicle (a bicycle? a scooter?) and mentioned only the police check.

21 On this capacity of the case file to transform reality into a "clear case", a "manageable problem", see Berg (1996).

22 There are many studies on the importance of material media and the reading they induce. About Richard Harper's documentary production at the IMF: "More specifically, research is suggesting that paper documents provide an organisation allowing the reader of a document to impute the relationships between document sections. Although this research is still rather incomplete, the key seems to be that paper-based documents allow and support a certain form of embodied interaction. In a single phrase, paper allows users of documents to get to grips. This is more difficult to do in, say, a hypertext environment, which makes the reading of hypertext documents quite different to the reading of paper documents" (Harper, 1998, p. 22).

23 On this effacement and the control of the writer's body it entails, see the cases of writing in a civil registry office (Fraenkel, 2008) or the preparation of expert opinions (Dupret, 2005).

24 For an exploration of the legal work involved in syllogism, see Dupret (2011).

25 It is understood that this very low referral or opposition rate also relates to other elements that go beyond the scope of this contribution. One example is the negotiations conducted locally between headquarters and the public prosecutor's office to agree on the type of cases that can be referred to, in order to reduce the risk of disputes.

References

Bakhtin, M. (1986) *Speech Genres and Other Late Essays*. Austin: University of Texas Press,.

Barton, D., Hamilton, M. and Ivanič, R. (eds.) (2000) *Situated Literacies: Reading and Writing in Context*. London and New York: Routledge.

Berg, M. (1996) 'Practices of reading and writing: The constitutive role of the patient record in medical work', *Sociology of Health and Illness*, 18(4), pp. 499–524.

Bowker, G. and Star, S. (1999) *Sorting Thing Out, Classification and Its Consequences*. Cambridge, MA: MIT Press.

Bruni, A. (2005) 'Shadowing software and clinical records: On the ethnography of non humans and heterogeneous contexts', *Organization*, 12(3), pp. 357–378.

Cole, M. and Cole, J. (2006) 'Rethinking the goody myth', in Olson, D.R. and Cole, M. (eds.) *Technology, Literacy and the Evolution of Society: Implications of the Work of Jack Goody*. Mahwah, NJ: Lawrence Erlbaum, pp. 305–324.

Dupret, B. (2011) *Practices of Truth: An Ethnomethodological Inquiry into Arab Contexts*. Amsterdam and Philadelphia: John Benjamins Publishing Company.

Dupret, B. (2005) 'Le corps mis au langage du droit: comment conférer à la nature une pertinence juridique', *Droit et Société*, 3(61), pp. 637–638.

Fraenkel, B. (2007) 'Actes d'écriture: quand écrire c'est faire', *Langage et société*, 121–122(3), pp. 101–112.

Fraenkel, B. (2008) 'How do you keep records?', *Langage et société*, 2(124), pp. 59–71.

Fraenkel, B. and Mbodj-Pouye, A. (2010) 'Les new literacy studies, milestones in history and current perspectives', *Langage et société*, 3(133), pp. 7–24.

Garfinkel, H. (1967) '"Good" organizational reasons for "bad" clinic records' in *Studies in Ethnomethodology*. Englewood Cliffs, NJ: Prentice-Hall, Inc., pp. 186–207.

Gonzalez-Martinez, E. (2006), 'The interweaving of talk and text in a French criminal pre-trial hearing', *Research on Language and Social Interaction*, 39(3), pp. 229–261.

Goody, J. (1977) *The Domestication of the Savage Mind*. Cambridge, London and New York: Cambridge University Press.

Goody, J. (1986) *The Logic of Writing and the Organization of Society*. Cambridge, London and New York: Cambridge University Press.

Harper, R. (1998) *Inside the IMF, an Ethnography of Documents, Technology and Organisational Action*. San Diego and London: Academic Press.

Heath, B.S. (1982) 'What no bedtime story means: Narrative skills at home and school', *Language in Society*, 11, pp. 49–76.

Heath, C. (1982) 'Preserving the consultation: Medical record cards and professional conduct', *Sociology of Health and Illness*, 18(4), pp. 56–74.

Hull, M. (2012) *Government of Paper. The Materiality of Bureaucracy in Urban Pakistan*. Berkeley: University of California Press.

Jones, K. (2000) 'Becoming just another alphanumeric code: Farmers' encounters with the literacy and discourse practices of agricultural bureaucracy at the livestock auction', in Barton, D., Hamilton, M. and Ivanič, R. (eds.) *Situated Literacies: Reading and Writing in Context*. London and New York: Routledge, pp. 67–86.

Knorr-Ctetina, K. (1981) *The Manufacture of Knowledge: An Essay on the Constructivist and Contextual Nature of Science*. Oxford: Pergamon Press.

Komter, M.L. (2006) 'Introduction', *Research on Language and Social Interaction*, 39(33), pp. 195–200.

Latour, B. (1987) *Science in Action. How to Follow Scientists and Engineering through Society*. Cambridge, MA: Harvard University Press.

Latour, B. (1990) 'Drawing things together' in Lynch, M. and Woolgar, M. (eds.) *Representation in Scientific Practice*. Cambridge, MA: MIT Press, pp. 19–68.

Latour, B. (2010) *The Making of Law: An Ethnography of the Conseil d'État*. Cambridge, MA and Malden, MA: Polity Press.

Latour, B. and Woolgar, S. (1988[1979]) *Laboratory Life. The Construction of Scientific Facts*. Princeton, NJ: Princeton University Press.

Lynch, M. (1985) *Art and Artifact in Laboratory Science: A Study of Shop Work and Shop Talk in a Research Laboratory*. London: Routledge and Kegan Paul.

Lynch, M. (2015) 'Turning a witness. The textual and interactional production of a statement in adversarial testimony' in Dupret, B., Lynch, M. and Berard, T. (eds.) *Law at Work. Studies in Legal Ethnomethods*. Oxford: Oxford University Press, pp. 163–189.

Meehan, H.J. (1986) 'Record-keeping practices in the policing of juveniles', *Urban Life*, 15(1), pp. 70–102.

Roussel, G. (2014) 'L'essor de l'ordonnance pénale délictuelle', *Droit et Société*, 88, pp. 607–620.

Scribner, S. and Cole, M. (1981) *The Psychology of Literacy*. Cambridge, MA: Harvard University Press.

Star, S.L. and Griesemer, J. (1989) 'Institutional ecology, "Translations", and Boundary objects: Amateurs and professionals on Berkeley's museum of vertebrate zoology', *Social Studies of Science*, 19(3), pp. 387–420.

Street, B.V. (1984) *Literacy in Theory and Practice*. Cambridge: Cambridge University Press.

Suchman, L. (2000) 'Making a case: "knowledge" and "routine" work in document production' in Lufi, P., Hindmarsh, J. and Heath, C. (eds.) *Workplace Studies, Recovering Work Practice and Informing System Design*. Cambridge: Cambridge University Press, pp. 29–45.

Vigour, C. (2018) *Justice Reforms in Europe: Between Politics and Management*. Louvain-la-Neuve: De Boeck.

Weller, J.-M. (2018a) 'Les appuis matériels du raisonnement juridique' in Colemans, J. and Dupret, B. (eds.) *Ethnographies du raisonnement juridique*. Paris: Law and Society collection, LGDJ.

Weller, J.-M. (2018b) *Fabriquer des actes d'Etat. Une ethnographie du travail bureaucratique*. Paris: Economica.

Zimmerman, D.H. (1969) 'Record-keeping and the intake process in a public welfare agency' in Wheeler, S. (ed.) *On Record: Files and Dossiers in American Life*. New York: Russel Sage, pp. 319–354.

7 Verbatim records and the testing ceremony

On the production of decidability in German asylum hearings

Thomas Scheffer

The ongoing refugee crises have a number of interrelated collective causes such as organized violence and military conflicts (Zolberg, 1989) or the rising shortage of water and food due to rapid climate change (White, 2011; McAdam, 2012). Contrary to these humanitarian crises and their "existential problems" (Scheffer, 2018, 2020), the state management of the refugee movements seems to focus nearly to its entirety on the militarisation of borders, the increasing internal control, and the expansion of deportation efforts. In Western democracies, these 'hostile' measures are to be based on the "rule of law". Once refugees reached German territory, the treatment of refugees derives from procedural case-by-case reviews. The following article investigates how the ability to refute on legal grounds is accomplished methodically in each and every case. This ability is grounded in the verbatim records (VR), kept by the officer in charge in the course of the asylum hearing. Especially the interplay of two recording styles ('monological narration' and 'dialogical challenge') enforces the transformation of collective threats into an individual claim to be testable. The recording styles apply what sociologists call "methodological individualism", meaning the breakdown of a social phenomenon in individually attributed properties. The record-keeping is part and parcel of an entitlement-testing ceremony.

For the case-by-case review, the state agency demands for an oral statement by the asylum-seeker. The German asylum procedure regulates the treatment of the oral statement as follows: "The hearing is to be recorded in writing which contains the foreigner's essential information." (§25 Asylum Procedure Law, *author's translation*) The written record provides the basis, and in most cases the only basis, for the review of the asylum application. The case appears in terms of an oral account on how and why the asylum seeker escaped from "political persecution" (Article 16 German Constitutional Law). This minimal basis implicates a restricted "burden of proof": The federal court decided that a refugee cannot be expected to prove her or his case by material evidence such as identity papers, medical certificates, confirmation of prison sentence, or verifications of the escape route. Carrying such evidence could jeopardize the flight itself and, in return, could invite doubts that its carrier has never been a refugee in the first place. Due to these rulings, the VR turns pivotal.

The VR is meant to render the asylum decision accountable and justifiable. Reasons for or against the individual application can be drawn exclusively from this VR. The VR is the only procedurally relevant object that is left after the hearing. Only by the VR, the officer can demonstrate that 'his/her' interview conformed to the procedural rules: e.g., a fair questioning and the right to be heard. Thus, the text gives the interviewee's narrative *and* narrates a version of how it was taken (Suresh, 2018). A basic assumption constitutes this substitution of the actual interview situation by VR: the talk should precede its documentation, meaning what is being said is neither distorted nor affected by the text-production. This basic assumption allows the protocol's official utilization as *the* facts of the case to be decided upon. The record thus materializes "truth and power" (Foucault, 2008).

I examine the production of VRs during hearings in the context of my ethnography of the German asylum procedure. In general, VRs are of great importance as they provide the vital basis for determining 'what the case is' and how it can be treated.[1] Next to the asylum procedure, record-keeping is key in/for police interrogations (Komter, 2006), court hearings (Scheffer, 2010), or social scientific interviews (Lynch, 2002). Here, the participants interactively, routinely and in an organised way co-produce the materials that enable further steps of reality construction. The written form is a structuring element of such moments since it shapes the accounts as they are given off *and* transforms them.[2] In this sense, ethnomethodologists insisted right from the start (Garfinkel, 1967) that written records are constructs 'in-and-out' and cannot be reduced to an original core.

The following analytics, developed from grappling with methodically arrayed materials (observation notes, audio recordings, official publications), presents what I call a trans-sequential analysis (Scheffer, 2007, 2010, 2018). As a study of a 'judgement-in-the-making', it reminds of other reconstructions of institutional fabrication. Documents play a major role in Knorr-Cetina's (1984)[3] laboratory study, where she contrasts the early and the final version of a research report after it passed the lab as inscription apparatus. Cambrosio et al. (1990) offer a case study on a political dossier travelling through a ministry, gaining several social meanings on the way. Smith (1985) analyses psychiatric accounts and how they construe mental illness. All these seminal case studies, however insightful, do not deal with the document-in-the-making and how this making is itself more than just writing (Smith, 2000). The officer's documenting is embedded in strategic, retrospective and prospective activities beyond the mere text: interrogation and auditing. I understand this multi-modal work as a channelled decision making process trans-sequentially *distributed* across episodes and sites.

Record-keeping requires a trans-sequential analysis on the production of speech/text 'as it happens'.[4] The process of putting-something-in-writing refers to interactive "episodes of documentation" (Zimmerman, 1969, p. 340).

Here, we encounter a core technique of the state apparatus-in-action turning the production of decidable cases into a regular achievement. The routine bridging of text and talk is a powerful part of governing people. This state-apparatus produces decidability by methodological individualism. It refers to and tests facts only to infer individual qualities. This methodology secures certain symbolic effects (such as certain refusal/approval ratings); it does so by bracketing out collective dynamics (such as civil wars, hunger crises, ecological disasters) even in refugee crises.

The article investigates this specific "adjudication in action" (Dupret, 2011) by undertaking the following analytical steps:

1. *The dictation styles for record-taking*: In this section, I present and compare the distinct methods of dictating employed by the officer in charge during the asylum hearing. I show how linkages to oral contributions are created in various ways and how talk is geared towards these usages. Contrary to what the record-keeping implies, what is put into writing is not what was said; people rather say what can be written.
2. *The final revision*: The officer is tasked with finalizing the eventual version. The resulting VR should perform a successful entitlement-testing ceremony by allocating good reasons for a judicial decision in this specific case. In this line, the final revisions produce not just a legally binding, but also a materially conclusive resource. This resource is identical with the case and renders it decidable.
3. In the *résumé*, I specify how the strategic record-keeping provides for the conditions of the entitlement-testing ceremony. This way, even collective existential problems such as war or ecological disasters can be individualized.

The dictation styles for the record

The VR, it is assumed for all procedural purposes, replaces the situated hearing and renders the latter available to a wide range of known as well as unknown readers (including the recorder her- or himself). This is how it is used by the procedural publics, such as judges, lawyers or NGOs, to evaluate the applicant's account or the caseworker's doubting: 'the applicant knows a lot', 'she contradicts herself', 'answers remain rather vague', 'the account does not provide grounds to grant asylum'; or as well 'the officer did not conduct the hearing well', 'questions appear as rather unfair', 'the refusal is unsubstantiated'. In this context, let us consider legal reviews conducted at the administrative court in charge of checking allegedly 'wrong' asylum judgements:

> The judge determines on the basis of the record whether the appeal of the refused asylum seeker has any chance of success. At the hearing,

> he asks contrastive questions aided by the record. He compares the claimant's submissions with those made in the hearing and, for example, evaluates them as rather "boosted" and "enhanced". He criticises the officer's official investigation with regard to the lack of follow-up questions or questions for clarification. He finds the evaluation of the statements in the official notification of the Federal Office to be "partial" and "too general".

The use of the record in the court procedure 'naturally' postulates that the written is neutral to the spoken. Based on this postulate, one could suspect errors in the transfer from the spoken out to written down only.[5] My analysis does not attempt to pinpoint flaws or distortions. It rather takes recent studies that take the record-keeping as inherent of the asylum hearing. Officers have to talk *and* write the hearing. Their record-keeping disrupts the interview too often (not allowing for fluid narration) or too rarely (not memorising everything said) (see Töpfer, 1990, p. 116).[6]

It is true for both their utilisation in the procedure and the analysis of errors that "documentations ought not to be the cause of the actual event they record; the causality should all be in the other direction." (Goffman, 1986, p. 79) Speech constitutes – that is the normative presumption – the original which is then represented in writing. However, only when neglecting the transmission process can talk and text be idealised to such degree as 'pure forms'. But perhaps the various practical links and relations between text and talk should be taken more seriously. Perhaps the talking and writing mingle to an extent that no longer allows us to separate original and representation.

The following analysis focuses on exactly those many links between text and talk; not as chaotic mingling through, but as a bundle of methodical, even strategic discourse practices. It tries to understand those links or bridges as practical constituents of, what one could call, a ceremony of entitlement-testing. In order to conduct this analysis it seems not helpful to adopt the natives' concept of an objective talk-text-derivability or to simply separate the written product from a talk prior to them.[7] Rather, I will elaborate on the oral and the written trans-sequentially by tracing pre-, semi-, and finalised versions of certain speech/writing acts of doing procedure. I start this analysis by introducing a simple praxeological distinction of various rhythms of recording: close to the spoken word, thematic, or pairwise. They result in different interactional dynamics.

Proximate synchronisation

In the case of synchronising the recording in proximity to the spoken word, we find the interpreter's (I*) translation of the response – of course not the applicant's (A) words themselves – and the official's (O) dictation closely. This proximity is illustrated in the following excerpt from the transcript:

O Question Colon Can you now tell me in great detail and step-by-step what you and these people did or said once you had entered the airport building Next Line Response Colon
A # ~~~~~~
I* Erm
O <Erm
I* < When I entered the airport building, first of all, I checked in my bags, that is, I had them weighed and =then they were taken away
O *When I entered the airport building* comma first of all comma I checked in my bags comma I had them weighed and then dot
I* < they were taken away
O <they were taken away dot
I* <Then we went to the big departure hall for all
O *Then I went* to the big departure hall for all
I* <Excuse me? And then in the gate
I* <and then er to the =gate
I* # to the gate ( ) and then we were we were er
O <Dot Then we were
I* <taken to the airplane
O <taken *to the airplane* dot
I* <Then I entered the plane
O <Then I entered the plane
I* <and drove off
O <and dro departed dot next line

At the beginning, O attends to the task of asking a question by formulating *and* dictating it as a translation task for the interpreter.[8] By asking and dictating the question at once, O prepares the ground for receiving the applicant's response. This reception, however, is not a direct one.

The officer repeats the interpreter's delivery in a 'brash' way; in doing so, he treats the interpreter's words as the original wording to be repeated by dictation. To put different, I* is made to dictate the decision-maker's dictation. The words of the former are transported onto the audio recording and further into the written protocol. Here, I* is prepared to be actually echoed in this manner. The echo often already starts even before I* finished his turn. O delegates wording work to the interpreter[9].

At times, we can find short phases of negotiation amongst these unequal 'co-authors' of the VR. In the above example, an agreement is reached through a brief communicative 'nod' ("Erm", line 5). It is easy to forget in similarly unproblematic cases that the mode of dictation is accomplished *in* the situation. This is more evident when I* hesitates to signal his readiness to deliver ready-to-echo words:

A ~~~~~~~~~

I* <Yes, well, what I understood now is that ( ) as I said, I didn't know that I was in France, he said to me, er and afterwards when I moved = on erm

O *I did not know* that I was in France comma but that is what I was told dot. Afterwards comma when I moved on

I* <and was already in Germany

O < and was already in Germany comma

I* <thought I would still be in France

O <I thought that I was still in France new line dot

The interpreter's introduction can be understood as an attempt to lower the standard of the subsequent dictation. Such mitigation can often be found when a dictation that stays close to the spoken word is imminent. It points to the greater burden that I* is expected to bear. Here, the decision-maker's repetitions ignore the warning signs; in other cases, O reacts by changing the rhythm of synchronisation. In the following example, synchronisation is established as a quality standard step-by-step.

A ~~~~~~=~~~

O I want to know what your **what your** (hits the desk with his open palm) last job has been immediately before =your departure

I* *that comes now, he did* tell me about that

O Erm alright =okay

I* *that issue* goes back 10 to 12 months to his last job in which he has then continued to work

O <good, alright, now then

I* <Well, he was he didn't have any money, nothing to eat when a friend came to him = who

O *I was* unemployed at first comma I had no money left for my family comma we could hardly eat
anything dot

I* <I then met a friend

O I then met a family friend

I* <who gave me =ten Egyptian pounds

O *comma he gave me* ten Egyptian pounds

I* so that we =could buy something to eat

O *comma so that I* could buy something to eat dot

How is the synchronisation coordinated between interpreter and officer? First of all, I announces his delivery (4). He tries to make sure that the answer is accepted 'as it is' (6). The officer encourages I to deliver the 'translated answer' per start sign. This "now then" (7) reframes the weight of the words that would follow. From here on, I* has to accept that his contributions will be imported word-by-word into the record. Slowly, she adapts to the task: guided by O (9), she changes into the required first person as well as a fragmentation of clauses (12). She is speaking the 'verbatim record'-style.[10] During I's reporting and O's dictating, A is side-lined, nervously awaiting I*'s next question-translation.

Once the proximate synchronisation between O and I* is established, a major part of the ex post wording work is carried out by the interpreter, while O repeats after the former. The applicant's 'original' contributions, however, remain untouched by the 'invasiveness' of the dictation. They continue to be synchronised only within the sub-hearing between interpreter and applicant. I* commences his delivery (of fragmented dictation styles) when he obtains sufficient material to deliver a fitting answer to the question. The synchronisation in proximity to the spoken word stops at the language barrier. It embraces just I* as if she or he provided the applicant's tongue.

Paired synchronisation

The word-by-word echoing is given up in the recording style of paired synchronisation. Here, the officer would wait until the turn-pair of question/answer fit. This would be a typical example:

O … new paragraph question could you please tell me now how you came to Germany
I* ~~~~
A ~~~~~~~~~~~=~~~~
I* ~~~~~~ He starts off with his his
O <his grounds for asylum, yes, well I thought so
I* ~~~~
A ~~~
O From Ankara ~~~
A ~~~~~
I* To Istanbul by coach, from Istanbul to Frankfurt by plane
O Erm
A ~~~~
I* departed entered on the 12th of June 96 ( )
O Erm, yes question I see, could you please tell me now how you came to Germany new paragraph

(clack) Reply I travelled from Ankara to Istanbul by coach and then took a plane to Frankfurt dot It was the 12th June 1996 dot new paragraph question why did you fly from Istanbul were there no flights from Ankara

20 I* ~~~~

A ~~~~~~

I* because a friend of mine was waiting in Istanbul

O new paragraph question (clack) new paragraph upon further questioning I went from Ankara to Istanbul because a friend of mine was in Istanbul dot new paragraph question how...

As in cases of close synchronising, here we find a recorded question at the beginning (1). O vocalises a standard question for the record *and* for a new round of question-answer pairing-in-translation. Initially, when I* starts to deliver the response, it is still unclear whether or not this can make it into the VR and how. However, the interpreter's inquiry beyond the language barrier (4) and, even more so, his subsequent signal of indirectness ("He starts off ..."/4) indicate that at this point he seems unable to provide a useful 'response' for dictation. I* allocates the blame for the delivery problem to A. The applicant apparently started off already with "his grounds for asylum" (5), as A infers.

The officer adapts his dictation style to the 'obvious' difficulties. He waits until a fitting answer is given with his transfer for the record (14). On this occasion, he listens to his recorded question once again in order to control the 'fit' between question and answer. Two different pairings follow: In the first (14), a fit is achieved by a continuing dictation without correcting the original recording of the question; in the second (23), the question is re-recorded. The officer retracts the already recorded question for the benefit of the 'useful' answer.

The officer reacts to the imminent uselessness of the talk for dictation purposes by deferring the dictation. A close linkage seems improbable: this way, O can attune to necessary reconstructions, corrections, clarifications of words and phrasings. The low quality of the interpreter's deliveries can present a continuing problem in hearings – and render a dictation close to the spoken word unlikely. In such cases, O waits for all partial deliveries in response to a question, even without the interpreter's signalling. In doing so, he gains an overview as well as time, which enables him to construct accountable question-answer-pairs commensurate for record-keeping.

Thematic synchronisation

The talk-text rhythm changes, once again, in the thematic synchronisation mode. Here, O takes up the Dictaphone only after a certain matter is dealt with. Now she would finalize the section by recording it in a rather summary fashion. One theme entails, for example, the grounds for asylum, the description of the 'escape route', or a set of "quiz questions" (e.g. regarding one's claimed religious denomination or professional occupation in the home-country). Several question-answer-rounds are worked through by the members before, finally, the officer speaks consecutively for the record. This is illustrated by the following longer excerpt from one of my transcripts:

O Why did you have to leave your home country question mark Please tell me in detail about your
personal grounds for seeking asylum (clack) dot
I* ~~~~~~
A ~~~~~=~~~~~~~~~~~~~~~~~~~~~~~~
O *[speaks on the phone] Yes, good morning, can you check where and which files there are of my darlings here [reads out the file number of the applicant's brother's file] representation what erm could you order these for my file number [dictates the new number] … yep, alright [hangs up/ coughs]*
A ~~~~~~~~~~~~
I* on February the sixth ninety-four my brother had received a sub a court summons, that day he did he did actually never come back
O Mmh
I* Three days later ninety-four people came to us and wanted ( ) wanted to talk to me, erm I was in the garden well I just happened to be at home, they asked for money. I had, well I was about to hear what money they were talking about, they pushed me to the side and walked into the house and searched the house ( ) ~~~
A ~~~~~~~~~~~~~~~~~~~~~~
I* During the house search they found leaf er leaflets of the UDPS party. After the house search they took the leaflets and me as well.
O That's what they always say.
I* Yes ( ) They took me to Kalamu, I was detained for a month there. I was mistreated there ( ) I was made to confess that I ( ) that I was a member of UDPS, too ( )
A ~~~~~~~~~~~~~~~~~~~~~~~~~~~~~~~~~~
I* My mother had taken care of it, had pleaded with them and had liberated me, she had to spend nine hundred Dollars to have me released, but before I was let go I was in I was photographed first, erm when my mother picked me up when my mother wanted to pick me up, came they said to my mother whether she knew the story of Tombal Bai, Tombal Bai is the ex-president of Chad, who was murdered that is he and his whole family ( )
O Tombal?
I* TOMBAL BAI, that's how his name's written. (6) He is the ex-president of Chad, who was murdered and his whole family, too
O Mmh
A (8) ~~~~~~~~~~~~~~~~~~~~~~~~~~~~~~~~~

I* () Er my brother well up until September ninety-four I personally had no news from my brother, er we hope that one day my mother I was actually expected to at my brother's save the carpentry business, that was the best anyway, I was expected to make sure that again re reopens. Er, I then asked what about the brother, mother said said to me then in a grand manner, yes I have heard that he has fled, via Angola, he had helped by Major had been helped by Major, but he's also not here () I went and opened the carpentry, that worked for two weeks, two weeks long, but two weeks later (4) ~~~

A ~~~~~~~~~~~~~~~~~~~~~~~~~~~~~~~~~~~~

I* On the twenty-sixth of September ninety-four the soldiers came into our house () ER, we had the apprenticeship in front of my house, that is, my brother had had his carpentry business there, and mother had her own door and I had my own door and, at that moment, I was at my mum's for lunch. When the soldiers came and also generally to scare people off so that no neighbors actually come out it is quite usual that when they come in somewhere, first of all, they shoot = in

O Mmh

I* # into the air, yes. That's what they did as well when they came through the streets to us. When I heard that I looked out of my mother's window and fled and such a long time to Germany ()

O Erm new paragraph-answer-colon On the sixth of February nineteen hundred and ninety-four my brother received a court summons dot My brother complied with this summons and has not been seen afterwards dot He disappeared dot new paragraph Then comma on the ninth of February nineteen hundred and ninety-four comma some people came to our house and wanted to talk to me dot I was at home and they asked for the money dot I asked what money they were referring to comma [rewind] dot However comma they just pushed me aside and entered the house dot They searched the whole house and found leaflets of the UDPS dot Then they just took these leaflets and myself with them dot They took me to the prison in Kalamu where I was mistreat (clack) Erm o god I was (clack) mistreated dot I was made to confess to being a member of the UDPS dot I remained there for a month dot …

After recording his question the officer puts the microphone away. During the discussion between interpreter and applicant, he appears to be 'all ears'. She receives the interpreter's translations equipped with a notepad. This apparent deferment of the dictation in the ongoing hearing can be interpreted as an invitation to narrate. In any case, it has a stimulating effect: the applicant is now interrupted only by the interpreter. The talk is rather fluid. Only the officer's accompanying note-taking[11] enables such restraint. This temporary storage, consisting of keywords and (personal-use) abbreviations and combined with the decision-maker's working memory, provides the rudiments for his concluding dictation.

Here, the interpreter's role is more the one of a re-narrator: he is not required to deliver a perfect adjacency pair of question-answer; he is not meant to feed directly into the subsequent dictation; he merely recounts what has been accounted for on the other side of the language barrier. Comprehensibility is what is essential here. O confirms through repeated signals whether this request is being fulfilled. Only when the interview touches on epistemic details it becomes apparent that the spoken is part of a test to be put into writing. O requests, for instance, the spelling of a name ("Tombal?"). I*'s response is geared to the official note-taking. She would write it down for the officer in his block. The collated material is converted into dictation only after the story is completed. In the above case, completion is marked through a relatively long pause.

In the subsequent dictation stage, I* takes on another function in relation to the record-keeping:

O ... I was made to confess to being a member of the UDPS dot I remained there for a month dot meanwhile, my mother had tried to have me freed and had to pay a sum equivalent to nine hundred ~
I* *dollars*
O dollars ( ) Didn't you say €? =(clack)
I* *No* I told you dollars
O (turning to me) Did he say €?
TS Erm [looking through my notes] I've only got 900 written down here [I/O laugh]
O valent to (clack) nine hundred US dollars dot Before I was let go comma however comma they took a photo of me dot ...

I* acts as an editor safeguarding the correctness of the dictation. Her correction refers to a detail (4) in the dictation that does not conform to her delivery. Evidently, the correction is not about a word-by-word congruence between the spoken and the written. The correction rather focuses on data items that could become relevant in further rounds of testing, e.g. for contrasting queries: dollars instead of €, 11 instead of 12, December not November, arm not leg, KPI not SPI, etc. The interpreter's interruption is not considered a *faux pas* but as a commendable fulfilment of his duty – even though the officer does not immediately concede his mistake. In order to settle the matter, memory work is carried out jointly, including sometimes the ethnographer as a quasi-witness (7).

The interpreter undertakes the monitoring of the dictation. His correction work is only possible due to the officer dictating '*en bloc*'. At the same time, this mode of dictation seems to necessitate such correction work, as note-taking 'mistakes' may add to potential errors in hearing, communication and dictation. The intermediate storage results in an additional layer of bridging talk and text.

Summary

The analysis of synchronisations between the spoken and the written shows how speech is adapted to the subsequent processing via a set of preparations, configurations, and wording styles. The bridging of talk and text depends on the style of recording or dictating:

- A dictation in proximity to the spoken word would require a precise and careful oral submission that can be repeated word-by-word;
- a dictation following turn-pairs that involves the good pairing of question-answers and that allows for a rather sceptical reception of the communications' results;
- and a thematic dictation that follows on a report that can be reconstructed and summarized, thus requiring some recounts at length.

Orality and writing do not constitute separate registers but mutually inform each other. The oral contributions in the hearing are (more or less) geared towards their transcription. They vary by degree of their prefabrication and usability for the record. The written prolongs the oral deliveries and, depending on their production status, uses them as either material or templates. Considering the pre-, semi-, and finished products makes it impossible to grant the spoken the status of an independent reality, of an untouched originality. Rather, the 'subjectivity' of the oral, as test data, appears as the product of the written record: by formulas used to frame what follows, by markers of authenticity (1st person and 'direct speech'), by the interrelated styles of recording, by the applicant's signature. Dialogues, as they are found in records of hearings, have never taken place in exactly these words and sequences. In return, capturing the spoken words as text would generate a not very useful or even deficient document. Record-keeping, thus, involves the co-production of recordables and the anticipation of later utilisations of the protocol already in the hearing's course. It demands for a trans-sequential orientation towards the procedure, meaning beyond the here and now of just talk and its interaction rituals.

The officer's final revision

Irrespective of the (degree of) prefabrication of the oral delivery, it is the officer-in-charge who concludes the recording process. He or she creates a final translation in the language of the record with its specific rhetoric. I call this step the final revision. Depending on the quality of the pre-products, the final revision can entail refining a statement (close synchronisation), arranging question-answer-pairs (paired synchronisation), or carefully wording a report (thematic synchronisation). Hence, the final revision depends very much on the rhythm of dictation; it is as well geared towards the interrelated styles of recording as obligatory stages of the individualizing *ceremony of testing*.

When we examine how recording styles are transmitted to the written record, several modifications become apparent on the way. Modifications close the last translation gap between previously formulated styles and the final record. The modifications take various forms: *inter alia,* questions are cut out so that separate answers can be combined to whole monologues; questions are complemented by additional commentary in order to highlight the effort of testing, making the officer a professional sceptic; questions are dictated as mere standards (e.g. "upon further questioning"); one-syllable (negative or positive) answers are extended to full-sentence replies to highlight the test-completion; 'the obvious' or information from previous passages are added; qualifying additions are omitted to make test results more clear. All these 'stylish' modifications are necessary, I propose, in order to guide a generalized reader – the 'impartial' tester of the testing, the 'judicial' reviewer of the review process – towards potentially good reasons for a final judgement.

The modifications represent the officer's methods to accomplish a record for all procedural purposes. They are systematic and structural; they can be found in every recording; they come into play depending on the reached state in the chosen rhythm of recording. My core hypothesis is supported by a simple observation: the modifications are geared towards the ceremony of testing. The similar results show in each and every record in systemic combination. The record would no longer show the style and rhythm of recording. In other words: notwithstanding the different ways of asking questions, the more active or passive modes of translating, or the different rhythms of recording, the resulting VRs look the same. The modifications as the final review show the extra work necessary to accomplish this standard record, invested with potentially good reasons to refute the application at hand.

In order to demonstrate how modifications are turned towards the ceremony of testing, I chose (1) a single mode of dictation (here, the dictation close to the spoken word) as only then the modifications have a comparable status for the final version of the record. In a second step (2), the modifications are shown in systematic combinations leading towards a 'ceremonial' record of hearing. This way the interview is ultimately "moulded and modified to fit into the understanding and expectations of the society in which it is presented" (Goffman, 1956, pp. 22–23). The interrelated styles and the modifications necessary to accomplish them show how the hearing protocol is a way of *doing procedure* and a resource to guarantee a reasonable judgement in any case, however easy or difficult.

The officer's means of the final revision

In order to demonstrate systematic combinations or patterns of modifications, I present two transcribed extracts from two different phases in the hearing. I begin with a longer excerpt from early on in the questioning about the applicant's travel route.

O Asked about the exact travel route
I* ~~~~~~~~~~
A ~~~~~~~~~~~~~~~~~~~~~
I* <Mhm ( ) On the 26th of February I
O <On the 26th of February XXXX I
I* <left
O <left Egypt dot
I* <Erm, I was [hesitates and turns back to A] ~~~~~~
A <~~~
I* <First on my way until December
O ( ) Er. What mode of transport did you use when you left?
I* <~~~~
A <~~
I* <I departed by plane.
O *Mhm.* Mhm. [Quietly] Question did you have a passport with you
I* <~~~~
A <~~~~~~~~~=~~~~~~~~~
O I departed by plane dot
I* # I left with a forged Egyptian =passport.
O I left with a forged passport dot. ( ) Mhm. Err where did you arrive.
I* <~~~
A <~~~~~~~~~~~~~~~~~~~~~~~~~
I* <mhm ( ) I arrived in France but I don’t know where
O *I arrived in France comma but* I do not know where dot
I* < Err, one would have to ask again, I think he came here by train.
O: Mhm- that’s what I thought.
O ( ) What made you think that you had arrived in France and how did you realize that.
I* <~~=~
A ~~~~~~~~~~~~
O *Next line question colon What made you realize that you had arrived in France.*
A #~~~~~~~~~
I* <Yes. Well, what I’ve now understood is that ( ) I didn’t know, as I said earlier, that I was in France, he told me, err and then when I moved on mmm
O *I did not know* that I was in France comma but I was told so dot Then, when I moved on
I* <and was already in Germany
O <and was already in Germany comma
I* <I thought I were still in France

O <I thought that I was still in France next line dot. Err one moment, err, tell me once again what happened exactly after you had landed in France at the airport ( ) were you on your own or was there anyone with you and what exactly happened next
I* <Mhm, err ~~=~~~~~~~~~~
O Next line Upon further questioning colon
I* #~~~~~~~~~~~~~
A <~~~~~~~~~~~~~
I* <Mhm ( ) err err When I had arrived in France a man waits there for me
O <When I arrived in France comma a man was waiting there for me
I* < er this man had a description of me
O <comma who had a description of me dot ( ) he was some kind trafficker or what
A ~~~~~~~~~~~
I* #Mhm~~~~~~~~~~
A <~~
I* <I don't know whether he was a trafficker
O ( ) mhm, I do not know whether this man was a trafficker dot
A ~~~~~~~~~~~~
O # And this man then took you to Germany or what?
I* <~~~~~~~~~Alemania
A <~~=~~~~~~~~~~~~~~~~~~
O *This man then took me to Germany dot* ( ) And this man also told you that you arrived in France
I* <~~~~~~
A <~~~~~~~~~~~~~~~~~~~~~~~~
I* #Mhm, er he he told me that I were in France and that I should take a er a train er
O *This man told* me that I was in France and that I should take a train dot
I* <Apart from that, he didn't talk anymore
O <Apart from that, he did not talk to me at all dot
I* <He walked behind me
O ( ) Mhm. Did he then travel with you on that train?
I* <~~~~~~~
A <~~
I* <No
O <He did not travel with me on that train dot I travelled on my own dot ( )

What modifications from talk to text does the officer use in the above transcript, and how does she combine these modifications?

Filtering vagueness: The stumbling translation of the prehistory of the applicant's flight (4–10) is not pursued further, let alone dictated. A similar modification can be found where I* announces the delivery of a vague translation (25). Both deliveries do not comply with the unambiguity required for the statements in the record ascribed to the asylum-seeker. Filtering vagueness is part and parcel of producing decidability by compiling only statements that can be tested and, thus, falsified.

Constructing monologues: A question about the means of transport is raised (11) but not dictated. Only the answer (18) is transmitted into the record, so that it now appears as self-directed speech: a narrative. Monologisations are found here following the question about the destination airport (20 sq.), upon questioning about and clarification of the relationships between the protagonists mentioned (39 sq.), and following the question about the 'trafficker' (48) and his services (55). This points at one basic style of recording in line with the methodological individualism of the ceremony of testing. The recording creates a narrator and her/his uninterrupted narration.

- *Absorbing the conduct of the conversation:* Responses (65) can be filtered out if they are considered irrelevant. The officer prioritises a further question. Without recording the last 'digression', he asks a different question (66) which then yields an adequate statement (69). The first attempt is omitted from the dictation. The recording creates the impression of a smooth test situation and some kind of narrative interview, only requiring a few selected impulses for making the applicant respond in length and without hesitation or confusion.
- *Standardised rewriting of the question:* Instead of the question that was asked (38–40), a question-standard is dictated – in this case, only a reference to a given invitation to talk (42). The reader is expected to deduce the question from the reply. The record only indicates that at this point some 'further question(s)' was/were asked that triggered the respective answer. However, the questions are turned irrelevant here. The impression is fostered that the test situation is driven by merely smooth stimuli, followed by 'free' responses. In this style of recording, questions are not forceful or even deceptive.
- *Extending monosyllabic reactions to full sentences:* This operation is a special variant of the monologisation. The transcript shows that a mere 'yes' or 'no' (69) is sufficient to provoke a full narrative sentence (70). The officer's closed question provides the basis for this extension. It adds to the narrative by adding up brief responses to lists of routine questions.

- *Disambiguating replies:* Furthermore, narrative sentences are supplemented with information the officer considers as established (66). The officer's dictation turns a conjecture into a statement ("I travelled on my own."). Note that he only heard that the applicant "should take a train" (61), not that he did.

The modifications of the interpreter's deliveries altogether result in the following recording:

Asked about the exact travel route

R: On the 26th of February XXXX I left Egypt. I departed by plane. I left with a forged passport. I arrived in France, but I do not know where.
Q: What made you realize that you had arrived in France?
R: I did not know that I was in France, but I was told so. Then, when I moved on and was already in Germany, I thought that I was still in France.

Upon further questioning

R: When I arrived in France, a man was waiting there for me, who had a description of me. I do not know whether this man was a trafficker. This man then took me to Germany. This man told me that I was in France and that I should take a train. Apart from that, he did not talk to me at all. He did not travel with me on that train. I travelled on my own.

The combined modifications create a coherent 'statement by the applicant'. Questions, reactions, clarifications, and responses are strung together in one sequence. This produces a comprehensible and concise narrative section that can be fully ascribed to the applicant as author.

In the following extract from a later phase in the hearing, we find a set of rather different modifications. The modifications that guide talk into text aim for a different generalised reader's impression:

O # Next line question colon have you lost anything else on the way apart from your passport and the ticket question mark
A #~~~~
I* <I have lost my bag here in Germany

O ( ) Aha, what was in it?
I* <~=~~~~~~~~~~~~~~~~~
O I have lost my bag here in Germany
A #~~~~~~~~~~~~~~~~
I* <I was inside a phone box
O no I didn't want to know how it happened. I wanted to know what was in it
I* Yes
O #Were there any documents inside?
I* <~~~~~~
A <~~
I* <a passport was inside
O <Mhm, other than that, anything?
A <~~~~~~~~~~~~~~~~~~~~~
O <comma my passport was inside
I* <and the photos of my children and my wife
O <and the photos of my children and my wife dot Any other documents?
I* <~~~~~~~
A <~~~=~~
O *Other than that comma there were* no documents inside dot and you haven't lost anything else?
I* <~~~~~~
A <~~~
O I did not lose anything else dot next line question colon But what happened then with the flight ticket and the boarding pass question mark
I* <~~~~~~~
A <~~=~~~~~~~~~~
O [rewinds] *But what happened then with the flight ticket and the boarding pass question mark*
I* #The ticket =was
O *The* ticket was
A ~~~~~~~~~
I* #inside the passport
O <inside the passport dot Errm ( ) [very fast, more quietly] question colon Why did you not tell me that before comma I asked you several times comma after all comma what other documents you have lost question mark
I* <~~~~~~~
A <~~~~~~~~
I* <I didn't know what the question aimed at
O ( ) You even mentioned =the photos of your children I did not know what the question aimed at dot
A ~~~~~~~~~~~~~~~~~

O ( ) Mhm, well all right, you just said you lost these things, earlier you said they were stolen from you, so which one is it?
I* ( ) ~~~~~=~~~~
O *Next line* Presentation colon Earlier you have said that the documents were stolen from you comma now you have said throughout that you lost them comma now which one of these is true question mark
A #~~~~~~=~~~~
I* *I'm* not sure whether they've been stolen from me
O I am not sure whether they have been stolen from me dot

In a first phase (1–26) we find, once again, the set of modifications that gear the interview towards a monologue for the record. The questions regarding the contents of the bag (5), the specification of other documents potentially carried along (12), a concluding question (16), and two further questions (20, 23) are omitted in the record. Moreover, the officer strings the responses together, thus producing one coherent and uninterrupted statement.

After this 'doing monologue' the final revision shifts into a different style, performed by another set of modifications that guide the reader's attention to the applicant's reactions and on the officer's evaluations of those reactions. It is now the interviewee in his or her role as a challenged 'interested' applicant that is focal for the recording. Here are the modifications that accomplish this amplification:

- *Depicting a need for clarification*: After concluding the applicant's monologue with a *résumé*, the officer dictates an additional request (26 sq.). The subsequent reply does not appear in the record as a move in the narrative, but as an attempt at clarification. The initial question is later (30) freed from 'hasty conclusions' (that the documents in question actually existed at some point in time). The officer's test is performed as reasonable and adequate. An entitled applicant should be able to provide an answer.
- *Depicting the applicant's pressure of substantiation*: While the first combination neutralised or even neglected the conduct of the conversation, the latter is rather emphasised and amplified here. The applicant's attempt to resolve the issue is deemed insufficient by the officer with the next recorded question (35 sq.). The officer verbalises the insufficiency of the applicant's test performance by foregrounding earlier questions that he could have answered 'correctly' (36). Thus, the applicant's follow up reaction is framed as just another attempt to repair inconsistencies.
- *Recording 'meaningless' responses*: The applicant defends his 'insufficient' responses so far with a general reference to the fact that he did not realise what the question aimed at (39 sq.). Later, a further 'empty reply' (50 sq.) makes it into the record ("I am not sure..."). Whereas ambiguous exchanges were clarified in the first part, any hint towards

insufficient responses that would allow for inferences of not-knowing is highlighted in this part of the record.

- *Reinforcing a question*: For the record, a question is reformulated by referring to two incompatible positions (43 sq.) which result from contrasting the applicant's active and reactive statements. Apparently, the applicant first says one thing and then another. While the officer's contributions were previously omitted or standardised, here they are reinforced in order to demonstrate 'the contradiction'. The question was not asked this strongly and confrontational in the interview. The applicant, thus, was not warned that he may have offered a weak point or flaw.
- *Emphasising the current assessment status*: Here, questions are furnished with an indication of the assessment status. The term "presentation" (46) shows the reader which assessment phase is being applied at this point of the interview. It marks the revelation of a contradiction. The following response is measured against the question whether it is capable of eliminating the discrepancy. The next passage in the record will be about whether the applicant succeeds in this or not. We can take this as another strategically formulated indication for the generalised reader how to make sense of what follows.

The analysed hearing transcripts contain two systematic combinations of modifications that push the recording in opposite directions. The one combination or style produces the impression of a self-contained narration, whereas the other emphasises the effort that goes into formulating questions for the interview; the one style supplements the applicant's phrases with what seems rather obvious, whereas the other style carefully scrutinizes minor gaps and inconsistencies in the applicant's answers; the monologue style in the first phase omits vagueness, whereas the confrontational style of the subsequent second phase displays any kind of 'failed' explanation. Apparently, the second phase rests on the narration. It determines whether a statement can be weakened or not, whether it receives reasonable doubts or not.

The modifications, when properly combined, open up representation potentials for the record-keeper. The official can demonstrate how her or his interview is actually efficient in generating 'fact-based' decidability. In the following section I examine which kind of representation the record *systematically* aspires to. To this end, I extend the analysis of the transcript to all VRs. What combination of styles is used in each and every hearing record in order to warrant the hearing procedurally/legally valid? The sequence of recording styles is geared towards the refutability of the asylum application.

Developing and securing explanatory power in hearing records

The combinations of modifications separate the hearing into two phases: a monological and a confrontational phase. Independently of the modifications required, these phases can be found in all records of hearings[12]. The standard for 'doing procedure' prepares any passage in the first half of the VR to the officer's usages of those passages in the second phase of the hearing. What is more, the first half shields the VR against the applicant's attempts to undermine later 'confrontational' usages. The second part of the record-keeping accumulates potential reasons to reject the applicant's version. It emphasises the officer's doubts. Both parts together produce decidability.

The first schema accentuates that the applicant's statements are 'being uttered freely' and thus produces a special grounding for all procedural purposes. I want to refer to this grounding as the *ceremony of testing*:

- *The record depicts the applicant as capable of representing her or his interests.* In the preface to the record, statements that describe the applicant as capable of participating in the hearing – with regard to her or his health, her or his knowledge of the procedure (legal instructions) and her or his articulation (translation) – are obligatory. This export warranty can invalidate later excuses and exclude alternative interpretations. However, it is not sufficient to deal with these general standards in an introductory fashion only. Rather, they require further confirmation over the course of the record: the applicant's fitness to participate, for example, reveals itself in a certain willingness to narrate. This willingness is emphasised by undoing interruptions. Once the applicant is deemed capable of dealing with the situation, its specific conditions can be blocked out. The testing by the asylum hearing is treated as an objective experiment that is sufficiently introduced by its norms.
- *The applicant's statements are ,self-explanatory'.* The monologue style heightens the value of recorded utterances in so far "the criterion of non-direction" (Merton and Kendall, 1948, p. 545) is fulfilled. In the social sciences, this criterion is considered as a characteristic of non-directive interview methods. Questions are reliable since they just perform the interview protocol, no matter the current situation and its participants. Not only when substantiating the asylum entitlement but whole sub-narratives about single episodes of the flight, the persecution, political activities, etc. are depicted as being 'told freely' in one go. Alongside the aforementioned monologisation, the excessive invitation to narrate constitutes another means of framing: "Please describe the last distribution of pamphlets in full detail. Leave nothing out." or "Can you please tell me now – in all its particulars and without missing anything – how you were enlisted." The applicant is not actually expected to provide all details imaginable without any omissions. The pointedness signals what this is all about: the answer that follows should be understood as a freely chosen, unconditioned presentation by the applicant. This is the fictional basis for the ceremony of testing.
- *The record confers unambiguous, immediate truth claims.* The assessable explanatory power of statements is not only the result of the monologue style. I have shown that the individual contribution also appears in the

record as an unambiguous, immediate truth. *Unambiguous* means here: the contribution must present a claim to truth which can be proven wrong or right. Qualifying additions ("perhaps…", "I'm not sure but…" or "I was told that I…") are modified and altered into strict specifications ("I was there!", "It was at…", "Then, I went…"). *Immediate* means: not knowing derived from the lack of experience (as a refugee), but only one's own experience must count as valid. Only the latter generates material that is suited to evaluating the statement and justifying the finding. The applicant is, thus, attached to strong truth claims in order to be able to turn them into detectable lies and deceit.

- *In the record, the applicant is granted her or his right to be heard.* The monologue style is crucial in order to substantiate the asylum entitlement. What is displayed is not only that the applicant expressed himself in the form of a narrative but also that he had the opportunity to deliver the intended conclusion of this narrative: that she or he actually *is* a political refugee and deserves the state's asylum. The conditions for this conclusion are presented as ideal, since the monologue unfolds beyond time constraints and impatience[13]: the invitation to narrate is followed by the interviewee's narration; the phase is closed by the officer's last invitation complemented by a concluding statement.

Q: Why have you left Iraq and claimed asylum in Germany?
A: I was forced to join the army. My brother has been in the army for seven years. Actually, he should have been discharged from the army in 1991, but he hasn't been discharged yet. They have arrested my father and then they took me. When we got home, they searched our house and took my army book. They said they would take me to the army. They took my army book away. I still had this, what is it called, this document. Then I packed my things and went to Zacho. From Zacho I then came here.

Q: Are these all the reasons for your asylum claim?
A: Yes.

The applicant was, according to the performed sequence of styles, given unrestricted opportunity to express himself; he or she was granted a 'hearing in accordance with the law'. Whatever is not said here 'even so', does not have to be considered further on – unless it constitutes facts not known yet to the applicant at the time of the hearing. Entering facts ex post is restricted by certain doubt-provoking presumptions that rather highlight contradictions than offering remedy.[14]

- *The officer-in-the-record is fair and impartial*: The narrative schema depicts the officer as fair. The officer erases those utterances that could reveal a prejudice: early 'hunches' expressed to the interpreter or sociologist ("He isn't one!"), rants about "another standard story!", amusement about individual episodes, a bored follow-up question or rhetorical questions ("Are you serious!"). This 'background music' could give the impression that the officer had not approached the case with the adequate seriousness, the required impartiality, and necessary conscientiousness. The officer as she or he appears in the record complies 'in any case' with this procedural decorum.

The first style describes the *freedom of speaking for her- or himself* which the 'applicant-in-the-record' enjoys. The applicant enjoyed the unrestricted right to be heard by the representative of the state. The confrontational style depicts any *doubt* of the officer-in-the-record as *justified*:

- The officer-in-the-record should doubt the submissions: The fair, unprejudiced officer is, nonetheless, required to critically question the applicant's submissions, to test and confront them with doubts. The officer should appear in the record in this way: as professionally doubting. Unsuitable are doubts that the officer would express initially or prematurely. The officer-in-the-record should not give the impression to actually be biased, prejudiced, or even racist. In this style, sceptical questions are asked only on the grounds of the 'free-flowing narrative', that is, as follow-up and additional questions[15] to the statements piled up following the first 'descriptive' schema. Doubts, thus, demonstratively refer back to particulars of statements deriving from the 'free narration':

  You have said that you had an army book. Where did you get that?
  You have said that your father was arrested. When did that happen?
  You have said that you attended school for three years. What is the name of the school that you attended?

  In order to place doubts, the officer would rephrase statements 'as narrated'[16]. Such selective references can induce a whole round of sceptical questions, themselves emphasised in the VR following the 2nd procedural schema. As a consequence, the applicant is required to either refute the rephrased statement 'as wrong' or to defend it as 'his own' statement. Once the sceptical question passed, the rephrased statement is validated (once again).
- *The officer's recorded questions are appropriate*: Recorded sceptical questions, furthermore, have to prove their appropriateness by their referencing. Assessments must not, for instance, point at a disorientation of the officer, that he mistook a statement, or that he would alter what has been said. Accordingly, the sceptical questions should effectively bring up gaps, conundrums or even contradictions as recorded above. This maxim is performed by adding to the statements by means of expanding questions before or after inconsistency markers:

1 Have you lost anything else on the way apart from your passport and the ticket?
2 But what happened then with the flight ticket and the boarding pass?
3 Why did you not tell me that before, I asked you several times, after all, what other documents you have lost?
4 Presentation: Earlier you have said that the documents were stolen from you, now you have said throughout that you lost them, which one of these is true?

Initially, a follow-up question is raised, which concludes the narrative episode (1); after that, an inconsistency ("but... then") in the statement is implied; this is followed by a degradation of the explanation attempt (3); finally, the last answer is marked as contradictory (4). By using such question scales, responses are depicted as unusual ("So how have you...?"), incomplete ("And then...?"), in need of explanation ("But who provided him with that much money?"), implausible ("But why should this woman have helped you at all?"/ "Was there no hospital at all?"), vague ("When exactly was that?"), unfounded ("How do you know that?"), meaningless ("What does that even mean?"), or baffling ("You mentioned that you were detained for four months! But for what reason?"). Each question thus delivers its own legitimation – as fair, self-evident, factually justified and the applicant's liability. The statements that go hand in hand with the recorded questions thus fulfil a double function. They evaluate the previous answers *and* signify one's legitimacy to 'question'.

The 'watertight' record is capable of exposing the applicant: At the end of every round of questions we always find the applicant's reaction, which is supposed to 'speak for itself'. Applicants counter emerging contradictions by referring to: a suggested answer, the consequences of which were not clear (yet); a bad translation which distorted the original meaning; a misunderstanding; one's own confusion and nervousness, or a recording error. These 'excuses' are confronted by a record that presents functioning communications and emphasises the opportunities given to the applicant for justifying the asylum claim. The record is immunised against those objections. They call into question the examinee, not the examination.

In this schema, 'evasions' are marked by vagueness and relativisms: "I don't know anymore", "I didn't understand the question", "I didn't say that", etc. Reactions which might hint at the cogency of a doubt are reported. This includes attempts by the applicant to sabotage or avoid the assessment – according to the interpretation in the record: the refusal to give evidence, reading out a prepared written note, or the request of time for consideration. While the strict format of the truth claim governed the applicant's actions, his reactions can also be received differently.

Résumé

With the final revision the officer accrues a series of representational means and requirements. *Vis-à-vis* the hearing and its organisation she or he emerges as the *master of procedure*. She decides what is asked for and what is to be taken as an answer. She is questioner and record-taker at once. This double function enables her to maintain a shielded sphere of production. The record of hearing is, in conclusion, filled with good reasons for the decision. The VR, what is more, secures those reasons against anticipated attacks by the party decided upon – or better: against. The two interrelated styles should secure the production of decidability and its very protection further on. Following the styles, thus, safeguards the bridging of text and talk as the core mechanism of doing procedure, meaning to join power and knowledge. This is how 'the state' operates via its servants vis-à-vis those who seek acknowledgement of certain rights by this state.

With a view to the recording maxims, the officer appears and acts as the *servant of procedure*. He must serve the sequence of styles of (1) letting the applicant 'talk freely' and (2) of phrasing 'reasonable doubt'. This build up is necessary in order to produce good documented reasons for the final decision, or to put differently, to produce decidability – and more so, refutability – in the course of the hearing. Utilising the styles allows the officer to place the applicant's performance at the centre of the examination instead of the officer's contributions implying a certain attitude or even prejudices. The complete record of hearing constitutes a commendation of the procedural assessment as the very basis of the later judgement.[17] This is the basic way by which legal rules are performed here: the hearing is presented as a documented social encounter that inhabits the law 'routinely'.

Bridging text and talk according to the styles produces procedure and, on this basis, decidability. In a nutshell, this is achieved by swallowing the immediate exchanges: the ('in our ears') foreign palaver of the sub-hearing amongst interpreter and applicant, the gazes avoiding and crossing each other, the giving and taking of a cigarette, the tears and trepidation, the turning towards and away from each other, the aggressive and defensive gestures, the struggles to find words and the verbalising.[18] The specialisation and focus on direct speech as well as on the question-answer-game banishes the participants' physical expressions from the test(ed) account. A multitude of impressions remains 'in the air'. Thus, competencies to self-representation that rely on immediacy are thus devalued over the course of putting the exchange into writing (cf. Elwert, 1985, p. 5).

The exchanges serve the recording, not the other way round: The direct exchanges provide the verbatim recording with appropriate 'originals' and 'materials'. The record takes up those 'contributions for the record' by further framing, polishing, and sharpening them. The recording completes the use value of the verbal contributions in procedural terms. "Quotability" is one important property of spoken words that aim to enter the VR. Quotability changes depending on the hearing-phase and its amplification schema of procedural recording.

Recording is a kind of ghost-writing: If we confront the writing efforts that the officer and interpreter have contributed with the completed text of the record, they appear as ghost-writers. Ghost-writers make substantial contributions but bear no responsibility, as their participation remains 'in the dark'. The record swallows the wording efforts, the quibbling, the corrections; all the more effectively it puts a spotlight on the applicant and his case. The recorded questions have a central design function: they determine the status of contributions and comment on the latter. They announce points of reference and points of action. Asking questions plays out as a reading guide for the generalised readership (similar to a voice-over in documentary films): look here, pay attention there, compare x with y. If all goes well, only the examinee and his performance are in the spotlight of the procedure.

Recording follows certain sequential styles in order to carry systematic effects. By applying a monological style followed by a confrontational style this recording produces decidability in line with the ceremony of testing. This ceremony is based on these two steps: an applicant is free to give reasons for being granted the legal status, whereas the officer is obliged to test those reasons impersonally and methodically. On the ground of this ceremony, an applicant can be lawfully granted asylum or being deported. Hence, the ceremony produces decidability, not just in terms of the ability to decide, but as a decision for everybody to accept. The prospect of such general recognition is, however, clouded by the risky mechanisms that rendered the applicant's words effective. An asylum claimant can hardly keep track of how her or his statements are processed further; she or he is separated from the testing methods and testing effects. This loss of control might explain how the record of hearing frequently turns against the very person who is held accountable for it.

Notes

1 Moreover, the micro analysis of record-taking aims at contributing to a reported gap in the sociology of administration and law literature: "While the topics of 'law and language' or 'language in legal texts' have already been studied in detail especially in sociolinguistics, this is not the case with regard to the relevance of the written form" (Hahn, 1997, p. 31, *author's translation*).

2 Luhmann focuses on this transformation in the following passage:

> Often, it (someone's talk, *TS*) is recorded in a language which is no longer that of the speaker but that of the police, the court, the law; or it is retained in memories which are not his own, and it confronts him in the further course of the procedure as an object with which he has to identify himself.
>
> (1969, p. 93, *translation by TS*)

3 Knorr-Cetina approaches the lab "as a recording system aimed at capturing results in writing and at producing permanence and enable circulation, (i.e. effects, *the author*) which are generally associated with the written form. In the

broader sense, it is a system to generate and process signs" (1988, p. 91, *author's translation*). The hearing could be described along these lines.

4 My concern, however, differs from psycholinguistic works on "writing in real time" (Matsuhashi, 1987), on the author's writing rhythms, movements and experiences which are analysed based on video recordings of writing hands (see Eigler, 1994, p. 999; Engert and Krey, 2013).

5 "Studying filtering processes by means of a comparison of transcribed audio recordings of hearings with the written records of hearings then constitutes the first step that can point out record-keeping errors, i.e. transfer deficiencies" (Banscherus, 1977, p. 215, *author's translation*; see Kube, 1979).

6 "The elicitation of a truthful – or at least fruitfully analysable – account essentially requires that the witness is not repeatedly interrupted by record dictation. However, if the record dictation is delayed until the end of the statement, many details which would have been worthy of entering the record are inevitably lost (Bender and Nack, 1995, p. 196 sq., *author's translation*). Audio recording is recommended as a solution to this problem (see also Schubert, 1983). The authors argue that audio recording unburdens the official, provides an accurate representation of the events and is free of the distorting effects of subjectivity and limited receptiveness.

7 Such a research design is adopted in Knauth and Wolff's study of court files: "From an ethnomethodological perspective we examine accounts, fundamentally, not as representations of an objective reality that lies beneath them [...] We are interested in the social reality as emerging through and in these very accounts" (1990, p. 214, author's translation). Or in the programmatic follow-up study on the usage of conversation and documentary analysis: "Written texts are not being discussed here regarding their nature as representation of reality" (1991, p. 48, *author's translation*). In both cases, text production is reconstructed based on the finished texts alone.

8 At times, impressively complex passages are recorded, which are spoken 'off the cuff' without any errors and specifying punctuation marks, dot, comma, and paragraph tags. This requires skill and concentration; accordingly, sometimes corrections are necessary.

9 At times, I* may even make up an answer by the interviewee that nicely fits the interviewer's question and, thus, the record (Bjelic, 1999).

10 Notice that the dictation alters the "we" (15) to an "I" (16). I will analyse those changes from oral to written later on.

11 The preliminary character of her notes resembles that of barristers' note-taking in court (see Scheffer, 2006). The notes do not yet constitute finished material but an internal tool to remember, reconstruct, and script follow up questions.

12 There are parallels to a study of the "rhetoric of records". In their introduction Maanen and Pentland write: "They (records, *the author*) are designed – implicitly or explicitly – to produce an effect in some kind of audience, which itself actively uses records to interpret events. This is not to suggest conscious deceit or cynicism on the part of either record keepers or users [...]. Rather it is simply to acknowledge and open up for analysis the conditions under which organizational records are produced and used" (1994, p. 53; see also Donk, 1992).

13 In fact, the time for hearings rarely exceeds their scheduled length in the context of a day's schedule (of two to three hearings depending on nationality). Important pillars of workflow planning are the lunch break (between 12.30pm and 2pm) and closing time (between 5pm and 7pm). The hearings begin at 9am. All applicants for the day are instructed to attend at 9.00am.

14 These can involve the belated discovery of certain facts (e.g. through calling home, press reports) or the late occurrence of certain conditions (e.g. "post-flight reasons"). Whenever such reasons cannot be submitted or sustained, an

amendment is easily dismissed by the administrative court as an "enhanced claim".

15 This is consistent with the narrative interview. The narrative phase is followed by a phase for follow-up questions (see also Schütze, 1978).

16 This change of subject-matter from narrative to individual statement can be illustrated with a comparison of photographs and films as suggested by Berger and Mohr: "Surprisingly, photographs are the opposite of films. Photographs are retrospective and are received as such: films are anticipatory. Before a photograph you search for *what was there*. In a cinema you wait for what is to come next" (1982, p. 279). The narration should be thrilling, should head towards the ending and thus (should be able to) captivate the audience. In this 'film', the claims are still covered by the story's progression. In order to depict a statement, moments have to be isolated which can then be fixed like a photograph. Isolating enables a detailed examination, distancing and critique.

17 Works on "interrogation strategies" (Holly, 1981) sometimes equate what happens in the record with the unfolding of the interaction. Especially the often stated 'omnipotence' of the interrogator can be traced back to this framing error. Records exist in order to describe an assessment as successfully completed.

18 The inevitable selectivity of putting-into-writing is described by Luhmann:

> Indispensable elements of oral presentation, especially the simultaneous involvement of speaker and listener, the simultaneous utilization of several perceptual media, above all audition and vision, and the use of changes in the tone of voice, gestures, pauses, and the constant possibility of the audience intervening, of "turn-taking", cannot be translated into the form of a written text.
>
> (2012[1997], p. 153)

References

Banscherus, J. (1977) *Polizeiliche Vernehmung: Formen, Verhalten und Protokollierung*, Vol. 7. Wiesbaden: BKA-Forschungsreihe.

Bender, R. and Armin, N. (1995) *Tatsachenfeststellung vor Gericht. Vernehmungslehre*, Vol. 2. München: C.H. Beck.

Berger, J. and Mohr. J. (1982) *Another Way of Telling*. London: Writers and Readers Publishing Cooperate Society.

Bjelic, D. I. (1999) 'Frenching the real and praxeological therapy: An ethnomethodological clarification of the New French theory of media' in Jalbert, P.L. (ed.). *Media Studies: Ethnomethodological Approaches*. Lanham, MD: University Press of America, Inc.

Cambrosio, A., Limoges, C. and Pronovost D. (1990) 'Representing biotechnology: An ethnography of Quebec science policy,' *Social Studies of Science*, 20, pp. 195–227.

Donk, U. (1992) 'Als ob es Wirklichkeit wäre – Die formale Sicherung polizeilicher Beschuldigtenprotokolle' in: Reichertz, J. and Schröer N. (eds.) *Polizei vor Ort*. Stuttgart: Studien empirischer Polizeiforschung, pp. 85–108.

Dupret, B. (2011) *Adjudication in Action. An Ethnomethodology of Law, Morality and Justice*. London: Routledge.

Eigler, G. (1994) 'Methoden der Textproduktionsforschung' in Hartmut, G. and Otto, L. (eds.) *Schrift und Schriftlichkeit: ein interdisziplinäres*.Handbuch, Berlin and New York: De Gruyter, pp. 992–1004.

Elwert, G. (1985) 'Die Verschriftlichung von Kulturen', *Working Paper des Forschungsschwerpunktes Entwicklungssoziologie der Universität* Bielefeld, 55.

Engert, K., and Krey, B. (2013) 'Das lesende Schreiben und das schreibende Lesen. Zur epistemischen Arbeit an und mit wissenschaftlichen Texten', *Zeitschrift für Soziologie*, 42(5), pp. 366–384.

Foucault, M. (2008) *The History of Sexuality*. London: Penguin.

Garfinkel, H. and Sacks, H. (1986) 'Formal structures of practical action' in Garfinkel H. (ed.), *Ethnomethodological Studies of Work*. New York: Routledge, pp. 157–190.

Goffman, E. (1956) *The Presentation of Self in Everyday Life*. Edinburgh: University of Edinburgh Social Sciences Research Centre.

Goffman, E. (1986[1974]) *Frame Analysis: An Essay on the Organization of Experience*. Boston, MA: Northeastern University Press.

Hahn, C. (1997) 'Schrift und Gesetz. Zur sozialen Bedeutung der Aufzeichnung von Rechtsnormen', *Zeitschrift für Rechtssoziologie*, 18(1), pp. 31–53.

Holly, W. (1981) 'Der doppelte Boden in Verhören. Sprachliche Strategien von Verhörenden' in Frier, W. (ed.), *Pragmatik, Theorie und Praxis*. Amsterdam: Rodopi, pp. 275–319.

Knauth, B. and Wolff, S. (1990) 'Realität für alle praktischen Zwecke: Die Sicherstellung von Tatsächlichkeit in psychiatrischen Gerichtsgutachten', *Zeitschrift für Rechtssoziologie*, 11(2), pp. 211–233.

Knorr-Cetina, K. (1984) *Die Fabrikation von Erkenntnis*. Frankfurt a.M.: Suhrkamp.

Knorr-Cetina, K. (1988) 'Das naturwissenschaftliche Labor als Ort der Verdichtung "von Gesellschaft"', *Zeitschrift für Soziologie*, 17(2), pp. 85–101.

Komter, M. L. (2006) 'From Talk to Text: The Interactional Construction of a Police Record', *Research on Language and Social Interaction*, 39(3), pp. 201–228.

Kube, E. (1979) 'Protokollierungsprobleme bei Vernehmungen durch Polizeibeamte', *Archiv für Kriminologie*, 163, pp. 175 ff.

Luhmann, N. (1969) *Legitimation durch Verfahren*. Neuwied and Berlin: Luchterhand.

Luhmann, N. (2012[1997]) *Theory of Society*. Vol. 1. Stanford, CA: Stanford University Press.

Lynch, M. (2002) 'The living text: Written instructions and situated actions in telephonic surveys' in Maynard, O. W., Houtkoop-Steenstra, H., Schaeffer, N.C. and. van der Zouwen, J. (eds.) *Standardization and Tacit Knowledge: Interaction and Practice in the Survey Interview*. New York: Wiley & Sons, pp. 125–150.

Maanen, J. van and Pentland, B.T. (1994) 'Cops and auditors. The rhetoric of records' in Sitkin, S. B. and Bies, R. J. (eds.) *The Legalistic Organization*. London: Sage, pp. 53–90.

Matsuhashi, A. (1987) *Writing in Real Time: Modelling Production Processes*. Norwood, NJ: Ablex Publishing.

McAdam, J. (2012) *Climate Change, Forced Migration, and International Law*. Oxford: Oxford University Press.

Merton, R. K. and Kendall, P. L. (1946) 'The Focused Interview', *American Journal of Sociology*, 51(6), pp. 541–557.

Scheffer, T. (2006) 'The micro-formation of criminal defense. On the barrister's notes, speech-production, and a field of presence', R*esearch on Language and Social Interaction*, 39(3), pp. 303–342.

Scheffer, T. (2007) 'Event and process. An exercise in analytical ethnography', *Human Studies*, 30, pp. 167–197.

Scheffer, T. (2018) 'Spielarten der Trans-Sequentialität. Zur Gegenwartsdiagnostik gesellschaftlicher Problembearbeitungskapazitäten entwickelt aus Ethnographien staatlicher Verfahren' in Gießmann, S. and Röhl, T. (eds.) *Materialität der Kooperation. Reihe. Medien der Kooperation.* Wiesbaden: Springer VS, pp. 331–357.

Scheffer, T. (2020) 'Existentielle Probleme, soziologisch', *Zeitschrift für theoretische Soziologie* (ZtS), forthcoming.

Scheffer, T. (2010) *Adversarial Case-making. An Ethnography of English Crown Court Procedure.* Amsterdam: Brill.

Schubert, O. (1983) 'Die Protokollierung' in Schubert, O. (ed.) *Die Vernehmung im Ermittlungsverfahren: ein praktischer Ratgeber für Polizeibeamte und Hilfsbeamte der Staatsanwaltschaft*, pp. 101–124. Karlsfeld bei München: Jüngling, pp. 101–124.

Schütze, F. (1978) 'Strategischer Interaktion im Verwaltungsgericht – eine soziolinguistische Analyse zum Kommunikationsverlauf im Verfahren zur Anerkennung als Wehrdienstverweigerer' in Hoffmann-Riem, W. et al. (eds.) *Interaktion vor Gericht.* Baden-Baden: Nomos, pp. 67–156.

Smith, D. E. (1985) 'Textually mediated social organisation', *International Social Science Journal*, 99, pp. 59–76.

Smith, D. E. (2000) 'Writing the social: Critique, theory and investigations', *Revue Canadienne de Sociologie et d' Anthropologie*, 37(3), pp. 368–370.

Suresh, M. (2019) 'The 'Paper Case': Evidence and narrative of a terrorism trial in Delhi', *Law & Society Review*, 53(1), pp. 173–201.

Töpfer, A.-K. (1990) *Das Verfahren zur Feststellung des politischen Verfolgtseins vor dem Bundesamt für die Anerkennung ausländischer Flüchtlinge, Freie Wissenschaftliche Arbeit zur Erlangung des akademischen Grades ,Diplom-Sozialwirtin' an der Wirtschafts- und Sozialwissenschaftlichen* Fakultät der Friedrich-Alexander-Universität Erlangen-Nürnberg.

White, G. (2011) *Climate Change and Migration: Security and Borders in a Warming World.*Oxford: Oxford University Press.

Zimmerman, D. H. (1969) 'Record-keeping and the intake process in a public agency', in Wheeler, S. (ed.) *Files and Dossiers in American Life.* New York: Russell Sage Foundation, pp. 319–355.

Zolberg, A. R., Suhrke, A., Aguayo, S. (1989) *Escape from Violence. Conflict and the Refugee Crises in the Developing World.* Oxford: Oxford University Press.

8 Craft skills and legal rules

How Australian magistrates make bail decisions[1]

Max Travers

In at least one criminal court in the USA, the discretion exercised by judicial officers in making bail decisions has been replaced by computer programs that recommend outcomes from risk scores (Livni, 2017). Although we should not expect similar initiatives in other countries any time soon, those concerned about terrible offences committed by defendants who are at-large on bail,[2] or seeking to save costs, are considering alternatives to the current system.

The paper will start by comparing how the use of rules has been understood in the field of jurisprudence, from the perspectives of legal realism and the sociological tradition of ethnomethodology. It is written for a general readership concerned about fairness and justice in the same way as early ethnomethodological research about criminal courts (for example, Sudnow, 1965). Employing this approach, the central part of the paper presents empirical data obtained through observing bail applications in Australian magistrates courts, and explicates the practical, interpretive methods in applying these legal rules.[3] The third part of the paper will consider the extent to which judicial discretion can be controlled through legislation. Magistrates apply tests that make it more difficult to obtain bail, yet they still exercise discretion. The conclusion will review the implications for those advancing philosophical arguments about legal practice, and for current debates about bail policy.

Ethnomethodology and judicial discretion

A variety of disciplines seek to improve our understanding of law as a social institution. Many studies in the interdisciplinary field of law and society see the value of mixing together ideas from different frameworks and even entire disciplines, and assume that this can be done easily. This section will explain the similarities and differences between the realist tradition in jurisprudence and ethnomethodological research on law. The focus is on how each tradition understands and attempts to research legal rules.

Legal realism

Legal realism is a movement in legal thought that emerged in opposition to the philosophical view of law as a formal system presented by the late nineteenth-century establishment in law schools (Hunt, 1978; Twining, 1973). Legal realism was active between the 1920s and 1960s through three generations of thinkers. The early realists included Oliver Wendell Holmes (1841–1935), and Roscoe Pound (1870–1964). The best known later realists were Karl Llewellyn (1893–1962) and Jerome Frank (1889–1957). The law and society movement that brought together law and different social scientific disciplines starting in the 1960s, and subsequently the critical legal studies movement in legal philosophy, were both influenced by realism (Garth, 1998). Legal realism also was a political movement, since some proponents used ideas associated with it to argue for changes in legal education and the law itself (Pound, 1910). The central focus, as in jurisprudence more generally, is how to understand the legal rules applied or made by judges in the higher courts.

There are two elements to legal realism: rule scepticism and fact scepticism (Hunt 1978). Prior to the ascendancy of the realists, it was common to present judges as following case precedents and rules mechanically or scientifically. Christopher Langdell (1826–1906) promoted the view, as Dean of Harvard Law School from 1870 until 1895, that each new decision logically followed from underlying principles in the development of the relevant body of law. Accordingly, judicial officers followed established or pre-existing rules.[4] By contrast, Holmes (1881) as a rule sceptic argued that judges in the higher courts could make rules, as well as follow them, through drawing on different precedents and distinguishing facts. Llewellyn (2009) employed this approach to undermine the claims made by legal philosophers about the supposed objectivity of law.[5] Frank (2009) extended the approach to considering how decisions about facts were made by trial courts.

Investigating rule-use

Ethnomethodology developed as a research program in the late 1960s, some years after the legal realists advanced their critique of formalism.[6] There are several strands of enquiry, but the best-known research studies are ethnographies that investigate occupational practices in detail.[7] The field of conversation analysis originates in the work of Harvey Sacks developed in the 1960s and '70s and has become the larger tradition. A key theoretical argument made in early ethnomethodology was that human activities are not determined by following rules. Theoretical statements directed against Parsons include an essay by Thomas Wilson (1971) distinguishing the "normative" (rule-governed) and "interpretive paradigms". There are also empirical studies that advance this critique through examining different kinds of rule-following. These include Harold Garfinkel (1984a) on following coding rules, Don Zimmerman (1971) on a welfare agency, and D. Lawrence Wieder (1974) on the convict code in a half-way house for drugs offenders. In these empirical studies, ethnomethodologists focused on settings in which rules were explicitly employed in guiding actions. They recognised an indeterminate number of interpretive methods employed in accomplishing the objective character of any social setting that cannot be captured by understanding members as following rules.

Ethnomethodology is distinctive in recognising that even the most technical activities rely on common-sense methods and knowledge. One such method for making sense of factual information is what Garfinkel (1984) identified as the "documentary method of interpretation" (he adapted a concept used by Karl Mannheim). For Garfinkel, it is not a specialised method for scholars, but one used by virtually "everyone" including judges or juries making sense of evidence to reach a finding of fact in a legal case. Similarly, everyone employs an "ad hoc" method that Garfinkel (1984a, pp. 20ff.) called "Let it pass" when making a decision without adequate information. Judges often have to reach decisions quickly by drawing on imperfect information. In bail decisions, their burden is eased by not having to give systematic, structured reasons (or any reasons) for their decisions. "Everyone" also inevitably and unavoidably has to rely on our shared common-sense knowledge in assessing factual information (Garfinkel, 1984a).

Some ethnomethodologists, most notably Wes Sharrock and his collaborators (for example, Sharrock and Anderson, 1984; Sharrock and Dennis, 2008; Greiffenhagen and Sharrock, 2009), and also Michael Lynch (1993), have discussed rules as a central example in advancing a Wittgensteinian critique of conventional social science. This critique combats "skepticist" readings of Wittgenstein on how we understand and apply rules (Lynch, 1993, chap. 5), and advances an anti-foundationalist response to the "cognitivist edifice" in the human sciences (Sharrock and Dennis 2008: 35).

There are four sociological insights that one can obtain about legal practice from this Wittgensteinian literature. Firstly, it recognises that there are many types of rules which are part of complex "language games" (Sharrock and Dennis, 2008, p. 46). Secondly, it recognises that rules, once learnt, are "followed blindly" in the sense that practitioners do not reflect on the established practices they use for following them (Sharrock and Dennis, 2008; Greiffenhagen and Sharrock, 2009). Thirdly, it argues that not every activity involves following rules. As analysts, we can over-use the concept. Fourthly, it argues that rules cannot be understood in any general sense, but are learnt through participation in specific practices:

> *Part* of portraying an activity may well involve portraying rule-governed or rule-guided aspects of it, and even identifying the rules that the activity involves, but it should not be supposed that these are tasks *for the philosopher* or *the sociologist*.... This is, of course, the very thing that participants in the activity themselves must do".
>
> (Sharrock and Dennis, 2008, p. 46; emphasis in original)

This observation is part of a philosophical critique of conventional theorising in social science. It invites empirical investigations by ethnomethodologists into practices in different occupations that may involve following rules. It strengthens the philosophical foundations of ethnomethodology, but leaves much work for describing practices in a variety of occupational settings.

Legal realism and ethnomethodology

There is no direct way to connect debates between realists and formalists in law with Wittgensteinian arguments about science or mathematics. There is some similarity between realist arguments about the indeterminacy of legal rules with the "skepticist" reading of Wittgenstein in the sociology of science (Sharrrock & Anderson, 1984).[8] One difference is that the arguments advanced by realists could be viewed as part of legal practice, or as part of political debates about law.[9] This can be contrasted with purely philosophical debates about science or mathematics that do not affect or concern practitioners. Otherwise, legal realism and ethnomethodology have something in common in advancing a constructionist, sociological view of law that can be contrasted with legal formalism, and also with structural sociological accounts in which there is less focus on decision-making. They share an interest in how judicial officers understand and interpret legal rules in case-by-case judgements.

Bail decision-making

The next section of this paper is an ethnomethodological analysis of how magistrates make bail decisions. It is unusual in this setting to find these judicial officers discussing or openly interpreting legal rules. The legal rules offer guidance on making decisions, but also give magistrates considerable discretion. Nevertheless, these legal proceedings take place within a legislative framework.[10] They offer what Garfinkel calls a "perspicuous" setting for investigating judicial discretion.

There are no rules on how to conduct an ethnomethodological study about legal practice, although Garfinkel (1984a) recommended certain study policies, including that one should treat any fact or social phenomenon as an accomplishment. Conversation analytic studies are concerned with explicating conversational rules, including the specialised turn-taking system in courts. Ethnographic studies often demonstrate how practitioners, through their practical and interpretive work, maintain a set of sequential procedural rules (for example, Lynch, 1997; Burns, 2000). However, conceptual elaboration in terms of rules is not taken too far in analysing legal decision-making.

Most of Garfinkel's (1984b) study of jurors does not explicitly refer to rules, but describes how jurors draw on common-sense knowledge in establishing the facts of a case. But one could argue that the communicative and interpretive methods in establishing facts were employed by jurors in applying legal rules. In this spirit, the following analysis of bail applications examines the interpretive work of identifying facts and applying legal statutes. It explicates some of the situated methods and knowledge that constitute exercising judicial discretion.

An ethnographic study

This study was conducted over thirty days, in 2014–2015 and 2017–2018, in metropolitan courts in the four Australian States of Tasmania, South Australia, Victoria and New South Wales.[11] There is a comparative element to the project in that legislation differs between the States, and there is also a significant difference in the remand rate as measured by the Australian Bureau of Statistics: Victoria had a lower remand rate until recently.[12] The researchers conducting this project found, unsurprisingly, that in any magistrate's court, decisions are made through employing similar methods and considerations.

The rules relating to bail varied between the four States. This is significant if one is working as a lawyer in a particular jurisdiction. However, practitioners acknowledged that, despite differences in terminology and even in legal tests between States, there was largely the same purpose and content. This is evident when you consider that, in Tasmania, there has so far been no legislation on bail, and the criteria are set down in the common law case *R v Fisher*.[13] The criteria are what you might expect: the magistrate is asked to consider, through weighing up relevant factors, whether the defendant is likely to attend the next hearing or commit offences while at-large on bail. Similar criteria are set out explicitly in bail statutes. Here, for example, are some of the factors to be considered in determining whether there is an "unacceptable risk" under the Bail Act 1977 in Victoria:[14]

> (3) In assessing in relation to any event mentioned in subsection (2)(d)(i) whether the circumstances constitute an unacceptable risk the court shall have regard to all matters appearing to be relevant and in particular, without in any way limiting the generality of the foregoing, to such of the following considerations as appear to be relevant, that is to say -

a the nature and seriousness of the offence;
b the character, antecedents, associations, home environment and background of the accused;
c the history of any previous grants of bail to the accused;
d the strength of the evidence against the accused;
e the attitude, if expressed to the court, of the alleged victim of the offence to the grant of bail;
f any conditions that may be imposed to address the circumstances which may constitute an unacceptable risk.

In making laws in the higher courts, judges select and distinguish cases in order to achieve what they see as a legally correct or just outcome. In bail applications, magistrates exercise even greater discretion. They have complete freedom in weighing up the criteria and bail conditions for managing risk. They can, for example, give second or third chances after breaches. In contrast to decisions made in the higher courts, magistrates are not required to give reasons. A bail decision is not appealed. Instead, defendants can make a fresh application to a higher court.

In any bail application, the magistrate is required to establish the relevant facts, and apply a legal test about risk, assuming that the risk can be managed by an appropriate condition. In many applications, the prosecutor has to demonstrate that there is an "unacceptable risk". In others the defendant has to satisfy the magistrate that there is a low level of risk, or that the risk can be managed. There is, however, no technical discussion of the law in these hearings. Each magistrate hears submissions, establishes and weighs up the various factors, considers if the risk can be managed, and reaches a decision. Here it is helpful to look at an actual example of decision-making. The application was heard in Tasmania:

Application 1[15]

LA: He is pleading Not Guilty. The Prosecution are opposing bail.
M: I'll hear the grounds of opposition.
P: [Reading extracts from the police summary] Your Honor, there
are section 12 grounds. Previous convictions have been admitted.
There is a history of taking cars... and drink driving. ... My point
in bringing it up is to show there is a drink problem for this
defendant. The events of [ ]. The defendant is 27 years old and
lives at [ ]. He was living with [ ]. He moved to Tasmania from
Queensland and they have been living together for 3 months.
On [ ] they had an argument about his employment. ... The
defendant arrived home at 11.30pm intoxicated. He woke her up
saying she was "a fucking cunt, a fucking whore". She said she
did not want to be in the relationship. He held her on the throat
so it hurt. He pushed her into the stairwell and caused her to
hurt her head. ... The defendant again grabbed the victim by
the throat and squeezed the throat. The defendant only stopped
when two neighbors came over. The defendant closed the door on
them. The witnesses called the police.
[The defendant was taken to the police station, and charged
and bailed the next day after he had sobered up, under a police
Family Violence Order.]
The police attended the victim the next day. The defendant was
within 50 meters and so arrested and taken to the police station.
Your Honor, there was a Family Violence Order and he breached
it so he needed to be remanded under section 12. He plans to
move to Launceston so he might not answer to bail. There is no

surety. He cannot satisfy section 12. That is my submission.

M: Miss Wood.

LA: Mr. Roberts has been a chef the last three years, employed in different states in Australia. He is in reasonable good health. He had medication for [ ]. My instructions are that this was a brief relationship .... Mr. Roberts was recently offered the position of a chef in Launceston. He plans to move to Launceston tomorrow. We are trying to contact the restaurant owner. There was a breach but the police were present at the time. In any case he could attend with the police to retrieve his belongings.

M: He does not have a surety, I presume.

LA: No. There is the employer [who could be a possible surety].

M: [Two minutes of thought, with hand on chin]. I recognize this as being partly on the borderline and I'm frankly unclear on whether section 12 justifies remanding in custody or to put it another way justifies being bailed. So I'm going to adjourn the matter for a period of time for two reasons. One reason is, if there is no surety, it is important I receive confirmation of this. It is also confirmation that the defendant really is going to be employed and more important I receive that he is going to be living in accommodation in Launceston. ... If it were only the first reason, it could be done at 2.15. For the other points I need [documentary proof]. So we should meet at 9.45am Court 3 on [ ] for further submissions.

LA: Legal Aid lawyer, M: magistrate; P: prosecutor.

Establishing the facts

The magistrate heard submissions on risk from the defence and prosecution. The prosecution case was that there was some risk of harm to the complainant who alleged that she had been assaulted. However, there was apparently no medical report about injuries. The defendant was contesting the charge, but his version of events was not presented to this court, possibly because the lawyer did not want to reveal the defence case.[16] There was a breach of the Family Violence Order imposed immediately following the alleged assault (lines 24–25), but this was not an act of violence. After being released from custody, the defendant approached the complainant, breaching the fifty metres limit imposed by the order, while police officers were present.

The risk potentially would be reduced if the defendant could show that he was living in Launceston (lines 33–34). To understand the relevance of this possible move to Launceston requires local knowledge. Launceston is a three-hour drive from Hobart. Moreover, in terms of local geography, it is viewed as a long drive on a demanding road. It is difficult to know from these remarks whether this was the key factor that made this a "borderline" case, or whether offering a surety would be enough to reduce the risk of further offending (line 37). Normally, a surety is offered by a family member or friend who pays money into court that would be forfeited if the defendant fails to attend the hearing. The defence lawyer offered to approach the new employer, although perhaps neither the lawyer nor the magistrate expected that the defendant would obtain a surety.

The prosecutor made two submissions that were ignored by the magistrate, and which did not even result in a response by the Legal Aid lawyer.[17] It was suggested that, although the defendant had not committed previous offences relating to domestic violence, he did have a previous offence related to drinking. The magistrate did not, apparently, accept the implication that a drinking problem in itself might result in a violent assault on his partner. The prosecutor also submitted that there was a "flight risk", or rather that if the defendant was living in Launceston there was a risk that he would not attend the next court date in Hobart. This might be seen as a contradictory argument since the defence could respond that moving to Launceston would protect the victim.

Bail decisions do not, therefore, involve a decision-maker being faced with an agreed set of facts. Instead, the magistrate interprets, establishes and selects facts that make possible certain outcomes. The concept of the "occasioned corpus", employed by Don Zimmerman and Melvin Pollner (1971) in another critique of Parsons, is helpful for seeing how facts in legal hearings are products of local interpretive work. They define the occasioned corpus as those "features of socially organised activities which are particular, contingent accomplishments of the production and recognition work of the parties to the activity" (Zimmerman & Pollner, 1971, p. 94). This does not, however, mean that the facts cannot be established. In this application, the defendant was asked to supply documentary proof of the job offer and availability of accommodation in Launceston.

Applying the law

Section 12 of the Family Violence Act 2004 (Tasmania) reverses the burden of proof for defendants charged with offences that relate to domestic violence. They have to persuade the court that victims will not suffer harm if they are granted bail. This might seem a high hurdle, until you realise from observing hearings that fifty percent of applications are allowed (the same acceptance rate for applications that do not involve domestic violence). The magistrate noted that the application was "partly on the borderline". This is not an objective assessment of the risk. It is rather an indication of how this particular magistrate approached decision-making. The meaning is not clear, however. An observer who has not seen the magistrate decide other cases would not know how such borders are identified. What is clear is that the magistrate was collecting information methodically. There was a two-minute pause while the magistrate deliberated, indicating that each decision required thought. Like other judicial officers, he was required to weigh up the factors he thought relevant to the risk of reoffending and decide whether they could be managed by conditions in a bail order, such as a place restriction. We do not know how the magistrate weighed up each factor, and it is also impossible to predict the outcome of this bail application. Another magistrate might have granted bail even if the defendant was living in Hobart, subject to a place restriction.[18]

Fairness for all practical purposes

In hearing bail applications, magistrates tried to ensure that any custodial remand did not exceed the sentence of imprisonment that was appropriate for the substantive offences. Critics of the bail system have argued that many defendants spend long periods in custody, even though they do not ultimately receive a custodial sentence. There also are defendants who are likely to go to prison. In one case observed, the bail decision was intended to ensure that the time spent on remand did not exceed the anticipated time in prison. This was a rare hearing in which we were able to interview the magistrate about how he came to a decision.

There were two hearings. In the first, the defendant was represented by a Legal Aid lawyer because her own private lawyer, who would not have received payment, could not attend court. The defendant had failed to appear for a hearing, and a warrant had been issued for her arrest. It was suggested that she had not appeared because she was caring for her mother. There was no information available about how she was pleading to a few charges. There was also a suspended sentence from a previous conviction, so if found guilty she would have to spend at least three months in prison. In these circumstances, the magistrate felt it best to keep her in custody overnight in the hope that her own lawyer could attend the next day.

The next day, before the defendant was brought into the court, the magistrate told the defence lawyer that she could spend a long time in prison. He understood that she was caring for her mother but had no further details. He had heard some basic facts, but not much in relation to the different matters.

Application 2

DL: Yes well I can certainly clarify those matters Your Honor.
CC: [The defendant is led into court from the cells]. Trish Gordon? Take a seat.
DL: I appear for Miss Gordon today.
M: Thank you for coming down today. I assume that the defendant is grateful.
DL: The first matter is [ ]. I am instructed Miss Gordon will plead guilty. For the driving offences she will plead guilty. For matter

[ ], she will plead guilty. For the breach of the suspended sentence, my recollection is that was at index 28.
M: Yes it is 4445. So I'll set that aside for the moment.
DL: Matter 29 is a common assault matter. That is a plea of not guilty. In terms of estimated hearing times, I suspect that will be two hours. Index 30 the stealing charge is old. From March 2006 she pleaded not guilty and I'm instructed that that is maintained. What is not apparent from the file is that there is no video footage so whether the prosecution would want to review that. There's an interview [ ] Matter at index 31 there was a previous plea of not guilty. I am instructed to plead guilty to counts 1 and 2 but plead not guilty to the assault on police officer charges. There are not any photos of the alleged injuries. That matter would take a couple of hours. The next matter of unlicensed driving. There will be a plea of guilty. The final matter is index 32 unlawful possessions. This is set for hearing. There are some issues with that matter [ ].
M: Traffic matters.
DL: There are potential subsequent offences punishable by imprisonment. They are noted.
M: They certainly are. What do you want me to do? I'm inclined to give bail. She was on bail, but failed to attend court. There were new matters of X and Y brought to court last time. There were no conditions attached to bail as I recall.
DL: My instructions are that she failed to appear for family issues. [ ] She has a child in care. She has returned to live with her mother who suffers from chronic illness.
M: I think she should be bailed. I say that for no reason other than the matters will take a long time to resolve. I think the defendant's residence seems stable. So I am considering bail before I am not sure if it is opposed or not [Prosecutor indicates there is no objection]. There is no surety. I know that [she faces allegations that would attract a period of imprisonment]. So those are the reasons and it may be I bail for mention on all the matters. One of the matters are from 9 years ago. The Prosecution should look at this. So there are some issues yet to be sorted out and it is not appropriate for her to be in custody.

DL: defence lawyer; CC: court clerk; M: magistrate.

When I spoke to the magistrate after the first hearing, it was still unclear whether or not this defendant would obtain bail. If the matters could be finalized quickly, it made sense to keep her in custody and backdate the sentence of imprisonment. But if, as turned out to be the case, finalizing the matters would take some time, it was "not appropriate" to refuse bail.

In this hearing the magistrate spelt out the reasoning, perhaps because this would help to understand the decision. I was left wondering what might happen if there were more offences whilst on bail. The magistrate gave this reply after the second hearing:

> Well, if there are more offences on bail, she then comes back before someone else as to whether she's re-bailed or not. It becomes quite messy...

One of the issues that magistrates are asked to consider in statutes on bail is the length of time a defendant will spend in custody (lines 36–37), and the likely sentence. However, in this state magistrates were not asked to consider such issues explicitly when making bail decisions. There was also no guidance on how to make an assessment. In this application, the number of charges was unclear, and it was also unclear when the matters would be finalised.[19] For example, it was not even clear if this defendant would be found guilty of a charge that triggered the suspended sentence (lines 9–10). This decision could be seen as orienting to a legal rule ("consider the length of time in custody before trial"). But it also has the character of a craft skill that cannot be learned from legislation, but only from experience in seeking to achieve fair outcomes.

This example illustrates that the formal considerations in statutes recognise the consequences of possible delay in scheduling hearings.[20] It also shows how the magistrate required advice from the right lawyer to make the decision. This defendant had committed numerous offences while on bail. There were various unresolved issues in the defendant's past record, and she would be sent to prison for breaching a suspended sentence. Any decision-maker, whether a police officer or a new magistrate, had to make sense of this prior record when considering a new bail application. Finally, fairness achieved was in ethnomethodological terms "for all practical purposes" (Garfinkel, 1997). To produce a fair outcome, the magistrate was required to work with whatever resources and information were to hand.

Making decisions from within

Ethnomethodology is perhaps most distinctive in revealing how decisions are made in real time within occupational practice. This has similarities with the realist critique of formalism, although realists do not describe judgemental work in much detail. There is still a tendency among legal theorists and law school teachers to see black letter law as a rational activity, based on applying rules to facts. When conducting research, it is easy to assume that, if only there is access to the information in every file, it should be possible to explain decision-making as a response to causal factors. In contrast, when you have the opportunity to spend time with practitioners, it is evident that they often have imperfect and limited information.

On one occasion, I was fortunate enough to accompany a Legal Aid lawyer who was about to take instructions from defendants before a hearing.[21] Each interview was completed under ten minutes. The only information available to the lawyer was a fact sheet for the breach (nothing was known about the original, substantive offence), and a list of prior convictions. It was not clear how long the defendant had been in custody.[22] There were defendants who were homeless and had mental health problems and drug habits. But the lawyer went into court without any details of the history or what medication was currently prescribed. In other cases, there was no time to contact family members who could supply a surety. Yet working together, the practitioners in court quickly made a bail decision with this incomplete information, before moving to the next application. What might be called "low stakes" defendants were released after guilty pleas, with the condition that they seek appropriate medical help, and with the warning that, if they continued to offend, they would be given a custodial sentence.

Legislation and judicial discretion

Magistrates in Australia are criticised by commentators on each side of the law and order debate. Most criticism comes from right wing "shock jocks" and politicians responding to a series of terrible offences committed on bail. Magistrates and states with allegedly soft bail laws are criticised for not protecting the public. It is, however, difficult to assess whether tough bail laws change judicial practices. They may only have symbolic or political value. Two applications illustrate the difficulties.

A "show cause" application

In the legislation in New South Wales, a defendant can be asked to "show cause" in certain circumstances, such as when an "indictable" (more serious) offence had allegedly been committed on bail. This reverses the burden of proof and makes it difficult to obtain bail. The test in the legislation is more complicated in that, if the defendant does "show cause", the prosecution can still seek to prove there is an "unacceptable risk".[23] There is a dual test, which sends a strong message politically that it should be difficult to obtain bail.

In the following application, the defendant had breached a bail condition that required him not to drink in a public place. He was also charged with a new offence of affray, for threatening an officer with a fork. A magistrate accepted the defence argument that the prosecution had over-charged the defendant in order to take advantage of the "show cause" provision:

Application 3

1 DL: Release application
2 P: And detention application. Not to be intoxicated in a public

place.
M: A detention application.
DL: There was a condition of not being intoxicated in a public place. He thought that drinking in a bar was OK. That's all I'd say on that Your Honor.
M: [reads] Yes Mr. Jones.
DL: Yes in relation to the show cause it seems to be a case of common assault. He was holding a fork eight centimeters away there was no physical contact. But the prosecution have laid affray charges that sets off the show cause. An affray charge causes a greater maximum penalty. Certainly in terms of affray it is at the lower end. It was handled by the police officer there and the fork was only taken so he could eat. There are other factors in the antecedents. He is a painter and is not on Centrelink.[24] He owes money on his childcare payments. If he was in custody, this would go away. They are the main factors I would raise to show cause. And also if the offence related to his family, it would be a whole different category.
M: Mr. C. You are charged with affray so there is a show cause provision. Were the situation otherwise it would be a simple common assault. In addition [because you are pleading not guilty to the first substantive charge] you could spend a significant amount of time in custody. On that basis, the court is prepared to come to the view that you have shown cause.
P: Your Honor bail is not opposed. Our concern is the safety of his family. The prosecution will press for a residence condition. Also there should be an alcohol restriction.
[M questions the custody officer about the defendant's address]
DL: I can't say anything on the conditions. The address should be .... We'd ask that the conditions be replicated and perhaps it could be made clear what that means.
M: [writes]
M: Mr. C this matter goes to the [ ] court on 6 June 2017 9.30. There is conditional bail to continue to reside at .... And there is an express condition not to consume alcohol in a public place. This includes pubs and clubs. You can drink in a private dwelling.

In this application, the magistrate quickly accepted the argument on over-charging (lines 21–25), and the prosecutor immediately withdrew his opposition to the bail application. The key reason for the decision stated by the magistrate is that, if the defendant was remanded, he would spend more time in custody than was justified by the original offence (the details were not available to the researchers). The subsequent offence of affray might appear to attract a longer sentence, but the magistrate made it clear that he viewed this as over-charging. Exercising discretion in this application involved both interpreting the law and assessing the factual basis of a charge (it is difficult to separate the two). Although this is only one case, it illustrates that not every magistrate made tougher decisions as a consequence of this law.

The "exceptional circumstances" test

In Victoria, there were considerable concerns about bail, following the Gargasoulas case (see note 1 on "the Bourke Street rampage"). The Coghlan report (2017) recommended that defendants had to supply a "good reason" why they should be granted bail. However, the revised Act requires defendants to demonstrate that there are "exceptional circumstances". One magistrate explained the law to each defendant in uncompromising terms: the only way of satisfying the test would be if you were "diagnosed with a brain tumour". It might appear that, in this State, no one will be granted bail. Even so, there is room for discretion. There were successful applications. One magistrate accepted a combination of circumstances, for example undertaking drug counselling and providing a surety, as satisfying the test.

Conclusion: in defence of discretion

This paper has supplied an account of the work of magistrates making bail decisions that contributes to an under-researched area of legal sociology. It demonstrates the extent of discretion in judicial work, and shows in some detail how this is currently exercised. Although magistrates employ common-sense knowledge and reasoning, they also employ craft skills that can only be learnt and employed in this occupational setting such as how to calculate "reasonable" periods in prison, and how to interpret legislation.[25]

The first part of the paper explained the distinction between legal realism and ethnomethodology. This is difficult because there are few points of contact between the two traditions, partly because their arguments were advanced within different disciplines. I hope to have demonstrated that ethnomethodology offers a coherent alternative to both formalism and rule scepticism, and to the structural bias of contemporary realists (Mertz & al., 2016), through describing in some detail how legal decisions are made. I also hope to have shown that the Wittgensteinian critique of "skepticist" readings of Wittgenstein in the sociology of science and mathematics is relevant to understanding constructionist arguments about legal practice.

An important principle in ethnomethodological research is that one should be "indifferent" to the moral and political questions that interest other sociological traditions (indifferent, not in the sense of callous disregard, but in the selection of cases deemed worthy of intensive analysis). The focus of this paper has been on explicating how magistrates employ discretion, rather than commenting on whether this level of discretion is a good thing. Ethnomethodology as a program, or set of research agendas, has sought to reveal the interpretive practices apparently concealed behind organisational charts and legal rules. There is no political agenda in this program: it can be understood as a debate with other traditions in sociology and legal studies on how to investigate and represent social reality. Nevertheless, ethnomethodological findings can also have political or policy implications. Studies about technology often suggest that new devices or organisational initiatives will not work unless they take account of the social organisation of human practices. This paper on judicial discretion may assist those making policy arguments about bail reform.

Perhaps the most striking finding is the extent to which the current bail system is based on discretion. Employing discretion is experienced as normal, and unavoidable, by those working in courts. This can be demonstrated through descriptive statistics, but is particularly evident when talking to practitioners. Magistrates are untroubled by the possibility that another magistrate might decide the same case differently. It is accepted that some magistrates refuse most applications, and others accept most applications. There are also magistrates who carefully weigh up the factors in each application. Some of the interpretive processes involved in assessing evidence, and applying legal rules to facts, have been described in this paper.

Discretion in bail decision-making involves being given the authority to reach an individualised judgement. It means not being accountable to managers or colleagues, or subject to external controls. Magistrates can interpret the law differently, and they can express different understandings of the facts. This may seem unsatisfactory, given the outcome of a bail application depends on the magistrate making the decision. This was the critique made by legal realists. But an ethnomethodological approach reveals that many magistrates consider evidence carefully, and employ craft skills to achieve what they consider "fair" outcomes.

There are many critics who would like to tame or standardise the unruly human work of bail decisions, and sentencing (Travers, 2012). Those concerned about offences committed while-at-large on bail have already achieved tougher legislation. Those favouring a more generous policy in the USA have sought to influence decisions through actuarial guides based on assessing risk (VanNostrand & Keebler, 2009). Discretion is not removed but displaced into coding decisions by welfare agencies (Castellano, 2011). It seems unlikely that there will be significant reforms that reduce judicial discretion in Australia. Nevertheless, because these arguments are being canvassed, ethnomethodologists can contribute to this policy debate by describing judicial work.

Notes

1 This chapter was previously published in *Ethnographic Studies*, Vol.16 2019, pp. 147–166.
2 A recent example in Australia is what became known as the Bourke Street rampage (McKay & Zervos, 2017). A mentally disturbed offender was granted bail, and the following day drove at speed into a crowded shopping mall, killing five people, including a baby.
3 This approach owes a great deal to my doctoral research in the ethnomethodological studies of work tradition supervised by Wes Sharrock at the University of Manchester in the late 1980s (see Travers, 1997; Travers & Manzo, 1997). Rod Watson has also influenced my work on studying individualised discretion through examining transcripts of legal hearings.
4 It would be a mistake to see this Langdellian view of law as only having historical interest, since "we are all realists now". When I gave my first paper to a law school in the early 1990s, a legal philosopher took the view that the arguments made by different sociological traditions were interesting but only related to the "surface" of legal activities. There were underlying universal principles that law students discover through engaging with different fields of black letter law.
5 For a recent demonstration of the indeterminacy of law that employs similar methods in de-constructing judgements, see Constable (2014), chapter 2.
6 Ethnomethodology developed through Harold Garfinkel's engagement with questions raised by Talcott Parsons on how to explain the orderly nature of society, and with philosophers in the phenomenological tradition, particularly Alfred Schutz. For an overview, see Heritage (1984).
7 For recent studies about judicial work influenced by ethnomethodology, see Dupret (2011) and Geraldo (2015); and for a study about a distinctive French appeals court Latour (2009).
8 In both cases, theorists argue that rule-use depends on external conventions, making possible a relativist argument. Those ethnomethodologists combatting a "mis-reading" of Wittgenstein argue that "rules contain within themselves what comprises compliance with them": in the technical terms of this philosophical argument, there is an "internal relation" between rules learnt in different activities and how they are applied (Sharrock & Dennis 2008, p. 42).
9 It is possible that even John Rawls (1955), whose ideas are discussed in Greiffenhagen and Sharrock (2009), does not sufficiently recognise this aspect of legal practice, exemplified by the realist tradition, when he distinguishes between "two concepts of rules". Most lawyers follow procedures "blindly", but there are also reform movements within law. Some practitioners even question the value of imprisonment.
10 Michael Lynch described the work of judges in managing hearings in a Canadian court. However, he acknowledged that "an analysis from the gallery has an indefinite, and uncertain, relation to the intelligibility of court proceedings for the principal parties" (Lynch, 1997, p. 104).
11 This project about bail decision-making and pretrial services in Australia was funded by the Criminology Research Council in 2017–2019. The investigators were Max Travers, Rick Sarre, Isabel Bartkowiak-Theron, Emma Colvin, Christine Bond and Andrew Day.
12 In 2011, the remand rate per 100,000 in Victoria was 19.6, while in New South Wales the remand rate was 49.1 (Brown, 2013). In 2018, Victoria had the highest remand rate.
13 In common with many judgements, this case from 1964 is not available in a law report or computer data base. Nor is it regularly consulted. When visiting a magistrate, I inquired if it might be possible to see the case. After some searching by an administrator, a typed loose-leaf volume of reported cases in 1964 was located in a store room.

14 For changes following the Bourke St. rampage, see the Bail Amendment (Stage 2) Act 2018 (Vic).
15 All identities in the transcripts are anonymised.
16 It is possible that another lawyer would have done things differently, although this was still a correct submission in the circumstances. See Travers (1997).
17 Not every argument made in submissions is given the same weight or even acknowledged by the magistrate in a summary.
18 Some magistrates in this court would still give a second chance if the defendant breached the place conditions.
19 A case would be finalised when there was a trial date for charges in which the defendant had entered not-guilty pleas, following preliminary hearings to review evidence. This defendant was also pleading guilty to some charges.
20 The only estimate in this hearing was that "the matter would take a long time to resolve".
21 See also Sudnow (1965) and Travers (1997).
22 There was a department in the prison service that had this information, but the line was often engaged.
23 This does not do justice to the complexity of the New South Wales legislation. An attempt by the Attorney General's Office to reduce the number of tests failed after political pressure to strengthen the bail law (Brown, 2013).
24 The welfare benefits agency in Australia.
25 A reviewer suggested that the decision made in application 1 could have been made "in the pub". Even so, a magistrate is making the decision within a legal framework, knowing what is possible with the resources available, and with the skills to address legal and procedural issues if they arise.

References

Brown, D. (2013) 'Looking behind the increase in custodial remand populations', *International Journal for Crime, Justice and Social Democracy*, 12(2), pp. 80–99.

Burns, S. (2000) *Making Settlement Work: An Examination of the Work of Judicial Mediators*. Aldershot: Ashgate.

Castellano, U. (2011) *Outsourcing Justice: The Role of Nonprofit Caseworkers in Pretrial Release Programs*. Boulder, CO: Lynne Rienner.

Coghlan, P. (2017) *Bail Review: Second Advice to the Victorian Government*. Melbourne: Victorian Government.

Constable, M. (2014) *Our Word Is Our Bond: How Legal Speech Acts*. Stanford, CA: Stanford University Press.

Dupret, B. (2011) *Adjudication in Action: An Ethnomethodology of Law, Morality and Justice*. Aldershot: Ashgate.

Frank, J. (2009) *Law and the Modern Mind*. London: Routledge.

Garfinkel, H. (1984a) 'What is ethnomethodology?' in Harold Garfinkel (ed.) *Studies in Ethnomethodology*. Cambridge, MA: Polity, pp. 1–14.

Garfinkel, H. (1984b) 'Some rules of correct decisions that jurors respect' in Harold Garfinkel (ed.) *Studies in Ethnomethodology*. Cambridge, MA: Polity, pp. 104–115.

Garfinkel, H. (1984c) 'Good organisational reasons for bad clinic records' in Harold Garfinkel (ed.) *Studies in Ethnomethodology*. Cambridge: Polity, pp. 186–207.

Garfinkel, H. (1997) 'Practical sociological reasoning: Some features in the work of the Los Angeles suicide prevention center' in Travers, M. and Manzo, J. (eds.) *Law in Action: Ethnomethodological and Conversation Analytic Approaches to Law*. Aldershot: Ashgate, pp. 25–40.

Garth, Bryant. (1998) From legal realism to law and society: Reshaping law for the last stages of the activist social state. *Law and Society Review*, 32(2), pp. 409–472.

Geraldo, P. (2015) 'Practical solutions: Praxeological analysis of judgments in civil hearings' in Dupret, B., Lynch, M. and Berard, T. (eds.) *Law at Work: Studies in Legal Ethnomethods*. New York: Oxford University Press, pp. 63–85.

Greiffenhagen, C. and Sharrock, W. (2009) 'Two concepts of attachments to rules', *Journal of Classical Sociology*, 9(4), pp. 405–427.

Heritage, J. (1984) *Garfinkel and Ethnomethodology*. Cambridge, MA: Polity Press.

Holmes, O.W. (1881) *The Common Law*. London: Macmillan.

Hunt, A. (1978) *The Sociological Movement in Law*. London: Macmillan.

Latour, B. (2009) *The Making of Law: An Ethnography of the Conseil d'Etat*. Cambridge, MA: Polity Press.

Livni, E. (2017) 'In the US, some criminal court judges now use algorithms to guide decisions on bail', *Quartz Media* (28 February). Available at: https://qz.com/920196/criminal-court-judges-in-new-jersey-now-use-algorithms-to-guide-decisions-on-bail/ (accessed 17 February 2019).

Llewellyn, K. (2009) *The Bramble Bush: On Our Law and Its Study*. Oxford: Oxford University Press.

Lynch, M. (1993) 'Wittgenstein, rules, and epistemology's topics' in Lynch, M. (ed.) *Scientific Practice and Ordinary Action: Ethnomethodology and Social Studies of Science*. Cambridge: Cambridge University Press, pp. 159–202.

Lynch, M. (1997) 'Preliminary notes on judges'work: The judge as a constituent of courtroom "hearings"' in Travers, M. and Manzo, J. (eds.) *Law in Action: Ethnomethodological and Conversation Analytic Approaches to Law*. Aldershot: Ashgate, pp. 99–130.

McKay, H. and Zervos, C. (2017) 'Blackburn South woman dies in hospital after Bourke St. rampage', *Herald Sun* (31 January). Available at: https://www.heraldsun.com.au/news/national/blackburn-south-woman-dies-in-hospital-after-bourke-st-rampage/newsstory/80819d24ec868a4b14f35c2bb6df7ebe (Accessed 19 February 2019).

Mertz, E., Macaulay, S. and Mitchell, T. (eds.) (2016) *The New Legal Realism: Translating Law-and-society for Today's Legal Practice*. Cambridge: Cambridge University Press.

Pound, R. (1910) 'Law in books and law in action', *American Law Review*, 44, pp. 12–36.

Rawls, J. (1955) 'Two concepts of rules', *Philosophical Review*, 64(1), pp. 3–32.

Sharrock, W. and Anderson, R. (1984) 'The Wittgensteinian connection', *Human Studies*, 7, pp. 375–386.

Sharrock, W. and Dennis A. (2008) 'That we obey rules blindly does not mean that we are subservient to rules', *Theory, Culture and Society*, 25(2), pp. 33–50.

Sudnow, D. (1965) '"Normal crimes": Sociological features of the Penal Code in a Public Defender Office', *Social Problems*, 12, pp. 255–276.

Travers, M. (1997) 'Persuading a client to plead guilty' in Travers, M. (ed.) *The Reality of Law: Work and Talk in a Firm of Criminal Lawyers*. Aldershot: Ashgate, pp. 93–124.

Travers, M. (2012) *The Sentencing of Children: Professional Work and Perspectives*. Washington, DC: New Academia Press.

Travers, M. and Manzo, J. (eds.) (1997) *Law in Action: Ethnomethodological and Conversation Analytic Approaches to Law*. Aldershot: Ashgate.

Twining, W. (1973) *Karl Llewellyn and the Realist Movement*. Cambridge: Cambridge University Press.
VanNostrand, M. and Keebler, G. (2009) Pretrial risk assessment in the Federal Court. *Federal Probation*, 73(3), pp. 3–28.
Wieder, D.L. (1974) 'Rules as explanations of action' in Wieder, D.L. (ed.) *Language and Social Reality*. The Hague: Mouton, pp. 29–45.
Wilson, T. (1971) 'Normative and interpretive paradigms in sociology' in Douglas, J. (ed.) *Understanding Everyday Life*. London: Routledge, pp. 80–104.
Zimmerman, D. (1971) 'The practicalities of rule use' in Douglas, J. (ed.) *Understanding Everyday Life*. London: Routledge, London, pp. 221–238.
Zimmerman, D. and Pollner, M. (1971) 'The everyday world as a phenomenon' in Douglas, J. (ed.) *Understanding Everyday Life*. London: Routledge, pp. 80–104.

Statutes and cases

Bail Act 1997 (Vic)
Bail Amendment (Stage 2) Act 2018 (Vic).
Family Violence Act 2004 (Tas)
R v Fisher 1964 (Tas)

9 Vernacular visions of viral videos

Speaking for evidence that speaks for itself[1]

Michael Lynch

Formal organizational and legal investigations typically include laypersons as well as professionals, and the transparency and intelligibility of the public display of evidence to non-specialists is an important part of the conduct and accountability of such investigations. Even in investigations of evidence in which laypersons do not render judgments of fact (as in a jury trial), the formulation of final judgments are publicly accountable and are presented in natural language. Testimony in formal tribunals is conversational in the way it runs off as dialogue between interrogator and witness, with occasional objections and other interventions by other parties, but rules of evidence as well as commonplace procedures for narrating and questioning accounts place restrictions on interrogators and witnesses.

Despite the emphasis on public accountability in formal legal proceedings, conflicts sometimes arise between 'lay' understandings of evidence and professional legal judgments about such evidence, leading to a distinctive variation on the theme of reality disjuncture (Pollner, 1975). One contemporary focus of such conflict has to do with video evidence of violence, particularly so-called "viral videos" of police shootings and beatings of suspects and persons in custody, and controversial military attacks (Jayyusi, 2015; Mair et al., 2012; Watson, 2016). This paper examines cases of police shootings and beatings that involved conflicting treatments of video images by large segments of the 'lay' public and specialized treatments of such videos as evidence in official investigations. After discussing some formal rules of evidence concerning testimony and documents, and their relationship to ordinary practices and understandings, the paper takes up a "paradox" formulated by Lena Jayyusi (2015), which involves a disjuncture between, on the one hand, popular understandings of such videos as unequivocal evidence of excessive and unwarranted force, and, on the other, official treatments of such videos as insufficient evidence of legally actionable violations. The first of these orientations can be called "popular vision," in contrast to the "professional vision" described in a well-known article by Goodwin (1994). Popular vision refers to a demonstrably public reaction to viral videos as unequivocal evidence of violence, [2] whereas professional vision (which in this context might better be called "the official version") is a treatment of the video evidence under the auspices of formal investigation and legal rules of evidence. Also salient in many of these cases is the "racialized vision" of the predominantly white juries and investigative panels that review the evidence. Using a recent case as an example, I discuss one of a very few instances in which a lengthy series of official investigations resulted in a criminal conviction of a police officer for shooting a suspect. In most cases, however, rules of evidence and other formal restrictions on the presentation and evaluation of evidence work in favor of accused police.

Giving evidence in conversation and formal rules of evidence

In a study of *giving evidence* as an ordinary conversational practice, Anita Pomerantz observes that "[t]he practice of giving evidence is usually thought of as strictly belonging to the institutionalized resolutions of disputes, e.g., in trials, hearings, inquiries, etc. Yet the practice is a constitutive part of activities in other settings too" (Pomerantz, 1984, p. 607). Without attempting to give an exhaustive definition of "evidence," Pomerantz proposes, contrary to the commonplace assertion that "the evidence speaks for itself," that "evidence speaks to something outside of itself; it suggests that some particular state of affairs exists in relation to some particular concern(s)" (p. 608). Accordingly, to give evidence is not simply to announce, declare, or assert something, it involves showing or attesting to a basis for what is said.

Pomerantz (1984, p. 612) gives an example of a brief exchange involving three passengers as the train in which they are riding approaches a stop in the English Midlands:

A TO B: Leamington is the next stop.
C: I think it's the second stop.
(*A* LOOKS AT *C*)
C: I was told it's the second stop.

Pomerantz observes that C does not take A's assertion at face value, and instead offers a correction, prefaced by the mitigating expression "I think". It seems possible (though Pomerantz does not mention anything beyond the parenthetical note in the transcript), that A's look toward C, following C's initial intervention in the exchange between A and B, expresses disagreement or at least a questioning orientation toward what C had just said. Pomerantz then treats C's next utterance as giving support or justification by indicating "that her information is based on someone else's knowledge and authority. Whether or not it is convincing evidence involves, in part, whom she is citing" (p. 612). In a footnote, Pomerantz observes that if the unidentified source of the information in question had been understood by the recipients to be a British Rail employee, then it would be more credible than countering A's assertion with a reported assertion from nobody in particular. However, the way the source is displaced is itself notable: C's second utterance is a repeat of the just prior one, with the prefatory "I was told" replacing "I think," thus repositioning C from being the source to being a relay for information from an unidentified, non-present source. Whether or not we figure that a speaker's report that she was *told* something is more credible testimony than saying what she *thinks* is so, C's modified repeat displaces responsibility for the claim.

Pomerantz's analysis of this example inadvertently highlights the confusing relationship between two vernacular formulations: *giving information* and *giving evidence* to support such information. Although C's second utterance presents a possible fact (Leamington is two stops ahead, and not the next stop) in the form of second-hand evidence, Pomerantz describes it as a *first-hand* report of *how C knows* the possible fact. In formal legal terms, the report would count as "hearsay" evidence of what was *told to* the speaker by someone else, which under most circumstances would be inadmissible in a courtroom as a statement of fact. A second-hand statement can be admitted as evidence under certain exceptional conditions, but generally is not treated as equivalent to the reported statement.[3] For example, if a witness in a trial testifies that his cellmate told him that he had committed a murder for which another man was convicted, under some conditions the testimony can be treated as a factual account of what the cellmate *said* to the prisoner, but it would not be treated as equivalent to the cellmate's admission under oath in court testimony, in a deposition, or in a signed and officially witnessed document.

Rules of evidence for court systems, such as the US Federal Rules of Evidence, provide disciplined versions of what counts as evidence. These rules are analogous in some respects to disciplined versions of evidence in the empirical sciences. In those fields, formal rules define what counts as (legitimate) evidence, and procedures are specified for reaching, testing, and verifying conclusions derived from such evidence. Formal rules of evidence and procedures for presenting claims and testing them tend to restrict what might otherwise appear to be reasonable bases for judgment and proof, but when viewed with the advantage of hindsight they can be seen to introduce peculiarities and even absurdities. The apocryphal 'tests' used in the witchcraft trials of centuries ago may seem patently absurd today, but less dramatic variations in the administration of proofs, and associated conceptions of testing, objectivity, and credibility, also have been chronicled and critically discussed in histories of law, science, and the relationship between the two.[4] Changes over time and concurrent differences between national and local legal institutions provide some insight into such administrative variations. Such variations include, for example, the use of juries, judges, and panels of specialists as triers of fact. Within systems that deploy juries, such as the Anglo-American system, there have been historical variations in the preponderance of jury trials, numbers of jurors in a panel, and methods of jury selection. For example, prior to the late eighteenth century, jurors were chosen from members of a community with first-hand familiarity with the dispute or crime featured in the trial, whereas later such persons were deemed potentially prejudiced and were excluded from consideration as jurors (though not as potential witnesses) in favor of persons without prior knowledge of the parties and the relevant events.

Such systemic changes point to variations in conceptions of bias and administrative objectivity. *Administrative* objectivity is a term that can be used to gloss the various procedures in science, law, and other organized fields that are designed to publicly display determinations of fact as fair, reasonable, and governed by impersonal standards (Lynch et al. 2008, pp. 136–137). Outcomes of such procedures are achieved for all practical-organizational purposes and may be open to challenge and revision. Courts of law include criteria for admitting expert evidence in trials, and flexible standards for reaching verdicts, such as "moral certainty," "beyond a reasonable doubt," and "preponderance of evidence."[5] It is important to keep in mind that these are proximal *administrative* procedures and flexible standards with a highly circumscribed relation to epistemological conceptions of objectivity and certainty.

As a mundane matter, we might suppose that, in the case Pomerantz describes, locally adequate proof or disproof of what C asserts would become available to the parties when the train arrives at the next station and/or the station after it, but what is unremarkably accepted in one organizational context does not necessarily apply to others. In formal academic and legal circumstances, such direct proof is rarely at hand, and testimonial, documentary, and circumstantial evidence is all that is available. Giving evidence often is associated with proving or confirming an argument, proposition, hypothesis, personal identity, criminal charge or litigant's complaint, and a large amount of literature (including legislative records and legal reference sources) is devoted to articulating the conditions under which a statement, document, observation, test result, or material object can be proffered as evidence and accepted as proof.

Speaking for documentary evidence

The presentation of evidence in a trial court or other public tribunal is particularly interesting for the way the formal proceedings are designed to 'test' evidence that in other circumstances would likely be taken as transparent and unremarkably obvious. In such proceedings, natural language *testimony* has priority for presenting, authenticating, and explicating written documents, photographs, surveillance videos, and other forms of mechanically produced and reproduced evidence. Such documentary evidence is not allowed to speak for itself without independent testimony or accepted forms of written authorization to vouch for it. In other words, the testimony establishes the documentary information *as* admissible evidence; information that otherwise would be excluded under the *hearsay* rule. This exclusion does not simply provide a formal version of a commonplace "entitlement," as Harvey Sacks once called it, for a storyteller to tell stories based on first-hand experience,[6] since it applies to documents and accounts that in other circumstances would not be challenged. The relation to testimony is reflexive: after a document is vouched for through testimony as an exhibit, it can then be used to leverage further testimony.[7]

There are many exceptions to the hearsay rule. One exception that the US Federal Rules of Evidence (Rule, 703) allows is for an *expert* witness, not only to report upon direct observations of relevant events, but also to testify about the reliability of specific types of evidence, including ordinary eyewitness testimony as well as various types of technical evidence. In addition, the Rules allow a witness who is deemed by the court to be qualified in a relevant field of study or through extensive practical experience to convey opinions to the court about matters that were not directly witnessed, but were based on her expert training or experience. So, for example, an expert with relevant academic or experiential qualifications can advise a court on the history and reliability of fingerprint examination, without also rendering a judgment about whether the particular fingerprints used as evidence in the case match the suspect's prints (Risinger, 2000; Cole, 2001).

Rules of evidence are formally codified, but during a trial they often are invoked in terms of vernacular action categories, such as when an adversary counsel raises an objection against an interrogator's leading question or a judge admonishes an interrogator for "badgering" a witness. Such objections and admonishments are occasionally enunciated in the course of testimony in terms of formal legal rules, standards, and definitions, but they are used in a flexible and discretionary, rather than rigid, way.

Formalized rules of evidence associated with law, science, and other rationalized endeavors draw upon natural language competencies associated with the amorphous domain of common sense reasoning. Studies by Pomerantz (1987) and many others in ethnomethodology and CA have described how formal courtroom discourse draws upon competencies with assessing the credibility of accounts, ascribing motives to actions, piecing together plausible narratives, and countless other understandings and judgments.[8] Such competencies can be viewed as a foundation for both lay and professional participation in such tribunals. Indeed, in his brief and dense chapter on jurors' decision making, Garfinkel (1967, p. 110) surmised that "[a] person is 95 per cent juror before he comes near the court." Nevertheless, Garfinkel also observed that jurors explicitly defer to the "official line" (from jury instructions and other sources) that defines a "good juror's" judgmental deliberations, though he adds that they do not simply substitute "the rules making up the official line" for the "decision-making rules of daily life" (1967, p. 112). Garfinkel speaks of an ambiguity in the relationship between the two orders of rules and argues that the rules associated with the "official line" become most clearly salient retrospectively in justifications for decisions made by other means. In the cases described in the present paper, rules of evidence become particularly salient when used to justify official determinations that override video documents that were widely treated by large segments of the public to provide unequivocal demonstration of criminal and racist conduct by police officers.

Viral videos

The vernacular expression "viral videos" refers to video clips that are disseminated internationally with great rapidity through the internet. The analogy with a virus suggests a rapid transmission through a large population; a technologized acceleration of the way gossip or a rumor spreads through a community. Like a virus, such spread is afforded by one or another communicative infrastructure, but instead of transporting food, water, air, or waste, the infrastructure transmits digital compositions from one site to another. The analogy with contagion might seem to have ominous connotations, but it is frequently used as a reference to benign videos of funny cats and other amusements that become popular for a short or long time, with millions of cumulative 'hits' recorded on the sites that host them. Prior to widespread use of the internet, media outlets, such as the popular television shows starting in the late 1980s that broadcast collections of 'best' or 'funniest' home videos, became central points of dissemination. Although viral videos often circulate widely because of their entertainment value, in some instances they are taken as evidence of wrongdoing that may become focal to protests and end up being used as evidence in formal proceedings.

In the past decade, an immense amount of public attention and public protest has been generated by videos that have provided massive numbers of viewers with what many take to be unequivocal evidence of excessive and unwarranted violence perpetrated by police and military personnel. Some of these videos are recorded by civilians using cell phones, while others are taken by surveillance cameras, vehicle dashboard cameras, or body cameras worn by the police or military personnel. Such videos become viral after being "leaked" deliberately or unwittingly to the public, or released unwillingly as a consequence of a court order. Prior to the murder in 2020 of George Floyd by a Minneapolis police officer, three of the most notorious cases included the violent and fatal administration of a chokehold of Eric Garner in 2014 by a group of New York City police, the fatal shooting of Laquan McDonald by a Chicago policeman in 2014 (the video was not made public until 2015), and the videotaped shooting of 12-year old Tamir Rice by a Cleveland policeman.[9] Footage of military actions includes numerous on-the-ground videos taken by residents of Gaza during Israeli attacks (Jayyusi, 2015), a cockpit video examined during an inquest concerning a "friendly fire" incident during the second Gulf War (Mair et al., 2012), and other video clips released through WikiLeaks of bombings and helicopter gunship attacks during recent military campaigns in the Middle-East. Such viral videos of shootings and beatings commonly include the following features (see Elsey et al., 2018).

1 They tend to be short clips. In many cases, the fragment that circulates is edited from a longer sequence.
2 Although they often have a soundtrack, voices of key people rarely are audible or easily understood, and the visual action is the primary focus.
3 They are presented with a brief commentary to identify the scene, the characters, and their actions.
4 What is happening seems transparently obvious "at a glance" and morally overwhelming.
5 Subsequent investigations by designated experts rarely result in criminal action against the alleged perpetrators.

Viral videos are rarely more than a few minutes long and are introduced by narratives or overlaid text that identifies the parties, the setting, and the sequence of action. Longer versions of the video from which the viral clips are edited sometimes are available online as well, along with news stories, blogs, and other commentaries that elaborate on their circumstances and significance (see Christensen, 2014; Schneider, 2015; Wilke, 2017; Mair et al., 2016). In the most widely known cases, the immediate popular reaction has been horror at the unjustified and excessive violence used by police and military agents. Such reactions tend to treat the video evidence as giving direct access to what really happened, contrary to the official accounts given by police and military organizations. In cases of videos of police shootings and beatings or military attacks on civilians, viral videos often become notorious in the popular domain before being used as evidence in official investigations. In some cases, such videos became publicly available following relatively brief in-house investigations that resulted in no sanction against the agents and agencies responsible, but the public reaction then led to further, more public and prolonged, investigations.

More often than not, after public reactions lead to official investigations and tribunals, the accused perpetrators are exonerated, but far from quelling the public controversy the exonerations often touch off further controversy and litigation.

Despite widespread popular reactions that treat such videos as unequivocal evidence of brutality by police or military forces, the official investigations usually dismiss or override their evidentiary value with other evidence that is not shown or not obviously seen. Despite such dismissals, on-the-ground footage also provides a source of hope for individuals and groups concerned with the inscrutability and impunity with which members of state organizations have been able to act.

A notorious and exceptional case, which will be discussed further in this paper, is that of Chicago Police Sergeant Jason Van Dyke, the officer held responsible for the McDonald shooting. The case became the subject of a highly public series of investigations, after internal police investigations exonerated Van Dyke and other officers at the scene from any culpability. A series of news exposés and public protests led to the public release of the video nearly a year following the shooting, leading to more intensive and widespread protests, with substantial political fallout in the Chicago city government. Eventually, Van Dyke was charged with first-degree murder, as well as other charges, and nearly four years after the shooting he was convicted on a reduced charge of second-degree murder, as well as 16 charges of using excessive force against McDonald (one charge for each shot he allegedly fired over a 13 second period).[10] Although it was highly unusual that criminal charges were pursued and a conviction obtained, many elements of the case were not so unusual.

Jayyusi's paradox

Lena Jayyusi (2015, p. 276) discusses what she calls a "paradox" that emerges when videos taken at the site of a military or police action evidently contradict official versions of what occurred. Often, after an official investigation is convened in response to strong public reactions to viral videos of police shootings or fatal attacks on civilians by dominant military forces, the evidence is deemed insufficient to meet legal standards, and "no official finding of a crime [is made] by the parties with authority to make such a judgment." As Jayyusi formulates the paradox, "despite the fact that in the judgments of the law there may not have been a crime, 'everybody' may 'know' *nevertheless*, that a crime indeed had been committed: here common moral discourse and legal discourse diverge, even as they meet at the moment when the wheels of inquiry are instigated" (p. 276, emphasis in original).[11]

What Jayyusi calls a paradox is not paradoxical in the sense that each of the two contradictory positions negates the other, but it is more akin to Melvin Pollner's (1975) conception of "reality disjuncture" in which one party insists upon an experiential account that is incommensurable with another's equally insistent account.[12] As Pollner observed, courtrooms provide a good place to find such disjunctures. An additional element with Jayyusi's paradox, however, is the systematic difference in the evidential basis for the contrary accounts: the authorized or official account claims a more comprehensive body of evidence for a ratiocinated judgment that contradicts "what everybody knows" from having viewed the readily recognizable actions shown on the video:

> … in the world of *legal* norms and procedures, that public and material body of "facts" was not yet "evidence" of actual violations; instead, it was evidence that there *may have been* such violations. The publicly visible activities thus held the status of "candidate evidence" of crime -evidence that an "inquiry" was called for.
>
> (Jayyusi, 2015, p. 274, emphasis in original)

Although official investigations provide tentative legal resolution, they do not necessarily put public reactions to rest, as "common sense judgments may, for ordinary persons, be seen to defeat judgments based on authoritative decision-making" (ibid.). Jayyusi also speaks of "the 'gap' between the common-sense moral judgments and the legal findings" through which "the ordinary actors/reasoners may have occasion to locate and read the 'political'" (p. 277).

Although official findings do not necessarily settle the public dispute, they allow accused parties and official spokespersons to dismiss what "everybody knows" as the untutored and partisan impressions of a rabble. Jayyusi identifies two understandings of the concept of *prima facie* evidence that come into play in such disjunctures: one is of an initial appearance ("at first sight") prior to investigation, while the other is of "plain and clear" evidence that is sufficient for a verdict for as long as it is not rebutted. The testimony of officially designated experts is often crucial for establishing such rebuttals during formal inquiries, but those who continue to hold the video documentation as self-evident may not be persuaded that expert testimony is even necessary (Mezey, 2013). Though without recourse to formal "proof", such lingering resistance recalls the proverbial line made famous by Bob Dylan in *Subterranean Homesick Blues*: "You don't need a weatherman to know which way the wind blows."

Professional versus popular vision

Charles Goodwin's well-known and widely cited article "Professional Vision" (1994) examined the use of video evidence in court testimony. Viewed in retrospect, the videotape in question may have been the first viral video that vividly and graphically depicted (alleged) use of excessive force by police officers during an arrest – in this case, by Los Angeles Police officers who arrested Rodney King in 1991. The technological context was different from today's viral videos, which spread through YouTube and social media: the footage was taken with a home videotape recorder and then disseminated through television newscasts. However, many prototypical elements of more recent viral videos were present in this instance. The tape was recorded by an uninvolved citizen, who happened to witness the episode from a nearby residence. The footage showed an unarmed African American man lying prone on the pavement, as a group of uniformed police officers (most of whom were Caucasian) stood surrounding his body while some of them repeatedly beat him with "side-handled batons" (a modernized version of what used to be called "nightsticks" or "Billy clubs"). Many viewers of the tape, including criminal prosecutors for the state of California, took it to be a self-evident document of actual police brutality. Following the public response to the video, several of the participating police were charged with criminal conduct. The prosecution emphasized the self-evident documentation provided by the videotape. According to the Chief Prosecutor in the criminal trial, "What more could you ask for? You have the videotape that shows objectively, without bias, impartially, what happened that night. The videotape shows conclusively what happened that night. It can't be rebutted" (Mydans, quoted in Goodwin, 1994, p. 616). A similar conception of video evidence has persisted to the point of becoming a political program for counteracting police power, as indicated in a slogan promoted on the website of copBlock.org: "Recording your interaction preserves the truth for anyone to see. The camera is the new gun. It is the great equalizer. Film the police!"[13]

The trial was televised, and Goodwin analyzed excerpts of the direct testimony and cross-examination of a few witnesses for the defendants. As Goodwin shows in his analysis, the witnesses (particularly Sergeant Charles Duke, who was presented to the court as an expert witness who had experience with training police in the exercise of force) testified that the accused officers were following the standard protocols for arresting a demonstrably dangerous suspect. Goodwin likened the rhetoric and graphics used by Duke and other defense witnesses to the "professional vision" used by scientists to elucidate and highlight non-obvious features of graphic data displays. In this case, the expert witnesses repeatedly replayed key segments of the tape and 'instructed' the jury to see the responsible enactment of professional protocols for restraining a potentially violent suspect. The largely white jury found the police officers not guilty of using excessive force during King's arrest. Others, particularly many African-American inhabitants of Los Angeles, were not persuaded, and the verdict touched off massive protests and localized rioting. Months later, in a civil lawsuit in Federal court, some of the participating police officers were held liable for violating King's civil rights.

Rules of evidence for criminal trials were significant features of the trial. In the criminal trial (and not in the later civil case), the prosecution had the burden of proof to demonstrate guilt "beyond a reasonable doubt", while the defense was only required to convince the jury that what the videotape showed was *in*conclusive, and that when viewed from the perspective of the police, the police actions *could be seen as* an exercise of "reasonable" police practice under the circumstances: the circumstances being (according to the defense narrative) apprehending a large, aggressive, inebriated suspect who had just led the police on a lengthy high-speed chase, had resisted arrest after being pulled over, and had yet to be fully subdued at the time the video was recorded.

Goodwin does not suggest that the defense attorneys and their expert witnesses were correctly showing, through their analysis of the tape, what actually happened during the arrest of Rodney King. Nor does he suggest that the defense of the police misled a credulous jury with a concocted "technical" account. However, his analysis becomes caught in a dilemma between the contrary versions of *prima facie* evidence that Jayyusi identifies. From the vantage point of the "professional vision" articulated by the accused police officers' defense, the videotape was *prima facie* only in the sense that it was an evidential document whose *apparent* sense "at first sight" was subject to expert reinterpretation; a reinterpretation that delved into greater detail and elaborated on the context in such a way as to expose the superficiality, naïvety, and bias of the initial impression conveyed by the viral video.

Borrowing from Jayyusi's discussion, we can view the counterpart of Goodwin's conception of "professional vision" not as "unprofessional" or "naïve" vision, but as "popular vision" – what "anybody" should be able to see. In this case, a popular (though certainly not universal) view was that any reasonable person who viewed the videotape would conclude that it gave "plain and clear" evidence of police brutality and that an exercise in expert reinterpretation would be unnecessary and even absurd.

Viewed in retrospect, the prosecution may have mischaracterized the video evidence as unassailable, but the very fact that the trial occurred could be attributed to the strong and widespread popular reaction to the "plain and clear" evidence shown by the videotape. Although US courts increasingly rely upon expert witnesses, it remains the case that the legal system pays conspicuous tribute to vernacular language and commonplace judgment. In trial courts, and even in Supreme Court rulings, judges often appeal (albeit tendentiously) to the ordinary meanings of the words used in legislation and common law, and they cite commonplace maxims such as, "I know it when I see it." Furthermore, jury trials are based on the assumption that "common-sense" evaluations of available evidence (as opposed to specialized legal or scientific evaluations) are adequate for judgments about "ordinary" evidence, and special considerations to preserve the jury's role in factual determinations are administered in legal proceedings. The judiciary is conspicuously reluctant to supersede the "common-sense" of juries in many cases.

Admissibility hearings are an important institution for vetting expert witnesses in jury trials, and a key question that arises in such hearings is whether a juror would *need* to rely upon an expert before reaching a reasonable conclusion about specific matters in evidence (Burns, 2008). In a generally favorable discussion of Goodwin's analysis, Sheila Jasanoff (1998, pp. 723–724) comments that he "underestimates the contingency of courtroom demarcations between lay and professional vision" and that a crucial issue "was the court's willingness to admit Duke as an expert on police brutality, an issue that could as easily have been left as a matter for lay determination." Jasanoff (1998, p. 720) refers to a "legal doctrine ... *res ipsa loquitur* (the thing speaks for itself)" that courts use to support the idea that lay jurors should be competent to understand particular kinds of evidence without the help of expert witnesses, and without the potential confusion engendered by contradictory testimony from adversary experts.

Ordinary police officers are excluded from being expert witnesses, but the defense in the Rodney King police trial got around that exclusion by presenting police officers such as Sergeant Duke as experts in the training of other police officers on the procedures for arresting suspects; in other words, they were treated as second-order experts who were credentialed for commenting on the normal practices of the police. In an insightful remark, Goodwin suggests that the testimony of such witnesses was part of an "ethnography" conducted by the defense: "To successfully make this claim [that the impression of an excessive beating was a misconception of reasonable police practices], the defense provided the jury with ethnography about police practices …". In this case, the ethnographers had gone native well before being asked to convey to the court "perceptions" consistent with a typified police officer's "domain of professional competence," and to show "that these perceptions are not idiosyncratic phenomena restricted to individuals but frameworks shared by a profession …" (Goodwin, 1994, p. 616).[14]

A dilemma that arises in Goodwin's analysis is hidden by the very use of "professional vision" as a covering term: the more basic issue is whether the intervention of experts and their "theories" is necessary to assist jurors to make sense of particular items of evidence. Even if one supposes that "[a]ll vision is perspectival and lodged within endogenous communities of practice" (Goodwin, 1994, p. 606), the question remains as to whether a specialized analysis is required to supplement, instruct, or correct what members of an "ordinary" community sitting on a jury would otherwise determine through deliberation with one another. This dilemma is at the center of democratic politics, as well as particular institutions such as the jury system. Perched on the horns of the dilemma are the polar perils of populist demagoguery and what might be termed expert 'technogoguery'. In this political context, evidence that "speaks for itself" is not an expression of naïve realism but an expression of trust in the entitlement of 'anybody' (any 'reasonably competent' member) to make sense of particular items of evidence.[15]

The Rodney King police trial provided a vivid demonstration of how evidence, which vast numbers of viewers took to be unassailable, could be 'deconstructed' in a formal proceeding. Some of the procedures used by the defense that Goodwin identified also have come into play in more recent trials of police officers, but for the most part the accused officers have been protected against incrimination by other, often more crude, means for bringing investigations to a close, often prior to any indictment of the police officers involved. These relatively crude tactics were evident in the protracted series of investigations and protests that preceded the trial of Jason Van Dyke for murdering Laquan MacDonald.[16]

The Laquan McDonald shooting

The viral video of the 2014 shooting in Chicago of Laquan McDonald was a portion of a dashcam video taken from a police vehicle as it sped through city streets until pulling up behind a person (identified as McDonald, a 17-year old African American) who is shown walking at a rapid pace down the middle of the street. As the vehicle in which the camera is situated comes to rest, McDonald continues walking away from the camera, approaches and passes to the right of a parked police car, with its warning lights flashing, and slows his pace while swinging his right arm and holding something (later identified as a knife). Another vehicle pulls in at the left side of the video frame, slows momentarily as it nears McDonald, and then speeds up, pulls ahead of the parked vehicle, and quickly parks to the left and slightly ahead of McDonald's path. Two police officers get out of the vehicle and stand 10 or 15 feet to the side of McDonald with guns drawn as he passes by. McDonald continues walking and veers slightly away from the two policemen, but as he passes them one officer (identified as Van Dyke) begins shooting. McDonald's body spins and falls to the pavement, and while he lies on the pavement for a second or two his arm makes an apparent movement – whether he is reaching for something or moving involuntarily from the impact of the bullets is difficult to tell. The shooting continues, and debris from bullets ricocheting off the pavement can be seen near the body. Soon after he stops shooting, the officer walks over toward the body and kicks away something (identified as the knife) lying on the pavement next to the body. Another police car arrives from the opposite direction, parks near the body, and two officers exit the vehicle, casually walk over to McDonald, who at this point is lying completely still as they stand nearby without attending to his body.

Readers may have noticed that this brief account of what the video shows is infused with narrative elements derived from news reports. It is difficult even to imagine what a viewer would see without at least minimal narrative preparation. The various video clips available online have a hazy quality: the scene takes place at night, colors are faded, and outlines are blurred. At least with versions of the video available online, it is difficult to see if the vehicle that pulls over is a marked police van, or if the two people who arise from it are wearing police uniforms. The identifications of those two people as police officers and of McDonald as a 17-year old African American male, are consistent with the video but not readily visible without supplementary commentary. The identification of the source of the video as a police dash-cam also is consistent with the scene, but again not derivable from it alone. Details of relevant actions – that, for example, McDonald is carrying a knife and that Van Dyke shoots 16 times – also are consistent but not directly visible in the video.

Although some key details were contested, many narrative elements in this case, like those in other legal cases, can be consigned to "agreed facts of the case" (Lynch, 1982, p. 292). Facts such as that the person shot was Laquan McDonald and that the shooter was Jason Van Dyke were not contested. Nor was there any dispute over the fact that Van Dyke was the only shooter, and that he shot McDonald numerous times, and that McDonald was holding a knife when he was shot. Further narrative elements frame the videotaped segment with details that precede and follow it, thereby providing "context". These include accounts of McDonald's actions that preceded the shooting, such as that he had brandished the knife to threaten police officers, and had slashed a tire of a police vehicle. They also include information derived in the aftermath, such as the autopsy report of McDonald's fatal wounds, the blood evidence that he was on drugs, and ballistic reports of how many shots were fired from Van Dyke's gun. Background information on prior complaints about Van Dyke's use of excessive force against suspects and McDonald's impoverished and troubled biography also were turned up. Although some of these facts only became public after initial investigations by journalists and police organizations, and there was no guarantee that they would remain uncontested throughout the subsequent inquiries and tribunals, they were not "theories" analogous to a defense "theory" that would narrate the event with the aim of specifying Van Dyke's actions as a reasonable response by a police officer to a threatening situation.

The conjunction of the video with what, for the time being, were uncontested narrative elements left plenty of room for alternative accounts, but it seems clear that the video evidence made a substantial difference, and that this was recognized by the different parties who clamored for and resisted its release. Various accounts of the shooting were presented during different phases of investigation. The video was not made public immediately after the incident, and it took a protracted effort by journalists and activists to force its release almost a year later. In the meantime, initial in-house investigations exonerated Van Dyke from culpability by emphasizing McDonald's possession of the knife and his threatening actions. The initial police report stated: "Officers confronted the armed offender, who refused to comply with orders to drop the knife and continued to approach the officers. As a result of this action, the officer discharged his weapon, striking the offender" (quoted in Austen, 2016). The "armed offender" in this narrative was McDonald, not Van Dyke. A narrative of the shooting as an action compelled by McDonald's armed threat also was given by a spokesperson for the Fraternal Order of the Police (the police union). This account asserted that McDonald "wasn't dropping the knife, and he was coming at the officer … with a strange gaze about him," which left the officers (the plural was notable) "no choice at that point but to defend themselves" (ibid.).

After the video was made public, the immediate threat posed by McDonald at the time of the shooting was widely questioned.[17] The scene shown in the video of McDonald walking past the two officers and veering slightly away from them just before Van Dyke opened fire proved crucial for questioning the in-house report's account that he had threatened Van Dyke with the knife. Following the release of the video, Van Dyke's defense attempted to sustain the perception of threat by reference to a police department bulletin in 2012, two years prior to the shooting, which warned of knives possessed by criminals that were capable of shooting bullets or that had detachable blades that could be spring-loaded and launched as projectiles. Van Dyke's continued shooting then could be seen as a reaction to the incipient movement of McDonald's arm toward the knife as he lay prone on the pavement.

In addition to apparent discrepancies between in-house investigation reports and the widespread public reaction to the video, other evidence was cited to support a theory of police and city government cover-up. Investigative journalists and other investigators turned up evidence of a bystander whom the police ushered away from the scene, and of a mysterious gap that appeared in a surveillance video taken from a nearby fast-food restaurant after the video was examined by two police officers shortly after the shooting. As in cases of political scandal (and this case involved political scandal as well as a criminal investigation), the cover-up of evidence was itself cited as inculpatory evidence.

There were many other aspects of the case that came together and culminated in Van Dyke's conviction.[18] The video (or videos, as there were others) may have been more effective for stirring and sustaining public pressure against the Chicago city government and police, than it was as legal evidence. Without such pressure, it seems unlikely that the case would have been pursued beyond the initial investigation. Also salient was the fact that this case occurred while a national movement, Black Lives Matter, was building momentum on the basis of a series of earlier cases involving (predominantly) white police officers and black defendants. Previous cases in which police were not charged or were exonerated after being charged were available as precedents, though not in a formal legal sense.[19] Popular outrage expressed through numerous forms of public protest and media criticism of racial injustice was exacerbated by official exonerations.

Racialized vision

The context of public protest against racial injustice points to one of the possible contingencies in the Rodney King police trial that Goodwin's focus on "professional vision" misses: the "racialized vision" of the jury. The Rodney King police trial was held in Simi Valley, a predominantly white and conservative suburb in the greater Los Angeles metropolitan area (among other things, it is the site of the Ronald Reagan Presidential Library). Although the jurors' deliberations were held in private, it was widely speculated in the media that, in line with Sgt. Duke's testimony, they would be more inclined to empathize with the "perceptions" of the police than they would with the African-American suspect. Harvey Sacks (1992) presents a brilliant explication of racialized vision in a lecture on a story about an incident related in a series of recorded phone calls.[20] During one of the calls, 'Estelle' tells her friend 'Jeanette' (the names are pseudonyms) about an incident she witnessed near the entrance of a department store where Jeanette works.

(Sacks, 1992, p. 180)

E: An'there was two p'leece cars across the street, anleh- colored lady wan'tuh go in the main entrance there where the silver is an' all the [(gifts an' things,)
J: [Yeah.
E: And they wouldn' let'er go in,

Sacks observes that Estelle's characterization of the characters and the scene implies – without saying in so many words – that the 'colored lady' is a suspect whom the police had apprehended for a possible theft of valuable goods from the department store. Sacks points out that Jeanette later corrects Estelle for having completely misread the scene, but he goes on to examine how the constituents of the story exhibit how Estelle "sees" the scene. Sacks very interestingly delves into the grammatical and referential details of the story, but a summary point he makes is highly pertinent to our discussion. He points out that Estelle's story portrays her relation to the scene as an innocent witness who has nothing to fear from the presence of the police:

> … there's no hint that she had any fear that somehow, e.g., that policeman was about to turn to her and ask her what she was doing there. The massive comfort in her innocence, and in that legitimate audience status that she has, is something that we should give real attention to, in at least this way: It's the kind of thing that we know can be readily shaken. There are times and places where some Estelle would not feel all that comfortable, but, passing such a scene – and you can readily imagine it – she would figure "Oh my God here I am, the first thing that happens is they're going to figure I'm involved." And that never dawns on our Estelle. And until it dawns on her she can have no sense of an empathy with, e.g., a kid in the ghetto. Her sense of innocence affects the whole way she sees the scene.
>
> (pp. 185–186)

Given the salience of police "perceptions" in the cases we have discussed, a jury full of 'Estelles' would be inclined to see the police as benign custodians of public order and safety, and Rodney King as a potential threat. The "professional vision" conveyed by Sergeant Duke would then be compatible with the "racialized vision" of the jurors.[21]

The public protests and media publicity that built up from case to case before and during the lengthy period of the investigations and litigation associated with the McDonald shooting, primed large segments of the public (and possibly the jury) in the Van Dyke trial to see the video as a document, not only of a young black male on drugs threatening violence but also of an unwarranted exercise of lethal force by a police officer.

Conclusion

In cases where police officers are suspected or explicitly charged with wrongdoing while on duty, official investigations provide them with unusual protections. In brief outline, these include the following sources of advantage.

1 Control over the crime scene and evidence collection: The McDonald shooting occurred at a crime scene, if only because McDonald himself would have been charged with several criminal acts had he survived. Prior to the shooting, a growing number of police vehicles and officers

had gathered at the scene and were monitoring McDonald's movements and controlling the access of other individuals to the scene. After the shooting, the scene was sealed off, and the police controlled access to it. Police officers also spoke to bystanders and checked a nearby fast-food restaurant video, and afterwards were suspected of having suppressed potentially incriminating evidence concerning Van Dijk's actions.[22]

2 Priority in the temporality of investigations: initial investigations are done 'in house' by police agencies, and often investigation is closed with a report exonerating the shooter. In the Van Dyke case, like many others, the initial investigations of the police at the scene were done by the police. The investigations not only were conducted by police organizations, but many of the key witnesses were police officers at the scene, whose testimony exonerating Van Dijk was incorporated into the report. Had it not been for the efforts of a few journalists, activists, and whistleblowers, it seems likely that (as in so many other cases) investigation would not have proceeded beyond the initial report, and the video of the shooting most likely would have remained hidden from public scrutiny.

3 Police solidarity: members of militarized police forces tend to be high on solidarity, and are represented by strong unions whose spokespersons support the officers involved in 'line-of-duty' violence and object strenuously to criticism of those officers. They also resist efforts to proceed with further investigation and indictment, and even professional sanctions such as suspension or firing.

4 Prosecutorial conflict of interest. As is often pointed out, prosecutors and police work closely together in criminal justice systems, and in the vast majority of criminal cases police are on 'the same side' as the prosecution. As Sudnow (1965) points out in his classic article on plea negotiation, prosecutors use their discretion to manage criminal charges and outcomes to conform to an informal sense of what is normal and natural in a 'community' they share with police officers.

5 Public support for the police: as noted earlier, the Rodney King trial was held in a conservative area of the LA metropolitan area, where the majority-white jury would be expected to support the police. Although not all cases involving excessive force against suspects involve white officers and black defendants, many do, and when, as often is the case, investigators and 'triers of fact' are white, the verdict may be predictable.[23]

6 Criminal trial standards, particularly the "proof beyond a reasonable doubt" standard for conviction, compound the advantages of accused officers to resist charges. In cases, for example, where a police officer shoots a suspect who, according to the officer's testimony, was 'perceived' at the time to be reaching for a weapon that afterwards turned out to be something other than a weapon, "the legal standard focuses not on the guilt or the innocence of the person who is shot but on whether an officer would have perceived a threat in the encounter"

(Goldstein, 2016). The issue, then, for exonerating the officer for acting in self-defense, is not what the suspect *did*, as shown on a video and otherwise documented with material evidence, but what the officer 'perceived' the suspect was threatening to do. Even when the officer's apprehension turns out to be incorrect, if it is deemed "reasonable" it meets the legal standard. This "reasonable fear" standard greatly enhances the advantages of police defendants by treating their professed apprehension of the scene as materially important for characterizing their visible actions.

7 Temporality and contexture of evidence: formal investigations of video evidence both intensify and 'extensify' the examination of details shown on the tape. The frame-by-frame examination of the evidence that Goodwin (1994) describes is one of many ways such evidence is subjected to intensive re-examination. No less important are narratives about the actions of the parties before and after the episodes shown on video. Commentaries also play a part in supplementing what is shown in the video with accounts of what the video does not (or in some cases cannot) show. In the McDonald case, these include descriptions of McDonald's threatening expressions and of the officer's imagination of a projectile-knife. Although these evidential matters 'inform' the sense made of the video, their salience, visibility, and credibility must be taken on trust.

These features of formal investigation militate against treating video evidence as self-evident, and they also point to the immense advantages that defendants have in the criminal justice system when they can mobilize state, private, and reputational resources to resist litigation and conviction. In many cases, viral videos and the public reactions they provoke are sufficient to instigate and sustain investigations, but when subjected to the deliberative and contextualized investigation characteristic of formal inquiry they are deemed equivocal and insufficient as grounds for conviction, or even further investigation. *Rules* of evidence and associated procedural standards work against the leverage viral videos furnish to "popular vision," as there is an extremely heavy burden of proof for criminal accusations against officials and organizations who have particularly strong resources for contesting them, and who can count upon sympathetic prosecutors, jurors, and judges when pleading their cases. Under such circumstances, the popular view of video evidence as 'speaking for itself' stands little chance of surviving the analytic arts of taking it apart, frame-by-frame, animating it and reframing it with analytical commentary, and building a counter-intuitive narrative. This does not mean that it is impossible for accusers to win cases through appeals to popular, rather than professional, vision, but it does point to a severe disadvantage in meeting a burden of proof in a legal world that appears to be relying increasingly on expert, formal, and "scientific" conceptions of evidence and proof.

The leverage provided by viral videos is not inconsequential, however. To appreciate this, we can recall what Sacks (1992, p. 504) once called a "fragile story":

> Some rather complex events have happened, and a thing you're trying out is whether you can put together a more or less compelling version of them, that version isolating one or another of the happened things, to find "That's what happened, isn't it?" "I have a correct version of it, don't I?" What's involved, then, is that you may in some fashion present to your audience materials which are more complicated than your story has them, where your audience could suggest about the proposed upshot of your story that you may not have it right.[24]

The upshot of such remarks is not that the "evidence speaks for itself," but that it furnishes a surplus of materials for supporting or contesting contrary versions of it. There is no getting around the necessity of *speaking for* such evidence and, beyond that, mobilizing political resources to build "communities" that enable such speaking to be trusted as credible. Political hope as well as challenge rests in that possibility of speaking for such evidence.

Notes

1 Earlier versions of this paper were presented at: an international workshop, "Looking for Evidence: The Practice of Proving in Science, Humanities and Law," Ecole des Hautes Etudes en Sciences Sociales (EHESS), Paris, 16 March 2016; the Annual Meeting of the American Sociological Association, Seattle, WA, 11 August 2016; and a workshop on "Interpreting Images of State Violence," Wilfred Laurier University, Brantford, Ontario, 14 July 2018. I am particularly grateful to Patrick Watson, Jay Meehan, Baudouin Dupret, and three anonymous referees for specific suggestions and links to relevant sources on controversies over police violence.

2 Popular vision is not unanimous or even in some cases representative of a majority of a population. The important thing is that it is made demonstrably public *as* popular. I owe thanks to Patrick Watson for pointing this out in a personal comment.

3 Definitions of the hearsay exclusion and exceptions to the exclusion are presented, respectively, in Sections 801 and 803 of the US Federal Rules of Evidence.

4 For historical accounts of evidence and conceptions of credibility in law and natural philosophy, see Schaffer (1992); Shapin (1995); and Shapiro (2002).

5 For accounts on changes in jury composition and standards of judgment, see Edmond and Mercer (1997); Laudan (2003); and Shapiro (1986).

6 See Sacks (1992, Volume 2, pp. 242–248), "Storyteller as 'witness'; Entitlement to experience," Lecture 4, Spring 1970; and Lynch and Bogen (1996, pp. 164–165).

7 See Lynch and Bogen (1996, Chap. 7) on "the documentary method of interrogation," used in the US House-Senate Iran-contra hearings to leverage testimony from recalcitrant witnesses. The practice is a distinct twist on Garfinkel's (1967) "documentary method of interpretation"; also see Watson (2018).

8 For a recent collection of such studies, see Dupret et al. (2015).

9 For an updated list and summary account of recent police shootings, some of which involved viral videos, see Park (2018).

10 See Watson (2018) for another case that resulted in a conviction. This was a shooting in 2013 of a young man, Sammy Yatim, who like McDonald was holding a knife. Yatim was videotaped from inside a Toronto street car while threatening passengers with the knife, and after passengers had fled, a group of police officers gathered outside the open door to arrest Yatim. One of the officers, Constable James Forcillo, repeatedly shot Yatim, and as in the McDonald case, the temporal pattern of successive shots was material to a guilty verdict against the policeman.

11 As I understand Jayyusi's phrase "'everybody' may 'know'," both 'everybody' and 'know' are used in a vernacular sense, where 'everybody' is not an enumerated totality and 'know' is a conviction that is not universally shared. In the polarized situations Jayyusi describes, 'everybody' is liable to be compartmentalized by others who refuse to countenance what they 'know', so that 'everybody' marks membership in an amorphous group or faction and what they 'know' is contestable by others.

12 It is not a paradox in the strict sense of a singular statement that, if true is false, and if false is true. The classic example such a statement is the liar paradox, "all Cretans are always liars," which when said by a Cretan contradicts its own truth.

13 For a criticism of proposals that invest naïve faith in the power of police camera video evidence, see Vertesi (2015).

14 Questions about police training and "perceptions" also came into play during investigations of the Tamir Rice shooting in Cleveland (Danylko, 2014).

15 For discussion of an English appeal case in which a judicial panel struggled to distinguish "common sense" evidence from "technical" evidence, see Lynch and McNally (2003).

16 This paper does not discuss the details of the Van Dyke trial. Currently, the trial transcript and materials from other police trials are being examined in a project led by Patrick Watson, in which Stacy Burns, Jay Meehan, and the author are participating.

17 I am glossing over an extended episode involving investigative journalists, whistleblowers, city officials, McDonald's family, and court rulings that culminated in the release of the video. Accounts of these matters are readily available online in news summaries such as Austen (2016).

18 The conviction might not be the end of the story, as appeals are possible. Also, McDonald's family and their proponents were dissatisfied that the conviction was on a charge of Second-Degree Murder, rather than the First-Degree Murder charge.

19 Lynch and Bogen (1996, p. 51) speak of a "popular archive" as recurrently used narrative and visual elements that circulate through the media to sustain running commentaries of a developing scandal. These elements include precedents that are not codified in law, as such, but which are recited in a way that link a current case to a past case. Familiar examples include appending "gate" to the designation of a scandal, or reciting the question "What did the president know and when did he know it?" to link the latest in a series of scandals to the precedent furnished by the Watergate scandal and hearings.

20 Sacks (1992, pp. 175–187), "Conveying information: Story-connective techniques; recognition-type descriptors; 'first-verbs'; understanding; differential organization of perception," Lecture 2, Winter 1970.

21 Such "racialized vision" is well-known to lawyers during jury selection and even in their efforts to find a favorable locale for a trial. Patrick Watson pointed out in a comment on an earlier draft of this paper that Jason Van Dyke's legal team requested a change in venue for the trial from Cook County to a Chicago suburb that would more likely result in a predominantly white jury.

22 Meehan (2000, p. 113) points out that after video and audio recording equipment was included in police vehicles, individual officers and police forces exercised

discretion over when and how to use it, and under what conditions to make recordings available to the media and as trial evidence.

23 One of Harold Garfinkel's earliest research projects explicated discrepant judgments and rationalities supporting verdicts in trials involving inter- and intra-racial homicides. See Garfinkel (1949).

24 Sacks (1992, pp. 504–511), "Fragile' stories; On being 'rational'," Lecture 15, Fall 1971.

References

Austen, B. (2016) 'Chicago after Laquan McDonald', *New York Times* (20 April). Available at: https://www.nytimes.com/2016/04/24/magazine/chicago-after-laquan-mcdonald.html (accessed 19 February 2019).

Burns, S. (2008) 'Demonstrating "reasonable fear" at trial: Is it science or junk science?' *Human Studies*, 31(2), pp. 107–131.

Christensen, C. (2014) 'WikiLeaks and the afterlife of *Collateral Murder*', *International Journal of Communication*, 8(10), pp. 2593–2602.

Cole, S. (2001) *Suspect Identities: A History of Fingerprinting and Criminal Identification*. Cambridge, MA: Harvard University Press.

Danylko, R. (2014) "*Examining Police Training: How Officers Are Taught to Deal with Armed Suspects*," Cleveland, OH: Northeast Ohio Media Group. Available at: http://www.cleveland.com/metro/index.ssf/2014/12/how_police_are_trained_to_deal.html (accessed 21 February 2019).

Dupret, B., Lynch, M. and Berard T. (eds.) (2015) *Law at Work: Studies in Legal Ethnomethods*. Oxford and New York: Oxford University Press.

Edmond, G. and Mercer D. (1997) 'Scientific literacy and the jury: Reconsidering jury "competence", '*Public Understanding of Science*, 6, pp. 329–357.

Elsey, C., Mair, M. and Kolanoski, M. (2018) 'Violence as work: Ethnomethodological insights into military combat operations', *Psychology of Violence*, 8(3), pp. 316–328.

Garfinkel, H. (1949) 'Research note on inter- and intra-racial homicides', *Social Forces*, 27(4), pp. 369–381.

Garfinkel, H. (1967) *Studies in Ethnomethodology*. Englewood Cliffs, NJ: Prentice Hall.

Goldstein, J. (2016) 'Is a police shooting a crime? It depends on the officer's point of view', *New York Times* (28 July). Available at: https://www.nytimes.com/2016/07/29/nyregion/is-a-police-shooting-a-crime-it-depends-on-the-officers-point-of-view.html (accessed 21 February 2019).

Goodwin, C. (1994) 'Professional vision', *American Anthropologist*, 96(3), pp. 606–633.

Jasanoff, S. (1998) 'The eye of everyman: Witnessing DNA in the Simpson trial', *Social Studies of Science*, 28(5/6), pp. 713–740.

Jayyusi, L. (2015) 'Discursive cartography, moral practices: International law and the Gaza war' in Dupret, B., Lynch, M. and Berard, T. (eds.) *Law at Work: Studies in Legal Ethnomethods*. Oxford and New York: Oxford University Press, pp. 273–298.

Laudan, L. (2003) 'Is reasonable doubt reasonable?' *Legal Theory* 9, pp. 295–331.

Lynch, M. (1982) 'Closure and disclosure in pre-trial argument', *Human Studies*, 5(4), pp. 285–318.

Lynch, M. and Bogen, D. (1996) *The Spectacle of History: Speech, Text, and Memory at the Iran-Contra Hearings*. Durham, NC: Duke University Press.

Lynch, M., Cole, S., McNally, R. and Jordan, K. (2008) *Truth Machine: The Contentious History of DNA Fingerprinting*. Chicago, IL: University of Chicago Press.

Lynch, M. and McNally, R. (2003) "Science", "common sense", and DNA evidence: A legal controversy about the public understanding of science', *Public Understanding of Science*, 12(1), pp. 83–105.

Mair, M., Elsey, C., Smith, P. V. and Watson, P. G (2016) 'The violence you were/n't meant to see: Representations of death in an age of digital reproduction' in McGarry, R. and Walklate, S. (eds.) *The Palgrave Handbook of Criminology and War*. London: Palgrave Macmillan, pp. 425–443.

Mair, M., Watson, P., Elsey, C. and Smith, P. (2012) 'War-making and sense-making: Some technical reflections on an instance of "friendly fire"', *British Journal of Sociology*, 63(1), pp. 75–96.

Meehan, A. J. (2000) 'Transformation of the oral tradition of the police subculture through the introduction of information technology', *Sociology of Crime, Law and Deviance*, 2, pp. 107–132.

Mezey, N. (2013) 'The image cannot speak for itself: Film, summary judgement, and visual literacy', *Valparaiso University Law Review*, 48(1), pp. 1–39.

Park, M. (2018) 'Police shootings: Trials, convictions are rare for officers', *CNN* (updated 3 October). Available at: https://www.cnn.com/2017/05/18/us/police-involved-shooting-cases/index.html (accessed 21 February 2019).

Pollner, M. (1975) '"The very coinage of your brain": The anatomy of reality disjunctures', *Philosophy of the Social Sciences*, 5, pp. 411–430.

Pomerantz, A. (1984) 'Giving a source or basis: The practice in conversation of telling "how I know"', *Journal of Pragmatics*, 8, pp. 607–625.

Pomerantz, A. (1987) 'Description in legal settings' in Button, G. and. Lee, J.R.E. (eds.) *Talk and Social Organisation*. Clevedon, OH: Multilingual Matters, pp. 226–243.

Risinger, D. M. (2000) 'Preliminary thoughts on a functional taxonomy of expertise for the post-*Kumho* world', *Seton Hall Law Review*, 31(2), pp. 508–537.

Sacks, H. (1992) *Lectures on Conversation*, Vol. 2, edited and transcribed by Gail Jefferson. Oxford: Blackwell.

Schaffer, S. (1992) 'Self-evidence', *Critical Inquiry*, 18(2), pp. 327–362.

Schneider, C. J. (2015) *Policing and Social Media: Social Control in an Era of New Media*. London: Lexington.

Shapin, S. (1995) 'Cordelia's love: Credibility and the social studies of science', *Perspectives on Science*, 3, pp. 255–275.

Shapiro, B. (1986) '"To a moral certainty": Theories of knowledge in Anglo-American juries 1600–1850', *The Hastings Law Journal*, 38, pp. 156–193.

Shapiro, B. (2002) 'Testimony in seventeenth-century English natural philosophy: Legal origins and early development', *Studies in History and Philosophy of Science*, 33, pp. 243–263.

Sudnow, D. (1965) 'Normal crimes. Sociological features of the penal code in a public defender's office', *Social Problems*, 12, pp. 255–276.

Vertesi, J. (2015) 'The problem with police body cameras,' *Time Ideas* (4 May). Available at: http://time.com/3843157/the-problem-with-police-body-cameras/ (accessed 21 February 2019).

Watson, P. G. (2018) 'The documentary method of [video] interpretation: A paradoxical verdict in a police-involved shooting and its consequences for understanding crime on camera', *Human Studies*, 41, pp. 121–135.

Wilke, C. (2017) 'Seeing and unmaking civilians in Afghanistan: Visual technologies and contested professional visions', *Science, Technology, & Human Values,* 42(6), pp. 1031–1060. DOI: 10.1177/0162243917703463

Part 3

Meaning and emotions in legal interpretation

The question as to whether the reference to rules, in legal reasoning, obeys a purely formal logic is at least as old as the advent of codified positive law. The ideal of a dispassionate law, applied in a mechanical way, although it weakened from the First World War onward, is observable at any level, beyond the process of digitalizing justice. Part 3 of the volume questions this ideal and tends to show, while underscoring the irreducibly human competences of judges, the limits of a pretense to integral standardization of rule-based decision making.

Focusing on judiciary conciliation hearings, Barbara Truffin highlights the impact of rules on the emotional and practical performance of judges' daily and ordinary tasks. She describes, regarding the emotional meanings attached to the tasks undertaken by the judges in charge of conciliatory hearings, two opposite attitudes: a pedagogical engagement with emotional display versus a more classic and authoritative style of distancing. She also identifies the rules' temporal and spatial dimensions as key operators of judges' everyday tasks, and especially their instructive nature.

In a similar vein, Julie Colemans analyses how emotional expressions make it possible to understand how a family judge's decision is constructed. Emotional perceptions constitute a precious tool for decoding both the categorizations adopted by the judge and the problems of coordination which are due in large part to the disconnection between the language of legal professionals and that of laymen. Legal rules permeate practices; they form the basis of a legal culture integrated by legal professionals and remain an implicit reference, offering a horizon of shared expectations. This language remains hermetically closed to lay litigants. While lawyers translate the demands of their client into legal terms, interactions of litigants without counsel are less fluent. In such cases, judges have to act as translators and mediators, which is awkward when the magistrate is caught up in emotionally charged interactions.

Observing how judges, in different Muslim societies, adjudicate in cases related to homosexuality, Baudouin Dupret et al. show how the many cases exhibit striking similarities in the ways in which judges bypass gaps and silences in legislation via the selection of alternate rules efficient in sanctioning behaviours that are socially associated with, though not necessarily nor legally included in, the offenses constituting the basis for the indictment. The classical jurisprudential debate regarding the relationship between law and morality should be revisited in praxeological way: legal practical reasoning articulates around legal rules; judges search and interpret legal rules according to moral norms; the moral cognition of legal rules does not coincide with the equating of law with rules-and-principles; and the moral cognition of rules does not preclude relative determinacy and predictability.

10 Time to agree?

Rules, agreements and *consent judgements* in a Belgian family court

Barbara Truffin

During the last decades, successive legislative reforms have profoundly transformed Belgian family law.[1] These reforms – which are still ongoing – are praised for having implemented principles of equality between spouses and parents through legal rules, whilst giving an increased momentum to judicial conciliation and formal agreements between (ex-)partners. Assessing the extent to which new formal rules of equality, as applied by professional judges, have achieved (or not) the proclaimed legislative objectives of modern equality stands far beyond the scope of this chapter.[2]

My contention here is far more limited: I am interested in understanding how legal rules of "conjugal and parental equality" are processed and communicated through the everyday reasoning, assumptions and emotional labour[3] of legal professionals. Indeed, to shed some light on the "ordinary lives" of legal rules at the heart of consent judgements[4] – which have become common artefacts in contemporary family trajectories – can contribute to understanding the bigger picture.

In order to do so, I have chosen to undertake ethnographic fieldwork in a large Belgian Family Court, following a praxeological approach. I have especially focused on the routinized organization of the conciliation hearings – "Chamber of Amicable Settlement" – conducted by professional judges, in order to identify the mundane reasoning, emotional labour and practical necessities interwoven with legal rules in the making of consent judgements.

In other words, the present chapter offers an ethnographic analysis of the making of judicial agreements between parents in a Belgian Family Court and focuses on the role formal legal rules of parental and conjugal "equality" play in judicial settings placed under the figure of conciliation.[5] What are precisely the judges in charge of the conclusion of such agreements doing when applying legal rules? How do the practical necessities of the orchestration and production of such judicial agreements articulate with the moral and emotional dimensions of interaction, time and spatial framing?

In the first section of the chapter, I give more information on my ethnographic observations: I present the legal rules at the centre of the scenes along with the documents through which they are made visible; and

I describe objects and folders, as well as the actors of the scene, its time and space. The second section analyses the conversational devices and material objects which delineate and relate spaces of agreement and adjudication in ten cases. The last section of the chapter reflects on the relationship between time and rules performed through acts of language and written documents produced in the conciliation hearings.

Conciliation from legal texts to ethnographic fields and objects

The general transformations of family judges' role which have taken place in different continents have been widely documented in different bodies of literature.[6] The regulation of conjugal separation or children-care related conflicts through Family Acts is broadly summarized as follows: a priority given to agreements between parents over judicial adjudication when they are not contrary to rules of public policy; rules of joint parental authority (exclusive authority being an exception); and rules of preference for shared custody. State regulation of the domestic sphere has therefore been deeply reshaped and, when civil judges are to intervene into parental conflicts, it is less and less according to explicit standards consecrated by legislative dispositions but in articulation with open standards such as the best interest of the child or through the "public policy"[7]conformity check that parental agreements have to undergo.

In Belgium, the legislative promotion of agreements in the field of Family Justice has received its own place in the Family Court Act of 2013 with the creation of a special "Chamber of Amicable Settlement" inside the Courts.[8] These conciliation hearings epitomize the regulatory model of family justice promoted by Belgian positive law, even though agreements and consent judgements can also be reached and formalized outside the Chamber of Amicable Settlement[9]. In the 13 judicial districts that Belgium counts, the organization of these hearings is left to the President of each Court.

According to the data provided by the Clerk's office of the Family Court, there was a total of 165 cases fixed in the Chamber of Amicable Settlements for the reference year during which I conducted my four months of observation[10]. In addition to observing hearings, I have also informally interviewed judges during, after or before the hearings and consulted the files of the cases long after the hearings had taken place, in order to gain a more longitudinal perspective on them. I also took part in one professional training session on conciliation organized at the Belgian school of judiciary and shared some of my observations with the attending judges and professional trainers.

During this period of time, I had the opportunity to attend 5 hearings that considered 13 cases; the Chamber was presided by 4 different judges who were approached through personal contacts and referrals by other judges or colleagues. Chamber of Amicable Settlement's hearings were organized each week, through a rotary system between the dozen of judges who were available at that time. They took place after a first public hearing – called an "introduction hearing – had been held by another judge in order to evaluate the possibility of the case to go through conciliation.[11] The judges had also collectively decided to allocate a maximum of an hour for each case in the Chamber. This decision illustrates their organizational autonomy. Family Courts in the country have made different choices: they distribute the conciliation hearings to "specialized" judges in order to separate more firmly decisional and conciliatory functions and give more or less time to the cases admitted in conciliation hearings[12]. Judges who welcomed me at their hearings were interested in talking about this issue of organizational autonomy.[13]

From the 12 cases scheduled for the hearings I attended, 2 cases never reached the bench because agreements were made outside the court. Among the ten remaining cases I could attend, seven total or partial agreements were written in the "one hour" format imposed upon judges, lawyers and parents. This success rate corroborates the data I had access to later on for the entire Court. As already mentioned, the total of conciliation cases fixed during the year of observation reached 165. There were 101 consent judgements taken out of these cases: an impressive success rate!

The everyday work performed by family judges varies according to different dimensions: among them the high number of cases and the increased pressure created by managerial directives on judges' functions; the technical difficulties of the cases and procedures; the emotional intensity of conjugal and parental conflicts; the presence or the absence of lawyers and the quality of their work in preparing and managing their clients' participation at the hearings; the heterogeneity of social and economic conditions of litigants; the difficulties in assessing the best interests of the children; and the general inclination of Family Court judges to rely on psychological expertise in order to objectify it through professional and legitimated means. Alongside these general factors, there is another and specific dimension which is addressed in this chapter: the impact of the rules of law themselves and their historical transformation toward a model of shared or interchangeable parental roles and obligations in a negotiated frame. Indeed, the content of the rules mentioned above has everyday implications for the tasks and work performed by the judges: they require judges to assess both technically and emotionally if and on which issues agreements between parents and ex-partners can be reached. Regarding the technical nature of rules, it is their temporal and spatial dimensions which characterizes the everyday tasks undertaken. But the importance and priority given to agreements and conciliation by the rules of law also require the judges to adapt the emotional labor they perform. If as other judges, they "must regulate their own emotions and display of feelings and those of the court users, as an essential component enabling court users as to experience the legal process as fair, impartial and legitimate" (Roach Anleu and Mack, 2005, p. 593), the moral and legal importance of agreements puts the principles of neutrality and impartiality under another light. The judges have to assess the limits of their (dis)engagement with litigants' particular concerns and respective bargaining power, whilst maintaining their own legitimacy and expertise toward both sides.

Before further discussion of the judges' distinctive styles in relationships with the types of emotional labour they imply, a first point has to be made about what, from an ethnographic viewpoint, makes legal rules visible and concrete in this space. I will then conclude this first section with an overview of the available characteristics of the parents in conflicts and the role played by their respective lawyers in negotiating agreements.

The ethnographic sites of legal rules: written forms, coloured files and speech acts

As in other judicial or administrative settings, legal rules are present, made visible and concrete through written forms or documents upon which judges rely throughout the hearings;[14] Civil Code rules about custody, child support and parental authority are converted into "ready-made" forms archived in computers which are available during the hearings to clerks and judges in order to organize and address the issues of the specific cases.

Legal rules are oriented to through the "check lists" and "agreement models" the judges direct should be completed by the parties. In doing so, judges adapt a working canvas according to their analysis of the characteristics of the cases: adaptation and selection of entries into the different dimensions of the cases will depend on the written documents they have read beforehand and on the oral explanations given (or not) by the parents and their lawyers during the hearings.

In this working process, the cardboard folders stand as powerful objects for the judges to arrange the facts and issues to be addressed in the "one hour" formula of settlement – and it is not uncommon to find "good luck" memos from one judge to others in the file as they feel the case is a difficult one to settle (as the yellow post-it I found in the cardboard of case C2). The files I could analyse received their colour according to the year the case was filed in.

They are organized in an inversed chronology order – the more recent documents on top – and by types of documents such as "records of hearing", "judgements", "documents folder" and "procedure folder".

On their check list and preformatted forms, the judges seek to assess if joint parental authority is contested, [15] and what are the reciprocal claims and current measures regarding (shared or not) custody[16] and child support.[17] Other entries such as spousal maintenance and attribution of conjugal residency are also anticipated by the canvas and will be raised or erased depending on the marital status of the parties. This is also the case for issues of authorization to leave Belgian territory (cases C2 & A3).

These forms, provided in the computers which are used during the hearings, serve as grids of translation of the cases "for all practical purposes"[18] into pertinent categories. When they have assessed the legal characteristics of the cases, linking them to rules' factual predicates (Schauer, 2009; Dupret, 2018), the judges start with the issues on which parents appear to be most likely to agree and adjust their list accordingly. They might offer explanations of the legal rules they refer to according to the evolution of the dialogues between parents and their lawyers, but the strength of the rules mostly resides in the forms and agreement models the judges are verbally and physically canvassing during the hearing.

If written codes are of course not physically brandished as "the Tables of the Law" during the hearings to summon the power of legal rules, this power does, however, radiate in a more ordinary fashion through dialogues engaged by the judges, objects and written acts they use or rely upon.

The "radiative" power of the rules is quite clear in the following case (D2). The father and the mother, recently parted, have both verbally agreed on giving the mother the principal (physical) custody of the three children and visitation rights to the father. Having checked this point, the judge is now dealing with the provisions of art. 203 of the Civil code. The model of children maintenance provided by this article switches when parents do not share residency rights. In this hypothesis, supports provided "in nature" are not evenly balanced on each parental side. The judge looks at the father and begins to explain:

JUDGE: To contribute to child support is a rule of public order: in other words, the law obliges the parents to pay proportionally to their means and does not allow for a parent not to pay. This is why I'm doing the math (looking at him, after having entered the numbers of their low incomes and the percentage of respective contributive capacity in her calculator machine).[19]

This legal operation will then be condensed through the written formula of the final document: "The agreement is not manifestly contrary to the interest of the minor children having regard to the elements known by the Court. Consequently, it is suitable to homologate the agreement".

When having reached this point, the judge asks her clerk to print the adapted and finalized agreement. The hearing closes with the judge reading aloud, animating the written words with her clear voice, each parent and lawyer holding the documents, following the progression of the reading. Soon after what still looks like a ritual, they will leave the room with "their own agreement" signed but written in a language whose lexical and grammatical contents they apparently did not fully master minutes ago. The printed words and formulas will remain in their possession, reminding them, as the judge did verbally during the hearing, that the power of the paper stops at the threshold of their own common (future) decisional power.[20]

Finally, before shaking hands and having to decide, without a word being exchanged, how to coordinate properly to leave the small room, the parents have to sign the agreement to make and mark them as their own.[21]

As in other judicial settings, we can recognize in the Chamber of Amicable Settlement distinctive speaking slots, time constraints and a massive orientation toward procedural correction and legal pertinence in the coordination of the actions[22]. Quite clearly, parents' agreements are provided here with a very strong legal monitoring.

"Conciliation skills": individual emotional dispositions towards peaceful settlements?

Judges and clerks play a central role in the coordination of speech interactions and writing operations. All the hearings I have attended took place in a small room attached to the biggest public hearing rooms. A simple table with typical office chairs were arranged for the parents and lawyers to appear. If this physical and material setting did not change from one morning hearing to another, the style of the judges presiding the hearings did.

Two contrasting styles were adopted by the four judges I could work with: a more direct and pedagogical style for two of them, and a more technical or entrenched style for the others. Each style was clearly associated with distinctive modalities of emotional engagement.

The first style was typically associated with moments in the interactions during which the "pedagogical judges" tried to reduce adversarial logic or respond to the expression of anger or strong emotional status by making statements about the classical judicial atmosphere parties should give up: "*You have to leave the oppositional logic and look for a mutual agreement*". A statement typically followed by an explanation of the different stages of the procedures and specific role taken by the Judges in the Chamber of Amicable Settlement in order to better to push them into agreement:

JUDGE: I do not adjudicate here. If there is no agreement at the end of the meeting, that's not a problem. Nobody will hold it against you. We will simply send back the case to Judge X … and the classical procedure will be followed.

And later on, in her explanations:

JUDGE: I have to add here that everything said here will not and cannot be used before the regular Chamber of the Court, agreed? (Judge A referring to the confidentiality rule of Art. 1253ter/1, §3,(6) of the Judicial Code).

The other pedagogical judge declares, in her humorous way, at the opening of her morning hearings to the first couple facing her and quietly sitting with their lawyer in between:

> I do present myself, I am a Canada Dry Judge: I cannot quench the thirst.

She is alluding to a commercial, quite popular in the 80's, which claimed this beverage had the colour and the taste of alcohol... without being alcohol. This presentation of herself downplays her own decisional power ("I'm not a real judge"), as much as it assumes that Court users are expecting an authoritative stance she has, however, given up on. The Canada Dry joke is also an indication given by the judge to the ex-partners that they must collaborate with her and each other, make reciprocal concessions and avoid emotional excess: there will be no real (i.e. authoritative) judge if there are no confrontations.

She then draws a positive portrait of negotiations and agreements:

JUDGE: Never forget that what is written in a judgement can be undone by an agreement. The court is a crutch.... Sometimes the parents fear to stand aside the judgements....

She never hesitates to add a formula, stating in bolded fonts: "It is here specified that the parties can always derogate to the present agreed modalities through a written and prior agreement" (Judge B).

When confronted with an obstacle in the explanation of one or the other parent, fearing to lose the consensus she has previously built, she makes the parties speak about their past and present modes of communication, and quite directly invites the expression of their emotions. She invites everybody to "*speak freely*" and asks: "*Why should you fear such a thing*?".

The two other judges also explained the frame of the meeting but did rely much more on the presence of lawyers (both through eye contacts and spoken utterances) and scrolled down the issues through technical angles at a fast pace. Their emotional display was less engaged and personal; they appeared more reluctant to engage in any form of guidance through encouragement and recognition of good and reasonable emotions and demands than the "pedagogical" judges. Relying more on the presence of lawyers, they created a greater authoritative stance and would more readily ask for psychological expertise in case of intense conflict and emotional outburst.

Interesting as they might be, these differences in style and emotional labour appear not to be determinant in the judges' capacity to persuade parents to enter into (total or partial) agreements. Indeed, on the ten cases I could follow seven were concluded by such agreements, sometimes to the apparent surprise of the judges themselves who confided to me "*this one I was sure, I could not make it*". Judge B even obtained a rate of 100% in my observations, but also in the statistics I could extract from the data provided by the Court's Clerk. The figure and skills of this one specific (and particularly pedagogical) judge might temper the general conclusion that the capacity to reach agreements is not derived from specific individual emotional skills. Indeed, the success rates of the three other judges, during this specific year, was more heterogeneous: Judge C had a 79% success rate, whereas Judges A and F succeeded in one of two cases regardless of their differences in style.

The making of agreements seems therefore rather consistent and efficient whatever the "styles" and the type of emotional labour performed by the judges in charge with the Chamber. This stands as a supplementary reason to document what are the collective and ordinary techniques used by these judges when modulating the spatial and temporal dimensions of the rules of "agreement". Before jumping to this discussion, the characteristics of the conflicts, the parents and their lawyers have to be presented in order to get a better grip on the ten selected case studies.

Parents, conflicts... and lawyers

The factual configuration of the ten cases examined by the judges, as well as the sociological indicators their treatment disclosed, are diverse and reflects the heterogeneous demographical composition of the big city in which the Court is located.

First it should be noted that, contrary to the legislator who has expressed a clear (even if not mandatory) preference for shared custody rights, this model was chosen by only four ex-couples out of the ten. Five mothers had already obtained or fought for principal custody and one father was granted it by the time the conciliation hearing took place.

In the ten cases, only one (*C3*) came to the judge at the express request of the father, i.e. without passing through the referral procedure from the regular chamber of the Court in a classical procedure. Interestingly, this unique case in which a clear and exclusive demand for "conciliatory" model is made, is one of the three which did not conclude in the "one hour formula" by a partial or total agreement. It is also one of the two cases in which the parties were not assisted by a lawyer and where the emotional distress of the father at the end of the hearing was clearly disapproved by the judge who told him in a cold tone that he was not allowed to seek advice from her as she was a (i.e. real) judge. The other unsettled cases were also the more voluminous files with a timespan exceeding four years of judicial battles by the time I have reopened them and checked on their evolution. In these two cases, the long judicial battle had produced numerous new judgements (sometimes consent judgements) and among the documents folders, a considerable amount concerned complaints to the police (for violation of the visitation right of the mother who by that time had lost her principal custody right). The passing of time had a clear effect of intensification on the conflictual nature of the cases and making the written documents of which they are composed more complex.

A common point in the three "no deal" cases lies in their object. All three of them concerned challenging claims against the principal model of residency already in place for the children. In these three cases, the fathers challenged the principal custody given to the mother and sought to exercise it themselves. In the other cases, if modalities of shared or principal custody were discussed and eventually agreed, the main points of discussion related to child support and repartition of extraordinary expenses.

There were very few cases in which lawyers did not assist the parents: only two out of the ten in total. I said above that one of these cases was a "failed" one in which no other judicial developments were recorded later on by the Clerk of the Court (C3). The other case without lawyers (B2) was a case in which the parents were already totally aligned and presented no problem of communication between them. They had turned to the Court in order to have an official record of their personal agreement in order for the father to document his familial charge for the National Office of Employment.

This clear presence and participation of lawyers in the hearings and conclusion of agreements can easily be read as the natural prolongation of the strong legal monitoring given to conciliation in Court. Lawyers are full partners of judges in the orchestration of the interaction, sometimes downplaying their clients' claims or disaffiliating from them in order to push forward the agreement. Others, more aligned on the "technical type" of judges, negotiated strongly each chosen word of the agreement giving a very high speed and attentional range to the interaction. Whatever might have been their strategy, each of their moves reinforced the asymmetrical nature of the interaction between parties and legal professionals. An asymmetry, as we will see, that articulated in a peculiar way with the "horizontal" and individualistic model of agreement.

In between conciliation and decision-making: moving into the asymmetrical spaces of rules

How do judges convince parents to "agree for their own good" in the form of *consent judgements*? And how does the decisional (adjudicative) space connect with the more horizontal space of deal making? Socio-legal studies have already pointed out that judicial conciliation typically corresponds to decisional modes of settlements. The practice described by Carol Greenhouse as "exclusive mediation" fits particularly well here: i.e. the third party heavily resorts to explicit normative references and his or her neutrality is assured by an official status (Greenhouse, 1985).

But how does this "exclusive mediation" type of formula work in the concrete setting of the Family Court? As mentioned in the first section, the references to legal rules are not always made explicit in the Chamber of Amicable Settlement. Moreover, legal rules are not operating in a vacuum or without connection to the moral dimension of cognition (Dupret, 2006). Here, I will try to show that this connection between legal rules and morality works on the factual predicate of the "rule of agreement" itself.

As already explained, judges usually engage and move between the lines of their full adjudicative power and their more restricted power as deal makers. They are doing so by accepting the decisional capacity of the parties, literally praising the "private sphere" as being above the law.[23] In doing so, they are downplaying their own decisional power – associated with the domain of positive law and adversarial attitude – and are making their "offers" more acceptable.

JUDGE A: The law says nothing; you're the first to decide for your kids (...). Parents run the show. Everything is possible if you do agree together. If not, but only if not, we will turn down to (regular) judgement.

(...)

JUDGE A: None of you have ever experienced a decision imposed by a judge. Believe me it can be highly upsetting.

MRS AND MR (together and agreeing): Well, that's actually why we are here today ...

JUDGE A: So, please try to think about it and leave this room more at peace....

The true magic of this type of hierarchical presentation of the values of agreement is that it simultaneously aligns with the factual predicate of the rule (to agree is good) but also justifies a decisional takeover if the condition is no longer met. The disagreement is fundamentally presented as a threat against stability in its multiple and reinforcing dimensions. Disagreement hinders the coordination of the different actions and operations during the hearing: it supposedly threatens the psychological wellbeing of the children; makes impossible the exercise of joint parental authority; and will infringe upon a well-oiled shared custody model. The ability to agree and to perform accordingly, with an adequate range of emotional display, is then a condition put to the "autonomy" of the parents in the conciliation hearing.

In other words, the mobilization of the moral register of the "responsible individual" by the judges aligns itself, in a perfect shape, with the legal rules they are in charge to apply. The importance of agreement in the formal legal rules has practical and emotional consequences in the hearing: it requires communicational aptitudes, continuation of the relationship with both parents and encourages the capacities to adapt oneself to the other's utterances and of mastering the expressions of strong emotions (*self-control*). In such a configuration, the legal register can easily fade away and give place to other normative figures. As the coordination of the hearing goes on, the judge, whose decisional power is theoretically entrenched, appears to be an actor fully engaged in the good orchestration of interaction, including the regulation of emotions: sanctioning wrong utterances and therefore "*bad parents*" who cannot display sufficient communicative abilities or who are seemingly overwhelmed by strong and negative emotions.

Here, the connection with psychological discourse and expertise is quite high. In one of her cases, judge A explains her professional knowledge of parental conflicts in the following terms:

JUDGE: If you want the situation to remain bearable, you should actively search a way to communicate. We don't impose you to be friends but joint parental authority implies that you decide together. You have to find a decisional process. The "split kid" is a suffering child. If you take the time to read child-psychological literature, you will see that they agree

> at least on one thing: shared custody can work only if parents stay in contact in regard with what concerns their child. "There is such problem, what do you think of it?". That is remaining parents beyond the separation.
>
> At the practical level, children are heard by the judges when they reach 12 years old.... So, you have to find a way: the problem you have experienced during the last holiday cannot happen again. You child is 4 years old... You have 14 years more to go (*the mother is silently crying*, A3 case).

Not surprisingly, when the judges have to deal with an obstacle too big to sustain an agreement, they typically explain their decision to stop the conciliatory process by the need for psychological expertise, relying on its external power to deflate the "stubbornness" of the facts. This is what judge C does in case C3, when she explains that she is stopping the "deal making" process; she cannot meet the daughter in the conciliatory procedure and the parents radically diverge on the reasons why she does not want to stay at her father's anymore. Judge C said:

> Here, you don't have the tools you have in a regular chamber, there is no psychological expertise. And actually, we need it. The father quite upset, replied angrily«. But what are we going to do concretely? Should I renounce to see her? To which school are we going to register her?

Judge A in case D2 also drew on the strength of the psycho-moral repertoire in face of a father from an African nationality, who had filed no request for a visiting right to his young baby; a situation the judge did not perceive as "normal" even if it visibly did not hurt the mother' feelings.

JUDGE (TO THE FATHER): Does it frighten you?
MR: Yes, I don't know what to do when she poops...with the diapers and so on.
JUDGE: But you do go visit her at the mother's place?
MR: I'm still a little bit upset....

The judge asks the mother if it is possible for her to be in the presence of the father, at her place, in order for the father to visit their baby or if the risks of disputing are too high. The mother quietly replies that the risks are too high.

JUDGE: But then what have you done until today?! (*realizing he has not seen the baby for months*)
LAWYER (*of the mother but taking side for both parents and herself from congolese descent*): I have to say here that in Africa, it is not the task of the father to provide such 'care'.

JUDGE: "all right, I can perfectly hear that tasks can be distributed in every single way and that is really, really good. But, all the babies of the world need their two parents. The baby will not know that she has a daddy..."(*she goes on in arranging the agreement with a visitation day for the father at the mother's place).*

Here again, moral legitimacy clearly stands outside the legal rules and relates to a vague and supposedly universal human psychology. This specific moral grammar is articulated with the form of the conformity-to-public-order check usually performed by the judges. It is to be mentioned that red flags of "public policy" issues vary according to judges and cases but are always contributing to "abnormal" narratives of parenting.[24]

This grammar is therefore used in a predictive fashion against persistent disagreements and stubborn facts, promising multilevel failures ("it is not good for your kid") or to move the decision-making elsewhere (i.e. handing the case over to the regular chamber); but also in order to impose "good" modalities in the best interest of the children with a great scope of variation according to judges' background expectations towards the case.

Troubles in communication, including emotional outbursts, are sanctioned by a return of decisional and vertical spaces: the return to a regular chamber or more or less subtle reminders that the conciliator is .... judging you. As we shall see, this play on spaces and the possibility to "escape" judicial imposition and moral judgements articulates with the "instructive" nature of the rules of agreement and the relationship with time.

"The time to agree?": escaping decision through endless anticipation

When they are engaged in the making of an agreement, judges, parents and lawyers all display a specific orientation toward time. My contention here, following Dupret & Ferrié's inspiring text, is that this temporal alignment is related to the very woven nature of law in action as an objectified dimension of its grammar: "the legal threading of relevancies connects different sites and instances of production. The thread's coherence is produced in a retrospective and prospective manner" (Dupret and Ferrié, 2015,p. 33).

Dupret and Colemans describe each and every judicial operation as based upon implicit or explicit instructions through which an instruction is transforming itself into a description and is made "instructing"; such operations "lay the referential and normative groundwork for future actions" (Colemans and Dupret, 2018, p. 17). In other words, reaching an agreement is not only weaving factual predicates to salient elements of oral interaction and written pieces, as we have seen in the previous section. It is also playing with "the time of the rules" as the agreement determine a precise scope of the rules in which will fall future "facts". Therefore, the application of the "instructions" extracted from the legal rules in an agreement, is not merely a description – as in writing down other procedural acts – but the enunciation of new "private" instructions for the parties which can freeze the linear progression of time (or at least of the referential rule).

For judges, this anticipation is intrinsically linked with the ultimate threat they can always use, of handing over the case to the regular chamber in case of persistent disagreements, emotional outbursts or stubborn facts. In case Dl, the judge A literally stated that to reach an agreement requires to project oneself into time.

JUDGE: You know, I think it is gonna be too tight in the future, this system of one week/one week for the holidays. And if it does not work (i.e the proposed change), we can always come back to the (previous) judgement. Today, I have the feeling you are against the idea to enlarge the system and are trapped in it. But we never know what tomorrow will be made of and you don't have, by any means, an obligation to achieve.

The projection into what would be the decision of "another" (imaginary) judge concerned all child support discussions I have assisted to, including case A3 as already mentioned above. When discussing these issues, all conciliatory judges were rapidly converting the declarations of the parents regarding their respective incomes and expenses into Art. 203 of the Civil codes prescriptions with the help of their calculator; they then presented the results of their computation as the potential decision the judges of the regular chamber would take later on.

Lawyers actively contribute to this type of anticipation. In case A3, the lawyer of the father even added this comment after the demonstration made by the judge:

LAWYER: Well, that is precisely what I have already explained to Mr. X!! 'We should accept a 60/40 formula for the contributive capacity *(desolidarizing himself from the refusal of this client to meet the proposition of the other side; after this episode, the judge invited the parties to go in the hall to discuss the best options with their clients. When they re-entered the room, the deal was done).*

In case B3, this "temporal" and strategic play between professional actors was pushed even further. The judge neutralized a particularly vehement lawyer – she had known this person for a long time as she explained me later – referring to what he should know of the Court's habits when ruling on art. 203 as self-evident and indisputable. In doing so, she used him to ratify her own statement about the future application of the rule on the situation of the parents, and left him with no other alternative other than disaffiliating himself from her central and authorized knowledge.[25]

Not surprisingly, parents also display similar orientations toward the "future" of the rule. This can be seen in case A 3, when the mother burst out during the hearing:

MOTHER: It is impossible to speak with him. He has even told me 'I do what I want'.
FATHER: The father replied: I have never said 'I do what I want': I have looked at the case law.
JUDGE (*interested in his knowledge*): I am curious to know, now.
FATHER: Well I have researched Belgian and French case law, and I have understood that I should have taken my son back to school on that day.

The determination of the scope of the rules helps to stabilize the agreement which becomes the seat of individualized rules and standards for the future. As expressed by Dupret, the effect of such practical grammar of the rules is "in brief, to temporalize the eternal" (Dupret and Ferrié, 2015, p. 37).

Conclusion

Progressing from documenting the connections between rules and facts of the files towards the understanding of the temporal characteristic of deal making leads me to several concluding remarks.

First of all, it is not a surprise that the "egalitarian" model framed by formal legal rules and their encouragements to resort to judicially negotiated agreements does not escape the classical asymmetrical organization of legal activities. As we have seen, the entire chain of production of agreements relies upon a very strong legal monitoring of the parents, even if it also requires specific emotional labour from the conciliatory judges. Producing a consent judgement depends on many operations of translation from natural language towards legal categories and procedural correction. In this regard, it is highly revealing that one of the cases where it was not possible to reach a deal, was a case with no lawyers to assist or to "translate" and organize the stories. This meant that it was difficult to manage the feelings and emotional expressions of the parents in the one hour "format" chosen by the Court to fix conciliation hearings. It is also highly instructive that the operation of public policy conformity checks is more likely to challenge already vulnerable or "non-conforming" parents deals, exposing them to the strong "psycho-individualistic" morality of the judges' background expectations.

This analysis also shows that factual correspondence between opposite claims and parents' communicative and emotional skills are key ingredients for the judges to obtain a deal. Conciliatory judges are more likely to succeed and reach an agreement with cases in which the narratives and written pieces of the parents can easily be put at the same level and are kept in line with the rational deliberative model enshrined in the legal rules. In this context, emotional outbursts have to be transformed during the hearings because they threaten principles of co-parenting, but also the necessities of deal making and the legitimacy of the conciliator. The pedagogical "type" of judges employ an explicit discourse on the alliance between emotional self-control and the virtues of judicial conciliation. The "technical" judges are much more reluctant to engage in any positive guidance of emotion. However, both reach a similar amount of total or partial agreements.

Consent judgements are therefore more likely to be reached with reciprocal claims which do not support a radical change in the practical modes of organization, and with parents who can adapt their emotional status to the emotional regulation of the judges displaying mastery and self-control. They tend therefore to assure the already well documented "conservative" function of legal operations, as they can momentarily freeze time and formulate self-made rules of parenting.

Notes

1 Legal scholars and sociologists have classically used the concepts of privatization and desinstitutionalization of conjugal and parental relationships to account for this legal and judicial transformation taking place in many countries. See among others, Ronfani (1997), Théry (1998), Cardia-Vonèche and Bastard (2005); Le Collectif Onze 2013. For Belgium law, see De Scheemaeker (2009), Massager (2011).
2 On the discussions by socio-legal studies over the possibilities to measure successes or failures of legal reforms and mobilizations along with the theoretical complexities of the relationships between law and society it entails, see Mc Cann (1996) and (1994).
3 Roach Anleu and Mack (2005).
4 i.e. a formal judgement which gives legal force ("homologation", in French) to the agreement reached in front and with the help of a professional judge.
5 On judicial conciliation in different contexts see Ben Hounet (2018); Berthomé (2009); Nader and Todd (1978); Gulliver (1969), Greenhouse (1985), Silbey and Merry (1986).
6 See references in footnote 1.
7 On public policy and international public order in Family Justice, see among others Bernard-Maugiron and Dupret (2012).
8 Uyttendaele (2017); in a near future the legislator could even go further and make preliminary mediation meetings a mandatory and conditional step before accessing to Family Court, as it was proposed by the former Minister of Justice.
9 Article 1253 *ter*/1, §3, (1) and (2) of the Judicial Code according to which the Family Chamber has the discretionary power to attempt a settlement in the Family Chamber or to refer the case to the Chamber of Amicable Settlements of the same Court.
10 According to the official published judicial statistics, there were slightly more than 1,000 cases involving minor children opened before the Court during the same year. 165 of them passed through the new Chamber of Amicable Settlements.
11 "A referral can be made upon request of the parties or if the judge considers it necessary. There are no legal criteria to assess this necessity. A judge has the

discretionary power to decide when and why a referral to the Chamber of Amicable Settlement is necessary" (Raes (2019), § 45).

It is also possible for the parents to turn to the Chamber of Amicable Settlement directly (Article 1253 *ter*/1, §3, (1) of the Judicial Code. Among the 13 cases, 2 cases pertained to this category.

12 Such choices are alluded by Raes when underlining "geographical differences, resulting in unequal access to the Chamber of Amicable Settlement" (Raes, 2019: §69); see also Boone (2016).

13 Usual measures were agreed with judges and clerks in order to make people, place and time anonymous; my presence in the meeting was explained and could always be challenged by lawyers and parents in conflict.

14 See Weller (2011).

15 Art. 374 § 1 of the Civil Code states that:

> [§ 1er.] When parents do not reside together, parental authority remains jointly exercised and the presumption established in art. 373, al. 2 applies
>
> In the absence of an agreement on the organization of physical custody of the children, important decisions about his or her health, education, formation, leisure's and religious or philosophical orientation or in the case such an agreement is deemed contrary to the interest of the child, the Family Court might attribute exclusive parental authority to one of the parents.

It is to be noted that in the ten analyzed cases, none of them was a 'hard case' involving a discussion or claim for exclusive parental authority, even if one of them (C2) implied at least one recorded act of violence from a mother against her children, denounced by school authorities during the civil procedure between parents. For a discussion of cases concerning exclusive parental authority see Simon and Truffin (2018).

16 As explained by Simon and Lecoyer, the Belgian Civil Code prioritizes agreements between parties (article 374, § 2, al.1 of the Civil Code) and makes equal shared residency (i.e. custody) the reference model (article 374, §2, al. 2 of the Civil Code). "Failing agreement between parents, the law stipulates that the court must, if so requested by one of the parents, primarily consider the feasibility of an equal shared residency between the parents. However, if the court considers that equal shared residency is not the most appropriate formula, it may decide to order another arrangement (article 374, §2, al. 3 of the Civil Code). In any case, the court must rule with a particularly reasoned judgement that takes into account the specific circumstances of the case and the interests of the children and the parents (article 374, § 2, al. 4 of the Civil Code)" (Simon and Lecoyer, 2015, p. 191).

17 Article 203 of the Civil Code states: "§1. Father and mother have to provide, in proportion to their means, to housing, support, health, oversight, education, formation and well-being of their children. If formation is not achieved, the obligation is pursued after the civil majority of the child. § 2. These means include among others all professional incomes, immovable incomes and movable property incomes of the father and the mother, as well as all advantages and means by which they maintain their level of living and the living level of their children."

18 Garfinkel (1967, p. vii).

19 In doing so, the judge also refers, but without mentioning it to Art.1397 § 2 and Art. 1253 ter/4 §2 of the Judicial Code. She is putting words on the public order conformity check she is operating: not leaving room to alternative solutions but a fixed amount of money representing the child support due by the father who does not share physical custody.

20 It is quite close to Bastard's first descriptions of French Family Judges who praised the parents when reaching an agreement "for the active part they took in

the work of building the agreement and transfer to them the responsibility of the agreed measures" (Bastardn, 1996, p. 73).

21 On signature, see the classical works of Fraenkel (2008).

22 Atkinson and Drew (1979); Drew and Heritage (1993).

23 This sequence of interaction will never prevent the judge from performing, later on in the hearing, the conformity check with legal rules elevated at the level of public order as seen above.

24 Even if the ethno-national dimension of the cases – 2 of the 10 selected cases – was not systematically addressed by the judges through "abnormality" framing, it is clearly a reactive zone for background expectations as can be. For the place of ethnicity in family justice see e.g. Simon (2015); Simon and Truffin (2016); Bessière et al. (2018).

25 The rest of her strategic negotiations is also interesting. She explained me after the hearing that she felt she had pushed the mother's lawyer a little bit too much, but knew she could take this risk after having backed his protective position towards the mother when rejecting the lawyer's further proposition of a joint bank account for extraordinary expenses: a proposition she felt was not suited to the current situation "because it could be experienced by the mother as controlling".

References

Atkinson, M. and Drew, P. (1990[1979]) *Order in Court: The Organisation of Verbal Interaction in Judicial Settings*. Houndmills: Macmillan.

Bastard, B. (ed.) (1996) *Reconstruire les liens familiaux: nouvelles pratiques sociales*. Paris: Syros.

Ben Hounet, Y. (2018) 'Les rituels judiciaires et parajudiciaires: conciliations et arbitrages dans le Nord de l'Afrique (exemples algérien, soudanais, nigérien)'. *Oñati Socio-legal Series* [online], 8(3), pp. 1–14. Available from: http://ssrn.com/abstract=3102244

Bernard-Maugiron, N. and Dupret, B. (ed.), (2012) *Ordre Public et droit musulman de la famille. En Europe et en Afrique du Nord*. Marseille/ Bruxelles: IRD éditions/ Bruylant.

Berthomé, F. (2009) 'Démêler, racommoder. Analyse interactionnelle de quelques dispositifs de conciliation' in Bonhomme J. et. Severi C. (ed.) *Paroles en actes*. Paris: L'Herne, *Cahiers d'anthropologie sociale*, 5, pp. 139–161.

Bessière, C., Biland, E., Bourguignon, A., Gollac, S., Mille, M. and Steinmetz, H. (2018) ' "Faut s'adapter aux cultures Maître". La racialisation des publics de la justice familiale en France métropolitaine', *Ethnologie Française*, XLVIII(1), pp. 131–140.

Boone, R. (2016) "Twee jaar familie- en jeugdrechtbanken: tijd voor een evaluatie (interview met H. De Paepe, K. Gerets, K. Grisez, K. Vander Steene, J. De Ridder, W. Verhaegen, A. Bruneel, S. Brusselmans, L. De Meirsman, E. Raskin and S. Brouwers)". *Juristenkrant*, 336, pp. 8–9.

Cardia-Vonèche, L. and Bastard, B. (2005) 'Vers un nouvel encadrement de la parentalité ?' *Informations sociales*, 122(2), pp. 110–121.

Colemans, J. (2015) 'Ce que les émotions font faire aux professionnels du droit: Jalons pour une approche praxéologique des expressions émotionnelles dans la sphère judiciaire', *Social Science Information*, 54(4), pp. 525–542.

Colemans, J. and Dupret, B. (2018) 'Introduction' in Colemans, J. and Dupret B. (eds.) *Ethnographies du raisonnement juridique*. Paris: Droit et Société/ L.G.D.J, pp. 7–22.

De Scheemaeker, C. (2009) *Garde partagée: égalité parentale et intérêts de l'enfant enfin rencontrés*? Liège: Edipro.

Drew, P. and Heritage, J. (ed.) (1993) *Talk at Work: Interaction in Institutional Settings*. Cambridge and New York: Cambridge University Press.

Dupret, B. and Ferrié, J.-N. (2015) 'The practical grammar of law and its relation to time', in Dupret, B., Lynch M. and Berard T. (eds.) *Law at Work: Studies in Legal Ethnomethods*. Oxford: Oxford University Press, pp. 27–48.

Dupret, B. (2007) 'Legal pluralism, plurality of laws, and legal practices: Theories, critiques, and praxiological re-specification', *European Journal of Legal Studies*, 1, 296–318. Available at: http://www.ejls.eu/1/14UK.pdf

Dupret, B. (2010) 'Droit et sciences sociales. Pour une respécification praxéologique', *Droit et Société*, 75(2), pp. 315–335.

Dupret, B. (2011) *Adjudication in Action: An Ethnomethodology of Law, Morality and Justice*. Farnham: Ashgate.

Fraenkel, B. (2008) 'La signature: du signe à l'acte'. *Sociétés et Représentations*, 25, pp. 13–23.

Garfinkel, H. (1967) *Studies in Ethnomethodology*. Englewood Cliffs, NJ: Prentice-Hall.

Greenhouse, C.J. (1985) 'Mediation: A comparative approach'. *MAN*, 20, pp. 90–114.

Gulliver, Ph. (1969) 'Introduction' in Nader, L. (ed.), *Law in Culture and Society*. Berkeley and Los Angeles: University of California Press, pp. 11–23.

Le Collectif Onze (2013) Au *tribunal des couples: enquête sur des affaires familiales*. Paris: Éditions Odile Jacob.

Lecoyer, K. et Simon, C. (2015) 'The multicultural family in conflict: Legal and socio- anthropological perspectives on child residency', *Journal of Legal Pluralism and Unofficial Law*, 27(2), pp. 190–207.

Massager, N. (2011) 'Partie VIII – Autorité parentale et hébergement' in *Droit des personnes et des familles – Chronique de jurisprudence 2005–2010*. Bruxelles: Larcier, pp. 387–482.

McCann, M. (1994) *Rights at Work: Pay Equity Reform and the Politics of Legal Mobilization*. Chicago, IL: University of Chicago Press.

McCann, M. (1996) 'Causal versus constitutive explanations: Or on the difficulty of being so positive...'. *Law and Social Inquiry*, 21(2), pp. 457–482.

Nader, L. and Todd, H. (1978) *The Disputing Process: Law in Ten Societies*. New York: Columbia Press University.

Raes, S. (2019) 'Legal tools for amicable dispute resolution in Belgian (family courts)'. *Family & Law*, DOI: 10.5553/FenR/.000038

Roach Anleu, S. and Mack, K. (2005) 'Magistrates everyday work and emotional Labour', *Journal of Law and Society*, 32(4), pp. 590–614.

Ronfani, P. (1997) 'La déjudiciarisation du contentieux familial', in Meulders-Klein M.-T. (ed.) *Famille & Justice. Justice civile et évolution du contentieux familial en droit comparé: actes du congrès international*. Bruxelles: Bruylant/L.G.D.J, pp. 43-59.

Schauer, F. (2009) *Thinking Like a Lawyer: A New Introduction to Legal Reasoning*. Harvard, MA: Harvard University Press.

Silbey, S. and Merry, S. E. (1986) 'Mediator settlement strategies', *Law & Policy*, 8(1), pp. 7–32.

Simon, C. and Truffin, B. (2016) 'La diversité culturelle en procès: l'expérience de la justice belge par les familles à composante migratoire, quels enjeux pour le pluralisme juridique?'. *Anthropologie et sociétés*, 2, pp. 107–129.

Simon, C. and Truffin, B. (2018) 'Distances multiples et rupture communicationnelle dans la justice familiale belge. L'altérité culturelle dans la construction du raisonnement juridique' in Colemans, J. and Dupret, B. (eds.) *Ethnographies du raisonnement juridique*. Paris: Droit et Société/ L.G.D.J, pp. 195–221.

Simon, C. (2015) 'The "Best Interest of the Child" in a multicultural context: A case study', *Journal of Legal Pluralism and Unofficial Law*, 47(2), pp. 175–189.

Théry, I. (1998) *Couple, filiation et parenté aujourd'hui: le droit face aux mutations de la famille et de la vie privée*. Paris: Odile Jacob.

Travers, M.H. (2001) 'Ethnomethodology, conversation analysis and law'. *Droit et Société*, 48,pp. 349–366.

Uyttendaele, N. (2017) 'Chambre de règlement à l'amiable et autres modes amiables de règlement des conflits' in Van Gysel (ed.) *Le contentieux familial: Le Tribunal de la Famille et le Juge de Paix*. Limal: Anthémis, pp. 149–167.

Weller, J.-M. (2011) 'Comment décrire ce qu'on ne voit pas? Le devoir d'hésitation des juges de proximité au travail', *Sociologie du travail*, 53(3), pp. 1–21.

11 Law, emotions and categorisations

Lightning a judicial blind spot: on the role of emotions inside the magistrate's decision making

Julie Colemans

Belgian family law is particularly noteworthy for an extraordinarily high number of cases but also for organising an exceptional procedure in the court of first instance. The legislature provides for the fact that family litigation should be based largely on consensus. The amicable settlement chamber, the preference of the legislature to arrive at agreement in case of divorce, conciliation, the specificities of the introduction of legal proceedings (in particular, the joint petition) add a particular colour to litigation. The involvement of parties during hearings is therefore more important than in other disputes, with the added consequence of a tension between the lived situations of parents who reveal their intimate lives to a judge who is representing justice, and his ideal of rationality, impartiality, respect for rules and temperance. However, as soon as we become interested in the law as it is lived and not as defined by its designers, we cannot conceal its emotional dimension.

This contribution aims to show how emotions that are supposedly so far removed from legal rationality make it possible to get an intimate understanding of what happens at the heart of family court hearings. While criminal law has been the object of studies on the other side of the Atlantic, private law, and as far as we are concerned, family law, has been little investigated. And yet, as highlighted by Clare Huntington, "divorcing spouses may feel anger and resentment, children in foster care may experience abandonment and fear and parents who lose custody of a child to the state may suffer a deep loss". Her observation is indisputable: "the US family law system is not well attuned to the emotional needs of litigants" (Huntington, 2016). Analysing the scene of the hearing is consequently very important in order to understand how the decision is constructed. We will see that emotional perceptions constitute a precious tool for decoding both the categorisations adopted by the judge and the problems of coordination which are due in large part to the disconnect between the language of legal professionals and that of the layman.

Having set out the theoretical and methodological milestones of this type of approach, we will show how emotions contribute to understanding legal situations. Although always present and yet rarely documented, emotions are seen but unnoticed. Yet both lawyers and magistrates rely on the emotional expressions observed in the parties involved in the hearing. This is in order to reformulate a debate based on the magistrate's reaction in the case of the former, or to test a proposed statement during the conclusion, in the case of the latter. Emotions, then, are at the heart of the categorisations operated by the parties in the hearing.

Methodological milestones

The challenges linked to describing the action have informed ethnomethodological studies since the founding work of Garfinkel (1967) and Cicourel (1968). Breaking off from the Parsonian approach which saw action as the result of a process which was beyond the reach of the actors, ethnomethodology places the actor at the heart of his questioning. "The point of view of the actor and his role in the organisation of the action must be analysed by intrinsic tools and the categories of analysis must be those used by the participants themselves" (Fornel and Leon, 2000, pp. 133–134). The attention given to the endogenous production of phenomena of order and categories mobilised by the actors in the interaction has naturally driven the observer to give as authentic an account as possible of the interactions. Conversation, understood as an activity in itself, also becomes the preferred empirical material for ethnomethodological studies.

During the 1980s, the analysis of conversation was informed by studies carried out on prosody and body language in the production and interpretation of meaning in context (Fornel and Léon, 2000, p. 150). Goodwin (1981) and Heath (1986) were the first to introduce visual and body dimensions into conversational analysis. This multimodal approach was then extended by Schegloff (1984) and Mondada (2007), who studied body language, Rossano (2012) facial expressions and gaze, and Mondada (2009), the body in interactional space. In short, multimodality is understood as "including sonorous and visual language and bodily resources employed by the participants (prosody, phonetics, syntax, lexis, gestures, looks, facial expressions, head movements, body postures, etc.)" (Mondada, 2012, p. 130).

This way of looking at conversation in an unexclusively logocentric way[1] concurs with the works of Watzlawick et al. (1972) on the pragmatics of human communication. According to him, "behaviour does not have an opposite. In other words, there is no "non-behaviour" (Watzlawick et al., 1972, pp. 45–46). So, if we accept that during an interaction, every behaviour has a message value and it is a communication, it necessarily follows that it is impossible not to communicate, whether we like it or not. Activity or non-activity, words or silence, everything has a message value. Such behaviours influence others, and those others, in return, are unable to be unreactive to these communications and therefore they, themselves, communicate" (Watzlawick et al., 1972, p. 46). Going from the sender to the receiver, communication is separate from standards of intentionality.

In parallel with this and concomitantly,[2] the sociology of emotions became a legitimate object of research in the 1980s[3] (Hocschild, 1983). Sociologists became actively involved in an exercise of objectivization (Game, 1997; Bernard, 2007) and definition (Cislaru, 2008; Scherer, 2011) of emotions emphasising the cognitive and evaluative role of emotions in this work.

At the meeting point of the sociology of emotions, the multimodal approach of conversation analysis and communicative pragmatics, I propose to consider emotions from the viewpoint[4] of the actors engaged in the interaction. Emotions, therefore, have a heuristic virtue: they reveal, by shedding new light on some the dimensions of reality that are little explored when focusing on conversations, rationales or power relations. We are not proposing a sociology of emotions whose object is the definition and capture of emotions *per se*. It is necessary, on the contrary, to extend the interpretive sociology to the experience of the person who feels sensation and emotions, perceives, thinks, believes, reasons in context and in interaction. Comprehension is therefore multimodal and contingent. *In situ*, the actor draws on the speech, body movement, looks and prosody. "Many human emotions are exhibited by characteristic facial expressions and manifested in typical tone of voice – as in the case of fear, anger, love and affection" (Bennett and Hacker, 2013, p. 201). The senses are at the heart of the interaction and as such reassert the place of the body in sociological analysis, adding a level that comprehensive analysis has long neglected, being, as it was, too preoccupied with shedding light on the rationality of the actors.

Emotions are therefore studied as interpretative resources to understand the action as it occurs. Emotional expressions[5] complete the spectrum of indications available to the sociologist to document an event. By taking account of the emotional dimension present in the lived scenes, the observer colours the language exchanges and refines the description of the hearing. The perception of the actors of the legal scene is consequently at the centre of the researcher's attention. It is a question of grasping what the members in interaction perceive and how these perceptions participate in the course of action that is in the process of occurring. A praxeological approach to emotions involves taking an epistemological, non-ironic position (Travers, 2001; Dupret, 2006). It is about describing "how ordinary members of society understand their own actions, rather than being ironic on this subject" (Travers, 2001, p. 352). By refusing to adopt an objectivising point of view on the phenomena observed, this approach uses the practical categories of the actors in order to take account of their ordinary point of view, by focussing on their procedures of interpretation and their situational ways of working. Understanding emotions "in the second person" (Colemans, 2015)[6] is a part of this research approach by highlighting the practical skills of the actors, that is to say, their capacity to perceive and interpret the emotional expressions of the person with whom one is interacting.

In order to do this, a three-dimensional methodological approach has been created. Firstly, the observation of the hearings was recorded with the consent of the parties present and their lawyer. This enabled me to write down the language exchanges as well as the prosody. This audio material was completed during the hearings, together with note-taking that concentrated on the salient elements that drew my attention: particular elements of the story, the behaviour of the parties or the judge, the lawyers and the attorney as the case may be. While in the beginning, the notes were indistinctly directed towards the postures of the parties and lawyers, elements of the dossier and reactions of the judge, the progressive acquaintance with the magistrates changed my perception of the hearings. Having become familiar, the scene offered another level of reading, more focussed on the non-verbal language of the judges (sighs, shrugging of shoulders, note-taking, laughs and looks).[7] Thirdly, the observation of the hearings was completed by interviews of self-confrontation carried out directly after the hearings. The focus is placed on the perception of the judges: how did he or she perceive the parties, their emotional reactions, the context of the affair. This is an opportunity to compare the perceptions of the hearing by the observer and those of the judge.[8] The feedback on the way the observer perceives the emotional expressions of the judge constitutes a powerful methodological tool. The mirror effect created by such feedback makes it possible to revisit the real-time hearing and grasp the interpretations, perceptions, impressions and feelings of the magistrate with regard to the case, in a contingent though slightly delayed way. Much is learned about the categorisations used by the judge with regard to the parties and lawyers, the quality of a plea, the dilemma with which the judge is confronted, the perception of a family dynamic or the personality of the parents. The observation of hearings and one-on-one interviews consequently seem complementary and inseparable. The emotional dimension of the scene cannot be understood without this supplementary explicitation which is only relevant with regard to the situational incongruities observed. In wanting to grasp the emotional "ordinariness" in the hearing, the researcher shifts the focus to the periphery of the phenomenon studied in order to better chance penetrate to its core. This helps to avoid the often-prohibitive pitfalls of an a-priori definition of the problem. Emotions, therefore, are a methodological entry point to an understanding of the legal phenomenon. In other words, emotions are a "pretext" for uncovering things which are seen but to which little attention is paid.

Detailed account of the hearing

The hearing reported below took place during 2017. It was a classic case of the separation of an unmarried couple with two children. The parents were aged between 30 and 40. The mother was accompanied by her lawyer. Based on her stooped and bent posture and avoidance of eye contact, I concluded that she was nervous and fearful. The father appeared without a lawyer. His attitude was much self-confident. Although slightly stooped he lounged on the bench and looked the judge up and down with an air of defiance. In spite of his attitude a certain nervousness was evident from the fact that he was continually tapping his left foot on the ground.

It was a hot June day in the new chamber of the courthouse. The judge has long since removed her magistrates robe. Smiling, she enthusiastically welcomed the third set of parents of the morning. After inviting them to be seated in a friendly tone, she began her routine:

JUDGE: Sir, madam, please be seated.

She gets to the heart of the matter immediately. In a quiet voice she asks the parents:

JUDGE: So, are you partners or legal cohabitants?
MOTHER: Partners.
JUDGE: Partners. And when did you split up?
MOTHER: In 2015.
JUDGE: So, you **agree** on some points of the petition?[9] Perhaps I'll go over them again… To see whether there is **agreement** on certain points. So: joint parental authority with regard to A. and O. We are dealing with important decisions about the lives of two children. Do we **agree**?

Family disputes are influenced by an ideal of consensus, imposed partly by article 374 of the civil code.[10] The vocabulary used is aimed at finding an agreement. However, in order that the parents can reach this agreement, it is important that they examine the decision and commitments that are preparing to make. In order to accompany them, the judge defines the concept of joint parental authority, which is the norm. The litigant, who is little used to the language and legal forms rarely has a clear understanding of the essential aspects of joint parental authority, the reason why the judge clarifies the legal notion – "So, our primary **concern** will be the important decisions for the children's lives". The layman sometimes confuses parental authority with the children's accommodation arrangements. This semantic clarification is important to enlighten the judgement of parents who are expected to find an agreement on the ways to organise their lives after separation. The judge takes the position of a third party who communicates relevant information and records the terms of agreement found between the parties. Or at least, this is the spirit of the law. The father's response somewhat shatters the consensual mode of communication.

FATHER: Yes. 50–50.

The judge bristled at the father's response. Then, while taking notes, she raised her head and looked at the father. Her face revealed an almost imperceptible annoyance.

JUDGE: So, we set their mum's as the principal residence of the children, Sir?
FATHER: Yes, *okay with that*, I agree that they should stay at their mother's place.

The father stresses that he agrees that the children reside with their mother: his use of the words "with that", implies that the question of the children's accommodation is reserved. This is confirmed by the following exchange. Their mode of interaction goes from being consensual to a more conflictual one.

Accommodation arrangements: a naturally conflictual communication

According to whether the judge addressed the father or the mother's lawyer, the modes of interaction were different. Between professionals, the communication is symmetrical while the communication between the father and the judge is asymmetrical.

Asymmetrical communication

JUDGE: With regard to secondary accommodation, how do you manage for the moment?

FATHER: For the moment I just have them for...she just wants to let me have them during my days off, but ***I don't agree with that!*** [The father becomes more aggressive] *I want 50–50 for everything! We had them together and I think we should both be responsible for looking after them!*

The father clearly formulates his disagreement and enters into a fairly typical conflictual communication in tribunals or courts where the search for a fault and imputation of responsibility constitutes the main line of exchange between parties. This is the case when he says, "she just wants to let me have them during my days off".

Although the judge spoke in a friendly and soft voice, she changed her tone, the voice became progressively more assertive. The judge nonetheless adopted a relatively understanding attitude to the father who was not represented by a lawyer. She listens to his request for an equal share in the children's accommodation but without viewing it favourably. She had a somewhat pedagogical attitude as far as the father was concerned.

JUDGE: Yes, but you are separated, you have been separated for two years, right? If my calculations are correct... And for the last two years you have been taking them for how many days per week, give or take? [Her voice became calmer]

FATHER: At the start, it was somewhat *à la carte*, and a few months ago she began to let me have them for two days...during my days off.

JUDGE: Yes, but I don't live with you Sir, so I don't know when you have time off [laughing but a little firm at the same time. Laughter often allowed the judge to keep a distance from proceedings]

FATHER: So, I have four days when I work, two days off in general, except when my last day of work falls on a Sunday, when I have three days off.

The mother's lawyer takes advantage of the last statement to present her suggestion to the judge:

LAWYER FOR THE MOTHER: What we suggested, in fact, is that Sir should take them for his two days off, but that changes every week, but Sir has his timetable for the year, isn't that right?
FATHER: That's right yes
JUDGE: You tell me that you agree that the principal place of accommodation for the children is their mother's and then you tell me you want a 50–50 arrangement. I am not sure exactly what it is that you want Sir.

The judge once again keeps the distance that the legal professional who has a knowledge of legal language has to which the layman doesn't have (to?)

FATHER: Well, I just want 50–50 for everything. So, I would like her to take them for a week then I take them for a week…for the holidays…

Despite the response of the father, the judge appears to be deaf to his request for equal share in the children's accommodation arrangements. She refocuses the exchange on the inaction and the responsibility of the father in the situation. There are only a few exchanges in this sequence, however, because the words of the father and the judge do not seem to meet. They develop in parallel, with the judge asking a question about the time that has elapsed since the separation and the father consistently reiterating his request for equal share in the children's accommodation.

The judge cuts him off: But *why* haven't you made this request before, this situation has lasted for two years and you decide on the day of the hearing, it's a bit *odd*.

FATHER: I went to get the documents a month ago. Long before then, we still had well…physical relations together. I left because I wanted to break up with her, but she didn't want us to separate and wouldn't let me be. This was followed by emotional blackmail then things calmed down again. We got on okay…sometimes things were okay and sometimes we argued.

The judge cut him off abruptly.

JUDGE: So, broadly speaking, there was nothing for two years…it's astonishing…that you should make this petition…Personally, I like periods of transition so I am not going to go from two days to equal accommodation because the **children** must come first. But I am trying to understand your reasons, because you took no action for two years and now, I get the impression that the petition is a reflex action and I need to know if it is for the benefit of the **children.**

FATHER: No, it's not a reflex action. The girls need to be with me as much as they need to be with her. I'm not trying to take the children away from her, I don't want to limit her access to them. I was never in agreement with two days per week when she said she would let me have them during my days off. And now...

It was clear that she was distancing herself from the father. The tone of the exchange changed:

JUDGE: Yes, but you took no action, that is what I find a little *odd*...
FATHER: It's only been like this for a few months, before that she let me have them for two or three days or more.
JUDGE: When Madam said you have been separated since 2015, I did not hear you say "no, it's not true".
FATHER: No, it has not been two years.
JUDGE: When she said it, *you did not challenge her*. So, your attitude seems to me to be a little *odd*.
FATHER: No, it's not.

The judge closed the discussion about the children's accommodation arrangements with the following sharply worded sentence:

JUDGE: I shall be the one to decide.

This ended the second phase of the hearing. Then the judge gathered information in order to set the contributive share. Interactions are emotionless.

JUDGE: Okay, what are the respective situations of the parties with regard to employment and income?
MOTHER'S LAWYER: Madam receives unemployment benefit as head of household.
JUDGE: Is that €1,100?
MOTHER'S LAWYER: 1,060.57.
JUDGE: Have you worked before Madam? Are you doing any courses?
MOTHER: I have worked; I am a care assistant.
JUDGE: And you work regularly?
MOTHER: I worked until January of this year. Up to January 26th.
JUDGE: And your plans now...
MOTHER: I plan to return to work eventually, yes.
JUDGE: Eventually, but you are doing some courses for the moment, are you actively seeking employment?
MOTHER: I want to train to be a nurse
JUDGE: Where did you register for your course?
MOTHER: I am going to get information at the forem.

JUDGE: So, for the moment there is nothing from your active search. How much is your rent or mortgage?
MOTHER: A rent of 400.
JUDGE: Do you live alone?
MOTHER: I live alone.
JUDGE: And you Sir, what do you do for a living?
FATHER: I work in public transport.
JUDGE: At the TEC?
FATHER: That's right, yes.
JUDGE: What is your income?
FATHER: An average of 1600–1700 euros.

The mother's lawyer laughed and shook her head. It was a signal frequently sent by the lawyers who wanted to cast non-verbal doubt on the allegations of the opposing party. When I asked the judge the question during the auto-confrontation interview, she told me she agreed with the lawyer.

JUDGE: And do you pay rent, or do you have a mortgage?
FATHER: 650 euros
JUDGE: Rent?
FATHER: A mortgage
JUDGE: Do you live alone?
FATHER: Yes
JUDGE: OK. So, about your working hours, Sir, can you tell me what they are?
FATHER: Well, in fact, there is one week when I start in the afternoon
JUDGE: Give me your hours, I need to know what they are over a 15-day period, I'm listening.
FATHER: So, the first week is a week of afternoons which begin usually at 15:30–16:00 until midnight roughly.
JUDGE: Yes, and for how many days is that?
FATHER: For two of the days my shift finishes late, in fact, when the third day is an afternoon, the last day is a morning.
JUDGE [beginning to get annoyed]: So, week 1: 15.30- midnight. How many days?
FATHER: 2
JUDGE: 2 days. On the other days of this week 1, what are your hours and how many are there?
JUDGE: Week 1, for two days, you work from 15.30- midnight. There are 5 days left in the week. What other days do you work and what are the hours each time?

The judge was visibly becoming impatient.

FATHER: The day after it's usually 11:00–19:00.
JUDGE: Yes.
FATHER: The last day is a morning, 06:00–14:00, it depends on the day.

During the exchanges between the father and the judge, the mother shakes her head to show that she does not agree with the hours given by the father. No longer able to contain herself, the mother intervenes:

MOTHER: It's not 06:00 it's 04:30.

The judge then questions the father while replying to the mother's objection:

JUDGE: Even 6 o clock. How do you propose to manage with the children then?
FATHER: My girlfriend is often with me.

The judge responds with both surprise and annoyance:

JUDGE: You have just told me you live alone, Sir!
FATHER: My friend, my girlfriend, or whatever you want to call her. Officially, I live alone but my girlfriend visits...
JUDGE: So, *you want all the advantages but none of the disadvantages.* You say you live alone but you are going to ask your friend to come and take care of the children in the morning. How long have you known this friend Sir?

Theses sentences marked a new distance taken by the judge with regard to the father who was now the object of an evaluative judgement on the part of the magistrate who continued with the following exchange.

FATHER: Six years
JUDGE: Well, well! you are very active indeed Sir.

The judge pauses. This allowed her to refocus on the problem linked to the children's accommodation arrangements and to avoid discussing the father's love life. She adopted a semi-understanding semi-reproachful tone.

JUDGE: Listen, I know the working hours of TEC workers are difficult. But given the hours you work; how do you propose to take care of the children?

Although the judge adopted a conciliatory tone, trying to be instructive and make the father see reason, there was a new breakdown in communication. The father replied in an aggressive tone:

FATHER: I'll stop you there.

The judge raised her voice to silence the father and continued her line of reasoning:

JUDGE: One week in two with children, O. is not yet 7 so we are not dealing with 16 or 17-year-old teenagers who can manage on their own! A. is 10 years old, so how does that work? It seems that it is always an outsider who doesn't actually live with you but who will come and look after the children? *How is that in the children's interest? My concern must be the children's interest and not yours.*

FATHER: The interest of the children is that I can drive them to school in the morning and my girlfriend can pick them up at 15:30.

The judge cuts him off again, raised her voice and insisted:

JUDGE: There has to be **personal** availability [she insisted heavily on this word] to avail of equal accommodation. The lack of personal availability is one of the red lines set by the legislator!

The framework of the exchanges became more and more legalistic. Having invoked the interest of the children which is at the heart of new family law, the judge invoked the availability requirement laid down by the legislator.[11] The judge gained the upper hand on the father and treated him more and more like a child, using a semi-moralising, semi-lecturing tone. She tried to get the father to see reason but without success.

FATHER: What am I supposed to do, go on the dole? So that I can see my children?

JUDGE: Nobody here is asking you to go on the dole. Does a relationship of quality require you to have the children half of the time, or even if it is not qualitity time?

FATHER: I want to see my daughters as often as possible, [like a scolded child who keeps repeating that he wants a sweet]

The judge repositioned the exchange while also showing some empathy. The tone was softer:

JUDGE: Sir, put your **children's interest** above your own, even if it is painful… …

FATHER: I am thinking of my children's interest: they need to be with their father!

JUDGE: So, you think the **interest of the children** is to be taken care of by your girlfriend when they could be snug and comfortable in their mum's house?

FATHER: And my mother can also take care of them, put them to bed and pick them up from school.
JUDGE: I'm afraid it's clear that you don't want to listen Sir. [She ends the discussion on this point]

The attempt to make the father see reason failed. The judge then considered that to continue the exchange would be pointless and decided to move on to a different subject. She ended the discussion very firmly and returned to her notes on the father's working hours.

JUDGE: So then, week 2, what are your hours?
FATHER: Week 2, it's a late shift and two afternoons

The judge cuts him off abruptly: I want exact hours please, Sir.

FATHER: 14:00–22:00
JUDGE: For how many days?
FATHER: 1 day
JUDGE: Then
FATHER: 11:00–19:00
JUDGE: 11–19 during how many days?
FATHER: 1 day. 10–18 during one day
JUDGE: 10:00–18:00 on one day, correct?
FATHER: And then one morning
JUDGE: And the morning time?
FATHER: 06:00–14:00 on average
JUDGE: Or half past four, it depends
FATHER: Yes, that's right.

A minute goes by without any exchanges, then the judge thought she was taking note of the hours over a 15-day period, but the father continued.

FATHER: The third week, is a week of mornings, then it starts again it goes in a three-week cycle, in fact.
JUDGE A LITTLE SURPRISED: Ah, so, it is three weeks. Okay, so tell me about the third week, I'm listening.
FATHER: The week of mornings is from 11:00–19:00
JUDGE: For how many days?
FATHER: 1 day
JUDGE: yes
FATHER: The second day is a morning 06:00–14:00, the third and fourth days too. On average.

The judge closes the questions relative to working hours and ended with the following sentence:

JUDGE: OK. Understood Sir.
FATHER [aggressively]: No, I haven't finished
JUDGE [laughing]: I'm the one who decides, Sir. Let's allow Madam to speak.

This last sentence was unequivocal. The communication between the father and the judge was asymmetrical. This was due, not only to the lack of a grasp of the rules and language of law on the part of the father, but also to the perception of the father's limited attitude.

Symmetrical communication

The mother didn't speak but her lawyer began her plea by describing the situation in detail.

Mother's lawyer: Thank you, your honour. So, there are two little girls, A. who has just turned 10 and O. who will be 7 in July. As Sir has confirmed and Madam has already told you, they have been separated for some time. Basically, they had attempted to find an amicable solution without going down the legal route.

So, there were some recurring problems when Sir had the children, they were systematically late for school. Their homework wasn't done, and you have some photocopies of the class diary which attests to the fact that there was a big **problem** with regard to the children's school progress, even when Sir only took them during his days off. As you rightly pointed out, Sir never petitioned to have them more than before, but now that Madam has drawn attention to the problems and the need for remedial measures, he wants equal custody. Another **problem**: Madam knows very well what she is talking about: the children are all too often witnesses to very violent disputes between Sir and his new partner, so this is a **problem** and Sir needs to be made aware of this **problem**. While it's good that Sir works, he has variable hours and my client has told me that the hours he has given you [the lawyer clearly shows by her smile that she has doubts about the hours given by the father] are not the exact hours he works: he starts at 04:00 in the morning but he tells you that he starts at 06:00. He tells you that in week 2 he only does one "early" shift while he actually does 2 or 3. Unfortunately, Sir does not have official proof of these hours. My client knows his hours well because the system has been the same for several years, and I get the impression that somebody is trying to pull the wool over your eyes. In addition to these **problems**, as you can see, Sir has been violent with Madam on several occasions, on December 7th, 2016, December 9th, 2016 and March 13th, 2017. You have medical certificates and photographic files attesting to the fact that Madam had her wrist fractured. I also submit a psychological report by psychologist Della

Giustina who clearly states that she aided my client with mental problems linked to finding herself in a situation of complex trauma, a variant of post-traumatic stress due to being in a relationship involving violent episodes as well as psychological abuse over many years. Therefore, we have a **concern**. And in addition, there is also a **concern** in relation to the children. I also submit the speech therapy assessment for O. which states clearly that ongoing care is needed. And so, your honour, for the moment the speech therapist is working with her parents so that her parents can help with the supervision of O's schoolwork. O needs these speech therapy sessions which Sir does not want to pay for as he considers them to be a waste of time. And so, we have a situation where Sir wishes to assume his responsibilities but does not want to pay for the speech therapy lessons. According to the assessment for O., she should have 70 sessions per year which is a considerable amount. With regard to A, we also have **concerns**. She is ten years old and is going to repeat her third grade again. With regard to the school PMS, speech therapy and ORL are required. Sir is against all these therapies, he refuses to pay for them, insults the grandparents who are helping A. and O. Basically, we are in a very **problematic** situation at the moment. So, *what Madam suggested*, in order to see whether Sir would act in good faith, was that he would pay for the sessions given that he has two days per week at least, it's obvious that he should cover the cost of ORL and speech therapy etc.

The father intervenes aggressively:

FATHER: I refuse to pay!

This intervention was directly ignored by the judge. The father was excluded from the debate between professionals. The asymmetry between the father and the legal professionals and the contrasting proximity between the lawyer and the judge could be felt here.

JUDGE: Do not interrupt, Sir, we are not in the Batte[12] here.

Having described the context, she formulated her different demands.

Mother's lawyer: Sir needs to show unequivocally that he has calmed down and we can assess the situation. So, what we contend, it is that *our request* concerning these two days which are not fixed will correspond with Sir's weekly timetable. Half of the school holidays, we have no problem with that, we petition that the daily journeys be assured by Sir as it will be complicated for Madam to make the journeys based on Sir's work hours which are not fixed. And so, with regard to the contributive share, I was surprised to learn that Sir gets 1,600 euros per month; my information, although I don't have the documentary proof at this stage [The Mother turned to look at her ex-partner to tell him it was not true] is that the approximate monthly salary is 1,900 euros; he has holiday pay of 500 euros...

JUDGE: I am going to petition a notice of assessment[13] in order to see all tax refunds.

MOTHER'S LAWYER: So, he has an overall monthly revenue of 2,400 euros. I am petitioning a payment of 200 euros per child per month. The children's allowance is 402 euros. There you have the information you need, and I submit it to you.

The judge is surprised:

JUDGE: For the contributive share, nothing has been paid for the moment?

MOTHER'S LAWYER: No

JUDGE [stunned]: Nothing at all??

MOTHER'S LAWYER: No, and Madam's parents help her to make the exceptional payments (speech therapy, etc.) because Madam earns 1,400 euros per month. The children…

The Father then became aggressive and intervened:

FATHER: At which point can I defend myself?

JUDGE: You have already spoken a lot, Sir. I will allow you two minutes to address the issue of money. How much do you want to offer Sir?

FATHER [on the defensive]: Offer what?

JUDGE [calmly]: How much of the contributive share are you offering?

FATHER [with an air of defiance]: I am offering nothing at all!

Seemingly impassive, the judge noted the father's refusal. This last exchange further eroded the thin veil of communication between the father and the judge. The communication became more and more strained.

JUDGE: Right, OK.

The father stood up and showed the cardboard folder he has with some fifty pages of printed documents. This was the beginning of the last phase of the hearing which would result in a breakdown in communication between the father and the judge.

The contributive share: breakdown in communication

FATHER: Take a look. May I?

JUDGE: Remain seated Sir, *if this has not been communicated you may not.* But you can explain to me what you want to say.

The father gets up again and holds up his file of documents.

FATHER: She spent all her money buying clothes on e-bay during our relationship, PayPal [he showed a file of receipts and credit card statements]

The judge is flabbergasted; she stammers:

JUDGE: And... and ... and
FATHER: This is all she did with the household money.

This was the last thing the judge expected. The documents could have been a tax certificate, payslips, a statement of income in order to set the contributive share, but certainly not a detailed account of his ex-partner's online spending.

The judge exploded:

JUDGE: And what has that got to do with the children?
FATHER: When there were end-of-year bills, I was the one who paid them.

Then a dialogue of the deaf ensued which broke the tacit rule of turn-taking organised around questions asked by the judge and the response of the father. This marked a definitive rupture in communication. The father would no longer reply to any question by the judge but would continue arguing his point about his ex-partner's poor money management.

THE JUDGE SHOUTS: What has that got to do with the children Sir?
FATHER: Give her money so that she can go and spend it on clothes? Buying a jacket worth 400 euros!

The judge wanted to put an end to this argument for the third time:

JUDGE: OK

But the Father continues in an aggressive voice:

FATHER: Accusing me of not giving money and saying I didn't want to contribute to the speech therapy fees? I have proof of payments to the effect that I paid money to her parents each time they asked me to contribute to the speech therapy.

Faced with the aggressivity of the father the judge decides to withdraw from this interaction. She put an end to an escalation which saw them raise their voices more and more to get the upper hand in the discussion. She decided to change the tone and keep a cold but amused distance.

JUDGE: Rightly so. In any event, the accounts will be calculated with the lawyer. There is no problem with that and for the exceptional payments, we expect these payments to be made every three months.
FATHER: And I am being accused of behaving dangerously in front of the children. How many times has she attempted to commit suicide? Running after me with a knife, and I'm the baddie? I can clearly see that you judge me "ah you have been unfaithful, the unfaithful husband".

THE JUDGE (*smiles and says in a sarcastic tone*): Sir, if I judged unfaithful husbands like that, I would be busy from morning to night, that kind of thing has no effect on me, I can tell you. [She laughs while looking at the legal professionals].

The hearing is over as far as the judge is concerned. Her opinion is now fixed. She allows the father to finish with a certain distance which translates her complete disengagement from the interaction. The job is done, anything that could be said now would have an insignificant impact. In contrast, the tone of the father was becoming increasingly aggressive:

FATHER: She changes boyfriends like she changes her underwear and…

The father comes up against a brick wall. The judge keeps her distance, she leans back in her seat and observes the scene from a distance. Her tone of voice is neutral to the point of being sarcastic. The judge laughs, half amused, half annoyed.

JUDGE: Well, well, that's *very elegant*.
FATHER: it's probably not elegant but…
JUDGE: You do as you wish Sir.
FATHER: The image is apt. She needs to be assisted by her parents because she is not capable of looking after the children by herself. You don't do your homework.
JUDGE: We can see that you are *very flattering* in your comments!
FATHER: The school absences: how many Wednesdays did she fail to bring A. to school? How many times did she not bring her at all? I called her every morning and when they were babies, I was the one who looked after them at night and called her to ask: have you fed the little one, have you bought nappies instead of being in Belle-Ile exchanging your clothes? And then I am the baddie?
JUDGE: I find that your tone of voice is *not very classy*. But everybody can express themselves… as long as it doesn't go too far. If you do go too far, I will be obliged to ask you to leave.

The judge called for a pause in proceedings and wrote in her file saying:

JUDGE: This file is outside the Ministry of Public Administration despite the context of domestic violence. The case is closed, and the judgment will be made on the xx/xx/xxxx.

The judgement was to be pronounced 3 weeks later. It would take into account the details that emerged during the hearing.

With regard to parental authority

It would remain joint

Accommodation

1 The father petitioned an equal share in the living arrangements of the children;

The mother was not in favor of this.

2 An equal share in the children's living arrangements is the model recommended by the legislator.

This cannot be deviated from except where there is a justifying factor or factors.

3 The mother claims there are various justifying factors:

Lack of personal availability of the father: he works for the TEC, in three-week cycles: during each of these weeks, he starts work very early (04:30 or 06:00 in the morning) and/or finishes late (22:00 or midnight) on average 2 or 3 days a week. The father lives alone.

No supervision of schoolwork: copies of class report are submitted;

Recurrent arguments between the father and his girlfriend,

Refusal to pay for the children's speech therapy care. During the hearing on X/X/XX, the father did not contest this last point.

4 The working hours of the father are long and are not suited to an equal share of the living arrangements of two children aged six and ten.

The father claims that he does not live with his current partner but claims that she can look after the children in the mornings and evenings when he is working…

This type of arrangement is not acceptable, because the relationship is not stable: and the father explained that he had known this woman for 6 months although the parental separation began in 2015…and the father and mother did not regularly "see" each other until March 2017.

The shortcomings with regard to schoolwork and speech-therapy care were also problematic.

The main living arrangements for the children would be at the mother's house.

5 As the father could not suggest an acceptable arrangement for the secondary living arrangements for the children, the mother's house would be the principal place of accommodation for the children (which corresponded to the current arrangement practiced by the parties).

The legal framework: where are the rules?

The family litigation is evidently particular. Based on an ideal of consensus, it goes against the grain of the classic dynamics of the trial based on the conflict and the opposition of the parties and their point of view. The judgement of law in the matter of family law does not decide between the parties – the parents in this case – with regard to the way in which they legally apprehend the events that took place in the past. Family litigation is prospective: it is intended to practically organise the life of separated or divorced couples through a binding legal framework.

Consequently, hearings acquire great importance in the decision-making process because the judges generally have the petition[14] but no conclusions.[15] The magistrate then has to construct a decision based on interactions during the hearing (in contrast with most civil affairs where the file (citation, conclusions, a dossier of documents) occupies a fundamental place. Here, the procedure is largely verbal, and the hearing constitutes the reservoir of contextual data which the judge will draw on to decide what measures will be imposed on the parents. Therefore, the judges observed took a lot of notes during the hearing. These serve as an outline – sometimes a very detailed one – of the judgement. The work of note-writing begins during the hearing and ends on the same day or some days later. The points which form a basis for agreement are noted and confirmed by the judge who will then rule on the points of disagreement.

While no article of the civil code is invoked during hearings, the legal rules permeate the practices of lawyers and judges. They form the basis of a legal culture integrated by legal professionals. They form a relationship to others and to litigation in general and remain an implicit reference, offering a horizon of shared expectations. Rooted in everyday practices, they are only explained and activated by professionals when they are not respected.

The legal system of separation

The order in which the different points that organise the legal regime of separation and the lives of children are dealt with is a practical standard shared by the judges and lawyers. Judges direct debates and write their judgement by invariably following the same order, namely, parental authority first, the setting of living arrangements, the shared accommodation arrangements and finally, the contributive share.

During the hearings, a **"checklist"** appeared: the same questions systematically asked in the same order by the judge.

- "Were you partners or legal cohabitants"?
- "When did you separate"?
- "Parental authority: joint or exclusive"?
- "Where will the children live"?
- "For the living arrangements: equal or principal and secondary"?
- "What are you offering in terms of contributive share"?

This same structure is to be found in the judgement delivered like in the petitions made available to the parties by the court clerk.[16] The lawyers, for their part, write the proceeding form while observing this order. Woe betides any lawyer writing the petition while not observing the tacitly imposed progression. His opponent would not hesitate to mention this to him which would have the effect of weakening his case and casting doubt on the sincerity of his client. This is particularly the case when the petition for contributive share outstrips the question of parental authority or the accommodation arrangements.[17] In this case, the parent is suspected of introducing a procedure, not in the interest of his children but in his own financial interest. The first two questions have to do with the shared past of the couple and constitute factual questions. The other questions no longer aim to establish facts but to programme the future organisation of the family in its plurality, and particularly the welfare of the children.

Article 374 of the civil code[18] and articles 203[19] and 203bis[20] of the civil code constitute the fundamental legal kit for magistrates. They regulate the questions relative to parental authority, the living arrangements and accommodation of the children in the first instance and the contributive share in the second instance.

The interest of the child

Article 374 enshrines a legal concept whose boundaries are somewhat indeterminate: **The Interest of the child**. While it is the alpha and omega of the procedure, debates and judges', it is directly invoked by the judge who brandishes it as a criterion of evaluation of the legitimacy of the petition by the father for an equal share in the accommodation of children.

While the father formulates his petition – "I want 50–50 for everything", the judge asks him: "But *why* did you not act before, because this situation has lasted for more than two years and you decide on the day of the hearing, it's a bit odd". She tries to understand the reasons for the petition. This phrase is part of an understandable – "why didn't you act sooner"? – and evaluative – "It's a bit odd" register, which translates the incongruity of a norm that has not been observed. This way of doing things does not correspond with the expectations of the judge. The underlying pattern is the following: as long as the position of the parties doesn't change, there is no reason to modify the legal situation. The legal situation can be modified to adapt to a new factual situation (this is the spirit of the standing reference). On the other hand, when the factual situation remains unchanged, the judge is reluctant to change the legal situation.

JUDGE: Broadly speaking, there was nothing for two years…it's a bit, well, ***odd***… to ask that… Personally, I like periods of transition, so I'm not going to go from two days just like that to allowing equal accommodation I can tell you, because **as far as the children are concerned** they must be protected. But I'm trying to understand your motivations, because you took no action for two years and now, I feel it is a kind of demand reflex and we need to know if it is really **because of the children.**

The judge noted the petition for equal accommodation but let him know that she was not in favour of it for two reasons. Firstly, the father needed to show that this change was petitioned in the interest of the children. Also, the judge still did not understand why the father had "taken no action for two years".

A little later, the judge returned to the subject of the terms of the accommodation in order to note the working hours of the father who is a bus driver. The hours are changeable. The judge insists on the practical organization with two little daughters.

JUDGE: One week in two for two children, also, O. is not yet 7 so we are not dealing with teenagers who can manage fine on their own! A. is 10, and what do we do then? We always seem to be talking about an individual from outside your circle who doesn't really live with you but can come and look after the children. **How is that in the interest of the children? I am interested in the children's welfare and not yours.**

FATHER: The interest of the children is that I can drive them to school in the morning and my girlfriend can pick them up at 15.30. [...]

JUDGE: Sir, **put the interest of your children above your own** even if it is painful...

FATHER: I am thinking of my children's interest: they need to be with their father!

JUDGE: You think that the **interest of your children** is served by their being looked after by your girlfriend when they are in your house when they could be in the comfort of their mother's home?

Finally, when it concerned the contributive share, the interest of the children was again mentioned by the judge. While the father justified his rejection of the contributive share based on the profligacy of his partner, the judge invoked the interest of the children to demonstrate the unsuitability of the father.

FATHER: That was all she did with the money of the house.

The judge exploded:

JUDGE: And what has that got to do with the children?!

FATHER: When the end-of-year bills had to be paid, I was the one who paid them.

THE JUDGE (SHOUTS): **What has that got to do with the children,** Sir?

These three series of exchanges, where the interest of the children was the central concern of the debates while being a standard of reference to assess the current attitude of the father and his ability to care for his daughters into the future, were in contrast with the plea entered by the mother's lawyer whose main concern was the interest of the two little girls. She began her plea by speaking about the children and stating their ages. She then began to list the problems for the children which she imputed to the father (the children's schooling, violence, father's working hours, speech therapy care). She spoke very little about her client, but the way in which the father managed the education of the children. Consequently, there was a large asymmetry between the attitude of the father who had to be constantly reminded by the judge that he must act in the interest of the children, and that of the mother's lawyer who made this requirement an integral part of her argumentation.

The procedural framework of the hearings

The hearings are managed by a knowledgeable mix of the rules of the judicial code, professional usages, traditions linked to a jurisdiction and habitual ways of operating on the part of certain magistrates. While this practical knowledge accumulated during experiences in the tribunal is naturally understood by lawyers who are experienced in the area, it proves to be a minefield for the layman who is confronted by the extremely codified scene of the hearing. The speaking times and silences require a practical skill of judicial courts. Does one have the right to speak? Should one wait until given the chance to speak? Who speaks and when? At certain times, the parties who wish to react spontaneously feel as though they have been ordered to keep quiet – "we are not at the Batte here" – by the judge. On the other hand, silence, in the face of allegations made by the opposing party is noted by the judge, the absence of contestation is equivalent to an acquiescence to what is being pleaded. This is the case with the petition for an equal share in the accommodation of the children put forward by the father after two years of separation.

JUDGE: When Madam said that you have been separated since 2015, I didn't hear you say "No, that's not the case". So, it has been at least two years.
FATHER: No, it has not been two years!
JUDGE: When it was said, ***you didn't contest it.*** So, your attitude is a bit ***odd***.

"I didn't hear you say 'no'"; "you didn't object" said the judge. These exchanges throw up one of the practical procedural rules which organise debates and could be summarised by "who doesn't speak, consents". In contrast, the mother's lawyer doesn't hesitate to underline the points of divergence with the father's allegations. Therefore, when the father presents his working hours or his salary, the reactions of the mother and her lawyer are immediate. The non-verbal language is explicit each time: they shake their head. The lawyer had an amused smile while the mother was visibly outraged and angry. In addition, the lawyer returned to the two points she contests during her plea. "So, Sir has a job, that's good, but he has irregular hours and my client tells me that the hours he has just given you are not his exact hours: he starts at 04:00 in the morning but he tells you that he starts at 06:00. He tells you that in week 2 he only does one "early shift" while he actually does 2 or 3 early shifts [...] Sir, told you, and I was surprised by this, that he earns 1,600 euros per month, my information was that the average monthly salary is 1,900 euros per month although I do not have the documentation to back this up yet".

Mastering speaking in turns is also important when it is necessary to reply to questions asked by the judge even when it is delayed. The lawyer, who is used to this, did so quite naturally whenever she spoke. She replied to the question the judge asked the father concerning the reason why the request was being made two years after the separation of the parents. She then explained that the parents had tried to find amicable ways of organising things, but a series of problems made this way of doing things impossible. The father, on the other hand, did not answer this question at any point. Just as he didn't answer when the judge asked him why he refused to pay part of the contributive share.

Certain principles which organise judicial procedure are also reminded to parties appearing alone before the judge. The contradictory principle[21] even though not explicitly invoked, is tacitly invoked whenever it is flouted. Thus, when the Father wanted to show a file of documents which had not been communicated to the adversary, it was restricted by the judge who nonetheless agreed to hear the Father out on the contents of the file: "If it has not been communicated, you cannot, but you can explain to me what you mean." Similarly, when the Father was struggling to formulate his claim in adequate legal terms, the judge relied informally on the operative principle that the civil lawsuit is the "preserve of the litigant". In other words, without prejudice expressed by the parties, the judge cannot rule. But litigants come to court with their story and their desires which they are often unable to translate into procedurally correct and legally relevant claims (Dupret, 2006).

FATHER: For the moment, I only have them for..., she just wants to let me have them during my holidays, but ***I don't agree***! I want 50–50 for everything! We had them together and I think we should both take responsibility for them!

The father made part of his request even though it hadn't yet been formulated in the correct legal terms: The Father wants to have an equal share in the accommodation arrangements of the children. The entire challenge – which is not perceived at any time by the father – is to know whether the judge is going to translate the father's rough request into a legal one. She may well remain deaf to the request by adopting a formal attitude or be open and welcome the demand made in ordinary terms and reformulate them in legal terms. Consequently, faced with an absence of formulation, or a poor or hesitant formulation, the judge may react in a number of different ways. He may offer an understanding ear to the claimant, reading between the lines what the layman is unable to formulate by himself into appropriate legal terms. Either he will adopt a more formal posture, ruling simply on the fact that the parent is asking for nothing or is not in opposition to the request of his adversary. In the case studied, the judge welcomed the demand. Indeed, the judge stipulated in his judgement that the father "requests equal accommodation".

The categorisations at the heart of the hearing: the role of emotions in the qualification operation

The material collected offers three levels of categorisations. The father describes the mother as a spendthrift woman who cares little for her children and needs help with their education. He talks about her as a fickle person – "she changes boyfriends like she changes her underwear". The father is described by the mother as a physically and psychologically violent man, who refuses to collaborate and contribute to the education of the children and who is actually not available for his children due to irregular working hours. The judge also categorizes the attitude of the father with regard to the mother, mentioning the violence alleged by the mother.

During the self-confrontation interview, the judge confirmed that latter categorisation. Certain personality traits – disrespectful, violent and in poor faith – are used to describe the father's profile. This opinion was constructed progressively by means of an interrupted speaking, a heavy exchange of words and unsweetened stories. The judge constructed her perception of the context of the affair and the personality of the parents, step by step. After the hearing, she gave a sense of her feeling about the father which probably summarises the perception of the last exchanges which led to the break in communication. "I wasn't surprised when I was told about the violence. You **sense** it. Right from the start you get the **sense** that you are dealing with a guy who wants to control person, I feel. No, it's obvious that there were previous incidents, you just **sense** it. When you hear him speak, he is spitting his poison".

The decisions rendered contains some traces of these categorisations, the formalisation of the law having done its job of selecting and transforming an ordinary telling into a legal one. The suspension points that underline what the law cannot said should be noted, however. "The Father declares that he does not live with his partner but explains that she could take care of the girls in the morning and in the evening when he works..." or even "the relationship is not very stable: and for good reason, the Father explains that he has known this woman for six years although the parental separation dates back to 2015... and that the Father and Mother would have selectively "seen" each other until March 2017..." These suspension points are the clues that lead to the underground map of the judge's line of tough and which we understand by referring to what has been experienced during the hearing. They refer to the moral judgements that the judge formed during the hearing, but which must not be included when the judgement is written. Finally, it is remarkable that only the categorisations with regard to the Father penetrated into the judgement. One can hypothesise that the strong emotions felt by the judge, mainly anger and annoyance towards the father, led her to express them, albeit with restraint, in the final judgement.

Conclusions

Family court judges appreciate the parties being present at the hearings. According to them, these give colour to the file. What is at play during hearings? The perception of emotional expressions is part of the logic of judicial situations and allows us to better understand the decision-making process in courts and tribunals through the role played by hearings. Extensive "emotional" cues are used by judges to refine their judgements, whether they relate to the parties' personality (which corroborates or contradicts the narratives proposed in the pleadings) or to the credibility of their allegations.

Through the ethnography of a family tribunal hearing which followed the path of the emotional expressions of the actors, this contribution demonstrates the communicational and linguistic asymmetries between professionals and laymen. Indeed, lawyers and magistrates are members, to use the terms of ethnomethodology, of the same language community. This natural shared language remains hermetically closed to the lay litigants. When a lawyer represents the latter, he or she assumes the role of intermediary, translating the demands of his client into legal terms. By contrast, when the litigant decides to appear in court by himself, the interactions observed are frequently less fluent, the judge himself having to act as a translator and mediator. And yet, this role cannot easily be discharged when the magistrate is caught up in emotionally charged interactions.

Grasping the emotional dimension of the law perpetuates one of the great teachings of ethnomethodology: it is to take account of natural phenomena of action which are seen but unnoticed. Legal professionals are competent members, who, in order to understand each other, rely on sensitive clues (Thibaud, 2002, p. 10) that they judge to be relevant and which allow them to give meaning to the interaction.

Notes

1 "If we accept that all behaviour is communication, even for the smallest unit thereof that exists, it is evident that it will not be a monophonic message; we will be dealing with a fluid polyphonic compound of numerous modes of behaviour: verbal, tonal, postural, contextual, etc., each one of them specifying the meaning of the others" (Watzlawick et al., 1972, pp. 47–78).
2 For a historical approach to this field, see Deluermoz et al. (2013).
3 The American Sociological Association recognised the sociology of emotions as a branch of sociology in 1986.

4 Bennett and Hacker (2010) finely analysed the emotions and from this came a "conceptual complexity and diversity of emotions" which cannot be confined to a single concept. "There is no single paradigm of an emotion which can serve, as it were, as a conceptual prototype. Some emotions, when felt in appropriate circumstances and with respect to a certain range of objects, are closely associated with a pattern of sensations and characteristic facial expressions, as in the case of fear of physical harm, grief or anger. Others, such as hope, remorse or compassion, are not" (ibid. p. 205).

5 Speaking about emotional expression makes it possible to decide on the question of knowing whether emotions are observable or not. Damasio (Feeling of what happens, p. 42) claims that "you cannot observe a feeling in someone else. In contrast, Bennett and Hacker consider that "we can often see delight and rage in a person's face, joy, anguish or horror in their eyes, contempt or amusement in their smile. We can hear the love and tenderness, the grief and sorrow, the anger and contempt, in a person's voice. We can observe the tears of joy and grief, the cries of terror, joy or amazement, and the blushes of embarrassment or shame" (Bennet and Hacker, 2010, pp. 221–222). In other words, emotional expressions are available in the action.

6 For a broader development of the approach to emotions in the second person, see Colemans (2015).

7 The judge officiating in the court case of the family involved in the report laughed, for example, when she discovered the game the parties concerned were playing "I can see through it, I am nobody's fool" she said to me often.

8 This methodological position echoes the communicational pragmatics of Watzlawick et al. "The possible or supposed causes of a behaviour are only of secondary importance, but on the other hand, the effect of behaviour in the interaction between directly linked individuals becomes a criterion of enormous importance" (Watzlawick 1972, p. 41).

9 It was a unilateral petition introduced by the mother. The father is therefore the defendant in this hearing.

10 Article 374 of the civil code favours the agreement of the parties, both with regard to the conditions concerning the organisation of the children's lives after the separation and to the way the decision should ideally be adopted during the judicial procedure. It is quite remarkable to note that the principle of joint parenthood, based on the agreement of the parents in matters relating to the education of shared children, consequently, have an impact on the way in which the judge directs the debates. We will see that this consensual condition proves to be fragile. In addition, it raises the question of the principle of joint parental authority, where exclusive authority is the exception as is an equal share in terms of the accommodation of the children.

11 In reality the law does not directly impose such a personal availability, but exceptional circumstances can be taken into account to deviate from the model of equal accommodation. The spirit of exceptional circumstances can be found in parliamentary works (Doc. Parl, Chambre, 2004–2005, 1673/014, p. 17), in jurisprudence (Liège, 18 June 2013, *Act. dr. Fam.*, 2015, p. 116; Anvers, 23 May 2000, *A.J.T.*, 2000–2001, p. 937 and Civ. Dinant, 24 May 2004, *R.T.D.F.*, 2005, p. 241) as well as in the doctrine (see e.g. Massager, 2009, p. 382 s.; Leleu, 2016, pp. 557–758).

12 The Batte is a large public Sunday market frequented by tens of thousands of people where stallholders shout loudly to attract their customers.

13 Notice of tax assessment.

14 The petition is a document initiating proceedings which contains the petition of the party or parties according to whether it is joint or contradictory.

15 The findings constitute the written argument of the parties to the trial. They contain the facts, the claims and the applicable law.

16 For a view on the different forms of petition, see the following site: https://www.rechtbanken-tribunaux.be/fr/tribunaux-cours/tribunal-de-premiere-instance/tribunal-de-premiere-instance-namur-division-namur-0/formulaires/tribunal-de-la-famille-modeles-de-requete

17 Indeed, the contributive share depends to a certain extent on the terms of the children's living arrangements: equal accommodation by the parents does not require as high a contributive share as a principal dwelling place which is almost on a full-time basis, the parent taking care of the child must show that they have more money than the other parent who only sees his children occasionally.

18 Article 374 of the Civil code stipulates that "*[§ 1st.] When the mother and father do not live together, the exercise of* **parental authority** *remains joint, and the presumption provided for in article 373, paragraph 2, applies: Active from:14-09-2006> In case of disagreement on the organisation of the child's accommodation, the important decisions concerning his education, training, leisure time and religious or philosophical orientation or if this accord seems contrary to the* **'interest of the child**, *the competent [family tribunal] can confer the exclusive exercise of parental authority on either the mother or father. It can also set the decisions about education which can only be taken with the consent of both father and mother.*

It sets the terms under which the one who does not exercise parental authority maintains personal relations with the child. These relations can only be denied for very serious reasons. The one who does not exercise authority reserves the right to monitor the education of the child. He or she may obtain, from the other parent or third party, all useful information in this regard and address the family tribunal in the **interest of the child.** *In all cases, the judge determines the* **terms of accommodation** *of the child and the place where he is registered at a main address in the population register.*

[§ 2. When the parents do not live together and they bring their case to the[family] tribunal, the **agreement** *relative to the accommodation arrangements of the children is approved by the tribunal only if it is manifestly against the* **interest of the children.** *In case of disagreement, in the case of joint parental authority, the tribunal examines, as a matter of priority, on the petition of at least one of the parents, the possibility of allowing the parents to share the children's accommodation* **equally**. *In any event, if the tribunal considers that equal accommodation is not the most appropriate format, it can decide to set a non-equal accommodation arrangement.*

"The tribunal rules in all cases by an especially reasoned subject, taking account of the concrete circumstances of the cause and the **interest of the children** and the parents".

19 Article 203 of the Civil code states that "*Fathers and mothers are expected to assume, in proportion to their ability, the accommodation, upkeep, health, supervision, education, training and development of their children. If the training is not finished, the obligation pertains after the child has reached the age of majority*"

20 According to article 203bis of the civil code, "*§ 1st. Every mother and father contributes to the fees resulting from the obligation defined in article 203, § 1st, up to his share in the cumulative faculties. § 2. Without prejudice to the rights of the child, each mother and father can claim from the other his contribution to the fees resulting from article 203, § 1st. § 3. The fees include ordinary and extraordinary fees.*

The ordinary fees are the usual fees relative to the daily upkeep of the child.

By extraordinary fees, is meant exceptional, necessary or unpredictable fees which result from accidental or unusual circumstances and which exceed the usual

budget devoted to the daily upkeep of the child which served as a basis, where applicable, to the setting of alimentary contributions

§4. On the petition of the father or mother, the family tribunal can impose upon the parties to open an account with an agreed institution based on the law of 22 March 1993 relative to the status and control of credit establishments by the authority of financial services and markets, destined for the payment of contributions fixed based on article 203, § 1st. In this case, the tribunal determines at least: 1) The contribution of each of the fathers and mothers to the fees mentioned in article 203, 1st, as well as the social advantages accruing to the child which must be paid into this account; 2) The moment of the month when these contributions and social advantages must be paid; 3) The way in which the sums paid into this account can be spent; 4)The fees paid by means of these sums; 5)The organization of the control of spending; 6)The way in which the loans are discharged; 7) The appropriation of the surpluses paid into this account. The payments of contributions effected in execution of this article are considered as payments of alimentary such as defined in article 203, § 1st."

21 In application of the contradictory principle, each of the parties is bound to give a copy of the documents they will use during the hearing to the other (article 736 to 740 of the judicial Code).

References

Bennett, M.R. and. Hacker, P.M.S. (2003) *Philosophical Foundations of Neuroscience.* Oxford: Wiley-Blackwell.

Bernard, J. (2007) 'La gestion des émotions aux pompes funèbres, une compétence reconnue ?', *Formation emploi*, 99(3), pp. 61–74.

Cicourel, A.V. (1968) *The Social Organization of Juvenile Justice.* New York: John Wiley & Sons.

Cislaru, G. (2008) 'L'intersubjectivation des émotions comme source de sens: expression et description de la peur dans les écrits de signalement', *Les Carnets du Cediscor. Publication du Centre de recherches sur la didacticité des discours ordinaires*, 10, pp. 117–136.

Colemans, J. (2015) 'Ce que les émotions font faire aux professionnels du droit: Jalons pour une approche praxéologique des expressions émotionnelles dans la sphère judiciaire', *Social Science Information*, 54(4), pp. 525–542.

De Fornel, M. and. Léon J. (2000) 'L'analyse de conversation, de l'ethnométhodologie à la linguistique interactionnelle', *Histoire Épistémologie Langage*, 22(1), pp. 131–155.

Deluermoz Q., Fureix, E., Mazurel H. and Oualdi M. (2013) 'Écrire l'histoire des émotions: de l'objet à la catégorie d'analyse', *Revue d'histoire du XIXe siècle*, 47, pp. 155–189.

Dupret, B. (2006) *Droit et Sciences Sociales.* Paris: Armand Colin.

Game, A. (1997) 'Sociology's emotions*', *Canadian Review of Sociology/Revue Canadienne de Sociologie*, 34(4), pp. 385–399.

Garfinkel, H. (1967) *Studies in Ethnomethodology.* Englewood Cliffs, NJ: Prentice-Hall.

Goodwin, C. (1981) Conv*ersational Organization: Interaction between Speakers and Hearers.* New York: Academic Press.

Heath, C. (1986) *Body Movement and Speech in Medical Interaction.* Cambridge: Cambridge University Press.

Hochschild, A.R. (2003 [1983]) *The Managed Heart: Commercialization of Human Feeling*. Berkley: University of California Press.

Huntington, C. (2016) *The Emotional Dynamics of Law and Legal Discourse*. Oxford: Hart Publishing.

Leleu, Y.-H. (2016) *Droit des personnes et des familles*, 3rd ed. Bruxelles: Larcier.

Massager, N. (2009) *Droit familial de l'enfance*. Bruxelles: Bruylant.

Mondada, L. (2007) 'Multimodal resources for turn-taking: Pointing and the emergence of possible next speakers', *Discourse Studies*, 9, pp. 194–225.

Mondada, L. (2009a) 'Emergent focused interactions in public places: A systematic analysis of the multimodal achievement of a common interactional space', *Journal of Pragmatics*, 41(10), pp. 1977–1997.

Mondada, L. (2009b) 'La production de l'intelligibilité de l'action: une approche multimodale des procédés de sélection des locuteurs dans les interactions en classe', *Éla. Études de linguistique appliquée*, 153(1), pp. 25–40.

Mondada, L. (2012) 'Organisation multimodale de la parole-en-interaction: pratiques incarnées d'introduction des référents', *Langue française*, 175(3), pp. 129–147.

Rossano, F. (2012) '*Gaze in Conversation*'. Wiley Online Library. Retrieved 21 February 2020, https://onlinelibrary.wiley.com/doi/abs/10.1002/9781118325001.ch15.

Schegloff, E.A. (1984) 'On some gestures' relation to talk' in Atkinson, J.M. and Heritage, J. (eds.), *Structures of Social Action*. Cambridge: Cambridge University Press, pp. 266–298.

Scherer, K.R. (2011) 'On the rationality of emotions: Or, when are emotions rational?', *Social Science Information*, 50(3–4), pp. 330–350.

Thibaud, J.-P. (2002) *Regards en action: ethnométhodologie des espaces publics*. Casablanca: Editions A la Croisée.

Travers, M. (2001) 'Ethnométhodologie, analyse de conversation et droit', *Droit et Société*, 48(2), pp. 349–369.

Watzlawick, P., Helmick, J., Beavin, D. and Jackson, D. (1972) *Une logique de la communication*. Paris: Seuil.

12 Playing by the rules

The search for legal grounds in homosexuality cases – Indonesia, Lebanon, Egypt, Senegal

Baudouin Dupret, Samer Ghamroun, Youmna Makhlouf, Marième N'Diaye, Ayang Utriza Yakin and Alexis Blouet

The positivist dogma contends that judges must base their judgments on rules that are clear and general, and whose application is predictable. In this sense, rules have a determinate meaning and judges apply them in a mechanical way. Against this dogma, the realist critique argues that legal rules and principles are indeterminate, malleable, filled with implicit assumptions, and open to interpretation. Between these two extremes, contemporary legal doctrine recognizes the fact that there is always a degree of indeterminacy in the interpretation and application of rules, but that this does not preclude the fact that, in most cases and especially those deemed "soft", there is little disagreement as to applicable rules, that people routinely understand rules, and that they more or less blindly follow them. In difficult cases whose legal basis is less explicit and necessitates a more stringent effort of interpretation, it is nevertheless true that judges' discretion is much wider and permeated by factors external to legal rules *per se*, like moral and political principles, standards of justice, and professional practices. In other words, law, which is logically distinct from morality, proves thoroughly moral in the operation of its cognition.

We want to use a praxeological approach to these theoretical questions. Specifically, we want to describe how judges play by, and with, legal rules. It appears that, on the one hand, even in cases in which the legal basis is thin or absent, judges seek rules on which to base their decisions. In that sense, judges are positivist legal practitioners who need legal rules to perform their professional duties. On the other hand, however, moral considerations seem to deeply influence the same judges' legal cognition. We aim to show how this unfolds in the concrete settings of four countries – Indonesia, Lebanon, Egypt, and Senegal – in cases relating to male homosexuality. In many respects, these four countries offer an excellent basis for the comparative inquiry into the morality of legal cognition.

Criminal law and the repression of homosexuality

Indonesia, Lebanon, Egypt, and Senegal have different, although comparable, historical, political, legal, and anthropological legacies. However, their legal systems belong to the civil law family. In this section, we briefly present their respective criminal systems and the legal grounds that are used to repress homosexuality.

Indonesian criminal law inherited many of its features from Dutch law, which itself was inspired by the French. In the Netherlands, the French Penal Code of 1811 remained in force until 1886, with only minor modifications, and as such became the law of the Dutch East Indies (Kelk, 2001, p. 5). Although the Netherlands adopted a new Penal Code in 1886, the colonial government only promulgated a copy, with some modifications, in 1915, which became applicable in 1918 (Jonkers, 1946, p. 2). After independence in 1945, the colonial Penal Code remained in force (Art 2 of the Transition Regulation of the 1945 Constitution; Presidential Regulation No. 2 of 10 October 1945). It became the Indonesian Penal Code (*Kitab Undang-Undang Hukum Pidana*, KUHP) under Art. 4 of Law No.1/1946. Despite several codification projects, this code still applies today (Utriza, 2013, pp. 328–332).

Indonesian criminal law, belonging to the civil law family, follows the latter's main principles, including that of legality. Art. 1, section 1 of *KUHP* states that: "An act cannot be repressed by criminal law unless it was previously prohibited and clearly established by law." Indonesian doctrine defines a crime as "an act violating a norm or a regulation promulgated by the state and condemned by sanctions decided by a judge in order to protect public order" (Lamintang, 2014). Accordingly, the act must: (1) be human; (2) conform to what is described in legal provisions; (3) be the act of a responsible person; (4) be contrary to the law; and (5) be punished by a sanction established by the law (Tresna, 1959).

Indonesian penal law penalizes homosexual acts only when committed by an adult on a juvenile[1]. Art. 292 of *KUHP* provides: "The adult who commits debauchery with a minor of the same sex, whose age is known or could be reasonably presumed, shall be sentenced to imprisonment for a maximum of five years." This is the translation of Art. 248 *b* of the 1886 Dutch Penal Code as amended in 1911.[2] The Dutch expressions for debauchery (*ontucht*) and same sex (*hetzelfde* geslacht) were translated into Indonesian by *perbuatan cabul* and *sesama jenis* respectively. Indonesian commentator Soesilo (2013) explains that 'debauchery' means "all acts that violate decency or morality or abusive acts, in the sphere of sexual desires, such as kissing, touching and groping the genitals, touching the breasts, masturbation, and intercourse." In 2017 the Constitutional Court ruled out an attempt to criminalize same-sex relationships.[3] In other words, Indonesian law does not criminalize homosexuality among adults.[4] As we shall see when presenting the Atlantis Gym and Sauna case, Indonesian judges do nevertheless have a circuitous means of prosecuting same-sex relationships, including Art. 36 of

Law No.44/2008 against pornography, which states: "Anyone who exposes themselves or other people in a show or in public in a way that exhibits nudity, sexual exploitation, sexual intercourse or anything containing pornographic acts as defined in Art. 10[5] will be punished by imprisonment for a maximum of ten years and/or a maximum fine of five billion rupiahs."

The 1858 Ottoman Criminal Code was applied, in what today constitutes the *Lebanese* territory, until 1843[6]. Closely based on the 1810 Napoleonic code, this Code made it superfluous for France, the Mandatory power (1920–1943), to impose new criminal legislation. However, a commission was created in 1939 in order to "replace a structure made for other times [...] by a legislative monument capable of controlling boundless criminal activity"[7]. It attempted to integrate French case law, but also European (Greek, Italian, etc.) doctrinal and intellectual developments. It consecrated principles such as the fact that both crimes and punishments must be defined by the law (Art. 1), a principle already mentioned in the 1926 constitution (Art. 8), and that of the strict interpretation of criminal law. The new code was promulgated by legislative decree number 340/NI, on 1 March 1943, as part a general legislative program that also produced the Obligations and Contracts Code (1934), the Civil Procedure Code (1934, replaced in 1983), and the Commercial Code (1943, amended in 2019). The Criminal Procedure Code was not adopted until 1948, five years after Lebanon's independence, and was replaced in 2001.

The new code had an important influence on Lebanon's neighbors (in 1949, Syria adopted a criminal code largely based on that of Lebanon). It was modified several times after 1943: in 1958 after the first civil war, and in 1983, as part of a major effort to update Lebanese codes, and then several times in the 1990s and 2000s through a number of legislative amendments. However, these amendments did not affect Article 534, which criminalizes "acts against nature". This last article comes within the general heading regulating offenses linked to public order and good morals (Book II, Heading VII, ch. II, § II). Homosexuality cases fall under the jurisdiction of a single criminal judge (*al-qâdî al-munfarid al-jazâ'î*) like most minor offenses (*mukhâlafa*) and misdemeanors (*junha*) as indicated in the new 2001 Criminal Procedure Code. This judge's decisions can be challenged before the Misdemeanors Court of Appeal (*mahkamat al-isti'nâf al-jazâ'iyya al-nâzira fî qadâyâ al-jinah*). More serious crimes, and linked misdemeanors, fall under the jurisdiction of the Criminal Court (Criminal Circuit of the Court of Appeal, *mahkamat al-jinâyât*). The rulings of both courts can be challenged, under some conditions, before the Criminal Chamber of the Court of Cassation (*mahkamat al-tamyîz*).

The repression of homosexuality is based on Art. 534 of the Criminal Code, which states that "any carnal conjunction running against the order of nature will be punished by prison up to one year". While the antique, Biblical, and medieval origins of the concept of "nature" used to regulate homosexual practices are well known (see e.g. Veyne, 1982, pp. 26–27;

Chiffoleau, 1990), the legislative inspiration of Art. 534 remains uncertain. It seems related to the Vichy Law No. 744 dated 6 August 1942[8] establishing sexual majority at the age of 21 for homosexual acts (as against 15 for heterosexual acts) and therefore making "acts against nature" illegal under the age of 21[9]. In cases involving transsexuals, Art. 534 is often used together with Art. 523 of the same code criminalizing prostitution.

Despite Lebanon's ratification of international covenants against discrimination and Art. 2 of the Civil Procedure Code making international agreements superior to national legislation, Art. 534 is often used to repress homosexuality. Lebanese judges justify this situation by the principle of non-direct applicability of international provisions, which is consecrated by Lebanese case-law.

In 2001, a new draft Criminal Code was proposed which included the suppression of Art. 534. It did not succeed, however, and the new draft submitted in 2017 reinstated the former provision. This legislative inertia, combined with hostility to homosexuality among political and religious leaders, convinced LGBT militants to explore alternative ways of changing the legal situation. In 2009, the Helem association for the defense of LGBTIQ rights sponsored a report reviewing dozens of rulings referring to Art. 534.[10] It showed that the latter, far from being marginal, was actually largely implemented by courts, fueling the hypothesis of repression that varied according to the social status of the people involved. In the same year, a ruling by the Batrun Criminal Court – whose single judge, in order not to punish homosexuality, for the first time interpreted the word "nature" of Art. 534 from the point of view of social and human sciences – stressed the potential benefits of taking the judicial path. Activists from the Legal Agenda association later developed a template document presenting arguments to be used by lawyers in order to organize the defense of people prosecuted before the courts based on Art. 534[11]. This was followed by several rulings of the same type, which were however confined to first-instance single-judge courts (in 2014, 2015, 2017). It was not until 2018 that an appellate court, following an appeal lodged against the 2017 ruling, for the first time took a decision partially based on this template, and avoided condemning homosexuality *per se*.

Today's *Egyptian* legal system is the outcome of a process that has lasted more than two centuries. During the nineteenth century, Ottoman governors, viceroys, and khedives strove to give the legal and judicial system a "modern" tone largely inspired by Western models (Ziadeh, 1968; Reid, 1981; Hill, 1987; Botiveau, 1989; Brown, 1997; Dupret and Bernard-Maugiron, 2002). From the late 1870s onward, mixed courts (*mahâkim mukhtalita*) and indigenous courts (*mahâkim ahliyya*) operated, together with religious courts (*mahâkim shar'iyya*), over matters related to personal status. A unified system of national courts was established in 1956; since 1979 it has been crowned by the Supreme Constitutional Court (*al-mahkama al-dustûriyya al-'ulyâ*).

The nineteenth century was also a time of intense codification. In Egypt, decrees and laws regulated criminal matters as early as 1829. Although a new Penal Code code was promulgated in 1852 that was largely identical to the Ottoman Penal Code of 1851 (Peters, 1995), French law massively permeated Egyptian law at the time of the promulgation of the Mixed (1876) and Indigenous (1883) Codes, of which Egypt's first modern penal code was a part. A new Criminal Code was issued in 1937, which applied to all Egyptian residents in 1949, when Mixed Courts were abolished and the judicial system unified. That 1937 code, amended several times, remains in force today. It has been complemented by several laws combating drugs, alcoholic beverages, money laundering, and – important in our case – prostitution (law No. /1961). Emergency laws, (nearly) continuously in force since the 1952 Revolution (and even before), outline special procedures when state security is deemed to be endangered, which actually means any situation involving a breach of public order.

The principles and general organization of Egyptian penal law are similar to other systems in the civil law family. Articles 95 and 225 of the 2014 Constitution affirm the principle of legality and of non-retroactivity of criminal rules and punishments. Three categories of crime are listed: contraventions (petty offenses), misdemeanors (punishable by short imprisonment and/or fines), and felonies (punishable by hard labor or death). The general theory elaborated by Egyptian jurists defines crime (*al-jarîma*) as "an illegitimate action produced by a criminal will for which the law stipulates a sanction or precautionary measures." (Husni, 1989, p. 40)[12]. This definition may be deconstructed as follows: (1) Crime supposes that an action (*fi'l*) be committed either actively (commission) or passively (abstention); (2) This action must be illegitimate (*ghayr mashrû'*) with regard to an explicit provision of criminal law and must not be committed under circumstances that can excuse it; (3) This action must originate in a "criminal will" (*al-irâda al-jinâ'iyya*), i.e. a human will that is capable of distinction and free to choose, yet that sought to perform this action and is therefore responsible for it; if this will intended the consequences of this action, jurisprudence speaks of "criminal intent" (*al-qasd al-jinâ'î*), whereas it speaks of "unintentional fault" (*al-khata' ghayr al-'amdî*) when the will did not intend the consequences of this action; (4) The law must stipulate a sanction (*'uqûba*) or precautionary measures (*tadbîr ihtirâzî*). Three basic elements therefore make up a crime: the legal element (*al-rukn al-shar'î*), the material element (*al-rukn al-mâddî*), and the moral element (*al-rukn al-ma'nawî*). The material element is made up of three components: an action, the consequence of this action, and the causal relationship linking the act and its consequence. The moral element corresponds to the will that accompanies the action, in the form of either criminal intent or unintentional fault. It conditions the infliction of a penalty on the commission of an offense by a human being. The legal element refers to the illegitimate status of the action and implies that there must be a text criminalizing this action, providing for the punishment of its perpetrator.

Egyptian law does not explicitly criminalize same-sex relationships.[13] However, as we shall see in greater detail in the next section, judges assimilate homosexuality with debauchery (*fujûr*) and use Law No.10/1961 on the repression of prostitution (*da'âra*)[14] as the legal element they need to establish the crime. Article 9 of Law 10/1961 stipulates:

> (a) any person who hires or offers in any possible way a place that serves debauchery or prostitution [...]; (b) any person who owns or manages a furnished flat or room or other place open to the public that facilitates the practice of debauchery or prostitution [...]; (c) any person who usually practices debauchery or prostitution is condemned to imprisonment for a period of no less than three months and no more than three years, and to a fine [...], or to one of these two penalties. When the person is arrested in this last situation, he or she may be subjected to a medical examination and, if it appears that he or she suffers from an ordinary venereal disease, to confine him or her in a medical institution until he or she has recovered [...].

The 1965 Criminal Code in *Senegal* is "the daughter of French legislation, however adapted to Senegalese reality" (Diouf, 1965). Nevertheless, it refers neither to customary nor to religious rights. With the exception of family law, Senegal's legal arsenal was wholly secularized in the name of the principle of "evolution", which moves "in the direction of giving up customary law", the latter being perceived as a "politically dangerous" choice for nation building and development (M'Baye, 1970).

The principles that guided the Preparatory Committee's work included the "protection of the family" on the one hand, and the "protection of childhood and of moral health" on the other (Diouf, 1965). This is why penalties concerning "indecent acts committed by an individual with a juvenile of the same sex" were made more serious. Art. 319–3 stipulates that "... any person who commits an act that is either indecent or unnatural with an individual of the same sex will be punished with imprisonment of from one to five years and a fine from 100,000 to 1,500,000 CFA Francs. If the act was committed with a juvenile under 21, the maximum penalty will always be applied".

However, it should be noted that the repression is not against "homosexuality" but against "an act against nature". This is the legacy of colonization: contrary to British law, the French Criminal Code never explicitly condemned homosexuality, with the important exception of the abovementioned Vichy Law No.744/1942. As in France, however, homosexuality was the object of moral reprobation (Teunis, 2001). It is considered to be a "social scourge" threatening to destabilize families and society, which must be protected by the law. In that sense, penal and family provisions must be understood together: acts against nature are acts against the family, which is conceived of on a heterosexual basis.

In practice, judicial indictments are not limited to acts against nature and include the supposed sexual orientation or identity of an individual. It is up to judges to decide the definition to give to the notion of "acts against nature", notwithstanding the fact that they can use other legal provisions to condemn the accused or make the penalty more severe. On the one hand, they give a wide interpretation to the notion of flagrancy (Art. 45 of the Code of Criminal Procedure), understood by jurisprudence as "the time neighboring the crime", in the absence of evidence of the materiality of the act, so as to encompass acts that are anterior or supposedly planned by individuals designated as homosexuals. On the other hand, the provision regarding conspiracy (Art. 238 of the Code of Criminal Procedure: "any association whatever its duration or the number of its members, or any agreement constituted with the aim of preparing or committing one or several felonies or crimes against people or property") allows penalties to be made more severe based on Art. 319 for the reason that gatherings of homosexual people would have the objective of preparing acts against nature. To summarize, judges can, by playing on past and future times, condemn individuals in the absence of any evidence of flagrancy, which shows that homosexuality is specifically targeted and not only acts against nature.

Looking for relevant rules: homosexuality at the bar

We turn now to cases in which accusations of same-sex intercourse were dealt with judicially in our chosen countries. It is important to note that we are interested in the *legal and judicial* mode of reasoning, not in public opinion about homosexuality. As we shall see, the legal and public spheres are not impervious to each other, and commonsense categories often permeate the ways judges address cases related to public order and good morals. It is however essential to the understanding of our analysis to stress that common sense is considered here from the point of view of 'legal cognition' (Dupret et al., 2019) rather than for its own sake. We therefore refrain from making any assumptions, regarding, for example, the prevailing morality or the Muslim-majority structure of society in the four countries.

The *Indonesian* case is known as the "Atlantis Gym and Sauna" affair, after the name of the sport and meeting club in which the accused were arrested. The case can be summarized as follows. On patrol on 20 April 2017, the North Jakarta police received information from inhabitants of the neighborhood that the Atlantis Gym and Sauna intended to organize gay parties on the following 7, 14, and 21 May. Based on this information, the police sent two officers in civilian dress to investigate. According to the police record, they found gymnastic facilities on the first floor, male striptease shows on the second, where naked men were dancing while staring at, dancing or masturbating with male striptease dancers on the stage, and private cabins on the third. Drawing on these preliminary investigations, the police raided the club on 21 May and arrested 141 men, including men from Malaysia, Singapore, and the United Kingdom. After three days involving long interrogations, the arrested men were nearly all released without charge. However, ten men were kept in custody and charged for breaching the 2008 Pornography Law (see above). These men were submitted to complete interrogation (*penyidikan*), from 22 May to 10 June 2017, and full investigation (*penyelidikan*), from 11 June to 7 August 2017. The police eventually submitted the case to the Prosecutor who filed three different petitions to the North Jakarta Criminal Court on 28 July 2017[15]. The accused were four employees of the Atlantis Gym and Sauna, four striptease dancers and two partygoers, the last six having been caught *in flagrante delicto* of 'pornographic activities' during the raid.

The threefold trial started on 14 August 2017. The first trial (of the four employees) was held in 13 hearings, the second (of the four striptease dancers) in 17 hearings, and the third (of the two partygoers) in 16 hearings. Seven common hearings of witnesses were also held. The Prosecutors brought 18 witnesses before the judges, including two police officers, six employees, four striptease dancers, and seven partygoers. They presented more than 100 pieces of evidence in court, including condoms, lubricants, sex toys, CCTV recordings, striptease dancers' tips, mattresses, advertisements for gay shows, and mobile phones containing broadcast invitations. During the hearings, the Atlantis employees explained that the Atlantis Jaya Company intended to offer a gym center, a sauna, and a whirlpool as a meeting place for gay people. Moreover, 18 private cabins were provided for intimate relationships. Women were denied access. The club organized shows staging male striptease dances on a weekly basis. Police officers who conducted the investigation testified to the existence of pornographic and sexual activities in the club. Several witnesses said that they knew the Atlantis Gym and Sauna through the Internet and other social networks.[16] They all knew that the club was restricted to gay people. Visitors said that they came to the club to attend the striptease shows and that they were motivated to find sex partners. They all knew and said that "the club provides pornographic services and programs". Before the court, four striptease dancers said that they performed striptease dances in front of the visitors. With some of them, they would engage in further sexual activities. One of the striptease dancers said: "I know that performing a striptease in front of same sex spectators is forbidden by the law of the country."[17]

The trial lasted for seven months, from the arrest to the court decision. At the last audience on 14 December 2017, the judges declared the accused guilty of breaching the law. They based their ruling on Art. 36 of Law No.44/2008. They also referred to provisions of the Criminal Code referring to assistance and participation in a crime. Namely: Art. 55(2) of *KUHP*, which states: "Are found guilty of a crime: those who give or promise something by abusing their power or dignity, or with violence, threats or offense, or by giving an opportunity, means, or information by intentionally encouraging others to commit an act;" Art. 56(2) of *KUHP*, which stipulates: "Are convicted of the crime of assistance those who deliberately provide opportunities, means or information allowing a crime to be committed;" and Art. 55(1), which states: "Are sentenced as criminal offenders those who do, induce, or participate in a crime".

In order to establish the crime and to condemn the accused, the court had to examine whether criminally sanctioned crimes had been committed by criminally responsible people who acted intentionally and deliberately. On this basis, the court found the four employees guilty of assisting, procuring, offering, and organizing pornographic services. The manager of the club was sentenced to three years in prison and the three other employees to two and a half years, in addition to a one billion rupiahs fine (or six months in prison). As for the four striptease dancers and the two partygoers, the court found them guilty of participation in the criminal act of showing their nudity and performing sexual activities in public. It sentenced them to two years in prison and a fine of one billion rupiahs (or three months in prison).

In *Lebanon*, in 2015, following a petition from the inhabitants of Bouchrieh, a Christian majority neighborhood in Beirut, and a municipal campaign against places frequented by supposedly homosexual or transsexual people, the police arrested nine people in the street and transferred them to the Prosecution who remanded them in custody and accused them of violating Art. 523 (against prostitution) and Art. 534 (against unnatural relationships) of the Criminal Code. In his decision dated 26 January 2017, the first degree criminal judge of Jeidet el Metn, in Mount Lebanon, condemned only one of the accused for prostitution, while dismissing the argument regarding relationships "against the order of nature" on the basis of Art. 183 of the Criminal Code, which states: "There is no offense when the deed was committed in a non-abusive exercise of one's right". This provision is rarely used by Lebanese jurisdictions, but it is part of the aforementioned plea template on which the Jeidet el Metn judge directly drew.

In his argument, the judge identifies the three conditions upon which Art. 183 can be used, thus making it possible to exclude the criminal characterization of homosexual intercourse under Art. 534:

1 There must be an acknowledged right. In this case, it is the right to have intimate relationships with the individuals of one's choice (providing they are adults and consenting). The judge demonstrates the existence of this right through the Preamble of the Lebanese Constitution, the 1948 Universal Declaration of Human Rights, the 1966 International Covenant on Civil and Political Rights, which was ratified by Lebanon in 1972, and the principle of equality. The judge also gives his interpretation of Art. 534, arguing that "depriving homosexual people of their 'natural' right to have intimate relationships among them without any discrimination or the intervention of any other party, leads to impose upon them what is 'against their nature' in order to conform with the

'nature' of the majority", something that constitutes an assault on their fundamental rights. In other words, nature changes according to the party concerned; there are many 'natures' in society and it is the judge's duty to guarantee their peaceful co-existence.

2 It is the exercise of this acknowledged right that is being prosecuted. The judge seeks to demonstrate that (homo)sexual relationships represent one means of expressing the right to intimate relationships with the individuals of one's choice. He refers, for example, to Art. 12 of the ICCPR and its guarantee of the right to a private life.

3 This exercise must be non-abusive. This is the case, since the deed does not concern juveniles or non-consenting individuals.

In conclusion, the Jeidet el Metn judge considers that Art. 183 makes it possible to dismiss accusations based on Art. 534. This decision fueled significant public unrest, for example from the Committee of Muslim Ulamas, which considered that "this ruling violates what is stipulated by all divine rules as well as by logic", pointing out that "Lebanese law forbids interpretation (*ijtihad*) in the presence of a text". The Committee asked the Judicial Inspection Office to investigate the judge who took this decision that "seeks to legalize a perversion condemned by both the Sharia and the law" and to require the Prosecution Office to lodge an appeal, before calling for general mobilization to protect society and its family and religious values "against these phenomena alien to the Lebanese social body."

On 1 February 2017, the Prosecutor's office lodged an appeal against the decision. In its ruling dated 12 July 2018, the Mount Lebanon Appellate Criminal Court began by recalling what constitutes, in its opinion, the two fundamental rules regarding interpretation of legal texts: interpretation must be carried out in accordance with the goal pursued by the legal text; interpretation must be carried out in a manner that conforms to "social evolution". Referring to treatises on criminal jurisprudence, the court stresses the fact that Art. 534 of the Criminal Code is part of the section entitled "Outrages to public decency and good morals", which means that "the legislator's goal was not to punish sexual perversion, but outrage against good morals". This is something that must be evaluated with respect to social evolution, so that "the implementation of the text does not become inexplicable in terms of logic or social justice". Based on this assumption, the court considered that the assault on good morals in Lebanon today is "intercourse that deviates from the traditional conception of natural sexual relationships between a man and a woman, providing this intercourse takes place in the view of other people or in a way that allows them to hear, or in a public space, or with a juvenile who deserves protection". Thus, Art. 534 does not repress the sexual act between people of the same sex, but only its performance in public in a way that undermines good morals.[18] To summarize, the appellate court, while rejecting the first instance judge's argument that relativized the idea of "nature" and coming back to a more classical dichotomy between natural and perverse, confirmed his decision.

In his dissenting opinion, one of the three judges considered that there is no ambiguity in the expression in Art. 534: "carnal conjunctions against the order of nature", since "from the time of the Creation, human nature" supposes the coupling of different sexes. The evolution of ideas within society cannot mean a change in the meaning of 'nature', since nature is independent of practice. This judge considers his position to be mere application of the law: the legislator has "the obligation to accompany and take into account those people who have perverse tendencies with respect to nature, independent of the causes of this perversion which must remain private out of respect for each person's freedom and personal conditions". He adds:

> The evolution of ideas in society does not produce a change in the stable notion of 'nature,' as mentioned in Art. 534, and the notion of 'nature' should not be manipulated in order to adapt it to new ideas and notions, since it is not acceptable to naturalize a situation on the basis that it is spreading, because being progressive and open does not allow the judge to go beyond the text until it is abrogated or amended. [...]

Finally, he insists that the law does not punish sexual tendencies *per se*, but only the sexual act that proceeds from them and which has therefore to be established. This is, in his opinion, a strict reading of the law and not a stance against homosexuals:

> The insistence on the current application of the text should not be interpreted as rejection of any particular group, but as application of the law.

The *Egyptian* case is known as the "Queen Boat case". It followed a police raid, in May 2001, of a nightclub on a converted barge moored to a Cairo wharf. Several people were arrested on the basis of alleged homosexual practices. In fact, this raid was only one among many concluding a police campaign in the Egyptian capital's gay milieus, without information being available as to why this particular moment was chosen to engage in active repression of gay practices in Egypt. Among the 52 people who were prosecuted, 2 were also accused of contempt of religion: this was why the case was transferred to a state security court. There follows a summary of the grounds on which the State Security Prosecution based its accusation:

> Considering that the Public Prosecution filed the criminal petition against the abovementioned accused because, from 1996 until 11/5/2001, in the district of the police office of Qasr al-Nil, governorate of Cairo
>
> 1 The first and the second accused:
> both abused Islamic religion by propagating (*tarwîj*) and encouraging (*tahbîdh*) extremist thoughts (*afkâr mutatarrifa*) through speech, writing, and other means, insofar as they kept interpreting Koranic verses in a wicked (*fâsid*) way, they calumniated revealed religions and one of

the prophets, they came to [commit] actions contrary to moral behavior (*adab*) while attributing these [actions] to religion, they had imposed a prayer that was contrary to established prayer, they had founded a place for prayer to perform it, they had ranked perverse (*shâdhdha*) sexual practices among its rites and the practices [bound] to these ideas and had encouraged them among the other accused and yet other people, and this in order to denigrate revealed religions, to disdain them and to provoke sedition (*fitna*).

2 All the accused:

practiced debauchery (*fujûr*) with men in the way indicated in the investigation.

It [i.e. the Prosecution] required that they be condemned to [the penalty stipulated in] Article 98/7 of the Penal Code and Articles 9/3 and 15 of Law-Decree 10/1961 on the repression of prostitution (*da'âra*).

To substantiate the accusation, the Prosecution produced evidence, which is presented by the court as follows:

> Regarding what the court deduced from the examination of the documents and the investigations [...] as well as from the evidence submitted and what was related during the trial, [the first accused] adopted deviant (*munharifa*) ideas inciting others to hold revealed religions in contempt (*izdirâ*) and to call to abject (*radhîla*) practices and sexual acts contrary to revealed laws. [...] He undertook to propagate these ideas among his acquaintances and those who are bound to him and to call them to adopt [those ideas]; he is affected by sexual perversion (*musâb bi'l-shudhûdh al-jinsî*) and practices it with people who are bound to him by considering [these practices] one of their rituals; he and his companions set about organizing decadent parties (*hafalât mâjina*) every Thursday in their homes or on boats, among them the tourist boat "Queen Nariman" [...] which many of his sexually perverse acquaintances attended [...] He photographed these sexual encounters, then developed and printed the pictures [...]
>
> He set about diffusing pictures of these meetings as well as his confused (*mushawwasha*) ideas through the Internet [...] A warrant was sought to arrest these accused and the other regulars of the tourist boat "Queen Nariman."
>
> On the basis of the Public Prosecution's warrant [...], the first accused was arrested in the manner established in the record [...] and the following items were seized: (1) 10 books entitled "God's Lieutenancy on Earth"; (2) numerous photographs and negatives showing sexually perverse practices of the accused with many people; (3) numerous Muslim, Christian, and Jewish books; (4) numerous photographs of areas around Cairo, churches, mosques and tourist sites and one Jewish synagogue; (5) commentary papers from Military Unit 1057c; (6) one Star of David; (7) a number of hand-annotated documents; (8) a photograph of the

> President of the Republic and his wife, (9) photographs of the accused in Jerusalem and the Occupied Territories; (11) numerous photographs of the country's Jewish community and Jewish tombs in Basatin; (12) the Israeli national anthem, a copy of the book [...]; (13) two maps [...]; (14) two maps of Cairo churches; (15) many maps of Cairo mosques. [...]

In November 2001, the court issued a ruling condemning the first two accused to a punishment of five and three years in prison respectively, 20 other accused to penalties of two years in prison, and the last accused to a penalty of one year in prison. Nineteen accused were freed for lack of evidence. The principal accused was condemned for debauchery and contempt of religion, while the second accused was condemned for contempt of religion only. All the other accused were condemned for debauchery.

The characterization of debauchery, which is covered by Law No.10/1961, actually targets passive homosexual relationships – the only ones to which the forensic physician could testify, according to the judge.[19] The following shows how the judge made this criminalization of homosexuality explicit:

> The crime designated in [this text] is only committed when a man or a woman fornicates (*mubâsharat al-fahshâ'*) with people without distinction, habitually. When a woman fornicates and sells her virtue to whomever asks for it without distinction, she commits prostitution (*da'âra*) [...]; *fujûr* occurs when a man sells his virtue to other men without distinction.

Then the judge cites a 1988 ruling of the Court of Cassation that confirms this conception: "jurisprudence customarily used the word *da'âra* to [designate] female prostitution (*baghâ' al-unthâ*) and the word '*fujur*' to [designate] male prostitution (*baghâ' al-rajul*)."

In May 2002, the Military Governor, that is, the President of the Republic, refused to ratify the ruling against all those accused of debauchery and the whole case was transferred to an ordinary court. The latter, in a ruling dated March 2003, condemned the accused to even harsher penalties. However, the appeal court, in its June 2003 ruling, reduced the penalties of the accused to the time they had already spent in prison, making their release possible.

The Sicap Mbao case broke out in *Senegal* in December 2008. Following an anonymous tip-off, nine men were arrested at the home of the first defendant, a LGBT militant and the secretary general of Aides Sénégal. This arrest came shortly after the 15th International Conference on AIDS and STI in Africa (ICASA) in Dakar, during which the issue of the care of homosexuals was discussed. This conference re-ignited the homophobic climate that had prevailed since the "gay marriage" affair[20].

The police record makes no mention of any flagrant offense. The record concentrates on objects and documents that were seized during the search, that is, "dildos, lubricants, condoms, pornographic tapes and information for homosexuals". Based on this, the accused were arrested for "acts against nature and harm to good morals".

During their stay in jail, while awaiting their trial, the accused acknowledged their homosexuality but denied the accusations made against them. They stated that they were gathered for a dinner-debate about the use of condoms and the scourge of AIDS. During this period of two times 48 hours, the nine men received no assistance from an attorney. Later, when freed, some of them told the media that they had been mistreated in order to extort confessions.

The case was judged by the court in charge of flagrant offenses, on the 6th of January 2009. Claiming that it constituted an "act against nature" and a "conspiracy", the Prosecution required that the accused be condemned to five years in prison. According to the Prosecutor, the fact that this house was frequented on a regular basis by the accused, who acknowledged their homosexuality and their participation in condom distribution, constituted "constant facts" justifying their condemnation.

On the other side, the defense attorneys stressed the absence of material evidence and asked for the release of their clients, adding that the law does not repress the offense of homosexuality but only that of acts against nature. According to them, the objects that were seized do not constitute evidence but only clues. Moreover, the attorneys considered that an occasional or one-off gathering cannot serve to establish a conspiracy. They summed up by asking the judge not to yield to street pressure and to simply apply the law.[21]

However, the judge condemned the accused to a severe punishment exceeding the Prosecution's demands: eight years in prison (five for acts against nature and three for conspiracy) and a 500,000 CFA Francs fine. In his ruling, the judge defined an act against nature as "any act aiming at satisfaction of a sexual kind, whatever its form, outside the scope of normal sexual relationships". He considered that this act was established since the accused had acknowledged that "they have practiced same-sex sexual intercourse with men for at least three years". Regarding the alleged conspiracy, the judge claimed that it was motivated by the fact that, besides its aiming at establishing a care and solidarity network among gays, its goal was to prepare acts against nature, thereby establishing the existence of an "intended offense".

The severity of the condemnations contributed to the huge national and international media coverage of the case. The defense attorneys lodged an appeal on 12 January. Their team was reinforced with attorneys from RADDHO and ONDH, two Senegalese Human Rights NGOs. A defense committee was also created, bringing together local (RADDHO, ONDH, Enda Santé) and international (UN AIDS, FNUAP, FIDH, Solidarité Internationale LGBT) organizations. Their plea was based on the right to intimacy and a private life, an argument that avoided the debate on homosexuality, which is considered to be problematic even within human rights associations.

The case took a political twist after many French leaders made statements asking for the liberation of the nine accused. Bertrand Delanoë (Mayor of Paris), Roselyne Bachelot (Health Minister), and President Sarkozy expressed their concerns and invited the Senegalese authorities to review their decision. In Senegal, Islamic NGO Jamra stigmatized the inadmissible intrusion of French authorities and the President of the Bar Association criticized the pressure exerted by France on a pending case.

The appeal was heard in this highly politically charged atmosphere on 20 April 2009. The very short delay (only three months, while generally there is a lapse of at least six months) reinforced the idea that foreign pressure was influencing the functioning of Senegalese justice. According to the defense attorneys, it could be explained by the fact that the accused had been denied provisional release and by the danger they incurred in prison, where they were threatened and assaulted.

Procedural questions alone were addressed during the appeal hearing. The defense attorneys challenged the regularity of the police record (the search having been made outside legal hours and without a warrant) and reminded the court that the offenses of which the defendants were accused were not flagrant in the sense of Art. 45 of the Criminal Procedure Code. The judge accepted the defense argument and declared the police record and the subsequent procedure null and void, leading to the liberation of the accused. In his ruling, the judge recalled the fact that respect for procedures has the objective of "the protection of the individual and his domicile". According to a defense attorney, this ruling represented a victory for "the right to defense, the presumption of innocence, and the respect of the legality of penalties" (interview, Dakar, 2018). However, this ruling did not clarify the distinction between "homosexuality" and "acts against nature". Its concise wording and the lack of reaction from the Prosecutors' Office, which did not appeal against the decision at the Court of Cassation, demonstrated the discomfort that the case had created within the Senegalese judiciary. By concentrating on procedural rules, the court avoided discussing the content and did not directly disavow the first-instance judge, which means in fact the moral norms that served to justify the harsh sentences he handed down.

The liberation of the accused ignited the anger of several Islamic associations, which decided to create an "Islamic front for the defense of ethical values", whose objective is to prevent the spread of homosexuality in society and to ensure that culprits are prosecuted and punished for this crime. Ten years later, the situation has not evolved very much: homophobia (fueled by conservative groups and media) is still active and homosexuals are still subject to trial. At the judicial level, however, convictions are generally limited or even overturned at appeal, thus confirming the judicial intermingling of moral and legal repertoires.[22]

Facts, evidence, rules, procedures, and interpretation: legal reasoning in practice

Going further in the anthropology of judicial reasoning in cases dealing with sexual morality, we now explore the specific ways in which the courts transformed social situations into legalistic rule-based decisions. We address two specific issues: courts' search for procedural rules and legal relevance. It leads us to examine how courts identify and present the facts of the ongoing case, applicable rules, and conclusive evidence; how legal characterization is permeated with moral standards; and how moral issues are formulated in legal technical terms.

Facts

In most cases, the facts of the pending case are extensively based on prosecution accounts, which are themselves based on police records. In the Egyptian Queen Boat case, for instance, the facts are presented as follows:

> The court based its conviction on the facts of the petition and has no doubt with regard to their veracity. Regarding what the court deduced from the examination of the documents and the investigations [...] as well as from the evidence submitted and what was related during the trial, [these facts] amount to what was consigned in the record [...]. This information reached [the Prosecution] from secret and reliable sources, confirmed by its careful investigations, which suffice [to show that the first accused] adopted deviant (*munharifa*) ideas inciting others to hold revealed religions in contempt (*izdirâ'*) and to call to abject (*radhîla*) practices and sexual acts contrary to revealed laws. [...]

In the same way, the Senegalese ruling reads:

> Considering that, following the interrogation record of *flagrante delicto* dated 24 December 2008, the Prosecutor of the Republic called the defendants [names] before this jurisdiction, with the charge of having committed, on 24 December 2008, or in any case in a period which does not make public prescription applicable, acts against nature (*actes contre nature*), and having belonged in the same circumstances of time and place, to an association created with the purpose of committing crimes.

This way of relying on facts as established by the police and the prosecution office testifies to the inquisitorial nature of the judicial systems under study. Facts are not disputed by the parties, as in adversarial systems in which the parties have to present their respective versions to the judge who acts as a neutral arbitrator. In inquisitorial systems, judges have an active role that consists of not only weighing the parties' versions of facts, but also of conducting the debates and orienting them in a discretionary manner. From a practical point of view, there is a tendency for judges to base their version of facts on the narratives provided by the public institutions that have conducted the investigation (and have the considerable evidential force of the state on their side). They do this in a routine way – sometimes because of the heavy case load – by merely duplicating the summaries that have been submitted for their attention. However, they always have the option of dismissing evidence produced by the police and the prosecution, especially in rulings that overrule established precedents, as is the case in Lebanon.

The presentation of facts is even more summary in the Lebanese case:

> On 5/8/2015, the president of the municipality of Bouchrieh-El Sedd, Mr. Antoine Gebarah, referred to the Anti-trafficking and Decency Protection Bureau in the Department of general Criminal Investigations, a complaint filed by the residents of the region of Bouchrieh against "all the cafés and bakeries whose clients gather on sidewalks and in public places on the entrance of the town of Bouchrieh (Dawra roundabout), and which became a gathering point for groups from different nationalities including night girls (*fatyât al-layl*, i.e. *prostitutes*) [...] and homosexuals (*mithliyyîn*), and involving drinking alcohol and other substances, which caused disturbance to the passers-by and the residents of the place", and asking it to deal with this issue,
>
> And on 7/8/2015 the Appellate Public Prosecution charged the agents of the aforementioned Bureau to go to the place and arrest the girls there in addition to the transsexuals and those who contact clients in order to have sex in exchange for money,
>
> And therefore the defendants were summoned and heard [...]

In this case, facts are reduced to a complaint, a police round-up, summarized interviews, and confessions that do not concern specific sexual acts but general practices or reasons to be in such suspicious places, as may also be seen in the Egyptian and Senegalese cases. Judges do not seem interested in knowing more about the situation. This can be explained by the nature of the ruling itself, which denies the criminal nature of most of the facts alleged against the defendants, either because of their non-abusive nature (single judge) or because of their non-public character (appellate judge: "it was not proven that the accused committed some sexual act in such a way that they could be seen or heard by others, or in a public space, or with a juvenile; nor was it proven that the accused had the will to go against public morals"). It is interesting to observe that the same facts (public appearance in suspicious places and times) can lead to radically diverging conclusions: they either fully support the accusation (police and prosecution), based on a kind of ordinary knowledge of "normal crimes" (Sudnow, 1965), or they fall completely outside the scope of the law (single and appellate judges), which requires an overt breach of its restrictively defined provisions.

Rules

In this formally syllogistic game, it is not enough to have evidenced facts, judges need a rule legally characterizing them. Put simply, the alternative is between a readily available rule and a rule that must be made relevant; between the "soft cases" of rules that can be followed "blindly" (Wittgenstein, 1953, §199) and the "hard cases" of rules that must be discovered beyond prevailing uncertainty; between routine practice and high profile affairs; between socially produced "obviousness" and dogmatic principles (the law cannot be silent and the law does not speak for nothing). Actually, any case requires some reasoning and thus some quantum of interpretation, be it to just establish an equivalence between the paradigm embodied by the rule and the instance represented by the facts. As nicely shown by Lenoble and Ost (1981), neither facts nor rules are ever totally transparent. However, rules are more or less "entrenched" (Schauer, 1991) and the judges' work varies accordingly. In Indonesia, there is no legal provision criminalizing homosexuality. The judges, therefore, found it impossible to condemn the people who had been arrested by the police, unless they could be found guilty under the pornography law:

> Considering, that the defendants have been faced with trial [...], then based on the facts revealed, the judges chose to demonstrate the second accusation, that is, the violation of Art. 36 of UURI No. 44 of 2008 regarding pornography [viz. "Any person who exposes themselves or exposes other people in a show or in front of a public in a way that exposes nudity, sexual exploitation, sexual intercourse or anything that contains pornographic acts as defined in Art. 10 is punished by imprisonment for a maximum of ten years and/or a maximum fine of five billion rupiahs"] [...], which consists of three elements, namely:
>
> First element: "any person" is substantiated as follows:
>
> What is meant by "any person" or "anyone" here is what is referred to as the subject of law, namely, a human or a corporation, who has legal rights and obligations, which is submitted for trial and can account for all his/her actions legally; [...]
>
> Second element: "exposes themselves or exposes other people in a show or in front of a public in a way that exposes nudity, sexual exploitation, sexual intercourse";
>
> The police established that the visitors were nude, [...] the dancers came and [...] took off their clothes [...], [and] the dancers masturbated two partygoers [in public] [...]

In Senegal, there is a provision criminalizing sexual relationships against nature, and the judge takes it as a perspicuous rule without any further consideration:

> Considering that, according to the interrogation record of flagrante delicto dated 24 December 2008, the Prosecutor of the Republic summoned [names of the accused] before this court based on the accusation of having performed, in Dakar, on 24 December 2008, for a period that excludes any prescription of public action, acts against nature, and to have belonged in the same circumstances of time and place, to an association created with the purpose of committing crimes;
>
> These facts are provided for and punished by Art. 319 §3 and 238 sq. of the Criminal Code.

In Lebanon, the provision of the Criminal Code looks identical and led judges to adopt similar positions, as illustrated in the following dissident opinion reflecting the prevailing mood:

> [...] We do not see in the expression "carnal conjunction against nature" any ambiguity that requires interpretation, because, in human nature since the creation, sexual intercourse occurs between two different sexes, which constitutes the natural intercourse, and any other sexual intercourse like the one happening between two people having the same biological sex becomes against nature and penalized in application of Art. 534 C.C. [...]
>
> And whereas the Lebanese law did not criminalize sexual tendencies, but sexual intercourse in itself, conviction should only occur when there is sufficient proof of the occurrence of sexual intercourse, and not just proof that a person is of homosexual tendencies [...]

However, interestingly, the same legalistic attitude recently led some Lebanese judges to reach an opposite conclusion:

> And whereas the criminal legislator emphasized the principle of protecting the individual in the exercise of his rights, making any deprivation of these rights an exception, and translated this into the general rule of Art. 183 of the Criminal Code stating that "an act undertaken in exercise of a right without abuse shall not be regarded as an offence;"
>
> And whereas it appears that this article imposes three conditions on the decriminalization of any act, the first being the existence and acknowledgment of a right, the second being that the committed act should be a legitimate means to exercise that right, and finally that this right should be exercised without abuse;
>
> And whereas it becomes necessary to determine whether the homosexual relation is the exercise of a right without abuse in the sense of

> Art. 183 of the Criminal Code, which implies establishing the extent to which the three conditions contained in the aforementioned article are fulfilled in the current case.

In the judges' work, finding the relevant rule is paramount. This is illustrated in the Egyptian case in a paradoxical way, in the sense that, without any provision explicitly condemning homosexuality, judges, drawing from the Court of Cassation's case law, extrapolated a rule criminalizing debauchery (*fujûr*), to be understood as homosexuality (*liwât*), from Art. 9 of Law 10/1961 on the repression of prostitution (*da'âra*), which stipulates that:

> (a) any person who hires or offers in any possible way a place that serves debauchery or prostitution [...]; (b) any person who owns or manages a furnished flat or room or other place open to the public that facilitates the practice of debauchery or prostitution [...]; (c) any person who usually practices debauchery or prostitution is condemned to imprisonment for a period of no less than three months and no more than three years, and to a fine of no less than five pounds and no more than ten pounds, or to one of these two penalties. When the person is arrested in this last situation, he or she may be subjected to a medical examination and, if it appears that he or she suffers from an ordinary venereal disease, to confine him or her in a medical institution until he or she has recovered [...]

Master-narratives, counter-narratives, and procedural strategies

Albeit in a very formal way, judges present, and feel themselves constrained by, the necessity to base their judgments on rules, which both constrain their discretionary power and provide the opportunity for flexible reasoning. With rules, they produce and reproduce narratives as to how to understand and apply the law. This is the ordinary working of law. It puts forward legal master-narratives that correspond to what David Sudnow (1965) calls "normal crimes", that is, the routine understanding of legal situations and of their treatment. The Egyptian case is paradigmatic in that judges, despite the absence of any directly applicable rule, selected legislation that seemed to adequately fit the "moral though not formal condemnation of homosexuality" when it becomes public:

> The crime designated in [this text] is only committed when a man or a woman fornicates (*mubâsharat al-fahsha'*) with people without distinction, habitually. When a woman fornicates and sells her virtue to whomever asks for it without distinction, she commits prostitution (*da'âra*) [...]; *fujûr* occurs when a man sells his virtue to other men without distinction.

Indonesian judges could not proceed in the same way, either because of the lack of any alternative legislation or their unwillingness to give the case a maximal extension. Whatever their reasons, they restricted themselves literally to the only legislation they considered to be at their disposal, i.e. the law against pornography. A widely publicized case based, as far as the police were concerned, on alleged male homosexuality was reduced to a circumscribed condemnation of people involved in public sexual indecency (and thus not homosexuality per se).[23] The legislation selected by the judges could only target some of the people facing the moral condemnation of same-sex relationships. This was probably done on purpose: judges wanted to produce a master-narrative relating to commercial (homo)sexual practices – which explains why they found a way to convict the owner and the manager of the Atlantis club for participation – while not further prosecuting individuals for their sexual orientation:

> Declaring that the defendants [names] have been proven legally and convincingly guilty of committing a criminal act. They intentionally provided opportunities, means or information to commit crimes, namely displaying themselves (dancers and visitors) in performances or publicly portraying nudity, sexual exploitation.

The Senegalese judge transforms a confession regarding sexual orientation into the evidence of the crime of committing acts against nature, although this type of crime can only be established if participants are caught red-handed:[24]

> Considering that the accused acknowledged having had sexual relations with individuals of the same sex for less than three years, in accordance to the summons notified to them;
>
> That the crime of act against nature is therefore established in their respect.

In this case, the socially shared master-narrative is made legal, despite the uncertainty of its wording and the inadequacy of its evidence.

However, in general, master-narratives do not operate freely. They are constrained in several ways, e.g. evidential and procedural. In the Egyptian case, the judge decided to convict only those accused whose so-called "passive homosexuality" was established by (most dubious) forensic expertise. In other words, the judge felt his discretion was limited by evidence. We have already shown the extent to which this evidentially based statement reflects a socially shared moral representation (Dupret, 2011), but our point here is to stress the extent to which judges' subjective interpretations are felt from within as objective limitations. This holds true in the case of the Lebanese dissenting judge, who considers that there has been a "human nature since the creation" for which "natural" sexual intercourse occurs between different sexes, while sexual intercourse between people of the same sex is "against nature". Accordingly, this judge considered that the master-narrative is clear and offers no room for interpretation. The same holds true in Senegal, where the inadequacy of the evidence was only highlighted at the appeal level, [25] leading eventually to the case being overturned:

> Considering that [...] it is imperative that the investigating powers of agents representing public authorities be exercised in a way that conforms to the law in order to serve as evidential facts;
>
> When proceeding in the manner indicated above, investigators blatantly violated the provisions of Art. 51 of the Criminal Procedure Code; [...]
>
> It follows that the investigation record, on which the prosecution against the accused and the subsequent procedure are based, must be annulled;
>
> As a consequence, the warrants against the accused are required to be handed in.

If adjudication is about legally characterizing facts so as to attach to them legal consequences and therefore about producing legal master-narratives reflecting prevailing interpretations of rules, there must be some room for challenging these narratives and proposing alternatives. This is known in legal practice as a reversal of precedent, even though the expression concerns the case law of supreme jurisdictions and not the capacity of ordinary jurisdictions to overturn the traditional interpretation of specific provisions. Countering master-narratives is one of the main advocacy techniques used to promote specific causes and trigger changes in the manner some questions are dealt with at the social, political, or moral level. Most judicial work is achieved as part of a routine process in which precedents are more or less blindly followed, as conformism spares often overloaded courts' time-consuming effort.[26] Cause lawyering seeks to break this routine process by proposing ready-made arguments qualifying or reversing the prevailing master-narratives. Such was the case in Lebanon, where associations offered judges a reading of the Criminal Code that subverted the classical interpretation of the expression "carnal relations against nature" (see Section 3). It is a particular manner of functioning, as it does not oppose existing legal provisions, but proposes changes of focus and evolutive interpretations.

The single-judge court of Metn opted for an alternative focus in its dealings with people accused by the Prosecutor's Office of acts against nature. It emphasized that "its first and fundamental role is to protect public freedoms and human rights in a way that preserves human integrity and dignity in society without discrimination or favoritism", a role that is translated into the rule expressed by Art. 183 of the Criminal Code: "An act undertaken in exercise of a right without abuse shall not be regarded as an offence." The judge undertook to explain how having homosexual relations corresponds to "the exercise of a right without abuse in the sense of article 183 of the Criminal Code":

> The right:
>
> [...] and whereas it becomes the right of homosexuals to have human and intimate relationships with whoever they want, without any discrimination in relation to their sexual tendencies or any favoritism or intervention from any party, similarly to other people, since this is the simplest of their "natural rights" inherent to them as humans [...]
>
> And whereas, on the other hand, the deprivation of homosexuals' "natural" right to have intimate relationships between them without discrimination or intervention from any party, results in forcing them to behave in a way "contrary to their nature" so that it corresponds to the "nature" of the majority [...]
>
> The exercise of the right:
>
> [...] and whereas the right to physically express human relations, through sexual relations between two consenting adults, is a right inherent to any human, and homosexuals should exercise it similarly to other people without any discrimination or preference, especially those who can only live their sexual lives through their tendencies [...]
>
> Without abuse (*tajâwuz*):
>
> [...] and whereas it is necessary to confirm, within the aforementioned motivations, that the sexual relations that deserve to be protected, whether they are heterosexual or homosexual, are the relations that occur between two consenting adults, without any aggression or exploitation or damage to the other,
>
> Based on all the previous elements, and in application of article 183 of the Criminal Code, the prosecution related to article 534 of the same code should be invalidated.

The appellate Court of Mount-Lebanon opted for an alternative interpretation of Art. 534 of the Criminal Code:

> And whereas it is first necessary to emphasize two fundamental rules of the interpretation of legal texts and the determination of the scope of their application, the first rule stating that the text should be interpreted on the basis of the goal that was sought when it was written, and the second stating that the interpretation of texts should be consistent with social evolution; [...]
>
> And whereas, secondly, the text of article 534 C.C. forms part of section 2 of chapter 2 of part 7 of the Criminal Code, whose title is "Infringement of Public Habits and Morals (*al-ta'arrud li'l-adâb wa'l-akhlâq al-'âmma*)", which means that the legislator's goal in writing this

> text is not to penalize sexual perversion, but infringement of public habits and morals when perpetrating it;
>
> And whereas, therefore, one should apply the text to situations that constitute an infringement of public habits and morals in the light of social evolution, and the interpretation of the text and the determination of the scope of its application should always be consistent with this evolution, otherwise the application of the text becomes unacceptable from the point of view of correct logic or social justice;
>
> And whereas what constitutes the infringement of public habits and morals in the light of social evolution is the sexual act that is beyond the traditional view of natural sexual relations between a man and a woman, when it happens in a manner that is visible or audible to others or in a public space or when it is perpetrated with a minor who should be protected; [...]
>
> And whereas the conditions of article 534 C.C. are not fulfilled, it becomes necessary to confirm the first degree decision in relation to its result.

Besides literal interpretation of the rule on the statute book, an active search for substitute legislation in a case of legal silence, procedural maneuvers aiming to mitigate the strict implementation of the law, and evidential techniques supporting or undermining accusatory characterizations, the Lebanese case proves essential to showing the (possibly successful) capacity to seek, and find, alternative interpretations of legal provisions whose binding character does not look challengeable. The reversal of the master-narrative it offers does not come from a legal "revolution", in the sense of a change of paradigm external to existing law, but from a "transformative" process, that is, a change that is initiated from within the law currently in force. It is a means of by-passing ambient homophobia and asking judges to intervene in matters in which democratically elected representatives will never risk offending public opinion.

How to do things with rules: the reference to rules in the life of the law

Although empirical descriptions cannot solve conceptual issues, they can show how flesh-and-blood people deal with concepts and pragmatically ascribe an objective meaning to them. To make use of John Searle's epistemic square, lawyers produce interpretations that, while being ontologically subjective (that is, they emanate from subjects), are epistemologically objective (i.e., they are generally considered as impervious to subjective interpretation) (Searle, 1996). Such is often the case with legal interpretation: although it is produced by law professionals, it tends to be considered as objectively based. Our intention is not to confirm or challenge this claim, but to show that interpretation takes shape in the ordinary practice of legal reasoning in a way that is shaped by the epistemically objective character of legal categories.

Following Eric Livingston, we call the process of legal interpretation 'instructed action' (Livingston, 1995). By this, we mean that norms, including legal norms, inextricably combine formulation and actualization. In other words, the (legal) norm acquires its meaning only through the combination of its enunciation with the practices that orient to it, be it to implement, violate or dodge it. Formulation and actualization are internally related to one other – like fire and heat: they are logically inseparable, although one can distinguish them for analytical purposes. In sum, legal action corresponds to activities instructed by legal norms in a way that is never totally predictable though never fully contingent. It should be said, also, that whereas the theory of legal constraints made it possible to relax sociologically the formal understanding of the legal process, the concept of instructed action allows us to logically consolidate the sociological understanding of legal practice. Rules have an open texture (Hart, 1961), but it is more open for some than others. The more legal categories and rules claim to duplicate ordinary moral sense (as is probably the case in criminal law), the more some people can claim access to their essential meaning and literal interpretation. However, the more these morally-supported rules are presented as having an obvious sense, the less entrenched they also prove in their interpretation, as this sense depends on extra-legal criteria, e.g. "common sense", which is by definition evolutionary. It is as if the moral authority ascribed to law – which triggers what we call the privilege of literalism, that is, the possibility of economizing on legal argument on the grounds that the rule is literally stated – implies its practical malleability, which follows the "spirit of the age" (Dupret, 2003), and thus its possible re-characterization.

In fields in which the moral basis of law seems to prevail, rule-based decision-making is so important in judges' work that, where no direct criminalization is available, they seek, and find, alternative or partial characterizations. Rules are central to the life of the law. Of course, such centrality does not work in the way legal dogmatism claims. The consistency of rules with facts must be actively produced. However, judges would not dare act without a formal basis for their argument. For them, it is a matter of legal constraint, i.e. how things must be done to be logically, substantially, and institutionally correct. It could be argued, as in caricatured legal realism, that this is purely paying lip-service to formal principles, but this would amount to an "ironic" attitude with respect to judges' work, given that, most often, they take these rules as objective and their argumentation as compelling. On the contrary, the question raised by our jurisprudentially-informed praxeological research is not whether rules do play an effective role in adjudication; they do. What this research has arguably demonstrated is that they play this role in a way that is thoroughly informed and instructed by their interpreters' technical and commonsense knowledge of normative categories.

Notes

1 See for example case no. 522/Pid.B/2012/PN.SBG from North Sumatra, in 2012, where a 50-year-old man had homosexual intercourse with a minor and was sentenced to two years in prison. Indonesian law defines any person under the age of 18 as a juvenile. According to the Child Protection Act of 2002, as amended in 2014, anyone who commits or incites someone to commit child molestation and/or child abuse will be sentenced to 5–15 years of imprisonment and fined up to 5 bn Indonesian Rupiah (€4m).
2 By the Law Gazette (*Staatsblad*) no.130, on 20 Mai 1911.
3 *Mahkamah Konstitusi*, case no. 46/PUU-XIV/2016.
4 However, the western province of Aceh, which was allowed to have its own criminal law under the peace agreement, criminalizes homosexuality (*liwât*): in the *Qanun Jinayat* no. 6 of 2014 (which came into force in 2015).
5 "One is forbidden from exposing oneself or others to a performance or public appearance that exhibits nudity, sexual exploitation, sexual intercourse or other pornographic acts".
6 Report by the Chairman of the Commission for the Reform of the Criminal Code (President Fouad Ammoun), March 1939, "Rapport général sur la réforme pénale", in *Code pénal*, 2009, Beirut, Antoine Édition, pp. 16 et s.
7 *Ibid.*, p. 18.
8 The crime of sodomy was abrogated with the French Revolution. However, outrages against public decency were aggravated by judges in the case of homosexual acts (Art. 330, al. 2 of Criminal Code) and acts against nature with a juvenile under the age of 18 (Art. 331, al. 3). One should also note that Art. 175 of the 1871 German Criminal Code punished "acts against nature".
9 See Saghieh, 2009, p. 31.
10 Ibid.
11 The plea template can be accessed online on the Legal Agenda website.
12 We draw most of the information concerning Egyptian criminal jurisprudence from Husni, 1989, which Egyptian jurists unanimously consider the most authoritative reference in the field.
13 However, on October 25, 2017, several MPs proposed a five-article draft law criminalizing homosexuality, defined as "sexual intercourse with people of the same sex" (Art. 1) and support for or incitement to it.
14 In Arabic, the word *da'âra* also refers to the notion of debauchery. However, it seems that this particular law directly targets prostitution, even though the law gives no definition of the terms.
15 Case No.852/Pid.Sus/2017/PN.JKT.UTR against the four AGS employees.
Case No.853/Pid.Sus/2017/PN.JKT.UTR against the four AGS striptease dancers.
Case No.854/Pid.Sus/2017/PN.JKT.UTR against the two partygoers.
16 BBM (Blackberry Messenger), WA (WhatsApp), and Twitter.
17 The same holds true in Senegal, where investigators look not only for the accused person's confessions but also for their admission that they knew it was forbidden by the law and local mores (between which they wilfully make no distinction).
18 Moreover, in this case, the court adds that the act was committed by a man and a transsexual, which transforms it into an act between a man and a woman, "like any sexual relationship characterized as traditional".
19 As far as lesbianism is concerned, one can mention, the so-called "piano piano case" in Senegal, from the name of the bar where the defendants, five women accused of having kissed each other, were arrested on the night of 11–12 November 2013. Judged one week later for "acts against nature" and "public offense against

decency", they were eventually given the benefit of the doubt and released. To our knowledge, no case of lesbianism has ever been filed in Indonesia, Lebanon or Egypt.

20 In February 2008, a celebrity magazine published a series of photos, asserting they were taken during a gay marriage ceremony. Most of the men in the photos were arrested but were quickly released due to lack of proof regarding "acts against nature". This decision generated an unprecedented wave of homophobia in the country.

21 Note that this demand for the application of the law can be made for diametrically opposing purposes: condemning homosexuality, as in the dissenting opinion in the Lebanese case; releasing those accused of homosexuality, as requested by the attorneys for those accused in the Senegalese case.

22 Contrary to what happened in Lebanon until recently, where 'liberal' decisions taken by single judges used to be overruled on appeal.

23 "Public sexual indecency" plays a pivotal role, either, when established, as a basis for conviction (Indonesia) or, when absent, as a reason to preclude it (Lebanon).

24 In the case we described, this is what the Lebanese judges refuse to do, although formerly it was normal practice.

25 Mainly for procedural reasons related to the due process of law, while in Lebanon, the appeal court considered that evidence was inadequate because it did not prove the act and its public character.

26 This was already hypothesized regarding Senegal (see above). In Indonesia – and despite the Chief Justice Ordinance according to which first instance cases must be dealt with in less than five months – it may be considered that the trial (six months) was rather expeditious, considering the number of defendants. This can be explained by the fact that the judges were under media pressure. It can also explain the fact that the more "objective" Pornographic Act was used, despite what the judges considered to be aggravating circumstances, i.e. the attack on Indonesia's founding principles (*Pancasila*). In Lebanon, the whole procedure lasted about three years, a duration that is not abnormal but certainly not expeditious. Here, the opposite explanation may be suggested: the lack of a national and international political dimension did not incite the judges to speed up the trial.

References

Champeil-Desplats, V. and Troper, M. (2005) 'Proposition pour une théorie des contraintes juridiques' in Troper, M., Champeil-Desplats V. and Grzegorczyk, Ch. (eds.) *Théorie des contraintes juridiques.* Brussels, Paris: Bruylant/LGDJ, pp. 11–23.

Chiffoleau, J. (1990) 'Dire l'indicible. Remarques sur la catégorie du nefandum du XIIe au XVe siècle', *Annales. Économies, Sociétés, Civilisations*, 45(2), pp. 289–324.

Commission for the Reform of the Criminal Code (report of its President Fouad Ammoun), (2009 [1939]), 'Rapport général sur la réforme pénale', in *Code pénal*, Beirut: Antoine Edition.

Crottet, B. (2012) 'Une tentative de reformulation de la théorie des contraintes', *Jus Politicum*, n° 7. Available at: http://juspoliticum.com/article/Une-tentative-de-reformulation-de-la-theorie-des-contraintes-451.html.

Dupret, B. (2003) 'A liberal interpretation of a socialist constitution: The egyptian supreme constitutional court and privatization of the public sector' in Kienle, E. (ed.), *Politics From Above, Politics From Below: The Middle East in the Age of Economic Reform* London: Saqi.

Dupret, B. (2005) 'Le corps mis au langage du droit. Comment conférer à la nature une pertinence juridique', *Droit et Société*, 61, pp. 627–653.
Dupret, B., Ferrié, J.N. (2004) 'Morale ou nature: Négocier la qualification de la faute dans une affaire égyptienne d'homosexualité', *Négociation*, 2, pp. 41–57.
Frank, J. (2017 [1930]) *Law and the Modern Mind.* London: Routledge.
Garfinkel, H. (1967) *Studies in Ethnomethodology.* Cambridge, MA: Polity Press.
Hart, H. L.A. (1961) *The Concept of Law.* Oxford: Oxford University Press.
Jonkers, J.E. (1946) *Handboek van het Nederlands indische Strafrecht.* Leiden: Brill.
Kelk, C. (2001) *Studieboek Materieel Strafrecht.* Deventer: Gouda Quint.
Lamintang, P. A. F. (2014) *Dasar-Dasar Hukum Pidana di Indonesia* Jakarta: Sinar Grafika,.
Lenoble, J. and Ost, F. (1980) *Droit, mythe et raison. Essai sur la dérive mytho-logique de la rationalité juridique.* Brussels: Publications des Facultés universitaires Saint-Louis.
Livingston, E. (1995) *An Anthropology of Reading.* Bloomington and Indianapolis: Indiana University Press.
Llewellyn, K.N. (1951) *The Bramble Bush: On Our Law and Its Study*, 2nd ed. New York: Oceana Publication.
M'Baye Kéba (1970) 'L'expérience sénégalaise de la réforme du droit', *Revue internationale de droit comparé*, 22(1), pp. 35–42.
Saghieh, N. (2009) *Aqwâs al-qudât amâm aqwâs al-mahâkim. Al-mithliyyûn fî qânûn al-'uqûbât.* Beirut: Helem.
Schauer, F. (1991) *Playing by the Rules: A Philosophical Examination of Rule-Based Decision-Making in Law and in Live.* Oxford: Clarendon.
Schauer, F. (2011) 'Editor's introduction' in Llewellyn, K.N. and Schauer, F. (ed.) *The Theory of Rules.* Chicago, IL: Chicago University Press, pp. 1–30.
Searle, J. (1996) *The Construction of Social Reality.* London: Penguin Books.
Soesilo, R. (2013) *Kitab Undang-Undang Hukum Pidana (KUHP) serta Komentar-Komentarnya Lengkap Pasal demi Pasal* Bogor: Politeia,.
Sudnow, D. (1965) 'Normal Crimes', *Social Problems*, 12, pp. 255–276.
Tamanaha, B. (2004) *On the Rule of Law: History, Politics, Theory.* Cambridge: Cambridge University Press.
Teunis, N. (2001) 'Same-sex Sexuality in Africa: a case study from Senegal', *AIDS and Behavior*, 5(2), pp. 173–182.
Tresna, R. (1959) *Asas-Asas Hukum Pidana Disertai Pembahasan beberapa Perbuatan Pidana yang Penting* Jakarta: Tiara.
Yakin, A. U. (2013) 'La réception du code pénal français et du droit pénal d'Europe en Indonésie' in Jeanclos Y. (ed.) *La dimension historique de la peine: Origines et projections en Europe du Code pénal de 1810.* Paris: Economica, pp. 322–342.
Veyne, P. (1982) 'L'homosexualité à Rome' *Communications*, 35, pp. 26–33.
Wittgenstein, L. (1953) *Philosophical Investigations.* Oxford: Blackwell.

Index

Note: Page numbers followed by "n" denote endnotes.

For Product Safety Concerns and Information please contact our EU representative GPSR@taylorandfrancis.com
Taylor & Francis Verlag GmbH, Kaufingerstraße 24, 80331 München, Germany

www.ingramcontent.com/pod-product-compliance
Lightning Source LLC
LaVergne TN
LVHW021120300926
849160LV00010B/796